CHINA: museums

CHINA: museums

Miriam Clifford, Cathy Giangrande, Antony White

ODYSSEY BOOKS & GUIDES

Published in 2009 in the USA by Odyssey Books & Guides in association with Miriam Clifford, Cathy Giangrande and Antony White. Odyssey Books & Guides is a division of Airphoto International Limited 903 Seaview Commercial Building, 21 Connaught Road West, Sheung Wan, Hong Kong. Tel. (852) 2856 3896; Fax. (852) 2565 8004.
Email. magnus@odysseypublications.com

Distribution in the United States of America by W.W. Norton & Company, Inc., 500 Fifth Avenue, New York, NY 10110, USA
Tel. (800) 233-4830; Fax. (800) 458-6515
www.wwnorton.com

China: museums

ISBN: 978-962-217-804-5

Front cover photography: © Miriam Clifford

Design: Anikst Design, London
Editor: Sandra Pisano
Copy editor: Julie Pickard
Index: Joan Dearnley

Printed in China by Hong Kong Graphics and Printing Ltd on paper sourced from sustainable forests.

Frontispiece: Cave 332. Early Tang (618–704). Mogao Grottoes (no. 200), Dunhuang, Gansu Province

Contents

31. Lao She Museum
32. Lu Xun Museum Beijing
33. Mei Lanfang Memorial Museum
34. Military Museum of the Chinese People's Revolution
35. Museum of Ethnic Costume
36. National Art Museum of China (NAMOC)
37. National Museum of China
38. National Museum of Modern Chinese Literature
39. New Culture Movement Memorial Museum
40. Poly Art Museum
41. Sino-Japanese War Memorial Museum / Marco Polo Bridge
42. Songzhuang Artists' Village
43. Sony ExploraScience Museum
44. Soong Ching Ling's Former Residence
45. Tank Museum
46. Tian Yi Mu – Beijing Eunuch Culture Exhibition Hall
47. Today Art Gallery
48. Ullens Center for Contemporary Art (UCCA)
49. Xu Beihong Museum
50. Zhoukoudian Site Museum

Tianjin and the North

51. Jing Yuan in Tianjin: Exhbition Hall of Aisin Gioro Puyi
52. Museum of Chinese Opera
53. Pingjin Campaign Memorial Museum
54. Tianjin Academy of Fine Arts
55. Tianjin Museum
56. Tianjin Natural History Museum
57. Tianjin Science and Technology Museum
58. Hebei Provincial Museum
59. Yinxu Museum
60. Kaifeng Museum
61. Longmen Grottoes
62. Luoyang Ancient Tombs Museum
63. Luoyang Museum
64. Luoyang Museum of Ancient Arts
65. Museum of Zhou Capital and Royal Six-Horse Chariot
66. Henan Museum
67. Linzi Funerary Horse Pit Museum of the Eastern Zhou
68. Linzi Museum of Chinese Ancient Chariots
69. Qi State History Museum
70. Shandong Provincial Museum
71. Qingdao Municipal Museum
72. Qingdao Naval Museum
73. Qingzhou Municipal Museum
74. Yungang Grottoes
75. Former Residence of Lei Lutai

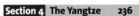

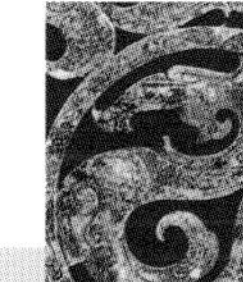

Preface

Gazeley is honoured to sponsor this distinctive museum guide showcasing China's ancient and contemporary cultural heritage. Numerous public and private museums, both new and refurbished, are opening across the country, displaying China's rich cultural traditions and artistry in world-class spaces. The extraordinary boom in museum building has transformed the cultural heartbeat of the country and is a fitting tribute to China's culturally fertile past and present.

This visionary mission is shared by Gazeley in response to the boom in China in warehousing and logistics. Having opened offices in China in 2006, success has meant we are now expanding further, providing logistics space in a sustainable way across the country. Our sustainable design concept is fully embedded in all warehouse buildings across the globe reinforcing our long-term commitment to sustainability and future generations. China has also set renewable targets. The combination of policy leadership and entrepreneurial savvy means China is now poised to become a leader in renewable energy, combining roaring economic growth with environmental solutions.

Gazeley is delighted to participate in this truly significant publication, celebrating China's desire for visitors to come away with a deeper understanding and appreciation of its glorious past and cultural wonders.

Pat McGillycuddy *Chief Executive Officer, Gazeley*
For further information please visit **www.gazeley.com**

赞助商代序

盖世理公司非常荣幸地成为此博物馆指南之赞助商，相信该指南定能成为展示中国古代和当代文化遗产之窗口。全国公立和私人博物馆或新建，或翻新，皆竞相开馆，向全世界展示中国之丰厚文化传统和艺术积淀。博物馆建筑之纷然涌现，令全国之文化气象焕然一新，亦为传播中国丰富的历史文化和近现代文化助力。

借中国仓储业和物流业欣欣向荣之大好局势，盖世理公司有幸能参于此文化盛举。我司已于2006年在中国成立分公司，并获巨大成功，公司业务不断拓展，在全国范围内开发可持续物流仓储空间。我们将可持续发展设计理念融入全球仓储建筑之各个领域，进一步履行我们坚持可持续性发展和造福下一代这一长远战略目标之承诺。中国亦同样不断设定崭新之目标。政策英明领导结合企业睿智头脑，意味着中国正在积极准备成为支持可再生能源之领先国家，在经济迅速发展的同时，着力处理好环境问题。

盖世理公司很高兴能参与这意义重大的出版项目，唯望来到中国之外国友人能对中国有更深入之了解，以更全面欣赏中国优秀灿烂之历史与文化。

Pat McGillycuddy　盖世理公司执行总裁
欲了解盖世理公司更多详情，请登陆公司网站：**www.gazeley.com**

Introduction

China is currently experiencing an explosion of museum building and expansion. In 1990, there were about 300 museums; by 2008, the official count included 2,310, excluding the newly permitted private museums, new art centres and vibrant districts and villages dedicated to contemporary art and culture.

Beginning in the Republican Period and accelerating after 1949, China established a system of national, provincial and city museums. New museums of world-class quality were opened, such as those in Nanjing and Shanghai.

Unlike in the West, these museums were concerned only with Chinese art. Traditionally, imperial and Confucian China prided itself on its cultural self-sufficiency. In all aspects of art, new generations referenced past generations. Most museums in China still contain almost exclusively Chinese artefacts, or those relating to China's history, but the situation continues to evolve.

The presentation of the collections in these traditional museums seems, by today's standards, to be horribly outdated and dreary – dark cases filled with unkempt objects, displayed on faded materials with signage almost exclusively in Chinese. All of this is changing now – and improving at remarkable speed.

China is opening up to the world to an extent that it has never done before. Its new museums and vibrant contemporary art scene are a testament to this phenomenon, and an interest in all sorts of collections and galleries is widespread among Chinese as well as foreign tourists. In early 2008, the Chinese government declared that by the end of 2009 all state museums and memorials except ancient architecture and site museums shall be free of charge. This has resulted in a huge increase in visitor numbers, proving that there is a great interest in culture and history.

The number of buildings undergoing renovation and modernization, as well as the construction of compelling and innovative new structures, is staggering. Every day, new private collections and government-sponsored museums open their doors. We have attempted to provide a representative and diverse introduction to a large variety of collections and institutions; a completely comprehensive list of both old and new museums would be impossible to provide in this period of growth. We hope soon to provide an interactive website to track this evolving situation and offer the very latest information.

Although we include the most famous of China's museums, such as the Shanghai Museum, the National Museum in Beijing and the Terracotta Warriors, we also aim to provide information on some of China's lesser-known cultural attractions, which may be quirky, off the beaten track or of special interest to particular collectors or hobbyists. Some of these offer little or no English (indicated in the entries) and therefore are rarely visited by non-Chinese. But, armed with this guide, a rewarding and eye-opening experience should be possible for the foreign tourist.

The Chinese people take pride in their country and its achievements, its newly created wealth and emergence as a world power. All art is to some extent about power; all museums to some extent reflect an ideology. Chinese museums are no exception and, in addition, the media in China are censored. The Ministry of Culture is dedicated to the preservation of cultural security, and this is inevitably reflected in the content and presentation of the museums in China today.

The key national and provincial museums, e.g. the Capital Museum in Beijing and the Shaanxi History Museum in Xi'an, present their displays historically. Every province has its own museum dedicated to the history and culture of that region. Exhibitions are didactic in nature, showing the development of Chinese history through its art, neatly compartmentalized by dynasty or material. Over time, these museums have also acquired newly excavated treasures in the wave of stunning archaeological finds after 1949. From this period as well, a fervent pride in the new state and its institutions emerged, leading to the founding of institutions such as the Military Museum in Beijing and the Naval Museum in Qingdao. Is the government's purpose to use the artefacts in these venues to highlight the creation of China as a unified centralized state, in addition to showing their aesthetic value? Foreign visitors are often left with this impression. The emphasis on viewing objects with an eye to history rather than for its own sake can be seen in the common practice of Chinese museums to exhibit copies of originals – and not always thus marked. This can occur even in a so-called 'Treasure Room', where a copy or cast is lovingly displayed as the real thing; it is not necessarily meant as a deception, rather the object itself may be deemed too valuable to risk exposure. This situation is likely to change with the creation of more modern museums, with ever better methods of conservation and tighter security.

Archaeological sites are now some of the most exciting art destinations in China, as new museums are built in situ and excavation pits are opened to the public – a trend that began with the Terracotta Warriors. Although, traditionally, the best finds went to the provincial museum or to Beijing, site museums are now able to start displaying their treasures in newly built, state-of-the-art galleries located at the excavation site. Great exhibitions of Chinese art are now being shown in the West, but, if able, do see the original collections in situ. No travelling exhibition can give more than a vestigial understanding of the impact of the Terracotta Warriors amassed in their burial pit the size of an aircraft hanger; or of the alternating intimacy and grandeur of the Forbidden City; or of the radiant magic of the great ancient bronze collection in Shanghai.

Excepting those in private museums, all objects are under the care of the Cultural Relics Bureau, both on a national and provincial level. Objects are assigned grades according to historic and artistic importance. Grade I is the top level, followed by Grades II and III. Lesser objects are classified as reference objects only. Generally, the larger the museum, the greater the number of national treasures, i.e. Grade I objects. You may see such notations in the publicity or signage in the museums.

This guide is arranged by region, province and city and covers many topics of interest – fine art, politics, archaeology, history, science and culture. Museums and sites that children might enjoy are noted. Opening times, exhibitions and even location change often, so do check details by phone, using the local listings or asking your hotel.

All the entries that have been included promise an enlightening experience. It is intended that the selection and presentation of museums will contribute to the quality of a visit to China and to the beginning of an enhanced understanding of Chinese art, culture, society and history.

1 Ancient Bell Museum of the Great Bell Temple

大钟寺古钟博物馆 *Dazhongsi guzhong bowuguan*

Jia 31 Beisanhuan Xi Road, Haidian District
北京市海淀区北三环西路甲31号

Tel: (010) 6255 0819 / 6255 0843
Open: 8.30–17.00; 16.30 winter
English booklet available
Kids

Housed in this temple complex built in 1733 under the Qing Emperor Yongzheng is a museum of ancient bells of all types including musical bells dating back to the Warring States period, Buddhist bells, Taoist bells, imperial court bells and bells for used for sounding warnings. There is even an exhibition hall devoted to bells from foreign countries. Originally called the Juesheng Si (Temple of Awakening), the complex was laid out as an imperial temple with the principal buildings (the Screen Wall, the Bell and Drum Towers and the Hall of Mahavira, among others) running south–north, flanked with side halls and east and west courtyards. At this sacred venue the Emperor conducted his rain-making rituals when drought was threatened. Later on, the giant Ming dynasty bronze bell known as the Yongle Bell was moved here from the Wanshou Si (Temple of Longevity). A new bell tower was built, consisting of a square lower part (the earth) and round upper section (heaven), to house the 46-ton bell, and the temple complex took on the more popular name of Big Bell Temple.

One of the principal buildings in the Temple of Awakening complex

Detail of prancing dragons on the Qianlong court bell

It's hard to imagine the size of the Yongle Bell until you see it. At 6.8 m high and 3.3 m in diameter, it is colossal. Very finely cast, it is inscribed with Buddhist texts (the Lotus and Diamond sutras) and attests to the consummate skill of the Chinese bronze casters. The bell is an important instrument in Buddhist services; monks struck the Yongle Bell on the eve of the new year with the resulting sound travelling up to 50 km and lasting for more than two

Big Bell Temple

minutes. The bell remains in mint condition, having been suspended for hundreds of years by three tiers of beams with the load carried by eight gigantic pillars decorated with dragons. For a small fee you can climb a set of stairs to one side of the bell and look down from above to get a better idea of its enormous size, as well as see the hole at the top where people once threw coins for good luck.

Bells in China

China's bell-making history is exceptionally long, starting with the production of the earliest bells anywhere in the world. Chiming bells were produced in sets for use in Shang and Zhou ritual music; single bells were musically meaningless. It is not easy to say how many bells there were to a chime. The one displayed in the museum is a reproduction of the famous set unearthed from the tomb of the Marquis of Zeng (433 BC) in Suizhou, and consists of 41 chime-stones and a set of 65 bells, all inlaid with gold inscriptions concerning pitches and scales. They were suspended from highly ornamented racks composed of three tiers with the top tier used for the smaller bells, and were struck with T-shaped mallets usually made of lacquered wood and ranging in size. It is believed that most musicians held two mallets rather than just one, allowing them to achieve quicker tempos by striking twice the number of tones simultaneously. A bell assemblage as big as the Marquis' probably was played by teams of two players (possibly more) positioned behind the rack. The playing of the large bells was the most precarious. Not only did the players have to swing quite a large mallet and be sure to hit the striking points of the A- and B-tones with exactitude (ancient bells often had these points marked with inscriptions hardly visible to naked eye), but they had to do it with just the right amount of force, or else the bells might crack.

Besides viewing the Yongle Bell, it's worth taking a look at some of the 500 other bells displayed throughout the complex. Skip the hall devoted to foreign bells as these are familiar and not all that spectacular. Instead, concentrate on the sections that demonstrate bronze-casting techniques and the area displaying other exquisite ancient bells. Among the ones that will surely catch your eye is the Qianlong court bell covered with dragons prancing through water and floating clouds, and the Taoist bell decorated with flying cranes, cast in the Ming period. The most admired bird in China, the crane is an auspicious symbol associated with the highest-ranked officials.

There is English signage throughout and a good Chinese–English guidebook for sale. Concerts featuring bells are also held here; check times at the entrance gate.

2 Arthur M Sackler Museum of Art and Archaeology

北京大学赛克勒考古与艺术博物馆 *Beijing daxue Saikele kaogu yu yishu bowuguan*

Inside the West Gate, Beijing University, Haidian District
北京市海淀区北京大学 西校门内

Tel: (010) 6275 1667
Open: 9.00–16.30 except public holidays; last entry 16.00
www.sackler.org/china/amschina.htm
Bookshop / gift shop

Arthur M Sackler (1913–1987) was an American scientist, physician, collector, philanthropist and benefactor of the arts. Besides the numerous medical institutions he established, there are galleries and museums in New York, Princeton, Cambridge, MA, London and Washington, DC bearing his name. The idea for a *teaching* museum at Beijing University sprung from his desire to create a bond between people through art and archaeology. Completed in 1993, the museum was built by Sackler's wife, Gillian, together with Beijing University after his death.

Because this museum was set up with a didactic purpose, it is the perfect place to begin one's journey through the art museums of China; a visit to the Sackler Museum offers a potted course in Chinese art history. When you have absorbed the information offered here, you are ready to tackle any of the larger, more complex museums you might visit, as well as appreciate more focused collections. This is certainly one of the 'must see' museums of Beijing due to the quality of the collection and its modern, uncomplicated and informative presentation.

Ox cart, Northern Qi burial, Hebei

Western Jin pottery warrior

The museum is set within the University grounds. Walk past the lovely Weiming Lake – The Unnamed Lake – which when frozen in winter becomes the University's skating park. It is well worth exploring the campus, which was once part of the Imperial Parklands. The American writer Edgar Snow, author of *Red Star over China* (1936) and protégé of Mao Zedong, is buried on a small hillside by the lake.

The Sackler Museum, carefully designed to be in harmony with the sur-

rounding University buildings, is based on a courtyard plan of the Ming dynasty. The Gillian Sackler Sculpture Garden adjoining the museum lies in part of the grounds of the Yuanming Yuan, the Old Summer Palace. The collection originally contained objects from the holdings and excavations of the University but has been expanded to include artefacts from other archaeological institutes and museums. As you enter, a sign explains the chronological layout of the galleries, which are arranged according to the archaeological periods used when teaching: Palaeolithic; Neolithic; Xia, Shang and Zhou; The Warring States; Qin and Han; The Six Dynasties, Sui and Tang; Song, Liao, Jin, Yuan and Ming. There are also three separate exhibitions illustrating the fieldwork carried out by the University: the Early Palaeolithic site of Jinniushan Man in Liaoning; the Neolithic village of Beizhuang in Shandong; and the Bronze Age (Western Zhou) Jin State site of Tianma-Qucun in Shanxi.

The Palaeolithic galleries contain stone tools and grinding stones, and human and animal fossils from Jinnian, while the Neolithic galleries have many fine pottery vessels from the Dawenkou, Yangshao and Longshan Cultures. Note the huge cooking vessel from Dawenkou marked with striations and a ring round the circumference, and the bold, geometric painted ceramics of the Yangshao.

In the Xia, Shang and Zhou gallery there are beautiful and characteristic examples of pottery and bronze vessels typical of the period. Notice the wonderful jumbo cooking pots, onc with distinctive 'rope' decoration. Look for the red-painted ceramic vessel with tripod legs from the Lower Xiajiadian Culture.

The time-line continues with objects from the Warring States period – note the ceramic roof tiles decorated with animals and birds, and the bronze mirrors.

In the 'Jin State Cemetery' exhibition, bronze objects, jewellery and horse trappings are exhibited, while the Qin and Han Gallery includes material from the burial pit of the famous Empress Dou of the Early Western Han. The faces of the ceramic figurines are serene, and their robes are expressive with their natural flowing lines.

Beijing University

Beijing University opened its doors in 1898 – at that time it was called Metropolitan University. In 1912, the name was changed to Peking University and in 1917 Cai Yuanpei became chancellor and the university became the centre of the pivotal New Culture Movement. Today the university consists of 30 colleges and has over 200 research institutions. It is generally considered the best university in Asia.

Pottery figure, Northern Qi burial, Hebei

The Six Dynasties and Sui–Tang period rooms contain wonderful examples of typical Tang ceramics: vessels, horses, camels and warriors. There is a large collection of figurines and ox-drawn carts in procession from a Northern Qi burial at Wanzhang in Hebei. Also included are some lovely celadon pieces and, notably, two formidable Tang *sancai* tomb guardians. The final gallery contains objects from the Song to the Ming dynasties. There are porcelains including Jingdezhen imperial ware and a Liao dynasty *sancai* plate.

Signage in each gallery, in both Chinese and English, offers a short explanation of the relevant period or excavation, and describes the highlights of the accompanying material culture. Lastly, there is a room for temporary exhibitions. The collection is a great pleasure to visit with its tasteful displays in well-lit cases, excellent and consistent English signage, and high-quality and well-labelled artefacts.

3

Beijing Ancient Architecture Museum

北京古代建筑博物馆 *Beijing gudai jianzhu bowuguan*

21 Dongjing Road, Xiannongtan, Xuanwu District
北京市宣武区先农坛东经路21号

Tel: (010) 6304 5608
Open: 9.00–16.00 except Mon

China's traditional architecture is a key component of its unique cultural make-up, from its walled towns, buildings set around courtyards and formal city layouts to the vast array of decorative elements and structural parts which meld together to produce a distinct style. As you wander round the country's temples, pavilions, hidden gardens and palaces, a better understanding of the elements of Chinese architecture will lead to a deeper comprehension of the two contrasting philosophies reflected throughout architectural settings: the Taoist belief that humanity and nature are one, and the need for order and harmony as laid down by Confucius. Insight into these schools of thought and the architectures based on them can be reached both inside the Hall of Jupiter (where this museum is located) and by exploring the surrounding complex of buildings – all that remains of the *Xiannongtan*, or Altar to Agriculture , which once occupied 3 square km. Unfortunately, signage throughout the complex is primarily in Chinese, but a good axonometric plan showing how this vast complex looked during the Qing dynasty can be seen directly ahead from the ticket booth at the entrance.

Even if you decide to skip the museum, this sister site to the Temple of Heaven, situated on the west side of the central axis leading south from the Forbidden City, is historically as significant and is certainly worth a visit. It was here that since 1420 the Emperors performed agricultural rituals and sacrifices at the vernal equinox. Clad in the yellow imperial silk robe and a blue coat, the Emperor would make his way from the Forbidden City with an escort of high officials and courtiers. Upon arrival he would proceed to the Altar to Agriculture, where he would make animal sacrifices to Xiannong, the legendary inventor of agriculture, and then perform the Tiling ritual, which consisted of ploughing furrows in the earth with the help of oxen followed by officials who would plant seeds and an old peasant who would cover them with earth. Once this was completed, the Emperor would celebrate in the Hall of Feasting. The Empress' duties involved feeding mulberry leaves to silkworms raised at the Altar of Silkworms and performing related rituals appropriate to women. Over the years, buildings were added and existing ones were renamed. During the Reign of Emperor Qianlong, the Ming wooden viewing platform was rebuilt in stone (it can still be seen surrounded by a white marble balustrade). Here a tent would be erected with an ancestor tablet inscribed with Xiannong's name in the centre and a table bearing meat from the sacrificed animals and dishes of cereals and vegetables as offerings to the gods. The last time the altar was used was in 1906 by Emperor Guangxu.

Han dynasty model of a multi-storey mansion

Unfortunately, until the Hall of Jupiter was renovated in 1979, the site was subjected to all kinds of abuse. Since 1997 various donations from international charities, including the World Monu-

ments Fund, have helped to fund the restoration of the Ju Fu Hall, the Divine Tablet Depository, the Divine Kitchen and its main gate, the Holy Granary and the Hall of Feasting, among others. A team of Chinese conservators have done their best to save as much of the original structures, paint work and mural paintings as possible. The Divine Tablet Repository and the Holy Granary are now museums, displaying objects relating to the First Agriculturalist.

The Hall of Jupiter is one of four halls enclosing a large paved courtyard, all exquisitely restored to their original kaleidoscope of colours, with tiled roofs and fabulous decorative features. The holdings include numerous beautifully executed models, images and diagrams which illustrate architectural advances as well as specific elements. Part 1 takes you swiftly through a survey of China's traditional architecture. One of the key displays here consists of wooden models illustrating the various shapes of *dougong* – a bracket used at the top of a column and composed of two elements: a rectangular block (*dou*) and a

Wooden model of the Flying Cloud Tower, Wanrong County, Shanxi

Exterior of The Hall of Jupiter

bow-shaped cross-bar (*gong*). Originating in early times, the *dougong* came into its own in the Tang dynasty, appearing more decorative and used according to sets of ratios graded to match the importance of particular buildings.

A selection of drawings and images illustrates the skills and the artistic input required for designing a Chinese garden. Further on is a much larger section devoted to the architectural evolution of the residence, starting with a Han dynasty funerary model of a multi-storey mansion which provides a useful glimpse of what buildings at that time looked like. The tiled roofs were supported by beams, and there were latticed windows as well as porches. Central to the elevated gallery in the exhibition hall is a 1:1000 three-dimensional map of Beijing as it looked in 1949 with its fortified wall still in place (it was removed in 1965 to build one of the outer ring roads). A stunning model of a corner watchtower of the Forbidden City built in 1368 shows its turret-style structure including its complicated triple-eave cross-ridged roof. Other models include the main hall of the Foguang Temple at Foguang Mountain near Wutai Mountain in Shanxi, one of the most important remaining wooden structures representing the apogee of Buddhist art and architecture during the Tang dynasty.

Walking back outside, you can examine several of the construction features you just saw in the gallery. These enormous wooden structures are true marvels. Take the time to notice the decorative paintings on the Hall of Jupiter:

Qing-style *hexi* painting with golden dragon patterns, divided by 'W' shapes, is the highest-ranked decorative painting, representing supreme nobility. The central sections of the beams show a pair of running dragons facing each other, as well as ascending dragons (facing upwards) on a blue background (heaven) and descending dragons painted on green backgrounds (water).

4 Beijing Ancient Coins Museum

北京古代钱币博物馆 *Beijing gudai qianbi bowuguan*

Arrow Tower, Desheng Gate, North Erhuanzhong Road, Xicheng District
北京市西城区二环中路德胜门箭楼

Tel: (010) 6201 8073
Open: 9.00–16.00 except Mon
English pamphlet available

The Beijing Ancient Coins Museum is located within the Desheng Gate, one of the two remaining arrow towers from the old Beijing inner-city wall, with eighty-two ports from which to shoot arrows. Imperial troops marched out of the city for battle through the Anding Gate and returned in victory through Desheng Gate. In 1664, when the bandit leader Li Zicheng led his army into the city to overthrow the Ming dynasty, he entered the city through this gate.

In 1993, the city government reconstructed the Zhenwu Temple and placed the Beijing Ancient Coins Museum here. On first entering the museum, there is a small pavilion consisting of a book and gift shop, which also has some introductory material displayed and a replica of a Qing dynasty bank from Pingyao, an ancient city in Shanxi, where the first banks in China were located until they were sidelined by the rise of a new up-and-coming financial centre: Shanghai. These privately owned banks, in Pingyao known as *piaohao*, date from the late Ming to early Qing period. Their existence is very important to Chinese Marxist historians, who point to them as evidence that China had developed its own brand of capitalism from feudalism. There is some English signage in this room, mainly just the titling. More detailed explanations of the displays are in Chinese only. There are also some numismatics books on sale, as well as various other small things and what the sales staff insists are genuine antique coins.

Paper money first appeared in the Northern Song dynasty

The galleries consist of two small halls in which more than a thousand ancient coins and paper money from the past 2,500 years are displayed. Metal coins in China date back to the Spring and Autumn period, when commerce first developed. Different types of coins were in use in different parts of China and at different times. In the north, the design of coins was based on agricultural implements, such as the spade. These types of coins, known as *bu* coins, were common during the Zhou, Zheng, Jin and Wei. In the south, coins shaped like a knife were used.

After China was unified under the Qin dynasty, round coins with a square hole were introduced. This design was based on the Emperor Qin Shihuang's belief that the sky was round and the earth square. This model of coin, one of the most common in the museum, remained in use for some 2,000 years. The history of currency is illustrated including the earliest paper currency, which dates to the Northern Song dynasty. These first notes, distributed from Chengdu in Sichuan Province, were called *jiaozi* – a word which readers may recognize as meaning dumpling. There is a fascinating but complicated etymological connection between the paper money, the ingots of gold or silver used before the *jiaozi* as currency, and the dumpling, traditionally eaten during the Lunar New Year because its shape is reminiscent of money and prosperity.

Among the many coins exhibited are copper coins that were cast in the Republican period (1911–1949) and 'folklore' coins, first minted in the Han Dynasty, which feature dragons or phoenixes. These were not used as legal tender but as precious objects to be given as gifts or collected. There is also an interesting display on the ancient technology used to cast coins, with an explanation in English.

Dasheng Gate

Museum entrance

The collection is neatly displayed, but more detailed English signage would be helpful for the foreign visitor. Also within the Desheng Gate grounds, to the left of the museum entrance, is a little tourist market hawking copies of ancient coins and other knick-knacks. In 1994, the museum established the first authorized coin-transaction market here. The museum's brochure says the market offers coin aficionados an ideal place to buy and sell coins, but our advice is: Buyer beware!

If you climb the steps to the watchtower above the temple area, there is a good view of the city below. In the tower is a privately owned contemporary art gallery called Beijing East Gallery.

5

Beijing Ancient Observatory

北京古观象台 *Beijing guguan xiangtai*

2 Biaobei Hutong, Dongcheng (intersection of Second Ring Road and southeast corner of Jianguomen Street)
北京市东城区裱褙胡同2号

Tel: (010) 6512 8923
Open: 9.00–16.30 except Mon

Sextant, Qing dynasty

Silhouetted against the high-rise filled and often hazy skyline of Beijing is a collection of astronomical instruments protruding from the top an imposing corner watchtower set in the ancient city wall. An intriguing sight in such a monstrous metropolis and, once you've located the entrance (via access roads), well worth visiting for the key role it played in gathering information about the heavens since it was built on this site in 1442, serving as the Imperial Observatory during the Ming and Qing dynasties and subsequently as the national observatory until 1929 when it ceased being used.

Prior to 1442 it had a rather chequered history, with some astronomical instruments arriving in 1227 with the Jin when they took them from the Northern Song capital of Kaifeng to Beijing and established the city's first observatory. When the Emperor of the Yuan, Kublai Khan, invaded he built a second observatory in 1279 just north of the present one and had instruments designed by the celebrated Chinese astronomer Guo Shoujing (at this time Arab-Persian astronomical instruments were being introduced into China). Later, after the fall of the Mongols under the Ming Emperor Zhu Yuanzhang, some of these instruments were moved to the new capital Nanjing. In 1420 Yongle, the third Ming Emperor, moved the capital back to Beijing leaving behind the originals and commissioning copies instead. Among these was the simplified armillary which measures the coordinates of celestial bodies and is now displayed in the observatory's courtyard. Guo Shoujing 'simplified' it by removing several of its rings.

Enter the gate of the observatory complex identified by Chinese characters and proceed through a small park containing a sprinkling of large stone tab-

lets carved with Chinese constellations, including that of the Green Dragon, a constellation that appears every spring in the eastern sky. A second gate leads into a classical Chinese courtyard strewn with a number of replica instruments interspersed between mature trees and park benches. Surrounding the courtyard are two museum buildings and connecting halls presenting a sweeping history of Chinese astronomical history from the Jin to the Qing. Displayed are an assortment of pictures, facsimiles of early star maps, and explanations of phenomena such as solar and lunar eclipses and comets, with minimal English signage. Also shown are some rather skilfully crafted Chinese astronomical instruments from the Ming and Qing dynasties and a section on the mathematical calculations used for the production of the Chinese calendar. Important in Chinese society, the Emperor's authority was secured by his ability to keep the calendar in harmony with the heavens as well as predicting eclipses. If the emperor failed to predict an eclipse, he would lose his 'Mandate of Heaven' or legitimacy to rule.

Visitors who have limited time should make a beeline to the narrow set of stairs which takes you up to the observatory platform where the treasures of this museum can be found. Surrounded by iron railings and enclosed by low stone walls is an assortment of eight bronze astronomical instruments dating from Qing. The story of their origin is as fascinating as the instruments themselves. During the sixteenth century Christian missionaries were making their way to China hoping to convert the Chinese to Christianity as well as write accounts about China to feed back to Europe. Among them were the two Jesuits, Matteo Ricci (1552–1610) and Adam Schall von Bell (1591–1666) who, using their scientific knowledge, re-worked the Chinese calendar and accurately mapped the imperial lands, gaining them coveted access to the court. Fr Schall's profound knowledge of astronomy gained him the title of the Directorate of Astronomy under the Shunzhi Emperor. Subsequently, a young Muslim was put in charge, but was soon replaced by the Flemish missionary Ferdinand Verbiest (1623–1688) whose knowledge of the Jesuit calendar so impressed the Chinese that he subsequently became director in about 1670 under the Kangxi Emperor. It was Verbiest who oversaw re-equipping the Imperial Observatory with six of the eight instruments which can be seen on the platform today. The design of the observatory was based on that by the

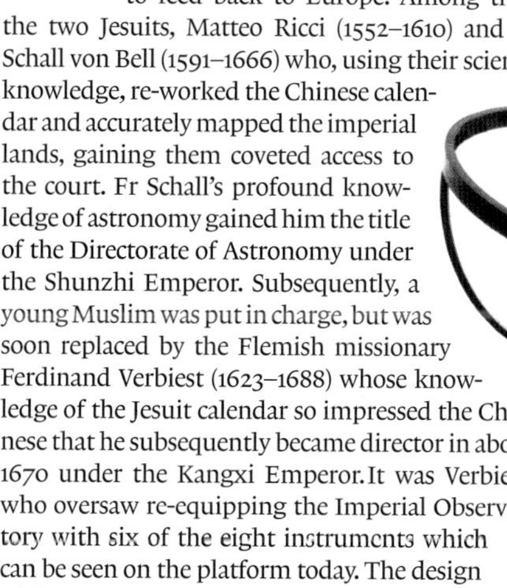

Ecliptic armillary, Qing dynasty

Simplified armillary, displayed in courtyard

Equatorial armillary, Qing dynasty

Danish sixteenth-century astronomer par excellence, Tycho Brahe, but did not include telescopes (although they had been invented). Among them are a celestial globe, a sextant, a quadrant, a horizontal circle for azimuth measurements, and both an equatorial and an ecliptic armillary sphere (the last two considered useless by Tycho). Several incorporate eastern decoration, including Chinese dragons. The other two instruments displayed, an armillary and azimuth, were built later. All were made of brass and used to produce star maps and compile astronomical tables showing planetary movements. During the Boxer Rebellion some of the instruments were looted by the French and Germans, but later returned and, in 1931, due to the threat from Japan, some were taken to the Purple Mountain Observatory in Nanjing for safe keeping. As a result, what is displayed is only a selection of what was there originally.

6 Beijing Art Museum, Wanshou Temple

北京艺术博物馆 *Beijing yishu bowuguan*

Wanshou Temple, Suzhou Street, Haidian District (100 m north of Zizhu Bridge on the West Third Ring Road)
北京市海淀区苏州街万寿寺

Tel: (010) 6841 3380 / 9391
Open: 9.00–16.00 except Mon
An introductory pamphlet is available but not on display

This lovely, uncrowded museum, set within a charming temple, is definitely worth the trip out to western Beijing. Sometimes called the 'mini-Forbidden City', it is built on the edge of the Changhe Canal, which connects the Summer Palace and the Forbidden City. It was once one of many temples lining the canal shore, almost all of which are now gone. The Wanshou Temple (Temple of Longevity) was built in 1577 during the Ming dynasty by Emperor Wanli for the purpose of storing Buddhist sutras and scriptures written in Chinese. During the Ming and Qing dynasties, the temple was often used for royal birthday celebrations; a thousand monks would chant sutras to celebrate the birthday of the Emperor's mother. The temple was continuously repaired and enlarged, and was used not only as a temple but also as a temporary imperial palace and garden; here the Empress Dowager Cixi would rest on her way to the Summer Palace from the Forbidden City. During the Republican period, the temple fell into disrepair, mainly owing to a fire in 1937 and the building's use by the Kuomintang army as an opium den. After 1949, it was used as a nursery school. In the 1960s and '70s, it became an army barracks. In 1979 the site was rescued when the Beijing government earmarked it as a 'key cultural heritage preservation site', and in 1987 the Beijing Art Museum was opened. Preservation and reconstruction of the buildings is still in progress.

When entering the first courtyard, visitors are directed to the Prologue Hall, where the history of the temple is explained and they can get a feel for the atmosphere of the Ming and Qing periods. There are excellent English trans-

lations and explanations of the exhibits throughout the museum.

The art is exhibited in the temple halls along the sides of the beautifully landscaped courtyards. The halls of Ming and Qing Buddhist art contain gilded bronze, stone, wood and crystal Tibetan and Han objects of worship. Some of these were not originally the property of the temple but come from the Bureau of Cultural Relics and are on permanent display here.

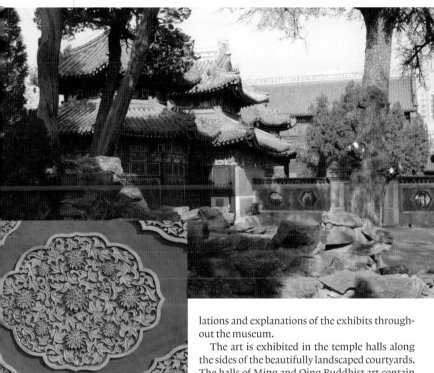

Temple buildings in the courtyard

Architectural detail from outer wall

There is a Gallery of Ming and Qing Arts and Crafts displaying wooden brush pots, ivory work, bamboo, inkstands and other objects. Alongside the artefacts are explanations of the use of some of the more obscure items; for instance, there is a display of thimbles made of a variety of materials such as jade or stone that were worn by ancient warriors as protection for their right thumbs when shooting arrows and which, in later periods, became valued as ornaments. Also on display are snuff bottles, bowls and cloisonné.

The Ming and Qing Porcelain Gallery displays mostly imperial porcelain, some of which was actually used by the Empress Dowager herself. Again, the exhibit is sensitively displayed with enlightening explanations of seals and especially interesting details regarding glazes and manufacturing or historical details. In the centre of the courtyard complex sits a large Ming period Buddhist temple. As you enter, you see a seated Buddha figure atop a bronze base of a thousand Sakyamunis. This exquisite and atmospheric old hall has eighteen *Luohans* lined up on either side and three big Buddhas behind. Note the beautifully painted ceiling. Be sure to walk behind the big Buddha and see the painted wooden bodhisattva Guanyin, the goddess of mercy.

The Wanshou Temple's Bell Tower was built as part of the original Ming temple and repaired in the Qing period. Tradition has it that the famous big bell of the Emperor Yongle's Reign – the so-called 'king of bells' – was hung in this tower and was to be rung by six monks every day. However, during the Reign of Qianlong, it was decided that the temple's location was inauspicious for the ringing of the bell, so it was laid on the ground. In 1743 it was moved to the Juesheng Temple, where it can be seen today in the Ancient Bell Museum.

In the temple grounds you can sit in the rock garden surrounded by magnolia trees and breathe in the atmosphere of Ming dynasty China. The eastern and western portions of the original temple grounds have, over the years, been taken over as residences; after you have looked at the museum itself, you can wander through the surrounding *hutongs*. People are living in the old temple buildings, which are now dilapidated, and you can see the ancient peeling paint, rotting roofs and pillars of the once grand structures among the detritus of modern life. On some walls you can even see the faint remains of slogans from the Cultural Revolution.

7

Beijing Aviation Museum

北京航空馆 *Beijing hangkongguan*

Beijing University of Aeronautics and Astronautics, 37 Xueyuan Lu, Haidian District
北京市海淀区学院路37号 北京航空航天大学

Tel: (010) 8231 7513
Open: 8.30–12.00 & 14.00–17.00 except Mon
www.digitalmuseum.buaa.edu.cn/index.jsp
Kids

The Beijing Aviation Museum was used by Beijing University as a showroom for teaching, practice and structural-design reference until 1986, when it was opened to the public. Unfortunately, there are no English explanations for any of the exhibitions.

The museum is divided into indoor and outdoor exhibition areas. The East Hall displays models and photos of various aircraft, as well as a model of the Chinese experimental communications satellite that was sent into orbit in 1984. In the West Hall are super-light aircraft which hang from the ceiling. The most interesting exhibits can be found in the yard to the back of the museum. On display are various aircraft from around the world and dating as far back as the 1940s. One of the most interesting is the P-61 night fighter, dubbed the 'Black Widow'. This name and a spider's web are prominently displayed on the front of this twin-prop plane, which was the first radar-equipped aircraft used by the Americans in the 1940s. Also of interest is a British Harrier jet. The P-47D fighter, aka the Thunderbolt, is easily identified by its chequered nose. Despite looking quite bulky, the P-47 was a fast aircraft and was used a good deal in

Military and civilian aircraft on display

Night Fighter, the 'Black Widow'

Europe in World War II. The museum is also home to several MiG fighters, including the MiG-15, which saw heavy duty in the Korean War. The sole helicopter in the collection was the first such aircraft to be developed by China.

Photography is permitted.

8

Beijing Museum of Natural History

北京自然博物馆 *Beijing ziran bowuguan*

126 Tianqiao Street
北京市天桥南大街126号

Tel: (010) 6702 4439; groups: 6702 4435, booking: 6702 7702
Open: 9.00–17.00 except Mon
www.bmnh.org.cn
Gift shop / café on second floor
Kids

Like so many museums of natural history, visiting this one is like walking into an oversized cabinet of curiosities, each exhibition hall – from the Ancient Reptiles and Invertebrates halls to Discovery World and the Aquarium – displaying the rare, the curious and the beautiful. This collection, however, unlike those founded in the great European cities, did not grow out of the wonders gathered by eighteenth-century men of science. Rather, it developed out of the National Central Museum of Natural History (founded in 1951) and consists primarily of indigenous specimens. Today, the museum boasts more than 200,000 items – a modest number compared to the many millions found in comparable natural history museums elsewhere – but its many unique specimens make it worthy of a visit.

Displays vary in quality; many of the newer ones, like those in the Palaeontology Hall and Discovery World, make use of ultra-modern methods of

Fossilized crinoids

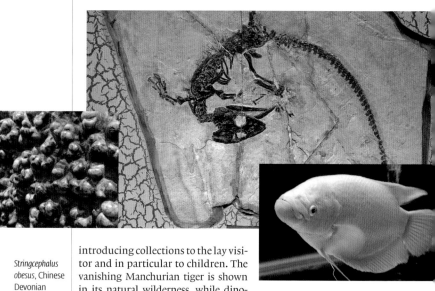

Stringcephalus obesus, Chinese Devonian brachiopod

Monjurosuchus splendens, proto bird fossil

A Severum in the tropical fish tank of the aquarium

introducing collections to the lay visitor and in particular to children. The vanishing Manchurian tiger is shown in its natural wilderness, while dinosaurs come to life – complete with sound effects and moving parts. Interactive displays allow school groups to learn through handling fossils and examining specimens, no doubt one of the reasons this is one of China's National Youth Science and Technology Education bases.

Overall the displays are well lit and described thoroughly in accompanying text, although only the main panels have highlights in English. Useful signage in the stairwells provides a layout of the museum indicating your current position and suggesting routes to follow, making it relatively easy to navigate the labyrinthine halls and exhibition areas.

If time is pressing, move to the large central dinosaur display entitled 'Dinosaur World' with full-size skeletons of a whole range of Chinese dinosaurs, some of which come alive as you approach, issuing sounds as they might have done in life. The long-necked *Mamenchisaurus jingyanensis* stands out. A gargantuan herbivore that lived around 150 million years ago, it had one of the longest necks of all known dinosaurs – 9 m in length – which allowed it to reach high in the trees to feed on leaves. Its 'second brain' in the hip area allowed it to control the movement of its hind legs and long, whip-shaped tail.

Another giant is the *Lufengosaurus huenei*, discovered by a Chinese dinosaur specialist and named after Lufeng, where it was found. Also plant-eating, its small, flat teeth with serrated edges enabled it to shred the plants it was able to reach while standing on its strong hind legs and using its big tail for balance. Also among the mix is the lake-dwelling *Tsintaosaurus spinorhinus*, discovered in and named after Qingdao in Shandong Province. Armed with a unicorn-like crest to which its name refers, this creature's large tail and paddle-like forelegs enabled it to swim.

Upstairs are displays of *Macroolithus* dinosaur-egg nests – the largest dinosaur eggs found in the world to date. Such nests have been found in various locations in China buried in sand or mud, sometimes as many as three deep, and date from the Late Cretaceous period.

Worth seeing are the cases crammed with beautifully displayed fossilized ammonites, sponges, shells and huge crinoids, or sea lilies. The computer-

generated images of these early sea creatures are stunning. Fossils of *Archaefructus liaoningensis* – an extinct genus of herbaceous aquatic seed plant from the Yixian Formation in western Liaoning Province – date from the Jurassic and are said to be the first flowers.

The basement aquarium is shabby but worth a visit if only to see the range of live specimens of fresh- and seawater fish; most impressive are the tropical fish. Also worth looking at, although rather dull in their formaldehyde-filled cases, are the two coelacanth specimens. A fish thought to be extinct since the time of the dinosaurs but rediscovered off the east coast of South Africa in 1938 when one was caught in a fishing net, these 'living fossils' date back 360 million years.

The Russian Tsar Peter the Great, who was renowned for his cabinet of human oddities, would have enjoyed seeing the hall entitled 'The Mystery of Humans' on the top floor. Displays of pickled body parts line cases around the walls while in the centre of the room, human cadavers with their heads hooded in black and feet covered with socks float serenely in coffin-shaped glass cases. Perhaps like Peter the curators hope these displays will inspire and above all educate; deformed fetuses and diseased organs are still used to support medical education and training.

The museum is active in scientific research across the disciplines of zoology, botany, palaeontology and anthropology. Fieldwork, often together with visiting scientists from institutions abroad, is conducted across China, and provides a constant stream of new discoveries. A host of publications highlights the latest research achievements, and the museum, in collaboration with the China Association of Natural Science Museums and the China Association of Wildlife Protection, publishes the scholarly journal *Nature* alongside more popular scientific books and papers. Mounting exhibitions abroad serves to not only publicize the collections and latest research but also to play an essential role as 'cultural ambassadors', promoting international collaboration.

As you leave the museum, look at the specimens of fossilized trunks of petrified conifers, some well over a metre high, standing outside in the forecourt. These are from the Mesozoic period and were found in western Liaoning Province, one of the most abundant areas in China for fossilized wood from the Jurassic–Early Cretaceous formation.

9

Beijing Planning Exhibition Hall

北京市规划展览馆 *Beijingshi guihua zhanlanguan*

20 Qianmen East Avenue, Chongwen District
北京市崇文区前门东大街20号

Tel: (010) 6701 7074 (group visit) / 6702 4559
Open: 9.00–17.00 except Mon
www.bjghzl.com.cn

This exhibition hall on the corner of the historic Qianmen follows the example of a similar and highly lauded space in Shanghai and other cities. Although the museum is stylishly designed with a hi-tech look, the experience here is a little disappointing due to the almost complete lack of English signage. The displays range in quality; some are quite contemporary in design. Some traditional, others kitsch. There is a huge wooden scale model of the Forbidden City which provides a fascinating peek into all the courtyards and areas closed

Scale model of Beijing in 2008

to the public; however, it is displayed with a tacky play of coloured lights and background music.

What *is* interesting and fun for the foreign visitor is a scale model of Beijing in 2008. Such models are included in all the planning museums of China. This 1:750 model is 302 sq m in size, and every building in town seems to be included. The floor of this enormous room is covered with an aerial photograph of Beijing in 2001. The problem is that one cannot get close enough to the centre of the model and the Second Ring Road to really get a look at individual buildings and point out those that you might know and use.

10

Beijing Police Museum

北京警察博物馆 *Beijing jingcha bowuguan*

36 Dongjiaominxiang Lane,
Dongcheng District
北京市东城区东交民巷36号

Tel: (010) 8522 5001
Open: 9.00–17.00
Kids, but see text

Situated on three floors, the Beijing Police Museum is thoroughly modern with well-lit cases, almost all with English signage. The content is thoroughly Chinese, including much political propaganda delivered in the tone of a party political broadcast.

The ground floor shows the history of the Beijing police from its beginnings in 1947. There are many photographs as well as documents, uniforms and old guns. On the wall is a huge photo taken from Tiananmen on the occasion of the 1 October 1949 ceremony in which Mao declared the beginning of the Republic. Also displayed are cannons, uniforms and other objects used by the participants in the ceremony. In contrast there are weapons, radio equipment, signed confessions, photos, signed denials and other relics of recalci-

trant Nationalist agents, spies and leaders. The usual pictures of visits to the museum by government officials and the high and mighty, including Mao Zedong and Deng Xiaoping, are also displayed on this level.

Upstairs there is a display of 'Judicial and Public Security Systems of Ancient Chinese Society'. There are a number of ancient artefacts such as a stone tablet dating from the Eastern Han found in 'a criminal's tomb' and inscribed with an account of his misdeeds. Also noteworthy is a Jin dynasty terracotta figurine of a man in handcuffs. There are Ming dynasty suits of armour, police

Beijing Concession District

This museum is housed in a former bank building in the old Legation Quarter of Beijing, an area well worth exploring as this neighbourhood is key to understanding China's domination by foreign powers. It begins on the southern edge of Tiananmen Square – called Qianmen – and is easily identified by the tower and clock of the old railway station – Qianmen Train Station – which has been recently restored.

After the First Opium War (1840–42) and the humiliating Treaty of Nanjing, the Qing government was forced, along with other degrading concessions, to allow foreigners to create a walled legation quarter in Beijing. All Chinese living in this district had to leave; no Chinese were permitted to enter without permission. Separated by walls, canon and armed guards, the area became an international town within Beijing – outside the jurisdiction of Chinese law. There were restaurants, hotels, cafés, delicatessens, post offices and banks in addition to the offices of the occupying governments which included Britain, France, Japan, Sweden and Russia. The tremendous resentment such indignities caused came to a head during the Boxer Rebellion of 1900 when the Legation Quarter in Beijing was besieged and the German ambassador among others was killed. After months of fighting and many deaths throughout China, the rebellion was ultimately crushed by an international force which sailed into Tianjin, and then marched to Beijing to lift the siege, looting and pillaging on their way.

Some embassies remained in the Quarter as late as 1959, but most of them moved much earlier to the Ritan Park area and Sanlitun. The newest embassy district of Beijing is in the Liangmahe neighbourhood. The old American embassy complex, together with Qianmen itself, has been restored and transformed into an elegant and upscale shopping and entertainment complex.

Although Beijing's Legation area is much smaller than that of Guangzhou and the Western-style architecture less remarkable than much of Shanghai, it still has an old world, colonial atmosphere. The streets are filled with solid old Western-style civic buildings and influences from German, British and French architecture can easily be spotted. Many of these buildings now house Chinese government offices. Some of the buildings that remain of the period include the Catholic Church of St Michael on the corner of Taijichang toutiao and Dongjiao minxiang, the buildings of the Belgian Embassy and a former French post office at 19 Dongjiao minxiang. The former Japanese Legation is on Zhengyi Lu and is now part of the Public Security Bureau. The Huafeng Hotel on Zhengyi Lu is still a hotel but was once the Grand Hotel des Wagon-Lits and was built in 1905.

Boxer rebellion. Soldiers outside the Wumen Gate

Qing dynasty policemen at station in Beijing

documents from the 1920s and 1930s, old maps of Beijing and photos of parades. Also displayed are some palace-guard uniforms and Qing dynasty police uniforms. Documents and photographs concern the travails of the police during the Cultural Revolution, when many members of the force were under attack. Even the Beijing police chief was persecuted and imprisoned. There are also some especially gory, graphic photographs depicting bombings, public uprisings, torture and murder – several of which are terribly gruesome and not suitable for children.

Photographs of and relics from particular crime investigations are displayed – such items can have a morbid fascination. Not surprisingly, there is no mention of the events of 4 June 1989.

At the top of the building is an exhibition of guns used by the Public Security Bureau from the past to the present. There is also a shooting gallery in which you can try your luck shooting at bad guys on a video screen.

11

Beijing Stone Carving Museum

北京石刻艺术博物馆 *Beijing shike yishu bowuguan*

24 Wutasi Village, Baishiqiao, Haidian District
北京市海淀区白石桥五塔寺村24号

Tel: (010) 6217 3543
Open: 9.00–16.00 except Mon
Delightful tea house

The National Library looming large on the north side of the Purple Bamboo Garden is your cue that across the street, along a rather quiet road and over the White Stone Bridge, is this museum within a temple complex. Unexpectedly peaceful and with a vegetarian restaurant attached, this delightful site is highly recommended for a brief respite.

Central to the complex is the handsome Wuta Si Temple, also known as the Five Pagoda Temple. Explore this first by going up the spiral staircase inside, as you will not only be enthralled by its carved decoration but from the top

you will get a bird's eye view of the museum's mostly open-air layout. Built in the fifteenth century to house five golden Buddhas and a miniature model of the famous temple of Mahabodhi at Bodh Gaya in India (where the Buddha attained enlightenment), it was originally known as the Zhenjue Temple. The building was renovated in the Qing dynasty, when it was used as an important imperial religious venue. It was badly damaged during the Japanese War, and what remains is a pagoda with a square base or throne and a large *shikhara* rising from four smaller ones. An enormous artwork in its own right, its surfaces are covered with the five sacred animals of Buddhism (lion, elephant, phoenix, horse, peacock), as well as the Buddha's footprints surrounded by lotus motifs, symbolizing his universal presence. Under each of the eaves are small shrines containing Buddhas.

The museum is divided into eight sections; displays range from tombstones to tools used to carve stone and fine examples of gilded stone tablets, all with very good explanations in English. A majority of the works are from the Beijing region with representative examples from various periods, many unearthed in recent years during construction work in the city. The stone tablets include one inscribed for a eunuch and others listing moral disciplines. Among the finest are twelve Ming and Qing tablets given by Emperors to their officials and generals and praising their achievements. Among the larger exhibits in the second hall is that containing more than a hundred stelae from the Tang to the Qing dynasties with inscriptions offering an encyclopaedic insight into the history, geography and politics of Beijing.

Decorative stone carvings for buildings and gardens (including arches, watchtowers, railings, balustrades and motifs such as dragons) demonstrate a diversity of styles and uses. Many of these were unearthed when demolishing the Ming wall in Beijing; particularly noteworthy are the stone lions which originally sat at the corners of foundation platforms in front of grand houses in the Yuan dynasty; the white marble decorated balustrade slabs engraved with dragons, phoenix and flowers; and the Song stone table listing acupuncture points. The third hall is devoted to the investigation and protection of carved stone objects in Beijing. In the 1950s surveys of carvings were launched in eighteen districts of the city to record, photograph and in some cases take rubbings. A map shows the distribution of these cultural relics. The survey's findings prompted the city to establish this museum in 1987.

Five Pagoda Temple

The area entitled 'The Art of Stone Carving' includes the oldest stone carvings in Beijing – from the Eastern Han dynasty – as well as Buddha statues from the Northern Qi and Northern Wei dynasties. Further on, gilded stone tablets from eight different provinces demonstrate the intriguing differences in regional cultures. There are stelae with Buddhist and Taoist inscriptions and images of the tombstones belonging to the Jesuits once buried in a graveyard here, thus demonstrating the cultural interactions between China and Europe.

12

Beijing Tap Water Museum

北京自来水博物馆 *Beijing zilaishui bowuguan*

Qingshuiyuan, A6 Beidajie Dongzhimen, Dongcheng District
北京市东城区东直门北大街甲6号
清水苑内

Tel: (010) 6465 0787
Open: 9.00–16.00 Wed–Sun

This is one of Beijing's newer technology-based museums. The subject may sound odd, especially given the fact that many people do not drink tap water in Beijing, but in fact the museum offers a compelling narrative of how this vital resource was and is delivered to the city's massive population.

Before there was any organized urban water infrastructure, Beijing's residents got their water from wells dug to reach underground springs. By around 1885 there were more than 1,200 such wells in the city. The water wasn't particularly satisfactory as it had a salty and bitter taste. Naturally, this would not have been suitable for the imperial family; their water was brought from a spring on Mt Yuquanshan in the west of Beijing.

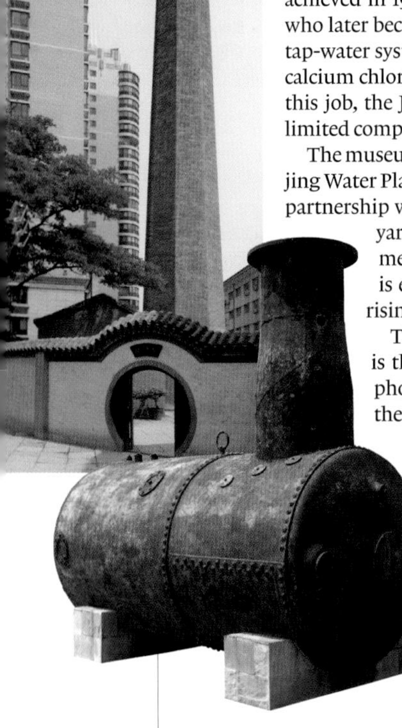

Original structures and equipment in the outside yard

How was the first public water system created? Apparently in the early twentieth century the Empress Cixi decided that a fire-protection system was needed for Beijing. For this purpose a source of water had to be available on the streets. This was achieved in 1907–08 when Yuan Shikai , the top Qing general who later became the first President of the Republic, initiated a tap-water system providing reliable, safe (as it was treated with calcium chloride) and plentiful water. The company created for this job, the Jingshi Tap Water Co. Ltd, was the country's first limited company.

The museum is housed in the original pump house of the Beijing Water Plant, making it close to a hundred years old. Built in partnership with the Germans, it is tucked inside a little courtyard – now an oasis – surrounded by high-rise apartment blocks and the Second Ring Road. Its location is evident from afar due to the tall brick steam pipe rising into the sky.

The exhibition is divided into three sections. First is the history of tap water in Beijing. On display are photos and artefacts as well as stock certificates from the Jingshi Tap Water Co. Ltd. There is a life-size model of a Beijing street illustrating how water was dispersed early in the twentieth century; it was available from a central public tap, where a man was stationed to distribute it. Residents had to buy water tickets. If they were unable to carry the water back to their homes themselves, they employed others to carry it for them. If you were wealthy, you could have your water delivered by standing order. A blue metal sign was posted above your door (all this can be seen on the reconstructed street corner).

A public tap in Beijing

The process of retrieving, storing, purifying and delivering the water is described and illustrated with original objects, photos and models. A model of the original 54-m-high water tower is also on exhibit.

The second section of the museum deals with the period from 1949 to 1979. Following the inception of the Republic, the Capital Iron and Steel Co. was established in Beijing, and the importation of foreign equipment for the city's tap-water system was stopped. The People's Army was ordered to take over water disbursement in the capital; there is a photo of the original document dated 17 March 1949 giving this order. They had their work cut out for them as only about 30 per cent of the population had access to tap water – even at this time most people were still getting their water from wells.

The final section of the museum deals with the present and the need for water conservation. There are models of Beijing No. 8 Water Factory, which uses water from thirty-seven deep wells, and No. 9 Water Plant, which uses surface water and is one of the biggest in Asia.

There is a lovely circular pillared building at the entrance of the complex built as a shrine to Guanyin. This building stood before the pool where water was collected in the early days. The original statue within it was destroyed, but at the time of writing this building was being restored, as was the charming park surrounding the pump house. Although the museum does not have much English signage, it is absolutely worth a visit, especially if you can bring a translator.

13

CAFA Art Museum

中央美术学院美术馆 *Zhongyang meishuxueyuan meishuguan*

Central Academy of Fine Arts, 8 Huajiadi Nan Street, Chaoyang District
北京市朝阳区花家地南街8号

Tel: (010) 6477 1575
Open: 9.30–17.30 except Mon; last entry 17.00
www.cafa.edu.cn
Book shop / café / conference facilities

This striking museum was designed by the prominent architect Arata Isozaki, whose work includes the Museum of Contemporary Art, Los Angeles. As an essential component of the Academy of Fine Arts, the museum's missions are to serve its students and provide visitors with an educational experience. CAFA is the only art and design institute in the country directly under the supervision of the Ministry of Education. Its goals are to improve communication between artists and the public, and to educate the younger generation from Beijing and the provinces.

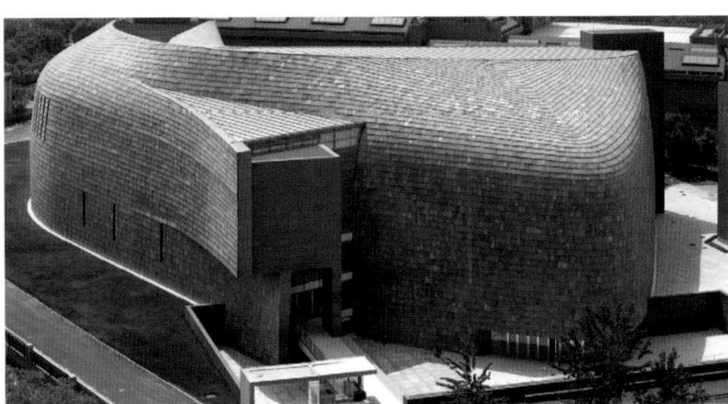

The museum has a collection of more than 6,000 pieces dating from the Yuan dynasty to the present. Tradition has it that graduates donate examples of their work to their alma mater, as well as a bequest after they die. As many of China's most famous artists attended the school, it has amassed a first-rate archive. The museum incorporates vast galleries with flowing lines and sharp angles – a feast for the eyes and a challenge for exhibition designers. The galleries are on four floors, with the second floor exhibiting local masters and the permanent collection. On the third and fourth floors the work of professors and teachers from CAFA is shown, as well as visiting contemporary exhibitions. Architecture, design, fashion and visual arts are all meant be represented in this venue, one of China's premier art establishments.

14

Capital Museum

首都博物馆 *Shoudu bowuguan*

16 Fuxingmen Wai Dajie, Xicheng District
北京市西城区复兴门外大街16号

Tel: (010) 6337 0491 / 0492; 6339 3339 booking
Open: 9.00–17.00 except Mon; last entry 16.00
www.capitalmuseum.org.cn/en/index.htm
Bookshop / gift shop offering a wide range of imaginative goods / café / tea bar

Han dynasty figurine

The original Capital Museum, although planned since 1953, was not opened until 1981.It was housed in the side halls of the Confucius Temple, one of the last idyllic sites of old Beijing. The original concept for the museum was twofold: to present a history of the development of the city of Beijing, its people, buildings and art; and to present a history of Chinese art, with an emphasis on artefacts collected in, or excavated in or near, the capital. The scale was small, the presentation and display unadventurous. The place was seldom crowded, and its charm was enhanced by the tranquillity of the surroundings.

Museum entrance hall

Full-size models of *hutongs* on display

From 1999 onwards both the municipal and state governments planned to move the museum to an altogether more grandiose site in Muxidi, west of Tiananmen and in the heart of modern Beijing. Construction began in December 2001. The new museum was designed by AREP together with China Architecture Design and Research. AREP, a Paris-based company specializing in transport projects, has had substantial experience in China, including work on the Xidan Bookstore a few kilometres down the road to the east on Chang'an Avenue, Beijing's central thoroughfare. The aim was to produce an intermingling of classic Chinese and modern architecture, in terms of both style and materials. Stone, bricks, timber and bronze are the major elements. The stone, from the Fangshan region, was commonly used in Beijing throughout its history. Elm, the most usual local construction material, is also used here. Decorative bronze features mirror locally unearthed Western Zhou ritual vessels. The massive overhanging roof is a modern essay on traditional low-slung Chinese roofs with eaves; the long stone curtain wall is intended to represent the ancient Chinese city wall, and a massive piece of stone carved with images such as dragons, phoenixes or clouds has been placed in the ground in front of the north gate.

The basic two-part collection remains the same as at the Confucius Temple. Although the physical plant and tech services are world-class (and designed to rival China's most modern museum to date in Shanghai), its scale (40-m high and 64,000 sq m) is deliberately in excess of the size of the collection. The museum's new building is therefore inextricably linked to its ambitious new exhibition programme.

The museum is made up of three main buildings: the Rectangular Exhibition Hall, the Oval Exhibition Hall, and the Office and Scientific Research Building. They are linked by a vast, towering reception hall and a naturally lit bamboo courtyard. The galleries devoted to the history of Beijing, housed on the second to the fifth floors of the Rectangular Hall, are the most interesting (sensitively and entertainingly arranged, they give a real picture of life in old Beijing, with a mass of architectural details, furniture, fittings, reconstructions of rooms and streets, toys, textiles, the Beijing Opera, and food and drink) and give a charming picture of the life and folk culture of the city as it was. They are not to be missed. The Beijing galleries are divided into History and Culture (second floor), Urban Construction (third floor), Chinaware and the Stage (fourth floor) and Old Stories and Folk Costumes (fifth floor). The exhibitions of fine art show highlights from the old Capital Museum on five floors of the Oval Hall and include painting, calligraphy, bronzes, jades, Buddhist art, and ancient stationery, writing materials and scholars' objects.

The building's huge scale leaves ample accommodation for multiple temporary exhibitions, and it has got off to a cracking start with major shows from the British Museum and the National Museum of Mexico, as well as some great provincial shows. Such high-quality exhibitions from around China will be of particular interest to the overseas visitor.

Russian-built MiG-15

15 China Aviation Museum

中国航空博物馆 *Zhongguo hangkong bowuguan*

Datangshan, Xiaotangshan Town,
Changping District
北京市昌平区小汤山镇大汤山

Tel: (010) 6178 4883 / 4882
Open: 8.00–17.30
Kids

Located about 64 km north of Beijing – approximately an hour's ride out of town – is the China Aviation Museum, among the finest aviation museums in the world. The museum displays more than 200 airplanes of a hundred different types, and provides an exciting hands-on look at the history of Chinese aviation. Opened in 1989, on the occasion of the fortieth anniversary of the Chinese air force, it is located on a former military air base at the foot of Datangshan.

The first thing you see upon arriving in the forecourt is a dramatic queue of surface-to-air missiles, anti-aircraft guns and a Chinese F-12 fighter. You

F-12 Fighter flanked by missiles and anti-aircraft guns displayed at the front gate

then enter an enormous, dark concrete hangar hewn out of the mountain with double anti-blast doors at both ends. Here, more than fifty airplanes, parked side by side in two rows, trace the development of Chinese aviation and the indigenous aircraft-manufacturing industry. The exhibit begins with a replica of a biplane, made of bamboo by Feng Ru, China's first aircraft designer and aviator. Born in Guangzhou, Feng (1883–1912) emigrated to the US as a child. In 1907 he began to manufacture airplanes in Oakland, California with a company he named the Guangdong Air Vehicle Company. In 1911, he returned to China with two planes and began to work with the Guangdong revolutionary government. In August 1912 he was killed in a plane crash while staging a performance.

The historical time-line continues with a replica of the first plane manufactured in China, 'The Rosamonde', named for Sun Yat-sen's wife, Soong Ching Ling. There is also a replica of the famous first aircraft of the Red Army: a plane captured from the Nationalist army and renamed 'Lenin'.

Following World War II, China obtained its aircraft from the Soviet Union, but the country soon began its own production, manufacturing Russian models under license. Therefore many early Chinese-made planes are very similar to their Russian counterparts. In the hangar can be seen the Chinese versions of Soviet F-2, F-5, F-6, F-7 and F-8 fighter planes. Also on exhibit are a Russian La-11 fighter, a Tu-2 bomber and a Mi-4 helicopter. Of special interest are MiG-15 and -17 fighter planes flown by Chinese and Soviet pilots during the Korean War. Some of these have stars painted below the cockpit – known as 'MiG Kills' – indicating how many American and South Korean planes they had shot down. Signage by the planes gives the names of the pilots responsible. Also notable is an American Mustang captured from the Nationalist army in 1949 and a Japanese Tachikawa Ki-36 used by the Japanese against Chinese guerilla fighters, as well as an Italian fighter aircraft – an F-104S – donated by the Italian air force.

Leaving the hangar, you see – parked by the side on the taxiway across from some gift shops and drink stands – a line-up of fighter planes from China and North Korea, including a rare FT-6 training plane. Finally you can wander out to the field where large aircraft of all sorts are parked. There are planes used during World War II and the early years of the People's Republic to transport senior leaders such as Mao Zedong, Zhou Enlai and Zhu De (commander-in-chief of the PLA). Here is an Li-2 used by Mao to inspect Guangzhou, Changsha, Wuhan and other areas in 1956. There is an Il-14 also used by Mao in 1957–58 which you can enter and see just as it was when Mao flew in it, his desk and bed, the carpet and upholstery all authentic and surprisingly austere. Displayed as well is the Y-5 transport, an all-purpose plane modelled on the Soviet An-2 which was used to scatter the ashes of Premier Zhou Enlai in 1976. You can even see a C-46 Transport Commando, flown over 'the Hump' by the US air force in World War II. After the Japanese took control of the Burma Road, the allies kept the Chinese Nationalists supplied by flying this treacherous route over the Himalayas. By the end of the war, more than 44,000 tons a month were being delivered, with a plane taking off every three minutes. More than 600 planes were lost.

The huge field is filled with every conceivable type of plane, both commercial and military, dating from World War II and later (helicopters, bombers and passenger planes; B-29 bombers from the 1940s, a MiG-21, a Red Flag F-20 fighter, even a water-ready flying boat). The list goes on and on. The planes have been left out in various states of decay. You can board many of them or clamber around outside, offering excellent photo opportunities and a great deal of fun. English labelling accompanies many displays.

For those with an interest in planes and aviation history, this experience is not to be missed.

16

China Millennium Monument World Art Museum

世界艺术馆（中华世纪坛）*Shijie yishuguan (zhonghuashijitan)*

A9 Fuxing Road, Haidian District
北京市海淀区复兴路甲9号

Tel: (010) 6852 7108
Open: 8.00–18.00 summer; 9.00–17.30 winter
www.worldartmuseum.cn

Built to celebrate the millennium this venue often hosts world-class national and international travelling art exhibitions. In 2001 it was the venue for the inaugural Beijing Biennale and has, over the years, hosted many high-calibre shows featuring contemporary, modern, classical and archaeological art both from China and abroad.

Check local listings to see what is on during your stay in Beijing.

17 China National Film Museum

中国电影博物馆 *Zhongguo dianying bowuguan*

9 Nanying Road, Chaoyang District
北京市朝阳区南影路9号

Tel: (010) 6431 9548
Open: 9.00–16.30 except Mon; last entry 15.30
www.cnfm.org.cn
Gift shop with legitimate DVDs / cafeteria / snack shops (including popcorn for movie viewing)
Kids

China National Film Museum

Since the release of *Ding Jun Shan*, China's first feature film, in 1905, China has had a thriving and innovative cinema industry. The film museum and cinema complex celebrates this past and present through exhibits and screenings. Unfortunately, there is little in English, but you can learn a lot walking through the museum's twenty exhibition halls with a Chinese friend. Content includes the history of Chinese cinema from its inception, animated and documentary films, the Hong Kong and Macao film industry and so on. Biographical information on stars and directors is displayed, as well as exhibits on special effects, sets and costumes, animation and the science of film photography. Hands-on interactive exhibits, which the kids might enjoy, allow you to try out camera and film technologies while making your own film. Shooting, editing, music, special effects and developing are covered. (Some of these exhibits are not always available during the week and when available may involve waiting in a long queue.) A variety of movies are also available for viewing. The museum has three 35-mm projection theatres, a digital-projection theatre screening panorama-format films with surround sound, and an IMAX theatre.

18 China National Post and Postage Stamp Museum

中国邮政邮票博物馆 *Zhongguo youzheng youpiao bowuguan*

Building D, No. 6 Gongyuan Xijie, Dongcheng District
北京市东城区贡院西街六号D座

Tel: (010) 6518 5511 / 5522
Open: 9.00–16.00 except Mon
www.cyzypm.com

The China National Postal and Postage Stamp Museum is located in the centre of Beijing in a new building. The exhibit is spread out over three floors, with postage stamps exhibited on the first floor, the early history of communications

Rare set of China Candarins

Stamp celebrating Mei Lanfang

and postal services introduced on the second floor, and China's modern postal system on the third floor. At the time of writing of this book, there were only very limited English explanations; however, the museum said English explanations would be ready soon. The stamp exhibition on the first floor, set in standing panels, covers the period from the Qing dynasty up to modern China. Stamps made in China up until the fall of the Nationalist government in 1949, which are against the wall on the left, have faded-looking inks and simple designs on cheap paper. It's only after 1949 that stamps become more colourful and themes begin to show a great deal of diversity.

The exhibition begins with Qing dynasty (1644–1911) in the 1800s. Prominent is the Dowager Jubilee, issued on 7 November 1894 to mark the 60th birthday celebration of the Empress Dowager Cixi. The stamp does not carry an image of the Empress Dowager, but rather a drawing of a dragon, possibly because it would have been considered improper to put the image of a member of the ruling family on a postage stamp.

The next period is the Republic of China (1912–49), featuring stamps with the image of Sun Yat-sen, the founder of the Nationalist Party that overthrew the Qing dynasty. Other stamps include Nationalist strongman Chiang Kai-shek, and sampans.

During the Revolutionary period, the 'People's Government', although not the official government of China, issued stamps in the areas under their control. A 1944 issue features Mao Zedong, then a guerrilla leader. There is also a workers' series issued in February 1949 showing an intellectual, soldier, postal worker and coal miner standing together in solidarity. The collection from this period also shows some actual envelopes bearing postage stamps and postal marks. A 1947 stamp celebrating the victory over the Japanese features Mao and Zhu De, in both perforated and unperforated editions, the latter for collectors.

The panels in the centre of the hall are devoted to stamps from around the world and modern China. This is a colourful collection, most of which is dedicated to Chinese culture. It includes stamps on historical sites around China – the Forbidden City, Temple of Heaven, Potala Palace, the Summer Palace and historical sites such as the old town of Pingyao and Confucius' hometown. There are also stamps on folk dance, Chinese instruments, Peking opera, traditional paintings, Buddhism and temples and mosques. Of particular interest is the series on Peking opera, featuring famous opera stars, including the legendary Mei Lanfang, who performed the *huadan*, or female role, in opera before women were allowed to perform.

A room to the left of the main hall features special exhibits that are held for six months to a year, featuring special stamps from the museum's collection.

The second floor is dedicated to the history of communications in China, and the connection with postal services is not always clear. The exhibits here feature the use of drums, fire from beacon towers and the use of horseback couriers – much as in the old West in the United States – to communicate between the long distances that separated frontier fortresses in ancient China. In the Ming dynasty a rudimentary postal system begins to take shape, and by the Qing dynasty we have postal regulations and a management system governing the courier stations around China. There is an exhibit on the birth of the non-government commercial postal system in the fifteenth century, and the appearance of overseas mail offices in the nineteenth century, established so that overseas Chinese could send letters and financial remittances back home.

'Stage Art of Mei Lanfang'

The exhibition traces the birth of the modern postal system in 1896 during the final years of the Qing dynasty, the advances under the postal system of the Republic of China, the Revolutionary period of secret communications instituted by the Communists, and the Red Post and Soviet Post during the Agrarian Revolution. On display here are black and white photos of early post offices, mail carrier uniforms, antique mailboxes, and other items related to the Chinese postal system.

The third floor is dedicated to China's modern postal system. Of especial interest is a video programme about a postal worker in the mountains of Sichuan province. The carrier is seen leading a white horse carrying two large mail bags over a wooden saddle up mountain paths, sometimes across snow-covered trails, as he delivers mail to far-flung reaches of the province, sleeping in tents in the evening. The trip takes him one month back and forth and museum staff say the man has covered a distance equal to six trips around the circumference of the globe. A mural also shows a woman mail carrier pulling herself upside down on a rope that stretches across a river in Yunnan province, in southwest China, where there is no bridge. The mural is devoted to the woman, who actually made this crossing regularly to deliver mail, becoming a national figure as a result.

The highlight of the floor – and possibly the museum – is the dark room where the museum displays its most valuable stamps under special lights. The collection includes an original Penny Black stamp from the United Kingdom, said to be the first adhesive postage stamp to be issued in the world, on 17 August 1839 (the date when the Penny Postage Bill was passed by Parliament, the stamp itself being issued for sale on 1 May 1840). The stamp, considered a masterpiece of the engraver's art, displays a profile of young Queen Victoria, reminiscent of the cameos of rulers on coins, wearing a crown.The stamp is framed by the words Postage and One Penny.

The rest of this floor is dedicated to modern postal technology in use in China today, from motorcycles and bicycles to stamping machines and computers.

19

China Printing Museum

中国印刷博物馆 *Zhongguo yinshua bowuguan*

25 Xinghua North Road, Huangcun Town, Daxing District
北京市大兴区黄村兴华北路25号

Tel: (010) 6026 1237
Open: 8.00–16.00 except Mon

Workers at the 'Directorate of Ceremonies' printing the Classics

Bi Sheng, inventor of moveable type

Although the museum building itself is rather unremarkable, its subject matter is not, for although it is common knowledge that Johannes Gutenberg fashioned the printing press in 1454, few know that he was neither the inventor of movable type, nor the creator of the first printed book.These firsts should actually be attributed to China. The exact dates of these inventions are rather murky. Probably as early as the seventh century, the Chinese were using carved wooden blocks to print Buddhist prayers on paper, although no examples to date survive. The oldest, extant printed scroll dates from between 704 and 751 and was found in a stupa at a Buddhist temple in Korea (written in Chinese characters). In China, the oldest printed book is said to be the Diamond Sutra scroll dating from 868 found in the Buddhist caves at Dunhuang. More recently, printed Buddhist charms (prayers known as *dharani* in Sanskrit rolled up and inserted into miniature pagodas) were discovered in a tomb in Sichuan, dating from around 757. It is certain that the Chinese developed the means to produce printed matter with the invention of writing 4,000 years ago and paper likely around the first century AD.

A further pioneering Chinese endeavour was recorded

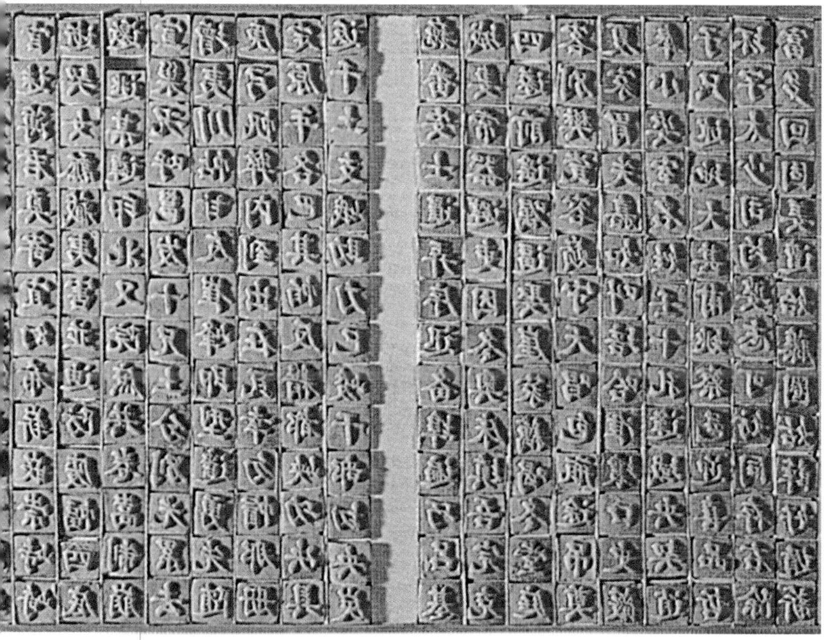

Reproduction of moveable type

in the mid eleventh century by Shen Gua (who wrote on the history of Chinese science in his *Brush Talks from Dream Brook*) who credited the invention of clay moveable type (ready made characters which can be moved and reused) printing to the engraver, Bi Sheng – an innovation which would later find its way to the West and be used by Gutenberg to print the Bible. As visitors enter the museum, a large bronze statue of Bi Sheng holding moveable type takes centre stage, highlighting this printing milestone which made it possible to accelerate the production of books. Three main display halls and three special exhibition areas over the museum's four floors trace the origin and development of printing through pictures, explanatory text (some in English), original objects and reproductions. Of these, the most fascinating exhibits relate to the invention of printing in China and elsewhere, from the earliest clay type to the later bronze used first in the Yuan dynasty for the printing of *The Imperial Examination Scripts*. Government as well as private printing were active during the Yuan with Hangzhou as the major centre in the south and Pingyang in the north, while during the Ming – known as the golden period of printing in China – the scale of printing grew exponentially, the quality improved and colour printing was invented. The second floor focuses on more recent printing advances such as planography (the technique of transferring ink to paper from a flat surface) and stencil printing and displays methods for specific types of printing, such as those used to print money (China was the first country to print a form of paper money known as 'exchange media' in the Southern Song) and stamps. The glamour of digital printing technology is touched upon on the first floor along with a concise history of printing in the West. An excellent publication entitled *An Illustrated History of Printing in Ancient China* (1998) chronicles this glorious history by means of excellent text and illustrations.

20

China Railway Museum

中国铁道博物馆 *Zhongguo tiedao bowuguan*

North of the Loop Line, 1 Jiuxianqiao North Road, Chaoyang District
北京市朝阳区酒仙北路1号

Tel: (010) 6438 1317 / 1517
Open: 9.00–16.00 except Mon
www.railway-museums.com/china_rm/
English and Chinese audio guides
Kids

Though somewhat difficult to find, this state-owned museum is well worth the adventurous journey. Just off the Fifth Ring Road and only fifteen minutes from the hip contemporary art scene at Dashanzi, this is a must-see for train enthusiasts. Housed in a large hangar-like shed connected to the China Academy of Railway Sciences Test Loop, the collection of locomotives and cars illustrates the development of China's railways from the nineteenth century to the present. Opened in 2002, the eight tracks can accommodate between eighty and ninety locomotives and carriages; sixty-nine locomotives are on display, twenty-nine of which were steam powered.

The first railway line in China was built illegally in 1876 by a group of Englishmen associated with Jardine Matheson, the Hong Kong trading company. They built a narrow-gauge line from Shanghai to Wusong, a distance of 15 km, to the mouth of the Huangpu River. This project was not approved by the Qing government, which purchased the railroad in 1877 and dismantled it. A standard-gauge railway was built by the English in 1881 from Tangshan to Xugezhuang for the purpose of transporting coal from the Tangshan mines. The first steam locomotive was constructed using the boiler and other parts

The oldest locomotive in China, 1881

of a portable steam winding engine borrowed from the colliery. This home-made 0-6-0 tank engine was known as 'The Rocket of China', and it was so successful that two more were ordered from the well-known manufacturer Robert Stephenson & Co. of Newcastle, making them the first to be imported into China. An example of these, as well as the oldest steam locomotive in China (fully restored after the 1976 earthquake in Tangshan), can be found in the museum.

Following the defeat of China in the Sino-Japanese War of 1894–95, the Great Powers proceeded to 'carve up' China, building railways as a key element of their spheres of influence. Russia built a railway across Manchuria to Vladivostock, Germany built the Jiaoji Railway from Qingdao to Jinan, France built the Sino-Vietnamese Railway in the southwest, and the British built the Kowloon Canton Railway. This explains the extraordinary variety of rolling stock in the country.

Among the highlights of the collection are:

- Foreign locomotives used in Republican China, such as the 1947 US-built steam locomotive Class KD 534. This train, built by Bowen Locomotive Co. and used for freight as well as passengers, was among a batch donated by the United Nations to help with economic recovery after World War II. It was called the 'Union Style' and was at the time the most technologically advanced in production.
- Famous multi-purpose locomotives built in Japan and named after revolutionary heroes such as the Class Zhu De and Class Mao Zedong.
- The Class SL3 No. 152 Japanese locomotive known as 'The Pacific'. Produced in 1942 and made by Kawasaki, it was the main passenger car used throughout the north and east of China, retiring only in 1981.

Zhou Enlai's official coach

Japanese locomotive 'The Pacific'

Zhan Tianyou

Zhan Tianyou (1861–1919) is the most famous person in China's railway history. Educated at Yale University in the US, and having been involved in other projects in China, in 1905 he was called upon by the Qing government to build a line between Beijing and Zhangjiakou. Zhan designed an effective method of constructing a rail line up steep mountains and invented the vertical-shaft construction method to create a railway tunnel at Badaling. He is also responsible for proposing a standard gauge and coupler to be used throughout the entire country – still the standard today. Zhan is buried at the Qinglongqiao station, where the line between Beijing and Zhangjiakou crosses the Great Wall. The museum nearby contains various artefacts, documents, photographs and prizes.

- A Russian Class FD 1979 steam locomotive made in the Soviet Union in 1931 and brought to China in 1958, when the country had a shortage of railroad transport capacity. It was used extensively in central China.
- Zhou Enlai's official personal coach, Class GW 97336, built in 1936 in Manchuria at the Dalian Works. Premier Zhou used this as his office when travelling in the 1950s and '60s. Visitors can enter the cars and view his and his wife's bedrooms, including her fuchsia-coloured bathroom suite.

The museum's audio guide is quite helpful, though spiced with patriotic formulas and political sermonizing. Plans are currently underway to add another building which will house artefacts connected with train culture, such as uniforms, equipment, tools and models. Anyone interested in further exploring the railway history of China can also visit the museum dedicated to Zhan Tianyou, the engineer known as the father of China's railways, near the Qinglongqiao railway station (see box).

21

China Science and Technology Museum

中国科学技术馆 *Zhongguo kexue jishuguan*

1 Beisanhuan Zhong Road
北京市北三环中路1号

Tel: (010) 6237 1177
Open: 9.00–16.30 except Mon & national holidays
www.cstm.org.cn/
Gift shop / snack bar
Kids

Although running a distant second to the glitzy Shanghai Museum of Science and Technology, there is no doubt that Beijing is serious about science education. This complex of buildings, including the main museum, movie theatre and special exhibition hall offers hours of scientific exploration, and a further expansion is planned. There are plenty of basic hands-on experiments, interactive exhibits and demonstrations with an emphasis on stimulating scientific curiosity and play. The exhibit on ancient Chinese science is fascinating. It features such early innovations as the winnowing machine, astronomical clock, moveable type, chain pump, odometer and clepsydra (water clock). Exhibits include aeronautics, energy, communications, material science and mechanics, information technology, life science and the environment.

22

China Sports Museum

中国体育博物馆 *Zhonguo tiyu bowuguan*

A new museum will open in 2009/10 as part of the Longtan Lake Sports Park, Chongwen District
北京市崇文区龙潭湖体育产业园

Audio guides / publications are planned

Han tomb brick with archer

Commemorative medal from the 1936 Berlin Olympics

At the time of publication this museum, which once stood inside the National Olympic Sports Centre, is closed with plans to re-open in Chongwen as part of the Longtan Lake Sports Park. Besides the museum, there will be a range of sports-related facilities in this, one of four major parks aimed at invigorating interest in sport for fitness and as entertainment. Until the new museum opens, temporary exhibitions of its collection are touring in Beijing and in other parts of China. Check local listings for details of these exhibitions.

The collection stands at some 8,000 objects and is growing daily, mostly amassed through donations from Chinese sports stars and athletes who have competed in international events. The red suit worn by Xu Haifeng when he won China's first-ever Olympic gold in pistol shooting in 1984 is a proud addition. Ancient objects trace the history of sport over 4,000 years and include a wooden comb from the Qin period featuring *jiaodi* (wrestling), in which the athletes are depicted wearing ox horns, and Tang images of polo being played. Hundreds of photographs and unique examples of equipment bring to life the variety of ethnic minority sporting activities like horse racing, hunting and archery. Objects dating from 1840 to 1949 map out the introduction of modern games such as gymnastics and sport as an extension of military training. Finally, a large collection of championship cups, world record-medals and images of famous Chinese attest to the country's sporting prowess, in particular at table tennis. No doubt there will be a section devoted to the 2008 Beijing Olympics.

23

Confucius Temple and Guozijian

孔庙，国子监 *Kongmiao guozijian*

13 Guozijian Street, Dongcheng District
北京市东城区国子监街13号

Tel: (010) 8401 1977
Open: 9.00–17.00

Confucius Temple – Kong Miao – is one of the few remaining unspoiled gems of old Beijing, a haven of peace in a city which is, according to taste, either destroying or re-inventing itself. It has two courtyards, four major buildings, fourteen Ming and Qing pavilions, countless precious stelae, and a wealth of ancient cypress trees, which even by Chinese standards, are varied, valuable and stunningly beautiful. Not least is a 700-year-old specimen with the alleged ability to distinguish the corrupt from the honest courtier who passed underneath. Open to the public since 1928, studious Beijing schoolchildren go to the temple to revise for their exams; traditional musicians rehearse classical and modern tunes on ancient instruments; and the discriminating tourist lingers.

The Dacheng Hall

Stone drums, stele and a bronze bell displayed on one side of the Dacheng Gate

Originally Confucius Temple was called Guozijian – Imperial College. This is now a separate but interconnected building immediately to the west (restored and re-opened to the public in 2007). Its function was the intensive training in classical studies of students for the imperial examinations, a training which created the administration to run the vast Chinese Empire. Here the Emperor himself would come to lecture. Once the teaching function was established in Guozijian, Confucius Temple became the ritual centre where the Emperor would sacrifice rather than lecture, and where the records of successful students were inscribed.

Confucius Temple was constructed in 1302; Guozijian was begun in 1308. Both underwent many changes, reconstructions and restorations.

The visitor enters Confucius Temple from the south through the Xianshi Gate (Gate of the Master). The buildings follow a south–north axis, passing through the outer courtyard (full of stelae and memorials) past the imposing statue of Confucius himself, then through the Dacheng Gate (Gate of Great Success) into the main courtyard with its pavilions. The Dacheng Hall is at the northern end. The main courtyard contains 198 stone tablets recording the names and origin of the successful candidates in the imperial examinations.

The actual temple where the Emperor would sacrifice – Chongshang Memorial Temple – is tucked away behind the Dacheng Hall. In the main courtyard there are fourteen pavilions, as well as offices and exhibition halls. Within the temple grounds are many historically important stelae, including the Thirteen Classics Stele, which took twelve years to be completed and contains 630,000 words; there are also records of 51,624 *jinshi*, the successful candidates for the imperial civil service examinations, from the Yuan to the Qing

dynasties. Other stelae record important events, the suppression of rebellions, a number of famous poems and the Sacred Edict. Every Emperor from Kangxi through the Ming and Qing dynasties inscribed a tablet on accession; the complete collection of nine tablets is displayed in the Dacheng Hall.

Confucius Temple was originally constructed with greenish-blue glazed tiles, but the Qing Emperor Qianlong ordered the reconstruction of the roofs of the halls of sacrifice with imperial yellow-glazed tiles. Other buildings were given green tiles and the side halls grey. The halls on the west side of the main courtyard house the Ancient Music House, a centre for the study of ancient Chinese instruments which has a pleasantly serious student atmosphere and a good shop. There is also a permanent exhibition devoted to the role of Confucius in history both at home and abroad, including, rather improbably, such Western luminaries as Voltaire and Ronald Reagan.

Returning south towards the main entrance, the visitor turns right in the outer courtyard to approach Guozijian, built on the same plan as Confucius Temple and with much of the same charm but somehow without the same atmosphere. Don't miss the Biyong Hall in the centre of the main courtyard, a stunning example of an open-plan wooden construction with a central throne from which the Emperor lectured his students. Its scale can be imagined from the fact that the Emperor Qianlong gave a lecture there in 1785 to no fewer than 3,088 students.

Confucius

Confucius was born in what is today Shandong Province and lived from 551 to 479 BC. A minor official, he toured the courts of various feudal rulers seeking to influence them with his radical teachings, which centred on a positive view of human nature and espoused the principles of respect for others, benevolence and sincerity, as well as filial piety. These teachings were collected into an anthology called the *Analects*.

In that early period, Confucius' views competed with many other philosophical and spiritual idea systems, including Daoist and Legalistic doctrines. In 136 BC, however, Confucianism, incorporating the ideas of both its namesake and other like-minded philosophers, became the exclusive state ideology of the Han dynasty. Subsequent centuries saw the importation and dominance of Buddhism, which in turn led to a counter-reaction in the eleventh century known as Neo-Confucianism. While reasserting key Confucian values, this system of thought raised the ancient philosophy to a metaphysical and religious level, taking on board elements of Buddhist and Daoist religions.

While Confucianism did not have an organized church or clergy, its religiosity was expressed in temples dedicated to its founder and to the worship of Heaven and of ancestors. It also grew to be one of the dominant philosophical trends in surrounding states in East Asia. In modern China, though, revolutionaries denounced the Confucian social hierarchy, which stressed the dominance of ruler, father and husband. More recently, as Marxist ideology has been de-emphasized, the Chinese government has returned to praising 'positive' aspects of Confucianism as a way to create cohesion and shore up civil society.

24

Dabaotai Western Han Tomb Museum

大葆台西汉墓博物馆 *Dabaotai xihanmu bowuguan*

Fengtai Lu, Fengtai District (680 m south of the World Park)
北京市丰台区丰台路
(世界公园南680米)

Tel: (010) 8361 3073
Open: 9.00–16.00 except Mon

Archaeologists excavated the Dabaotai Western Han Tomb in 1975 but were unable to identify whose tomb it was. It's likely, however, that the person buried here was a prince of the Liu family who died sometime around 45 BC. Tombs like this were normally constructed for emperors and princesses during the Han dynasty.

Two tombs were located here when the site was excavated in 1975.Tomb No. 1 is an underground burial palace with wooden frames. The inner coffin is made of Chinese catalpa, a tree with large heart-shaped leaves. It has three inner and outer wooden coffins enveloped by tens of thousands of large square beams, sealed with plaster to keep it dry, which may explain why the tomb is so well preserved. Some 400 funerary objects were uncovered, including ceramics, bronzes, and iron, jade and bone articles. The most striking items are the three lacquered chariots and eleven horses that were buried alive in a long, narrow passageway which opens at the entrance to the tomb.

Scale models of the chariots are on exhibit outside. There is also a small museum displaying several burial objects that were excavated in the tomb, such as jade carvings, miniature wooden burial figurines, bronze incense burners and a bronze door decoration resembling a beast. Tomb No. 2 once held the remains of the queen consort, but it was robbed and destroyed by fire in ancient times, and nothing remains.

25

Dashanzi and Caochangdi

大山子艺术区，草场地 *Dashanzi yishuqu, Caochangdi*

Chaoyang District
北京市朝阳区大山子艺术区
北京市朝阳区草场地

Sculpture by Wang Guangyi

These two neighbourhoods are the main focus for Beijing's rip-roaring contemporary art scene. The situation is so dynamic and developing at such speed that by the time you read this there may well be more areas to explore and, within these existing locations, many more galleries to investigate. The best way to do this is to arm yourself with a weekly or monthly entertainment guide – Beijing has a few excellent ones – and just start walking.

Within Dashanzi in northeastern Beijing is an area lined with factories and warehouses – some still functioning – known as '798' (*Qi Jiu Ba*). At its centre is Gallery 798, which was the first gallery here. This factory building, built around 1950, was designed by East Germans in the Bauhaus style. Its original function was as an electrical-equipment production plant – it is said that components for China's first atomic bomb were made here. Stencilled in red and still preserved along the inside walls of this building and on the interiors and exteriors of many others in the area are slogans from the Cultural Revolution such as 'Long Live the Great Helmsman Mao Zedong'. Since the opening of Gallery 798 and other early galleries, the neighbourhood has exploded with art venues – to date approximately 200, including the Ullens Center for Contemporary Art. Restaurants, bars and shops have followed, and the streets buzz with activity. Indeed, this neighbourhood has become one of the top tourist attractions in Beijing, leading some people to feel that it is now *too* commercial and has lost its once edgy feel.

There are too many galleries to name here, but a some of the highlights are 798 Space; 798 Photo Gallery; 798 Red Gate Gallery (a branch of the established, eminent Red Gate Gallery located at Dongbianmen Watchtower in Chongwen); White Space Beijng; and Beijing Tokyo Art Projects and the Pace Wildenstein Gallery.

Further east is a newer art district called Caochangdi. The original gallery here (still open and flourishing) is the China Art Archives and Warehouse, built seven years ago by the well-known artist Ai Weiwei. At that time, this village seemed far from the centre of Beijing, but now it has been urbanized. Although the galleries here are spread out and may seem hard to find, it is well worth the trip as this is *the* emerging area and houses some of the most exciting art venues in the city. Again, as galleries are popping up daily, it is necessary to check local listings.

At the time of writing the outstanding galleries included the Three Shadows Photography Art Centre, built by Ai Weiwei and the brainchild of the photographers Rong Rong and Inri. First-rate exhibitions are held here in a well-designed space. In addition there are a film theatre, outdoor film evenings, photographers' talks, children's workshops, darkrooms and digital rooms open to the public with an instructor available, a library open to the public, a gift shop and a café. This is a wonderful addition to the Beijing museum scene and a great place to bring kids for weekend workshops. Pekin Fine Arts is another place to visit. After leaving the well-known Courtyard Gallery, owner Meg Maggio set up in a new space also designed by Ai Weiwei. Gallerie Urs Meile is a Beijing space for the prominent Swiss gallery of the same name, while ShangArt is a branch of the distinguished Shanghai gallery. In addition, there is a separate gallery space called Platform in which a number of galleries cluster together. Finally, the Beors-Li Gallery is located in an old warehouse called Universal Studios. This warehouse gallery also has a popular café and bar.

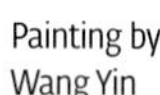

Painting by Wang Yin

Outdoor sculpture in Dashanzi

Be sure to check listings for galleries in both 798 and Caochangdi as opening hours vary. Some of these places may seem hard to find, but that's part of the fun.

26

Fahai Temple

法海寺 *Fahaisi*

Fahai Temple, Moshikou,
Shijingshan District
北京市石景山区模式口法海寺

Tel: (010) 8871 5776 / 3976
Open: 9.00–16.00
Books / pamphlets

Set on the foot of the Cuiwei Mountain, a short walk from the eunuch cemetery of Tianyi Mu, is the Fahai Temple or Ocean of the Law Temple. It was built with funds raised by the Ming dynasty eunuch, Li Tong, who hired fifteen of the very best painters of the period supervised by the imperial artists Wan Fuqing and Wang Shu. This Buddhist temple, built between 1439 and

Saraswati, Hindu goddess of wisdom and fortune

The waiting maid of Mahesvara holding a jade mirror

1443 under the Zhengtong Emperor contains original and extraordinarily beautiful Ming dynasties Buddhist wall paintings modelled on earlier Tang and Song dynasties traditions. The presence of Indian Hindu gods in these paintings are in keeping with the international influences so often seen in Ming dynasty art.

Originally the temple complex had many buildings all containing murals but the only surviving wall paintings are nine murals in the Mahavira Hall (*Daxiongbaodian*). These can be viewed (at an extra charge) and miraculously are in excellent condition with clear and bright paintwork. They are not frescoes but painted on prepared clay with mineral pigments in a glue medium. In some areas, especially on images of armour and jewellery, gold thread was added. In order to preserve the highly fugitive paint the temple is kept in darkness and visitors are provided with a torch and go in with a guide – at this time, Chinese-speaking only. The paintings survived the ravages of the Red Guards although the statuary at the temple complex did not (see box). Two reproduction temple buildings have been built up the hill from the Mahavira Hall – one of which exhibits reproductions of wall paint-

Mural detail of Upasaka, a lay follower of Buddhism

ing details. However, viewing the originals is well worth the added fee.

Entering the Hall the murals fan out along the three facing walls. Beautifully painted clouds, peonies, lotuses, lilies, flying apsaras, celestial beings, gods, kings and animals confront the visitor. On the north wall is the most famous mural of Fahai Temple. This is a triptych of three bodhisattvas: Avalokitesvara (Chinese: *Guanyin*) the goddess of Compassion, Manjusri (Chinese: *Wenshu*) representing wisdom and Samantabhadra (Chinese: *Puxian*) the god of truth. Guanyin, in the centre, is portrayed gazing at the reflection of the moon in the water. This represents the illusory nature of the material world. She is sensitively and naturally painted, wearing a swathe of white gauze draped over her shoulders and wrapped in pearl and jade necklaces. These figures are accompanied by other gods and attendants, a tame lion and Puxian's six-tusked elephant. The faces of humans, gods and animals in these murals are painted in an exquisitely sensitive and expressive manner.

On either side of the northern wall beside the entrance is a diptych known as 'Sovereign Sakra and Brahma', on one side, Brahma and other gods with attendants and guardians and, on the other side, the female Sakra with her retinue all going to a meeting. They are painted with individual expressions and with faces meant to reflect their individual characteristics – kindly, mighty etc.The bodies and movements are graceful and flowing.Although the mural is in two panels they relate to and reflect each other and through this symmetry are in effect one work.

The murals of Fahai Temple, although not nearly as commonly visited, are considered of comparable quality to those at Dunhuang and the Yongle Palace

Wu Xiaolu: Hero of the Cultural Revolution

The Red Guards were initiated by Mao Zedong in 1966. Their goal was to destroy the 'Four Olds' – old ideas, old culture, old customs and old habits.

Their methods were violent, destructive and murderous. Mainly students and young workers, they rampaged through China destroying art, architecture, libraries, temples and museums as well as publicly humiliating and even killing those they considered anti-revolutionary.

This story is told about Wu Xiaolu, an elderly caretaker of Fahai Temple at the time.

When the Red Guards arrived at the temple, they destroyed all the sculptures in the compound including one of Li Tong – the eunuch who built the temple in 1443. The Red Guards then left for the day. Mr Wu, was ready for them the following day when they came back to finish the job. Brandishing an axe and determined to save the murals, he told them they would have to fight him to get into the Mahavira Hall which he had locked.

At that moment – as the tale is told – the sky filled with black clouds and thunder and lightning followed. Mr Wu cried out – 'You see – you have angered the Buddha – now he will punish you!' The Red Guards, although intent on destroying the old traditions, could not quite handle this 'old' threat – they ran away in fear and the murals were preserved.

and represent the height of Ming dynasty wall painting.

The temple compound itself, in a charming bucolic setting, is a most pleasant place to spend some hours and like Tianyi Mu it is wonderfully underpopulated. One can relax there very comfortably in the shade of the two ancient white pines contemplating the marvellous paintings one has just been privileged to see.

27 Forbidden City and the Palace Museum

紫禁城，故宫博物院 *Zijincheng, Gugong bowuyuan*

Tiananmen
天安门

Tel: (010) 8511 1576 / 1567
Open: 8.30–17.00,
1 Apr–31 Oct; 8.30–16.30, 1 Nov–31 Mar
www.dpm.org.cn
Gift shop / book shop / museum guide available (written / audio),
Restaurant / coffee shop / shops and cafés situated at intervals throughout the site
Kids

Wumen, the Meridian Gate

The Palace Museum, along with the Forbidden City in which it is housed, constitutes one of the three most famous, and most visited, sites of China (the others being the Great Wall and the Terracotta Warrior Army in Xi'an). Surrounded by moated walls, covering an area of 720,000 sq m (of which more than 400,000 sq m are open to the public), and with nearly 8,000,000 visitors a year, the nature and history of the site merit study before planning to visit.

The Forbidden City was the palace of the Emperors of the Ming and Qing dynasties. The overall impression is one of breadth, not height, with a procession of grand central palaces running from south to north. There is a balance between vast open courtyards, long walled thoroughfares, and more intimate palaces crowded together behind long purple walls away from the central courtyards. The purple walls and yellow and green tiles take on different hues at different times of year. In summer the brilliant white light flattens the effect; in winter the sunlight draws out the purple so that it almost glows – an effect much heightened during snow. The Forbidden City was also the administrative and bureaucratic hub of a vast empire; by the sixteenth century no other country in the world could boast a palace of such size, complexity and grandeur from which was controlled, with more or less success, the daily lives of more than 120 million people – more than the entire population of Europe at that date.

The Palace Museum is not only the most famous building in China, it also houses a significant part of the imperial collection of art and artefacts – in total the greatest of all the collections of Chinese art and civilization. At the fall of the empire in 1911, some 1,170,000 items were in the collection, of which 600,000 are still in Beijing. A relatively small selection of these are housed and displayed in galleries open to the public spread throughout the site.

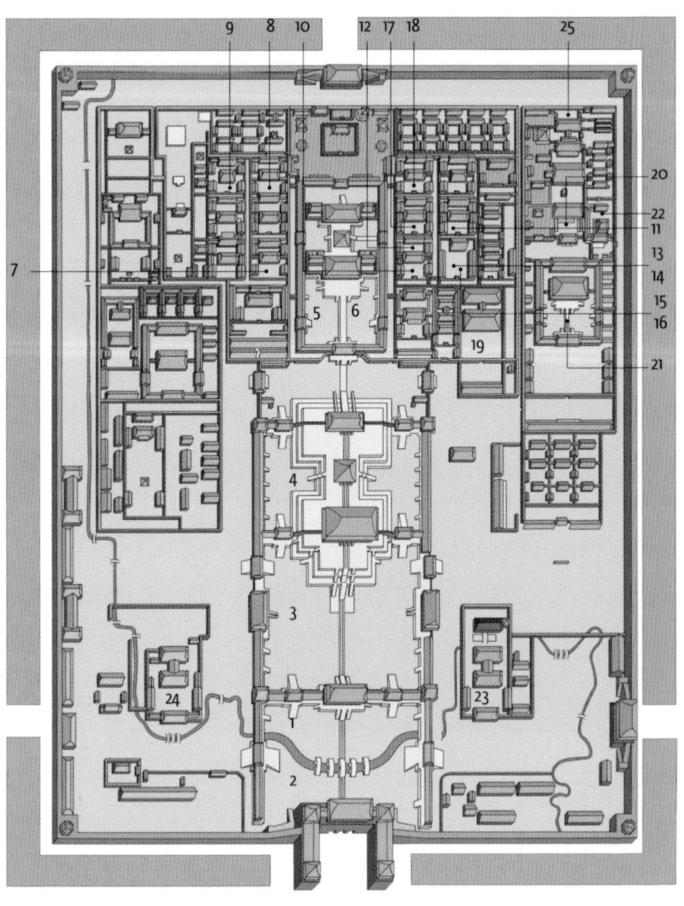

This was truly a working palace. The Emperor was the Son of Heaven – not just the absolute ruler of his subjects on earth but the appointed link between them and the deity. He was both the supreme legislator and the chief executive of infinite power – and he controlled a vast, dedicated Confucian-trained bureaucracy to enforce his will and also to report back to him from the world outside. The largest country in the world was also the most centralized – the sheer volume of paperwork and opinion that came to the Emperor for appraisal would have overwhelmed the ruler of any modern state. It is no wonder that a conscientious Emperor like the eighteenth-century Qianlong, who rose every morning at 5.00 to cope with the workload, took early retirement and built for himself a special Retirement quarters – The Studio of Exhaustion from Diligent Reign – in the north-east corner of the city (restored and opened to the public in 2008).

The Forbidden City was built on an axis centred between the four imperial temples of Beijing. Its ground plan perfectly fulfilled the geomantic requirements of *feng shui*, while its predominantly purple colour referred by literary

Forbidden City Exhibition Halls

1. Qing dynasty Court Insignia
2. Weapons of the Qing dynasty
3. Qing dynasty Ritual Music
4. Long Live the Royal House
5. Long Live the Emperor!
6. The Qing Emperors' Grand Weddings
7. Daily Life of Qing dynasty Concubines
8. Life of the Last Emperor, Puyi
9. Ruling from Behind the Screen
10. Hall of Donations
11. Bronze Mirrors
12. Artefacts donated by Zhang Naiqi
13. Digital Painting and Calligraphy
14. Shards from Chinese Kiln Sites
15. Imperial Porcelain with Royal Designs
16. Early Twentieth-century Architectural Folly
17. Ancient Bronze Vessels from the Shang and Zhou dynasties
18. Jade Carvings
19. Hall of Clocks
20. Imperial Treasures and Ornaments
21. Stone Drums
22. Opera at the Qing Court
23. Chinese Ceramics
24. Chinese Painting, Calligraphy and Printing
25. The Studio of Exhaustion from Diligent Reign

allusion to the Pole Star, and hence enforced the Emperor's pivotal role between heaven and earth.

Until 1911 the public knew nothing of the layout of the Forbidden City. Even ministers and civil servants had only strictly limited access to the outer courts, where the business of government was conducted, and no idea of what went on in the 9,000 rooms of the imperial residences at the eastern end. Those seeking access had to approach from the south through the Gate of Heavenly Peace (*Tiananmen*), on the north side of Tiananmen Square. From the balcony of this gate in 1949 Chairman Mao proclaimed the birth of the People's Republic, saying 'that the Chinese people have stood up'.

This is still the best approach for the visitor today. After one more gateway, the Forbidden City proper is reached through the Meridian Gate (*Wumen*). Thirty-eight-metres high, it is the tallest building in the Forbidden City and has a unique three-winged layout. The central gateway was for the exclusive use of the Emperor (with the exception of the Empress on her wedding day, and of the three examinees who passed top of the civil service examinations). It was where he reviewed his troops, where ministers who had failed were clubbed as punishment, and where officials with business within had to present themselves before daybreak.

The Qing dynasty was overthrown in the revolution of 1911, although the last Emperor, Puyi, was permitted to continue to live in the Inner Court – the imperial residence – until 1924. The Qing were Manchus from the northeast, and, after 1911, all their treasures from Chengde (originally Rehe) and Shenyang (originally Mukden) were brought down to Beijing and added to the imperial collection housed in the Forbidden City (although a significant number of Manchu relics were later sold off or pawned by Puyi himself).

A selection of the imperial collections was first shown to the public as the History Museum in 1914. The Palace

Taihemen, the Gate of Supreme Harmony

Museum itself was opened, to great fanfare, in 1925. Its history was driven by the turbulent happenings in China during the War against Japan, World War II, and the Civil War. By 1933 the invading Japanese were about to capture Beijing, and the collection was evacuated for safety, first to Nanjing, then to Sichuan, then to Chongqing and finally, in 1947, back to Nanjing, headquarters of the Nationalists. When the Nationalists were evidently finally losing the Civil War, they shipped, in 1948–49, 2,972 crates of relics to Taipei. After Liberation in 1949, many of the remaining relics were returned from Nanjing to Beijing. The Palace Museum is therefore one of three museums housing the old imperial collection, the other two being the Nanjing Museum and the National Museum in Taipei. In Beijing only a fraction of the entire collection can be shown at any one time; a selection of works are exhibited in a number of buildings scattered throughout the palace.

Gate of Supreme Harmony showing balustrades along the banks of the Golden Water River

The Forbidden City can also be entered from the Gate of Divine Prowess (*Shenwumen*) opposite Jingshan Hill in the north. However, entering via the Meridian Gate is recommended for a first visit, as walking from south to north gives a clearer picture of the palace's logical layout and follows the route taken by ministers, generals and civil servants and others with business at the court. The tunnel-vaulted entrance leads to a huge courtyard through which the Golden Water River (*Jinshuihe*) runs – it both feeds the moat and provides water for the palace complex.

Directly opposite is the Gate of Supreme Harmony (*Taihemen*), the gateway to the Outer Court, a vast 30,000-sq-m open space, with low, flanking buildings and a central route – the 'imperial road' – picked out in stone leading directly the Hall of Supreme Harmony (*Taihedian*). From Ming times the *Taihedian* was the central ceremonial hall, the site of imperial coronations, the starting point for all of the major ceremonies that punctuated the court's annual round, as well as for the reception of successful candidates in the imperial scholars' civil service exams. This is where the Emperor would meet and address those of his subjects who had business with him, having himself progressed south down the 'imperial road' from his private quarters in the Inner Court.

Behind *Taihedian* is a smaller central building, the Hall of Central Harmony (*Zhonghedian*), where the Emperor would put on his robes. The next palace, marking the end of the Outer Court, was the Hall of Preserving Harmony (*Baohedian*), used by the Qing for banquets, concerts and the im-

perial exams. Passing through this, you descend three massive marble stairways into an open space that divides the Outer Court from the Inner Court – the private quarters of the Emperor, his family, concubines, eunuchs and maids. The Inner Court is reached through a relatively small but ornate Gate of Heavenly Purity (*Qianqingmen*), outside which the Emperor would meet his ministers and supplicants and carry on the serious business of the day – more detailed and less ceremonial than that conducted in the Hall of Supreme Harmony. This was the northernmost point of his public functions.

The Palace of Heavenly Purity

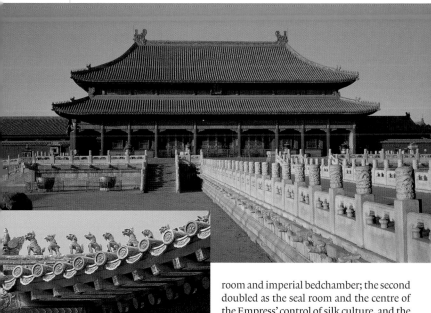

Proceeding through the Inner Court, there are three more central palaces: the Palace of Heavenly Purity (*Qianqinggong*), the Hall of Union (*Jiaotaidian*) and the Palace of Earthly Tranquility (*Kunninggong*). The first doubled as throne room and imperial bedchamber; the second doubled as the seal room and the centre of the Empress' control of silk culture, and the third as shrine and imperial bridal chamber.

To the north of the Inner Court lie the beauties of the Imperial Garden – to the west and east lie a mass of smaller palaces and pavilions, each with a role in imperial life, all interconnected. One of the great joys of visiting the Forbidden City is to wander through these palaces and discover unexpected angles and delights. Be sure to allow enough time to do this. The exhibition halls of the permanent collection are scattered throughout. They can either be visited individually or, although of necessity too briefly, as part of a general tour. A museum guide is available. There are small shops and cafés situated at intervals throughout the site.

Glazed ceramic beasts on a roof ridge, including dragons, phoenixes, lions, winged horses and sea horses

Exhibition Areas within the Forbidden City

At the time of publication, it is anticipated that all of the following permanent exhibitions will either have been opened or re-opened after reconstruction. These will be in addition to any temporary or touring exhibitions which may be open at any given time. The exhibition halls can be identified by the numbers on the accompanying plan.

Meridian Gate

1. Qing Dynasty Court Insignia
An exhibition of grand canopies, fans and insignia that were used in imperial ritual, housed in the corridors on the west side of the first courtyard after entering the Meridian Gate.

Outer Court

2. Weapons of the Qing Dynasty (1644–1911)
The first corridor on the west side of the Outer Court.
The Qing were Manchus from the northeast for whom horsemanship was the basis of their culture. An exhibition of their horsemanship and archery; and, from the reign of Kangxi (1662–1722), of their firearms.

3. Qing Dynasty Ritual Music
The Pavilion of Spreading Virtue (*Hongyige*).
An exhibition of Qing dynasty court music, including recordings.

4. Long Live the Royal House: Treasures from the Qing Palace
The corridor on the west side running north, beginning opposite the Hall of Supreme Harmony (*Taihedian*).
An exhibition of selected paraphernalia of the Qing Court, including articles of daily use, scientific instruments and a look at the history of the palace in the post-1949 period.

Inner Court
Central Inner Court, west side

5. Long Live the Emperor!: Imperial Birthday Celebrations (1644–1911)
The west corridor of the Palace of Heavenly Purity (*Qianqinggong*).
An exhibition of the birthday celebrations of three Qing Emperors and two Empress Dowagers, including the Kangxi Emperor, the Qianlong Emperor and the Empress Dowager Cixi.

Central Inner Court, east side

6. The Qing Emperors' Grand Weddings (1644–1911)
The east corridor of the Palace of Heavenly Purity (*Qianqinggong*).
An exhibition, including digital technology, of the rituals of betrothal, marriage, dowry and wedding presents, and the bridal chamber.

Western Palaces of the Inner Court

7. The Daily Life of Qing Dynasty Concubines
The Palace of Eternal Longevity (*Yongshougong*).
An exhibition of historical records, photographs, and artefacts illustrating the procedures for the selection and certification of concubines, their health, leisure, costumes, accessories and the registers of individual appointments with the Emperor.

8. The Life of the Last Emperor, Puyi
The back courtyard of the Palace of Preserved Elegance (*Chuxiugong*).
The sad story of Puyi, the last Emperor, who was allowed to remain in the Forbidden City until 1924, after which he was fatally compromised by the Japanese during the war period.

9. Ruling from behind the Screen: Empress Dowager Cixi (1835–1908)
The Palace of Universal Happiness (*Xianfugong*).
An exhibition of the costumes, trinkets and riches in daily use by the powerful Empress Dowager Cixi, the evil genius of the last century of Qing rule.

Eastern Palaces of the Inner Court

10. Hall of Donations
Palace of Great Benevolence (*Jingrengong*).
A selection of more than eighty donations to the museum, and an interactive screen with information on donors and their gifts.

11. Bronze Mirrors
The Palace of Supreme Harmony (*Yonghegong*) and the Studio of Equal Obedience (*Tongshunzhai*).
A small but high-class exhibition, with good explanatory signage, about the development, use and decoration of bronze mirrors in Chinese history, with examples from the fifth century BC through to the nineteenth century.

12. Artefacts Donated by Zhang Naiqi Palace of Great Benevolence (*Jingrengong*). An exhibition of ninety works donated by Zhang Naiqi (1897–1977).

13. Digital Painting and Calligraphy Gallery
Palace of Prolonging Happiness (*Yanxigong*) – second floor.
Four computer screens with digital images of a selection of the finest painting and calligraphy in the Palace Museum collection.

Interior: The Hall of Union

Exterior: The Hall of Preserving Hamony

14. Shards from Chinese Kiln Sites
The Hall of Prolonging Happiness (*Yanxigong*).
An exhibition of Qing shards arranged by kiln site.

15. Imperial Porcelain with Royal Designs
The Palace of Prolonging Happiness (*Yanxigong*).
An exhibition of Qing porcelain and designs from the Tongzhi and Guangxu periods.

16. Early Twentieth-century Architectural Folly: The Crystal Palace (*Shuijinggong*)
The Hall of Prolonging Happiness (*Yanxigong*).
The last Qing building, begun in 1909 and unfinished in 1911 when the dynasty fell, this is a garden structure with marble and ironwork, having five pavilions and an underground aquarium – a fitting fantasy for the last days of a dynasty.

17. Ancient Bronze Vessels from the Shang and Zhou dynasties (first millennium BC). The Palace of Celestial Favour (*Chengqiangong*).
A fine selection of ancient bronze ritual vessels.

18. Jade Carvings
The Palace of Accumulated Purity (*Zhongcuigong*).
An exhibition of jade from the Neolithic through the eighteenth century.

East Side of the Forbidden City

19. Hall of Clocks
The Hall for Ancestral Worship (*Fengxiandian*).
An exhibition of the Qing collection of clocks and timepieces, many of them British and Swiss. On most days a selection of clocks are 'played' at 11.00 and 14.00.

20. Imperial Treasures and Ornaments
Located in the corridors surrounding the Hall of Imperial Supremacy (*Huangjidian*), in the Hall of Cultivating Character (*Yangxingdian*), in the Hall of Joyful Longevity (*Leshoutang*) and in the Belvedere of Well-Nourished Harmony (*Yihexuan*).

21. The Stone Drums: Seal Script of the Qin Dynasty
The eastern corridor of the Hall of Imperial Supremacy (*Huangjidian*).
Drum-shaped stones carved with third-century BC script.

22. Opera at the Qing Court
The Pavilion of Pleasant Sounds (*Changyinge*) and the Hall for Viewing Opera (*Yueshi lou*).
An exhibition of costumes, masks, props and programmes from the resident opera companies at the Qing court.

Eastern Outer Buildings

23. Chinese Ceramics
The Hall of Literary Brilliance (*Wenhuadian*).
This recently opened, splendid permanent display is a chronological survey based on the imperial wares and collection, generously supplemented by the objects that have come into the collection since the Palace Museum was founded.

Western Outer Buildings

24. Chinese Painting, Calligraphy and Printing
Hall of Martial Valour (*Wuyingdian*)
Hall dedicated to rotating exhibitions of Chinese painting, calligraphy and printing.

Wallpaper (*tielo*) in the unrestored Jade Pavillion (*Yucui xuan*) in the Retirement Garden located in the northeast corner of the Forbidden City

25. Retirement Garden

Built between 1771 and 1776 by Emperor Qianlong as his retirement home, The Studio of Exhaustion from Diligent Reign (*Juanqinzhai*) is situated in the newly opened Qianlong Garden, an intricate mix of fine and curious rocks and precious trees. The lodge itself is one of the five most important interiors to survive from China's imperial past – the epitome of design and craftsmanship. It is meticulously decorated with bamboo marquetry, white-jade cartouches, trompe l'oeil murals and silk panels. The building is luxurious but small-scale and intimate – the complete antithesis to the grandeur and bombast of Qianlong's earlier surroundings. From 2003 to 2008 it was restored by an international team led by the World Monuments Fund and the Palace Museum. It opened with limited access in autumn 2008.

28

Geological Museum of China

中国地质博物馆 *Zhongguo dizhi bowuguan*

Yangrou hutong, 15 Xisi Street
北京市西四羊肉胡同15号

Tel: (010) 6655 7858
Open: 9.00–16.30 except Mon
www.gmc.org.cn
English and Chinese audio guides
Kids

Caudipteryx zoui

Shenzhousaurus orientalis

There is something here for everyone who is fascinated by the marvels of geological science, from the truly stunning displays of diamonds, rubies and huge specimens of native gold in the Gemstone Gallery to the magnificent exhibits of rock-crystal geodes, a dramatic calcite druse intergrowth with fluorite crystals, and the rare blue aragonite on show in the Mineral and Rocks Gallery. But the real stars are the treasure trove of late Jurassic and early Cretaceous fossils unearthed from Liaoning Province. Dating from more than 128 million years ago, these rare specimens include dinosaur remains

with evidence of proto-feathers – providing the evolutionary link between non-avian dinosaurs and living birds – as well as fossils of primitive aquatic and semi-aquatic animals with paddle-like limbs and, often, long, serpentine necks. If time is short and you cannot visit all four floors, head directly to the Prehistoric Life gallery on the third floor and view these wonders.

Among the first large fossil remains you encounter as you move counter-clockwise around the gallery is the specimen of *Hyphalosaurus lingyuanensis*, often called the *Sinohydrosaurus lingyuanensis*. This marine lizard probably descended from a land-dwelling progenitor, grew up to a metre in length, and is often referred to as a baby Loch Ness Monster. Recent discoveries have unearthed a two-headed fossil of this creature – a rare freak of nature. Not only did the new baby *Hyphalosaurus* specimen have two heads; it had two necks.

Although the first fossil feathers were discovered in 1861 in Germany on the 145-million-year-old bird *Archaeopteryx*, the first wingless feathered dinosaurs were unearthed in the early 1990s in Liaoning, just a day's drive from Beijing. Well preserved in what was once the marshy shore of a lake, the remains are incredibly fine and clear. Careful examination of the *Sinornithosaurus* specimen reveals its three different types of feathers: simple hair-like filaments, downy tufts and feathers in the modern sense. This fossil is the first evidence that animals other than birds had feather-like skins (not to help them to fly but probably to keep them warm). On display nearby is *Shenzhousaurus orientalis*, known as the Ostrich dinosaur because this species and related ones apparently behaved like modern ostriches. This bird-like creature had a beak with teeth.

Mineral display

Very rare is the fossil species *Confuciusornis sanctus* – the holy Confucius bird – discovered by a farmer in Liaoning. The skull, wing, two feathered legs and pelvis were found in ancient lake-bed sediments. This bird, around the size of a rooster, had a long, feathered tail and claws on its forearms, probably for climbing trees. However, unlike previously found avian fossils, it was toothless, making it the earliest bird known to have abandoned the toothy jaws of its ancestors. Its discovery revised the texts on the evolution of birds.

Equally important is the fossil *Protarchaeopteryx robusta* found near Beipiao City in Liaoning, with its tail and body feathers. It was unable to fly, but with its short arms and long legs probably was a fast runner. The size of a modern-day turkey, it represents a stage in the evolution of birds from feathered,

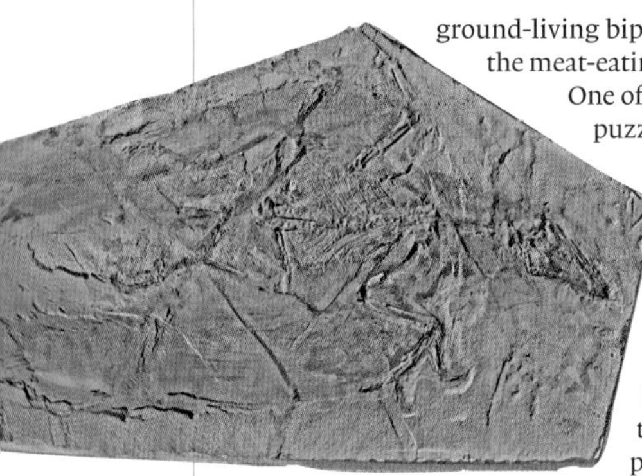

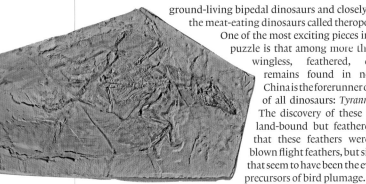

Confuciusornis sanctus

ground-living bipedal dinosaurs and closely resembled the meat-eating dinosaurs called theropods.

One of the most exciting pieces in the whole puzzle is that among more than a dozen wingless, feathered, dragon-like remains found in northeastern China is the forerunner of the daddy of all dinosaurs: *Tyrannosaurus rex*. The discovery of these creatures – land-bound but feathered – infers that these feathers were not full-blown flight feathers, but simpler ones that seem to have been the evolutionary precursors of bird plumage.

Also in this gallery are fossil finds recovered from what is known as the Chengjiang Fauna, a series of sites near Kunming in Yunnan Province where a large number of perfectly preserved fish and other soft-bodied fossils have been unearthed. The earliest examples date from the Lower Cambrian era, around 530 million years ago, extending the known time span of vertebrates back 50 million years and helping to solve the largest mystery of evolutionary biology – the origins of vertebrates. On this floor, displayed in well-lit and labelled cases, are stone implements and teeth drilled with holes – possibly indicating their use as ornaments – collected in 1933 from the famous cave site of Zhoukoudian, which has yielded the largest number of *Homo erectus* fossils in the world.

It's not surprising that this museum is visited by more than a million people a year – the modern cases (with excellent Chinese and English labelling) enhanced with digital imagery and covering all facets of geology (including the formation of the earth, volcanoes, gemmology and fossil history) making it a worthwhile visit for foreigners and a must for Chinese schoolchildren. There is a Specimen Care and Conservation Laboratory where you can watch specimens being cleaned and conserved, as well as have your own treasure – be it a fossil or mineral – identified by the museum's resident geologist.

Ongoing research within the museum and with various Chinese scientific bodies, including the National Natural Science Foundation of China and the Chinese Academy of Sciences, as well as numerous foreign institutions, make this a living museum where a stream of new finds and research are constantly challenging the enduring mysteries of the natural world.

Li Siguang

A bronze plaque in the museum's forecourt honours Li Siguang (1889–1971), the father of modern Chinese geology. Li studied geology from 1912 to 1918 in Birmingham in the UK. His contributions to palaeontology, glaciology and seismology are well documented, but he is probably best remembered for his work in geological mechanics (also known as engineering geology), which applies geological principles to civil and mining engineering, among other disciplines. His work in this branch of science played a significant role in the discovery in China of several large gas and oil fields and other mineral resources. To honour his contribution, the Li Siguang Geological Science Award is presented to outstanding Chinese geologists.

29

Guanfu Classic Art Museum

观复古典艺术博物馆/观复博物馆 *Guanfu gudian yishu bowuguan*

18 Jinnan Road, Zhangwanfen,
Dashanzi, Chaoyang District
北京市朝阳区大山子张万坟金南路18号

Tel: (010) 6433 8887
Open: 9.00–17.00
www.guanfumuseum.org.cn
English guide available:
no appointment necessary

According to the museum's own publicity materials, this was the first not-for-profit private museum in China. It houses, for the most part, the collection of Ma Weidu. Three other collectors are also contributors but less significantly. The collection has been housed in various places but now resides in this purpose-built museum in northeastern Beijing, not far from Caochangdi. It is somewhat tricky to find, so a telephone call in advance is recommended.

More and more museums are opening all over China exhibiting the collections of private art lovers who want to share their passion. This one is well worth your time. The objects are of the highest quality and are well displayed, and signage in English appears consistently alongside every object. The collection features porcelain, furniture, Qing dynasty windows and doors, lacquer, cloisonné, enamel ware and bronzes, modern paintings, sculpture and photographs. It also includes jade, but due to space problems, these objects are held in storage and are available for viewing only to scholars or students by appointment.

Cizhou white glazed *meiping*, Northern Song dynasty

The museum tour begins in the ceramics gallery, in which you can see objects from the Tang to the Qing dynasties. Every object has a mirror beneath it so you can have a look at the bottom. Breathtaking examples from the major kilns are on display. Song dynasty celadon from the Ru, Guan, Ge and Jun Kilns is exhibited, as is porcelain from the Yuezhou, Longquan, Yaozhou, Cizhou, Dingzhou Kilns – and more. Note a Jingdezhen shadow-blue-glaze foliate-mouth vase from the Northern Song. The gorgeous lip of this vessel delicately falls open like a wilting leaf. Be sure to see the Cizhou white-glazed *meiping* painted with a floral design from the Northern Song. Standing on its own in a case is a large *famille rose* vase with six floral panels on a dark blue background. Each panel represents one of the seasons. Every object on display in this gallery is a feast for the eyes.

The museum continues with a furniture collection from the Ming and Qing periods. About 300 pieces are displayed, organized by type of wood – mahogany, *zitan* and *huanghuali* – and in addition there is a complete family room (mainly using mahogany) and study (mostly *huanghuali*).

Mahogany, or 'red wood', was used from the mid Qing period and was imported from Southeast Asia. From the Qianlong and Jiaqing periods it was frequently used for court furniture. The mahogany furniture on view includes tables, chairs, chests, cabinets and so on; notice especially a very graceful pair of eighteenth-century horseshoe-backed armchairs.

Zitan, or 'purple wood', was used during the Ming period but was most popular in the early Qing. The density and weight of this wood make it feel substantial, so it was equated with value and wealth. The trees grow slowly, and the wood is not always useable. These factors, along with its inevitable expense, contribute to its relative rarity. It carves well, so in the Qing it was often elaborately decorated, although Ming examples are simple and plain. Note the *zitan* painting table on display, dated to the Kangxi period or earlier. This is the largest known Qing painting table, with a width of 96 cm and length of 182 cm, and is ornately carved with dragon panels.

Huanghuali (yellow-flowering pear), exhibited in one large room, was most popular in the Ming dynasty, and the majority of examples here are from that period. Chests, screens, beds and chairs are on view. Note the late Ming southern official's chair whose back is inlaid with multicoloured jade decoration of a bird on flowering branches.

Next are the galleries entitled 'Works of Art'; these contain cloisonné, enamel, lacquer, bronzes, carved jade and wooden objects ranging from folk objects to imperial wares. The museum also has a collection of photographs, including historical images, landscapes and portraits of famous people.

Upstairs is a collection of windows and doors in four rooms, mainly from the Qing dynasty. The patterns, history and craftsmanship involved are explained on panels in the galleries. Many of the windows are finely carved with much detail. One series of eight depicts trees with delicate, multi-textured feathery leaves of varying species of trees. A magnifying glass is available for careful examination. Most of the doors and windows are from southern China, where such lattice and cut-out design was the style (the weather in the north would not allow this). There are also examples of heavier solid doors from the north.

There is a gallery of modern painting (not the collection of Ma Weidu) which includes three paintings by Chen Yifei.

The displays in the museum are rotated every one or two years.

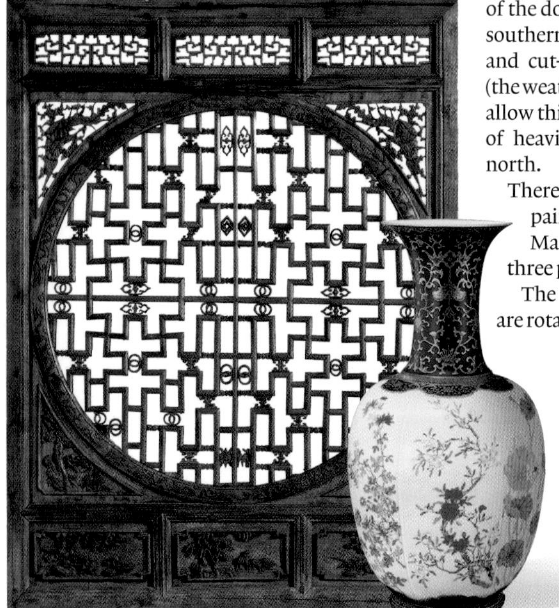

Qing dynasty window

Famille rose vase, Qing dynasty

30

Jiaozhuanghu Underground Tunnel War Remains Museum

焦庄户地道战遗址纪念馆 *Jiaozhuanghu didaozhanyizhi jinianguan*

Jiaozhuanghu Village, Longwantun Town, Shunyi District
北京市顺义区龙湾屯镇焦庄户村

Tel: (010) 6046 1906
Open: 8.30–16.30
www.bjjzhdd.com/zy.html (Chinese only)

During World War II the people in this tiny village dug an extensive interlocking series of tunnels linking up their houses and leading out to the countryside in an effort to resist the Japanese invaders. Entrances to the tunnels can be found in cupboards, stables, water-storage tanks, under beds and elsewhere. By 1946 there were 23 km of tunnels connecting the houses and even reaching nearby villages. According to the museum, from 1943 until 1948 the villagers fought more than 150 battles against the Japanese and the Nationalists, killing 130 and taking sixty prisoners. Visitors to the site can go into some of the restored village houses and enter the 650 m of tunnel now open. The famous film made about this place called *Underground Tunnel Guerilla War* is sometimes shown at the museum and is available on DVD in the shop. There is also a small outdoor snack bar. Look for the sign reading 'Anti-Japanese Food' to find it!

Monument to the heroes of the village

31

Lao She Museum

老舍纪念馆 *Laoshe jinianguan*

Fengfu Hutong 19, Dongcheng District
北京市东城区丰富胡同19号

Tel: (010) 6514 2612
Open: 9.00–17.00
www.bjlsjng.com/ (Chinese only)

This is one of the most charming of the courtyard residences and the home of one of China's best-loved writers, Lao She, from 1950 until his untimely death during the Cultural Revolution. He is best known for his 1936 novel *Rickshaw Boy* (*Luotuo Xiangzi*), which depicts a Dickensian Beijing at the turn of the century. Exhibits detail his biography, and his study has been left intact, with a seal carved by Qi Baishi, a jade ink box from Gen. Feng Yuxiang, and a calendar opened to 24 August 1966, the date when Lao She either committed suicide or was murdered by Red Guards.

32 Lu Xun Museum Beijing

北京鲁迅博物馆 *Beijing Lu Xun bowuguan*

19 Gongmenkou Ertiao,
Fuchengmennei, Xicheng District
北京市西城区阜内大街宫门口二条19号

Tel: (010) 6615 6548
Open: 9.00–15.30 except Mon
www.luxunmuseum.com.cn/default.aspx

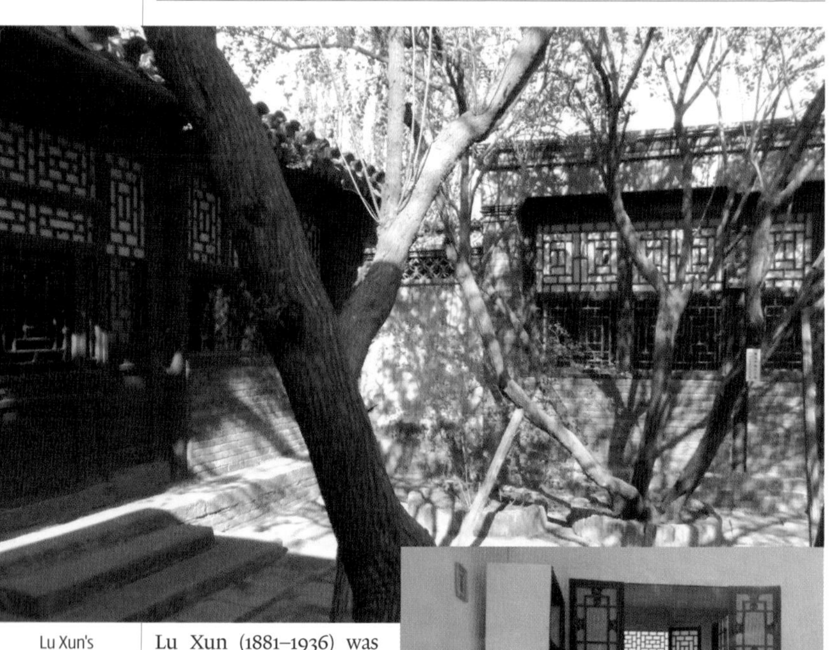

Lu Xun's house: courtyard and interior

Lu Xun (1881–1936) was one of China's most famous writers of the first half of the twentieth century. The museum consists of his house, in which he lived from 1924 to 1926, and, on its east side, a new museum, expanded and re-opened in 1994, dedicated to his work. The house, with its small courtyards, trees and simple furnishings, gives an authentic glimpse of a Beijing courtyard residence of the period – functional and modest yet attractive – which will appeal to any visitor. The new museum building is more for those interested in left-wing Chinese literature of the pre-war period. Lu Xun studied in Japan as a medical doctor until the oppression and poverty of Chinese society convinced him to change careers. He took part in the May 4th Movement and, although he became a leading socialist writer, he never became a Communist. Nevertheless he has been hailed since 1949 as one of the great modern novelists – he was a one of Mao's favourite

Lu Xun

authors. Lu Xun was internationally known, both translating progressive Western works and himself reaching a Western audience. He specialized in short, sharp satirical novels such as *The True Story of Ah Q* (1921–22). The museum houses a wide range of literary relics of the period and some fascinating photographs (including one of George Bernard Shaw). There is excellent English signage throughout the museum.

33 Mei Lanfang Memorial Museum

梅兰芳纪念馆 *Mei Lanfang jinianguan*

9 Huguosi Street
北京市西城区护国寺街9号

Tel: (010) 6618 3598
Open: 9.00–16.00 except Mon
www.meilanfang.com.cn/mlf/english.htm
Gift shop sells variety of books, DVDs and trinkets / illustrated pamphlet with some English

Mei Lanfang (1894–1961), the legendary Beijing opera performer, excelled in his performance of the *huadan*, in which all female roles were played by male impersonators. His fame stretched as far as Europe and the US. Mei visited America in 1930, and despite the fact that the country was going through the Great Depression, he performed in front of packed-out, enthusiastic audiences. He won glowing reviews in the *New York World*, which said he was one of the most extraordinary actors ever seen in the city. The legendary star made an even bigger splash in Europe, where his performance in Berlin made a deep impression on the dramatist Bertolt Brecht; it's said that Brecht's acting method grew out of his experience of watching Mei.

Mei, of course, also made a major contribution to the theatre in China. He boosted the status of actors, created a new type of design for opera costumes, and, through his excellence as a performer, lifted the art form to a new level. And, even though he himself played female roles, he broke the theatrical gender barrier when he accepted the actress Xue Yanqin as his student in the 1930s. Prior to this, there were few mixed-gender troupes in Beijing opera, making female impersonation a key characteristic of the genre. Xue went on to become one of the opera's greatest performers.

Mei Lanfang's siheyuan or courtyard house

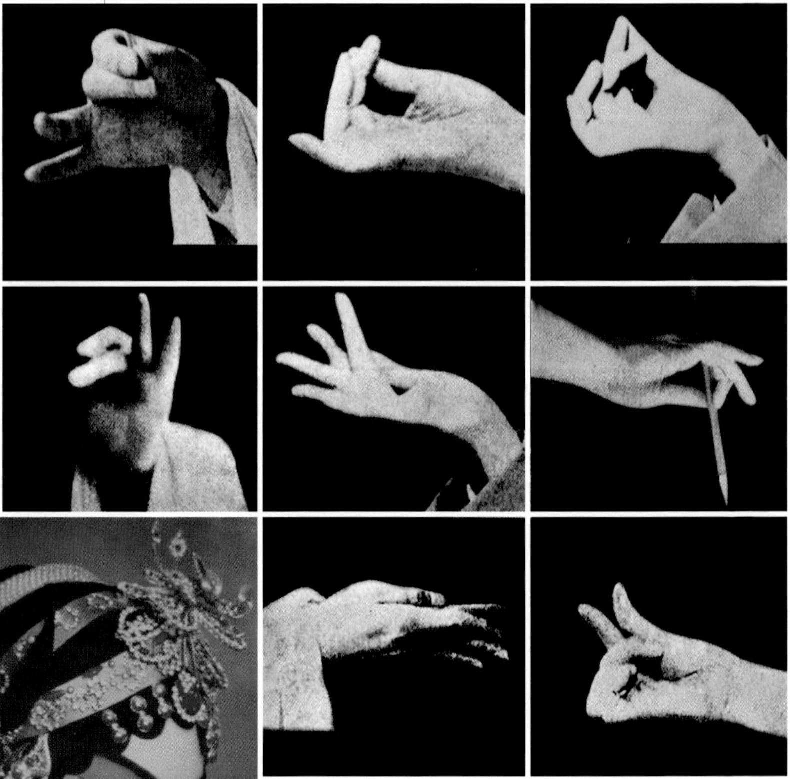

Mei's traditional courtyard home, an excellent example of its type, is reason enough to visit here. At the end of the nineteenth century, it was part of a much larger mansion that belonged to a prince. The house had gotten quite run down, but was renovated for Mei and fitted with both Chinese and Western furniture and fixtures, blending old and modern elements. The star lived here from 1949 until he passed away in 1961. During the Cultural Revolution, Red Guards slapped posters on the outer walls accusing the actor of leading a 'bourgeois life'. His family decided to leave the house, which fell into ruin, remaining closed until 1986, when it was renovated.

Hand positions in Chinese opera have specific meanings

Mei Lanfang in character museum

The first rectangular building in this complex features wonderful black and white and colour photos from Mei's life and of his many performances. There are also the ornate costumes he wore on the stage. There is also a monitor here showing videos of some of his performances. In the rear courtyard are Mei's living quarters – his living room, study and bedroom – all with the original furniture. In one room there is a wonderful poster showing his delicate hands expressing dozens of different operatic gestures, each expressing a different emotion. In the warmer months, chairs would be moved out into the courtyard so the family could enjoy the fresh air.

34 Military Museum of the Chinese People's Revolution

中国人民革命军事博物馆 *Zhongguo renmin geming junshi bowuguan*

9 Fuxing Road, Haidian District
北京市海淀区复兴路9号

Tel: (010) 6686 6114
Open: 8.30–16.00
Gift shop / café
Kids

This is an enormous museum – 60,000 sq m – of great interest not only to lovers of guns and violence but also to those interested in Chinese history, especially the 5,000-year history of the Chinese military. The building is a huge, recently refurbished Soviet-style monolith built as one of the key construction projects in Beijing during the Great Leap Forward. Its central tower is crowned by a military star with the characters '8.1', denoting the date of the birth of the People's Liberation Army (PLA) during the Nanchang Uprising of 1 August 1928. It dominates the wide Fuxing Road just south of Yuyuantan Park and beside the Millennium Monument.

On the museum forecourt there are tanks, rockets and the Trident jet used by Zhou Enlai and other top leaders during the 1960s and 1970s. For a small fee you can go aboard the aircraft and sit in the now tattered armchairs used by the founding fathers of Chinese Communism.

The entrance hall is dominated by a huge white marble statue of Mao Zedong surrounded by mural-sized photos of Mao as well as Deng Xiaoping and Jiang Zemin, to provide political balance. In the large halls on the ground floor are tanks, missiles, and space rockets and capsules. The tank collection includes American tanks captured from the Nationalist forces during the Civil War and from US forces during the Korean War. One can pay extra to swivel round on an anti-aircraft gun or to sit in the driver's and gunner's seats of a modern Chinese heavy tank. Prominently placed as you enter are two limousines used by Zhu De and by Mao, the latter given to him by Stalin. Also on the first floor is the Hall of the Agrarian Revolution, illustrating Mao's theory on the role of the peasants.

On the upper floors one can view a large collection of pistols, rifles, machine guns, flamethrowers, torpedoes and bombs from all over the

Sculpture on the façade

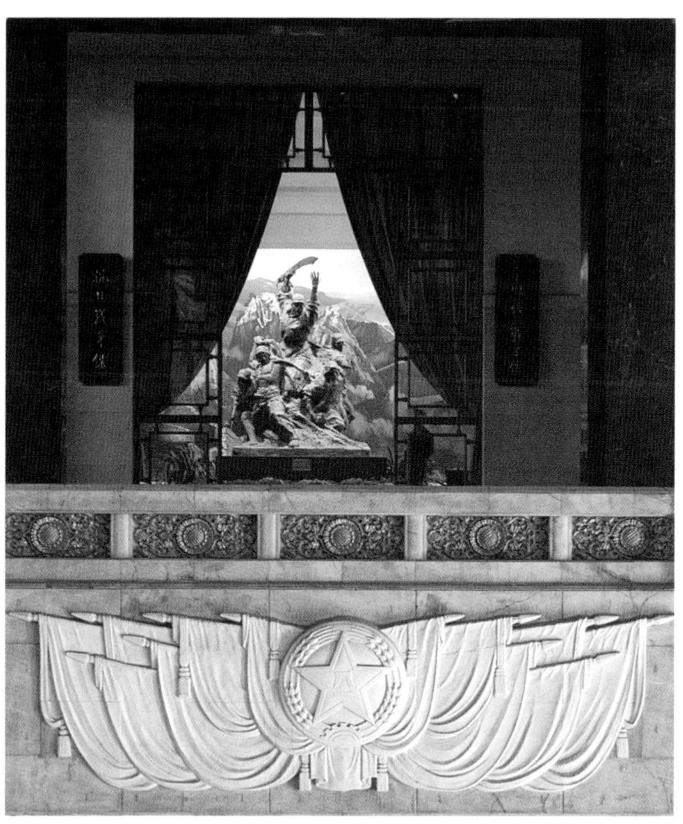

Interior displays

world. A sculpture hall features busts and statues of Chinese leaders and generals, as well as foreign luminaries such as Kim Il Sung. There is also a large collection of historical and archaeological material which deals with ancient Chinese warfare. In contrast to the other exhibits, there are plenty of English explanations in this exhibition. Ancient weaponry, both authentic and replicas, is on display. A few of the famous Terracotta Warriors are exhibited, as well as paintings, models, a replica of a fortified city wall surrounded by a variety of siege weapons, and many other fascinating objects telling the history of Chinese warfare up to the Opium War with Britain. Of special interest are ancient grenades, bombs and rocket-born arrows, demonstrating how gunpowder, a Chinese invention, was put to use for military purposes.

Other halls feature the War against Japan (World War II), the Civil War (against the Nationalists) and the War of Resistance against US Aggression and Support Korea (the Korean War). There are guns, uniforms, objects, paintings, photographs, relics such as an oil lamp used by Mao, flags and letters, as well as other personal effects and originals of documents written by the revolutionary leaders.

Except for the Hall of Ancient Warfare, English signage is sporadic, but in many areas major themes, at least, are noted in English.

35

Museum of Ethnic Costume

民族服饰博物馆 *Minzu fushi bowuguan*

A2 Yinghua East Road, north entrance of Heping Street, Chaoyang District (second floor of the Beijing Institute of Clothing Technology Building)
北京市朝阳区樱花东街甲2号 北京服装学院二楼

Tel: (010) 6428 8261
Open: 8.30–11.30 Mon & Tues; 13.30–16.00 Thurs–Sat
www.cnnc.org

This utterly modern and fascinating museum with excellent English and some French signage is well worth the trouble to find if you're interested in Chinese textiles and costume history. The textiles are exhibited beautifully. Only 5 per cent of the collection of more than 100,000 items is on display and includes all manner of textiles and related accoutrements from both the Han and some of China's ethnic minorities, and from ancient to modern times. All are the finest examples of their type. The museum claims to hold the most comprehensive collection in China, amassed largely at the end of the 1980s before prices for such pieces became prohibitive. The Institute of Clothing Technology is continuing to collect with funds from the municipal govern-

Selection of looms

ment. The range of textiles displayed includes embroidery, batik, weaving, brocade and printing on cloth.

Featured are such items as a nineteenth-century Han jacket made of bamboo beads. These jackets, although unusual, can still be found in antique stores around Beijing. Similar to the waterproof fish-skin clothing made by Native Americans is a suit of the Hezhe people also made of fish skin. The nomadic Hezhe, one of the smallest of China's minority groups, come from the north, and their clothing is traditionally made of fish skin and deer hide. One of the star pieces in the collection is a royal dragon robe with a Manchu-style pattern dating to the late eighteenth century. This is woven in the now obso-

lete *kesi* style, meaning 'carved silk' – a technique developed in the Tang dynasty that reached its apex in the Song. It was used when weaving detailed pictures and intricate motifs to create raised decoration.

Walking through the galleries while reading the explanatory panels, you can learn about Chinese textiles in general as well as regional variations. For example, they explain that the clothing of the north tends to be heavier and richer, incorporating fur, felt, silk and satin, while that of the south tends to be made of cotton, flax or silk. Various types of trimming are displayed with explanations of the different stitches used.

By understanding textile traditions you can appreciate Chinese culture and ethnic minority culture more deeply. For example, the Miao people illustrate their history and oral traditions through textile decoration. They believe that the butterfly is the ancestor of everything on earth – thus the butterfly is a common batik motif. The museum's collection of Miao costumes is one of the most complete in China, from the exquisite festive costumes of the Miao women in Shidong (Guizhou Province) to the collarless coats and pleated skirts of the Miao of the Nandan area of Guangxi Zhuang Autonomous Region.

Robe: eighteenth-century royal dragon robe

Scores of silver accessories and items of jewellery are also displayed with examples from about twenty branches of the Miao, as well as from the Tibetan, Mongolian, Jingpo, Dong, Dai, Yao and Hani peoples. These adornments include bracelets, earrings, combs, shoulder ornaments, necklaces and headdresses. Some incorporate inlay of pearls, jade, silver wire and gold. Amazing

are the thick, twisted silver chokers of the Dong people and the horn-shaped headdresses with chiselled dragon designs of the Miao people of Shidong.

Especially noteworthy for its elegance is a magnificent early eighteenth-century Mongolian silver headdress which belonged to a princess of the Chahar tribe. The headdress, in two parts, includes a decoration for the princess' plait and is decorated with gold chain and inlaid with coral. It was obtained by the museum from a male descendant of the princess following difficult negotiations as he did not want his people to abandon their cultural property. Ultimately, however, he was convinced that many more people would be able to appreciate its beauty if it were displayed in a public gallery in China's capital.

One gallery is dedicated to a unique collection of photographs taken by the well-known photographer and ethnographer Zhuang Xueben in the early twentieth century. Of great anthropological interest, they record wedding ceremonies, holiday celebrations and even wars by the tribes in western Sichuan including the Tibetan and Qiao minorities. The photographs bring to life and give context to the costumes that you see as you walk through the galleries.

Silver Jewellery

The cultural identity of the minorities of China is defined by clothing and jewellery. The Miao wear by far the most silver jewellery, followed by the Dong. Great displays of their ornaments occur during festivals when the women adorn themselves with several kilograms each. However, the most important role played by jewellery is during courtship. A family's wealth is defined by how much silver its daughter owns, and it forms part of her dowry.

Before Communism, the minorities of the south were the main providers of opium to the trade, thus earning the large sums of money needed to purchase high-grade silver and produce jewellery that was almost pure silver. As China does not have many silver or gold mines, the metal was originally traded along the Silk Route, later arriving by sea on Dutch ships. The Spanish were also providers of silver, particularly in the sixteenth and seventeenth centuries, when much of it came from Peru and Bolivia. Today, very few of the minority communities can afford high-grade silver, so most jewellery contains no more than 20 per cent silver or is an alloy of copper, zinc and nickel called 'alpaca'. Alpaca is also known as 'German' or 'Nickel silver' and is often referred to by the Chinese word *paktong*.

Photo by Zhuang Xueban

36

National Art Museum of China (NAMOC)

中国美术馆 *Zhongguo meishuguan*

1 Wusi dajie
北京市东城区五四大街1号

Tel: (010) 8403 3500 / 6400 6326 (ticket hotline)
Open: 9.00–17.00; last entry 16.00
www.namoc.org
Cafeteria at the back of the building

Beijing's museum of modern art, compared to those of other world capitals, has a long way to go. The museum was recently refurbished, but the results are highly disappointing. The collection includes modern and contemporary Chinese painting, folk art and crafts such as cut paper, kites and puppets, and sculpture, as well as a small collection of Western paintings donated by a couple from Germany. There is English signage in all of the galleries, but it is often garbled. The museum does have temporary shows and hosts visiting exhibitions. These can be of high quality. It is recommended that you check listings to see what is on while you're visiting.

37

National Museum of China

中国国家博物馆 *Zhongguo guojia bowuguan*

16 East Changan Avenue, Dongcheng District
北京市东城区东长安街16号

Tel: (010) 8447 9115
Temporarily closed for reconstruction
www.nationalmuseum.cn/gb/home/index.htm

The new National Museum of China is planned to open in late 2009 or early 2010. Some temporary exhibitions are being held during reconstruction.

The new museum was formed in February 2003 under the aegis of the Ministry of Culture by amalgamating the two existing museums on the east side

of Tiananmen Square: the National Museum of Chinese History and National Museum of the Chinese Revolution. The National Museum of Chinese History opened in 1912, re-opened in 1949 after the Revolution, and was re-housed behind its present façade in 1959. Its aim was to present a detailed history of China through its art and artefacts, including many of the greatest of national treasures from Palaeolithic times through to 1911. The National Museum of the Chinese Revolution focuses on China's modern history from 1911 to the present day. Its emphasis was more on political events than on art.

The two are now being brought up to date as well as merged. The total floor space will increase to 192,000 sq m, and the new institution's boast is that it will be the largest art museum in the world. It will certainly house one of the great national collections of Chinese art, which will be displayed to emphasize historical context and the complex development of Chinese history. The original 1959 façade will be preserved. Behind this a completely new building is being constructed by the German architects Von Gerkan, Marg and Partners. This firm, well known in China, specializes in the creation of new buildings on existing sites, including the reconstruction of the 1936 Olympic Stadium in Berlin. Their solution to this major new challenge is eagerly anticipated as is the final selection and display of the exhibits.

38

National Museum of Modern Chinese Literature

中国现代文学馆 *Zhongguo xiandai wenxueguan*

45 Wenxueguan Lu, Shaoyaoju, Chaoyang District (close to North Third Ring Road at Heping)
北京市朝阳区芍药居文学馆路45号

Tel: (010) 8461 9011 / 9071
Open: 9.00–16.30 except Mon
www.wxg.org.cn/Main1024.html

The museum defines modern literature as that of the twentieth century to the present and includes in its purview all works in Chinese including those from outside the mainland, i.e. Hong Kong, Macao and Taiwan as well as those written by overseas Chinese. The institution serves as a museum, library, archive and research institute and continually collects, conserves and organizes books, letters, videos, photographs, magazines, written reviews, mementoes – every-

Portrait of Qi Baishi by Wu Zuoren

thing collectable relating to the works and lives of modern Chinese writers. They also publish a quarterly journal and host retrospective exhibitions.

The museum has reproduced the studies of selected writers such as Lu Xun, Ba Jin, Cao Yu and others using their personal effects. Their desks, lamps, reading glasses and teacups are laid out as if they had just momentarily stepped away.

Complete libraries of luminary Chinese authors are in the collection such as those of China's beloved female writer Bing Xin, the playwright and journalist Xia Yan, Yu Pingbo, the persecuted essayist and poet and many others. The museum actively seeks donations from authors and collectors.

Their archive is impressive: The library holds over 80,000 volumes, 110,000 books are available on disc and thousands of actual manuscripts are in the collection and available for scholarly research. The holdings are all in Chinese and the English descriptions are limited.

39 New Culture Movement Memorial Museum

北京新文化运动纪念馆 *Beijing xinwenhuayundong jinianguan*

29 Wusi Dajie, Dongcheng District
北京市东城区五四大街29号

Tel: (010) 6402 4929
Open: 8.30–16.30 except Mon; last entry 15.45

The Museum of the New Culture and the May 4th Movements, which has two parts, closed for two years for refurbishment in September 2007.

The first section is located in the 'Red Building' of the old Beijing University – the University's original liberal arts college and offices. Cai Yuanpei lived here when he was Chancellor. The galleries are in the old classrooms and consist mainly of posters, in both English and Chinese, cogently explaining the New Culture and the May 4th Movements and the main players involved in them. There are also journals, documents, magazines and photographs of the period. Unfortunately many are reproductions due to problems with the museum environment. This should be corrected after refurbishment, and an English audio guide is also promised (at the moment only Chinese is available).

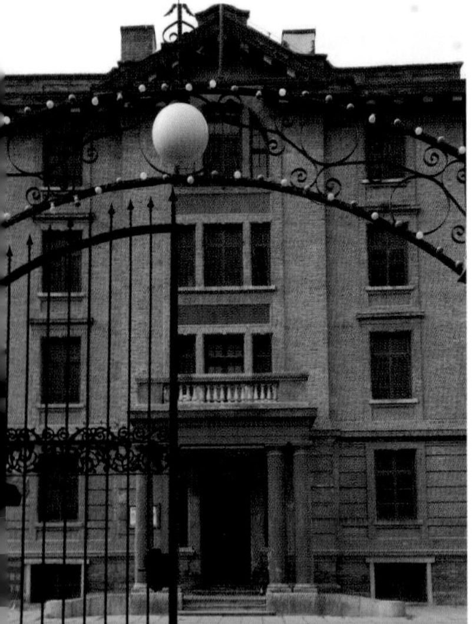

'Red Building' of the old Beijing University

This old building has plenty of atmosphere. The library still has the old tables and magazine racks, and – also on display – the pay book in which the meager salary of a library employee named Mao Zedong is entered. In one of the old classrooms a film is shown about the movement but only in Chinese. Across the courtyard is a purpose-built museum which continues the movement's story with photos and reproduction documents, but at the time of writing the displays were in Chinese with no English explanations.

New Culture Movement

Following the overthrow of the Qing dynasty and the establishment of the Republic, China's political situation remained in turmoil, with its social values firmly rooted in conservative Confucian principals. Around 1915 it was the New Culture Movement which took on the task of denouncing the old Confucian Culture and promoting Western liberalism. The movement, which endorsed science, democracy and women's rights, had an enormous impact on modern China and also heralded further radical change in 1919 with the May 4th Movement.

The leaders of the New Culture Movement began writing in vernacular rather than classical Chinese, which until then had survived as the official written language. This broadened social access to new ideas and fostered political change. A key leader of the movement was Cai Yuanpei, who in 1916 became Chancellor of the National University of Beijing – the nerve centre for both movements. He introduced reforms stressing the pursuit of learning over that of wealth and education 'above politics', hiring professors such as Hu Shi, the philosopher and essayist, and Chen Duxiu, who established the magazine *New Youth*, which became the flag-bearer of the New Culture Movement.

Another key figure was Lu Xun, the editor of *New Youth* and one of China's most celebrated writers, who took an uncompromising stand against the old culture, painting a black picture of 'feudal society'.

The decision of the Western Allies at Versailles following World War I to allow Japan to take over Germany's colonial interests in China's Shandong Province created the patriotic storm that culminated in the May 4th Movement. Anti-Japanese demonstrations in Beijing were followed by boycotts and strikes in Shanghai and elsewhere. The hypocrisy of the West and particularly the US in supporting Japan in this issue fuelled a widespread disenchantment with Western liberalism. Almost overnight, and in a move that has impact into the present day, China's intellectuals looked away from the West and towards Russia and the October Revolution. Chen Duxiu and Li Dazhao, librarian at Beijing University, became founders of the Chinese Communist Party in 1921. As an unknown student from Hunan, Mao Zedong worked as an assistant to Li in the University library.

Cai Yuanpei

40

Poly Art Museum

保利艺术博物馆 *Baoli yishu bowuguan*

2nd F, Poly Plaza, 1 Beidajie,
Chaoyangmen, Dongcheng District
北京市东城区朝阳门北大街1号保利大厦2楼

Tel: (010) 6500 1188 / 3250
Open: 9.30–16.30 except Mon & national holidays
Bookshop / gift shop

The aim of the Poly Art Museum, owned by the Poly Corporation, is to bring Chinese art treasures looted in the past back to China. Their most publicized purchase took place in 2000 at an auction in Hong Kong. Three Qing dynasty bronze astrological animal heads – a monkey, a tiger and an ox – stolen by British troops in 1860 from the Old Summer Palace went on the block. Amid great publicity, the Poly Corporation paid US$4 million for them. They are now on display in the museum.

Bodhisattva in meditation, Northern Qi

Wine vessel, or *you*, Western Zhou

The Poly Museum, recently relocated to the Poly Corporation's new headquarters across the street from the old gallery, has a first-class collection of art lushly displayed in modern cases with dramatic lighting. There is excellent English signage throughout the gallery, as well as useful placards with time-lines and visual explanations of the terminology used for Chinese pots and vessels. The collection mainly consists of bronzes dating from the Shang to the Tang period and Buddhist stone sculpture. These are separated into two galleries.

Some highlights of the bronzes include, from the Western Zhou, a set of eight bells and an oddly formed *gui* which is very organic in shape and looks like it was modelled from clay. Also from this period is an extraordinary *you*, or wine vessel. The body and lid are in the form of a face with eyes, nose and smile; the top of the lid has scalloped 'hair' and a bird perched at the centre. There is a high looped handle with fantastical bird decoration and two side handles in the shape of a mythical animal: a goat's head with an elephant's trunk. A dragon writhes around the base. This splendid piece should not be missed.

Bronze weapons from the Warring States period are also exhibited such as a *yue*, or axe, and a sword with gold inlay. There are various examples of arms and armour from the Shang and Zhou dynasties such as a Shang helmet decorated with animal faces. From the Western Han is displayed a tall, stemmed lamp supported by kneeling human figures armed with knives. Finally there is a Tang dynasty *hu* with dragon handles.

In the second gallery can be seen some very fine examples of Buddhist sculpture of the Southern, Northern, Sui and Tang dynasties. This new gallery is very impressive; each object is a treasure. All are elegantly displayed with clear explanations.

41 Sino-Japanese War Memorial Museum / Marco Polo Bridge

中国人民抗日战争纪念馆 *Zhongguo renmin kangrizhanzheng jinianguan*

101 Chengnei Street, Wanping Town,
Lugouqiao, Fengtai District
北京市丰台区卢沟桥宛平城内街
101号

Tel: (010) 8389 3163 / 2355
Open: 9.00–16.30 except Mon; ticket office closes at 16.00
www.77china.org.cn/index.php?id=1 (Chinese only)
Restaurants / souvenir shops

The location of this Memorial Museum is no coincidence as the 'Marco Polo Bridge Incident' is often cited as the beginning of the Sino-Japanese War. On 7 July 1937 tensions erupted into violence between Japanese troops stationed on one side of the bridge and the Chinese on the other. A prolonged battle ensued and after three days the Japanese ultimately took the bridge and the town of Wanping. From there they marched on to Beijing, seizing control on 29 July and Tianjin the day after.

The exhibits in the Memorial Hall are divided into three sections, focusing on Japanese atrocities, the war years and anti-Japanese heroes. Exhibits detail gruesome episodes during the Japanese occupation, including the use of germ warfare and the Rape of Nanjing. Some exhibits are quite graphic, including pictures of decapitated Chinese and implements of torture. While some exhibits include actual weapons (rusting swords, implements of torture and at least one skull, purportedly of a Nanjing massacre victim), most of the displays consist of photographs and original documents, with explanations of the most salient features in English and the rest in Chinese. This museum is not suitable for young children.

The *Lugou Qiao*, or Marco Polo Bridge as it is known in English, was built in 1192 and rebuilt in the seventeenth century by the Kangxi Emperor after it was washed away in a flood. There is no chance of such an incident repeating itself

today as the Yongding River has been diverted to supply the needs of Beijing. The bridge gets its English name from the fact that Marco Polo saw the bridge during his time in China in the thirteenth century and waxed lyrical over it in his book *The Travels of Marco Polo*. The magnificent span of this handsome granite bridge, held up by eleven arches, now extends across dry brush or grass depending on the season. But the bridge is still a sight to behold. It measures 235 m and has 250 marble balustrades supporting 485 carved stone lions – none of which are identical or in the same position. Many of them have smaller lions crawling on them or resting between their paws. On either side of the bridge is a commemorative stele, one built by the Kangxi Emperor on its reconstruction, the other by his grandson, the Qianlong Emperor. Tradition has it that the bridge is best seen while viewing the moon during the Mid-Autumn Festival.

While you are there you will be struck by the atmosphere of Wanping Town itself – the only walled town remaining in the Beijing area. It has recently been cleaned up to promote tourism but still has a special atmosphere of times gone by. You might want to stop at the Beijing Hutong Museum by the West Gate of the town which is open from 9.00 to 17.00. They have a modest collection of toys and folk figurines as well as a charming extended diorama depicting street life in Beijing's *hutongs*, with all sorts of traditional shops and crafts displayed in miniature.

Marco Polo Bridge

The Sino-Japanese War (1937–45)

This war is also referred to by the Chinese as the War of Resistance Against Japan. In 1931 the Japanese had taken full control of northeast China and in 1932 proclaimed there the puppet state of Manchukuo. Then in July 1937 the full-scale Japanese invasion of the rest of China began.

The Nationalist Party (KMT) government, which had enjoyed ten years of relative stability, was forced by the Japanese invasion to abandon the capital in Nanjing and flee to Chongqing in Sichuan where they held on tenuously through the war, with support from the Allies. The Japanese invasion and occupation of China was brutal. For example over a six-week period, the 'Rape of Nanjing' left several hundred thousand Chinese civilians murdered. Japanese atrocities in China still scar Sino-Japanese relations today.

Though Japan took over most of China, the occupation did not extend much beyond the cities and the major lines of communications. This gave the opportunity for the Chinese Communist Party (then in a United Front with the Nationalists) to conduct widespread guerrilla war behind the Japanese lines. Though the Chinese resistance pinned the Japanese down, the war in China became a sideshow after the US began its naval campaign in the Pacific and went straight to Japan.

The Nationalist Government emerged from the war greatly weakened. At the same time the war permitted the rival Communist party to gain nationwide legitimacy as well as territory which left them well placed to win the subsequent Civil War. Many historians believe the Japanese invasion was a key turning point in the Communists' rise to power.

42

Songzhuang Artists' Village

宋庄画家村 *Songzhuang huajiacun*

Songzhuang Town, Tongzhou District
北京市通州区宋庄镇

Tel: (010) 6959 8343 (for daytime tours)
Open: 9.00–17.00
www.chinasongzhuang.cn
Bookshop / café at visitor centre / restaurants in the village

This is not a quaint, rustic village but what most non-Chinese would consider a fair-sized town located in the eastern suburbs about 13 km from central Beijing. Its main thoroughfare, a wide boulevard, has the sort of shops and restaurants typical of many such Chinese towns. Songzhuang actually incorporates a number of villages centred on Xiaopu. During the early 1990s, many of China's up-and-coming young artists such as Fang Lijun, Yue Minjun, Liu Wei and Yang Shaobin left their community in Yuanmingyuan – the old Summer Palace – and began moving their studios to Songzhuang. The town became identified as an artists' centre, a reputation the local government decided to support and capitalize on. Today approximately 2,000 artists live in Songzhuang. Some allow passers-by to drop in unannounced, while others require that you call ahead. In addition there is something like 200 museums, art centres and galleries of various sizes and quality in the village. A day trip out here is great fun and highly recommended.

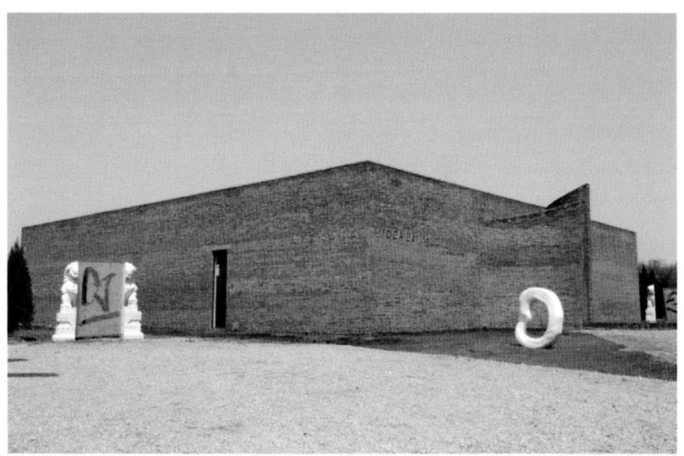

Songzhuang MoCA

The best way to get started is to buy a map of the galleries, available at the visitor's centre. A car is indispensable, as the distances are great. The galleries, museums and studios tend to cluster, so you can park in one area, look around on foot and then move on to the next area.

Among the major galleries is the Songzhuang Art Centre, a non-profit museum with large and airy galleries, built in 2006. It has featured exhibitions of work by many of the iconic contemporary artists residing in Songzhuang. The curator and director is Li Xianting, an early resident and one of the most respected names in Chinese contemporary art. An artist, critic and curator, he

Gallery in Songzhuang MoCA

organized the *Stars* exhibition in 1978, setting off the contemporary art movement in China. The Xiao Pu Culture Centre, a complex connected to the Songzhuang Art Centre, incorporates galleries, studios, storage and workshops. Finally, the Songzhuang MoCA is a beautifully designed space exhibiting temporary shows (see their website, www.bjmoca.com, for details).

During October, an annual art festival is held at the village.

43

Sony ExploraScience Museum

索尼探梦 *Suoni tanmeng*

Chaoyang Park, No. 1, Chaoyang Park Nan Lu
北京市朝阳区朝阳公园南路1号
朝阳公园内

Tel: (010) 6501 8800
Open: 9.30–18.00 Mon–Fri; 9.00–19.30 Sat & Sun; closed two or three days in the middle of each month (check website)
www.explorascience.com.cn
Kids

This interactive science and technology museum introduces Sony's newest digital technologies. It combines interactive educational exhibits from the Exploratorium in San Francisco with Sony's latest technologies to help young people explore and experience the attraction of science.

The museum has four different sections: Illusion, where visitors can ex-

plore optical illusions; Refraction / Reflection, where you can experience how light travels through space to carry information; Light / Colours, using spectroscopes and computer processing to see how the light we see each day is comprised of various wave lengths; and Sound, an invisible phenomenon that moves through space. Sony ExploraScience also puts on special exhibits that change every two months. Throughout the museum there are interactive bilingual screens that explain the exhibits. Photography is allowed.

44

Soong Ching Ling's Former Residence

宋庆龄同志故居 *Song Qingling tongzhi guju*

Houhai Beiyan 46, Xichengqu (north-east shore of Hou Hai)
北京市西城区后海北沿46号

Tel: (010) 6404 4205
Open: 9.00–17.00; 16.30 winter
www.sql.org.cn (Chinese only)

This is the Beijing residence of Soong Ching Ling (1893–1981), wife of Dr Sun Yat-Sen. The house, set among gardens on the north side of Houhai Lake, was her official residence and is basically unchanged since she occupied it. Exhibited are many photos and personal possessions of Soong Ching Ling from her childhood to the time of her death which document many of the historic events she lived through and took part in. There are also many mementoes on display recording her associations with renowned figures of China's recent history.

45

Tank Museum

中国坦克博物馆 *Zhongguo tanke bowuguan*

No. 88372 Army Unit, Yangfang, Changping District
北京市昌平区阳坊镇八八三七二部队

Tel: (010) 6675 9901; located on an active military base; you must call ahead before your visit
Open: 8.30–17.00 except Mon
Kids

Although the museum's building is somewhat dilapidated and the displays inside, consisting mainly of photos, do not elicit great excitement, a good selection of Chinese, American and Japanese tanks is displayed in the courtyard outside, making this a worthwhile stop for the tank enthusiast. Almost all of the displays are accompanied by good signage in Chinese and English giving detailed historical information as well as specifications. Plans are afoot to move some of the non-vehicle displays into a nearby building undergoing refurbishment.

Like other military equipment in the arsenal of the People's Liberation Army (PLA), many of the tanks are remakes of Soviet examples either licensed or purchased, including the Type 59 Medium Tank based on the Soviet T-54. Externally this tank was almost identical to its Soviet model, but its innards were made to Chinese specifications. Subsequent models with added improvements are also shown. The experimental 111 Heavy Tank was delivered in 1970 without its turret and was never completed due to the start of the Cultural Revolution. Among the several American tanks is the amphibious Landing Vehicle Tracked LVT variant (A)-4 produced in 1944 and designed for use in areas around water or in rice fields (where the Americans used it during the Vietnam War). The museum's example would have been captured by the PLA from the Nationalists during the Civil War.

T-54 Medium Tank

US LVT(A)-4 Amphibious Tank

46 Tian Yi Mu – Beijing Eunuch Culture Exhibition Hall

田义墓 – 北京宦官文化陈列馆 *Tianyimu – Beijing huanguan wenhua chenlieguan*

80 Moshikou Dajie, Shijingshan District
北京市石景山区模式口大街80号

Tel: (010) 8872 4148 / 2585
Open: 9.00–16.30
Small pamphlets / books (Chinese only)

Tian Yi Mu – the tomb of Tian Yi – is actually a cemetery containing the tomb of the eunuch Tian Yi (1534–1620). He served three Emperors of the Ming dynasty – Jiajing, Longqing and Wanli – under whom he rose to prominence, ultimately reaching the powerful position of Director of Ceremonies. The Emperor favoured him to such a degree that at Tian Yi's death he declared three days of public mourning and commissioned the creation of this cemetery.

Entering the memorial by the Divine Path, one is first confronted by two imposing facing stone guardians – on the left a military official and on the right a civil one. Beyond these are three pavilions, each containing a massive stone stele resting on a turtle's back and wrapped in a four-clawed dragon. These recount Tian Yi's good deeds and achievements as well as the imperial order to build the memorial.

The cemetery at Tian Yi Mu

Gates lead you to the cemetery down the Divine Path

Continuing on, there is a Qing dynasty stone temple which originally contained three rooms and had a roof. More eunuchs are buried here, acknowledging the respect commanded by Tian Yi even two centuries after his death. Walking on through the Shouyu Gate, the visitor symbolically leaves the world of the living and enters that of the dead. In this section a row of four marble tombs with mounded roofs contain the remains of eunuchs who wished to be buried near Tian Yi. These tombs are beautifully carved with scenes from traditional tales and depictions of auspicious creatures and plants. Facing each tomb is an altar table (for the adopted children of eunuchs to make their offerings), and between them is the entrance to the underground tomb of Tian Yi himself – unfortunately robbed in the early years of the Republic. You can still see the hole in the upper left of the heavy stone door where thieves hacked their way in. Now the dark, dank underground room holds only a few rotten planks of wood and an empty pit in which the coffin once lay. Tread carefully – you enter this chamber by a stone staircase lit by a single bulb. It may feel like an adventure, but sadly there is nothing left to be seen.

Notwithstanding the missing Tian Yi, this peaceful Buddhist graveyard has a wonderfully numinous atmosphere. It is empty of tourists, a bit overgrown

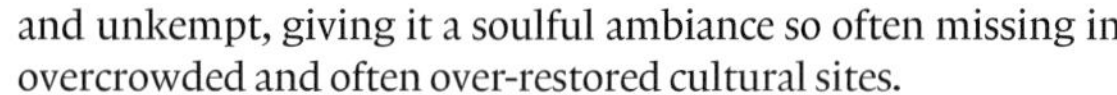

Stone sculpture of civil official

The Dowager Empress Cixi with concubines and eunuchs in the Forbidden City

and unkempt, giving it a soulful ambiance so often missing in overcrowded and often over-restored cultural sites.

At the time of publication a new museum is planned which will contain new material from other eunuch cemeteries but will no doubt also include information from the existing small exhibition room. In this gallery, by means of photographs of old documents and of eunuchs of the imperial court, a history of 'eunuch culture' is described. There are photos of Sun Yaoting (1902–1996), the last imperial eunuch, on a visit to Tian Yi Mu.

There is also a detailed explanation of the actual process of castration during the Qing dynasty – no doubt identical to that of earlier periods.

Eunuchs at the Imperial Court

Eunuchs at court date back to the eighth century BC, when captured enemies were castrated and enslaved. In later periods parents sold their sons for this purpose, and as the role became increasingly prestigious and lucrative, older boys and men actually volunteered for the cut.

Eunuchs were able to attain a powerful and influential position at court as they were uniquely privy to the machinations and connivances of both male and female segments of society in the 'Great Within', as the Forbidden City was known. Eunuchs were charged with much of the bringing up of young royals. Isolated within the Imperial City, these children were highly influenced by their mentors, who were often accused of introducing them to sexual excess and dissipation, ultimately creating compliant, even paranoid adults. These emotionally handicapped grown–ups would then be dependent on guidance and advice from their trusted eunuchs to navigate the complexities of the 'Great Without'.

In the women's quarters, the concubines of the Emperor were constantly scheming to gain his favour and attentions for themselves, their sons and their family. Eunuchs, since they were not a sexual threat, had almost unfettered access to the women in the harem and played a large part in these manipulations and intrigues, even to the point of murder. The royal eunuchs were reputed to be manipulative, debauched, treacherous, corrupt and ambitious. It sounds extreme but could be true. They were generally despised, but perhaps this was due, at least in part, to jealousy over their intimacy with the royals, their accumulation of wealth and a repugnance at their mutilation.

The actual operation was performed in a room in the Imperial City by a 'knifer'. Just before the cut, the patient was asked if he was absolutely sure he wanted to go ahead, given a herbal infusion meant to anaesthetize, and then held down and cut with a specially designed curved knife. A metal plug was inserted into the urethra, he was made to walk immediately, and no drink or urination was allowed for three days. The plug was then taken out. If the man could urinate at that point, he would probably live. The severed penis and testicles, known as the 'Precious', was carefully kept by every eunuch as they were required to be shown when progressing to higher levels of service. If lost or stolen, eunuchs would borrow or rent those of others to show. Eunuchs also were required to be buried with their 'Precious' in order to gain entry into heaven as men.

47

Today Art Gallery

今日美术馆 *Jinri meishuguan*

Building 4, 32 Baiziwan Road,
Chaoyang District
北京市朝阳区百子湾路32号4楼

Tel: (010) 5876 0600
Open: 9.00–17.00
www.todaygallery.com
Trendy café / well-stocked bookshop

This is a privately owned museum of contemporary art, both Chinese and foreign. Work is exhibited over four floors and is rotated regularly, usually every ten days or monthly. There is no permanent collection, and occasionally one gallery showcases work for sale. The building opened in 2006 and the space is modern and well designed. The shows are generally of a high calibre, and the museum is well thought of.

48

Ullens Center for Contemporary Art (UCCA)

尤伦斯当代艺术中心 *Youlunsi dangdai yishu zhongxin*

798 Art District, 4 Jiuxianqiao Lu,
Chaoyang District
北京市朝阳区酒仙桥路4号798艺术区

Tel: (010) 8459 9269
Open: 10.00–19.00 except Mon
www.ullens-center.org/
Excellent shop with eclectic and more usual items

Founded by a Belgian couple, Guy and Myriam Ullens, this state-of-the-art facility in the 798 Art District of Dashanzi has brought together a collection of more than 1,500 modern and contemporary works by three generations

Architect's rendering of the second nave turned into an open exhibition hall

of Chinese artists in a wide range of media. This is the largest single collection of Chinese contemporary art in the world, and with its opening in November 2007, the UCCA became one of the most comprehensive contemporary art institutions in China and the only non-profit art organization in the country supported by a private foundation.

The modern galleries were designed by the French architect Jean-Michel Wilmotte in collaboration with the Chinese architect Ma Qingyun in an old Bauhaus style factory. The UCCA's mission is to present both group and solo exhibitions exploring current developments in Chinese and international art, as well as site commissions and experimental projects by emerging Chinese artists. The inaugural exhibition, entitled '85 New Wave: The Birth of Chinese Contemporary Art', presented the revolutionary period in Chinese art from 1985 to 1990, when artists were 'breaking free from decades of socialist realism to begin a process of intense experimentation'. The permanent collection includes works by well-known artists of the period, including Wang Guangyi, Xu Bing, Geng Jianyi, Huang Yongping and Zhang Peili, among others. In addition to exhibiting artworks, documentary materials such as manuscripts, letters, sketches, photos and rare videos help to create a sense of this seminal period. To support the exhibition programme, tours, screenings, lectures and seminars are on offer.

Chen Zhen, *Human Tower*, installation, 1999

Fang Lijun, *Series Two No 4*, oil on canvas, 1992

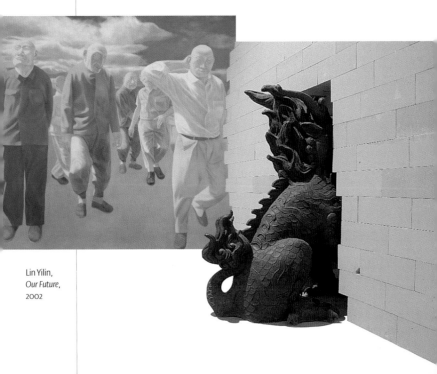

Lin Yilin, *Our Future*, 2002

49

Xu Beihong Museum

徐悲鸿纪念馆 *Xu Beihong jinianguan*

53 Xinjiekou Beidajie, Xichang District
北京市西城区新街口北大街55号

Tel: (010) 6225 2042
Open: 9.00–16.00 except Mon

Xu Beihong was one of China's most famous twentieth-century artists. Born in 1895 in Jiangsu Province, he was taught by his father and spent his youth with him as an itinerant portraitist. After his father's death, he went to Shanghai, where he worked and studied, soon becoming prominent in art circles. In 1917, he spent a year in Japan, then returned to China and taught at Beijing University. There he became politically involved, joining the revolutionary New Culture Movement. In 1919, Xu moved to Europe, studying and painting in Paris, Berlin and Brussels. By the time he returned to China in 1926, he was a well-known painter with a strong academic background and a solid technique in classical European-style drawing and oil painting. In 1927, he became the head of the Art department of the National Central University in Nanjing where he remained for the following ten years.

On his return to China, Xu began creating paintings combining classical Western realism with Chinese themes and contemporary political messages. Each message is spelled out for visitors by the curators of the Xu Beihong Museum. For example, the well-known paintings *The 500 Retainers of Tian Heng* and *Awaiting the Deliverer* are on exhibit. The sign below *Awaiting the Deliverer* (which the Museum has labelled *Awaiting Our Leader*) explains the meaning of the work: 'Under the dark rule of the Kuomintang government the people were eagerly awaiting to be liberated'. Similarly, on the label below *The 500 Retainers of Tian Heng*, it is explained that 'this picture was painted in the years of darkness when the Kuomintang reactionaries colluded with imperialism and imposed barbarous rule in China'.

Xu also painted in traditional Chinese style with brush and ink. These are his most famous works and mainly depict horses. *Galloping Horse* is especially famous. It was not on display at the time of the writer's visit although other horse paintings were on display, including the famous brush-and-ink *Kapok Tree*.

During the 1930s and early 1940s, Xu continued to travel, returning to Europe as well as going to the Soviet Union and India, where he painted a portrait of Mahatma Gandhi which can be seen in the museum. During this period, he also finished one of his huge patriotic paintings, *Yu Gong Removes the Mountain*, an allegorical work which was one of Mao Zedong's favourite paintings as its message describes relentless struggle leading ultimately to success.

Yu Gong Removes the Mountain (1940)

Xu died of a cerebral haemorrhage in 1953 after some years of poor health. The Xu Beihong Museum is situated in an older building next door to his original house and studio (no longer standing). The ground floor has two galleries of Xu's paintings and calligraphy on exhibit and one room with very poor-quality paintings by local artists for sale. Upstairs are further galleries with paintings by Xu, as well as a room containing a mock-up of his study and studio. Hanging on the walls of this room are photos of Xu throughout his life. The painting galleries, although a bit old fashioned, are clean, and the works are fairly well hung and lit in spite of being behind a wall of highly reflective glass, making them difficult to see. There is English signage throughout the galleries.

50

Zhoukoudian Site Museum

周口店遗址博物馆 *Zhoukoudian yizhi bowuguan*

Zhoukoudian Village, Fangshan District
北京市房山区周口店

Tel: (010) 6930 1272 / 8011
Open: 8.30–16.30
www.zkd.cn

About fifty miles southwest of Beijing is the Palaeolithic site of Zhoukoudian. It was here that the first *Homo erectus pekinesis* skull cap was excavated in 1929, later known as 'Peking Man'. This discovery ranked alongside Africa's Olduvai Gorge as one of the greatest stories in archaeological history and remains one of the most widely known prehistoric sites in the world.

The story began in 1899 with the German doctor and fossil collector K A Harberer. While visiting China Harberer collected what were then known as 'dragon bones' but were actually fossil bones. These were ground up and sold in pharmacies to be used as a cure for every sort of medical problem. Harberer had them analyzed on his return to Germany and found that they were actually the remains of many different types of extinct mammals, including sabre-tooth tigers, antelopes and hyenas. He also had collected a molar that looked somewhat human and was estimated to be up to 2,000,000 years old.

The story picked up again in the 1920s with the Swedish scientist Johann Gunnar Anderson, who was searching for 'dragon bones' at a limestone quarry near Zhoukoudian, when he was directed by a local resident to a site known as 'Dragon Bone Hill'. There Anderson and his colleague found

many mammalian fossils, as well as two teeth similar to those found earlier by Harberer. These molars, analyzed in 1927 by the Canadian Davidson Black, head of the Anatomy department of Peking Union Medical College, were identified as in fact belonging to a hominid and up to 2,000,000 years old. This caused an uproar in the archaeological community as the molars constituted the oldest known evidence of human fossils.

The site of Chou K'ou Tian (Zhoukoudian) became the focus of palaeontological research, with a large-scale excavation funded by the Rockefeller Foundation in America. Besides many fossilized animal bones of differing species, another similar molar was found, confirming Black's theory that these teeth came from a new and separate genus of hominid which he named *Sinanthropus pekinensis* – now classified as *Homo erectus pekinensis* – 'Peking Man'. Davidson Black became director of the excavation and – uniquely for his time – demanded that Chinese archaeologists working at the site be on equal footing with their European colleagues. He hired prominent Chinese scientists to work in the team, including Pei Wenzhong ,Yang Zhongjian and Bian Meinian.

At a dramatic moment at the very end of the 1929 season, in the midst of the Civil War, Pei Wenzhong, excavating a cave by candlelight, discovered a complete human skull cap. Between 1929 and 1937 several more skull caps were found, as well as eleven mandibles, various facial bones and about 150 teeth. These fragments confirmed the existence of forty individuals, males and females of varying ages – still the largest known sample of *Homo erectus* fossils ever found. The fossil remains tell us that *H. erectus pekinensis* had a long, sloping forehead and thick brow ridge. The jaws and teeth were much bigger than ours, and there was no chin.

In July 1937, as work at the site was progressing so well, everything was suddenly stopped due to the Japanese invasion. The Japanese occupiers took a great interest in Zhoukoudian. In order to protect the fossils from them, they were stored at Peking Union Medical College, and casts were made. In 1941 the originals were packed up to be sent to the US for safekeeping. Somewhere along the way to the port city of Qinhuangdao they disappeared, never to be seen again. Some say they were stolen by the US Marines who were guarding the boxes; others think the Japanese took them; still others believe they remain hidden away in an American university somewhere. There is no

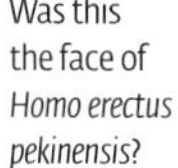

Was this the face of *Homo erectus pekinensis?*

A view from the cave site of the industrial city below

evidence for any of these stories. Research had to continue using the plaster casts made in the 1930s.

Excavation at the site was resumed after the war. Two more skull fragments belonging to one individual were found, as well as many more tools from the Early–Late Palaeolithic. Pollen analysis yielded information about the diet of the individuals and about the species of fauna during this period. Late Cenozoic fish fossils have been found as has evidence of ninety other mammal species, including hyenas, deer, bears and tigers.

On the evidence of the many stone tools found at the site (more than 100,000 artefacts) and many quartz-flake tools, it seems that these individuals subsisted mainly by scavenging. There has been controversy about the use of fire at the site. Evidence of ash was thought to remain from hearth fires, but now some say that the ash was caused by lightning-induced spontaneous fires and had been washed into the soil by flooding. On the other hand, burned bone associated with stone tools has been found, which would in fact indicate a controlled use of fire.

Interestingly, some scientists now feel that the caves themselves were actually the dens of hyenas – not the homes of Peking Man. The hominid fossils found do not include many long bones, hands or feet – they are mainly teeth and skull fragments, many of which show puncture marks. The theory is that the very large Pleistocene cave hyena was using *H. erectus pekinensis* as a food source; they would have taken their prey back to their caves and eaten the extremities in their entirety. There is also evidence of the skulls being split open and the brain removed. This fits the hyena theory well, although some feel it is evidence of cannibalism.

Homo erectus pekinensis is now believed to have inhabited Zhoukoudian from 550,000 to 400,000 years ago until about 230,000 years ago, giving the species a very long survival rate. In 1987 Zhoukoudian became a UNESCO World Heritage Site. None of the human fossils on display are originals – all are casts. The animal and fish fossils are real, however. Also on exhibit are large-scale dioramas depicting Peking Man in his natural habitat, including stone tools and bone implements. There is as well a display of the geological history of the site in conjunction with human and animal evolution. Large posters tell the story of the discoveries with biographies of the archaeologists.

At the time of writing, the museum cases and display were quite musty and outdated. However, the material exhibited and history of the site are so important that the site is worth a visit for those with an interest in the subject. You can also wander round the park-like site and visit (from the outside) the limestone fissures in which Peking Man was found. There is not a lot to see, but the levels at which the finds were made are well marked. If you call a day or two ahead, you can hire an English-speaking guide – very helpful when it comes to navigating the excavation areas. The museum has some English signage.

51 Jing Yuan in Tianjin: Exhibition Hall of Aisin Gioro Puyi

天津静园 爱新觉罗溥仪展览馆 *Tianjin jingyuan Aixinjueluo Puyi zhanlanguan*

70 Anshan Road, Heping District, Tianjin
天津市和平区鞍山道70号

Tel: (022) 2731 1618
Open: 9.00–11.00 except Mon

Puyi and others in the Jing Yuan

Aisin Gioro Puyi, the last Emperor of China, in Tianjin

Façade of the Jing Yuan complex (see over)

The beautiful Jing Yuan, or Garden of Serenity, was home to China's famed last Emperor and his concubine Wan Rong from 1929 to 1931. There is no more tragic figure in modern Chinese history than Puyi, a victim throughout his life of whatever political authority crossed his path.

Puyi was born in 1906 and took the throne nearly three years later on the death of his cousin, believed to have been poisoned by their aunt, the notorious Empress Dowager Cixi. His reign was brief, as he was forced to abdicate in 1912 following the Revolution. But the new Republican government permitted him to retain his title and to be treated as a foreign monarch.

His life, however, was like a black comedy. Six years after he abdicated, a Qing loyalist general tried to restore Puyi to the throne. Unfortunately, the restoration lasted just a few days, until another warlord dropped bombs from an airplane flying over the Forbidden City. In 1924, Puyi was driven out of the palace by Feng Yuxiang, the warlord dubbed the Christian General because he baptized his men with a fire hose.

Puyi then moved to Tianjin, but in 1931 the Japanese installed him as the reluctant Emperor of the puppet state Manchukuo, a former Manchu territory to the north. At the end of World War II, Puyi was captured by the Soviet army, and in 1950 Stalin sent him back to China, where he spent a decade in a re-education camp before Mao Zedong declared him reformed. During the Cultural Revolution Puyi was attacked by radical Red Guards who saw him as a symbol of feudalism. He passed away in 1967.

The Jing Yuan complex was originally known as Qian Yuan when it was home to Lu Zongyu, the Chinese envoy to Japan, but the name was changed to Jing Yuan after Puyi moved here. The main structure is a Spanish-style building of brick and wood. There are one-storey buildings on the two sides and a covered corridor to the west.

As soon as you enter Jing Yuan, you'll notice a small building on your left that has an exhibition about the life of Puyi, including photographs of him, other reminders of the imperial court, and some of his personal effects, histori-

cal objects and documents. Visitors can see Puyi and Wan Rong's bedrooms, reading rooms and offices.

Somc forty families moved into the house after Puyi left, and it was seriously damaged. A major renovation was carried out between 2005 and 2007 that returned the house to its former glory. Photographs show the stunning contrasts between its condition formerly and today. A small room on the west side, beside the corridor, houses a small gift shop with a few books on the life of Puyi, as well as an exhibition on the restoration of the house.

52

Museum of Chinese Opera

天津戏剧博物馆 *Tianjin xiju bowuguan*

257 Nanmenli Dajie, Nankai District, Tianjin
天津市南开区南门里大街31号

Tel: (022) 2727 3443
Open: 9.00–16.00 except Sun

The Museum of Chinese Opera, located on the site of the former Guangdong Guildhall (built in 1907), includes a magnificent traditional wooden opera hall and display rooms in the eastern and western chambers which have exhibits on the history of Chinese opera, primarily black and white photographs of China's legendary opera greats, opera dolls and costumes. Surrounding the back and two sides of the opera hall are glass-encased dolls dressed in colourful outfits representing characters from China's most famous operas, including *Sun Wukong*, or the Monkey King.

The Guangdong Guildhall served as a gathering place for businessmen coming to Tianjin from the provinces. The wonderful umbrella-shaped caisson which hangs above the centre of the stage is not merely decorative but also provides good acoustics, amplifying and transmitting the voices of the performers in a natural way without the need for a modern sound system. The centre of the opera hall has no columns – the beams being relegated to the sides – which means that there is nothing blocking the view of the audience. The windows at

Actors in the Beijing Opera *Lian Hua Hu* (Lotus Lake)

the top of the building allow natural light to penetrate so that no stage lights are needed for matinee performances.

The century-old grey-brick and wood structure with its courtyard is alone worth the visit. The design of the building is based on the style of buildings in Chaozhou in Guangdong Province.

There are no explanatory materials in English. Photography is allowed in the opera hall but not in the exhibition rooms.

53

Pingjin Campaign Memorial Museum

平津战役纪念馆 *Pingjin zhanyi jinianguan*

8 Pingjin Road, Hongqiao, Tianjin
天津市红桥区平津道8号

Tel: (022) 2653 5418
Open: 9.00–16.00

Chinese heroes at the entrance

This museum introduces the background to a famous large-scale strategic battle between Communist and Nationalist forces, one of three major campaigns launched by the Red Army in the final days of the Civil War to bring about the end of Nationalist rule. The battle, which lasted from 29 November 1948 to 31 January 1949, resulted in the fall of Tianjin, which in turn left Beijing (then known as Beiping) exposed.

The museum is made up of three sections.

Victory Square, at the front, displays dozens of tanks, artillery pieces, fighter aircraft and even small navy boats. There are also a number of bronze statues highlighting events in the war.

The main building has six exhibition halls and some 2,500 valuable relics, sculptures and paintings. In the Prologue Hall is a copper sculpture entitled *Marching to Victory,* which represents Mao Zedong, Zhou Enlai and other senior leaders of the time. Behind the sculpture, the walls are covered with colourful frescoes showing scenes of fighting, and happy views of the Red Army and local villagers.

Turning left, you'll enter the Campaign Decision Hall, where you'll be greeted by a wax figure of Mao Zedong sitting at his planning desk. On the surrounding walls are paintings, black and white photos of the battle, and original documents related to the campaign. Cross Prologue Hall and enter

Campaign Implement Hall, where there are photos, documents, objects and charts related to the campaign. Also on display are a sand-table model of the battle and the keys to Beijing's old city walls, which the defeated Nationalists turned over to the Red Army. In the People Support the Front Hall are paintings of Zhou Enlai making preparations for the war, a wax diorama of peasants working around a farmhouse, an old wooden cart and related objects.

Other items scattered throughout the two floors of the museum include dozens of machine guns, personal items belonging to former Communist officials and life-size reproductions of battle scenes. There is also a Multidimensional Demonstration Hall, which has a full-screen theatre showing scenes of the battlefield with sound effects.

Photography is permitted.

54

Tianjin Academy of Fine Arts Gallery

天津美术学院美术馆 *Tianjin meishuxueyuan meishuguan*

No. 4 Tianwei Road, Hebei District, Tianjin
天津市河北区天纬路4号

Tel: (022) 2624 1540
Open: 8.30–17.30 (when there is an exhibition)
www.tjarts.edu.cn

Although the city's contemporary art scene is not as effervescent as that of Beijing's, it has enormous potential, for not only is Tianjin just an hour by train from the capital, but it boasts the well-established Tianjin Academy of Fine Arts – founded in 1906, as well as Schools of Art, Design and Architecture. Many well-known Chinese artists are alumni and have returned to teach at the Academy; several have also displayed their work in the newly opened gallery. Over half of this five-floor modern edifice, built on a corner plot adjacent to Academy, houses temporary exhibitions of alumni and international artists' works ranging from contemporary and traditional painting, photography, sculpture and multimedia rotated several times throughout the year – while the other half comprises offices, conference spaces and artists' studios. New commercial contemporary galleries have also starting opening in the city. Those on the trail of the contemporary art scene in China should check local listings for upcoming shows at this gallery and the seemingly burgeoning commercial ones too.

55

Tianjin Museum

天津博物馆 *Tianjin bowuguan*

31 Youyi Road, Hexi District, Tianjin
天津市河西区友谊路31号

Tel: (022) 5879 3000
Open: 9.00–16.30 except Mon; last entry 16.00
www.tjbwg.com
Chinese audio and exhibition guides only
Bookshop

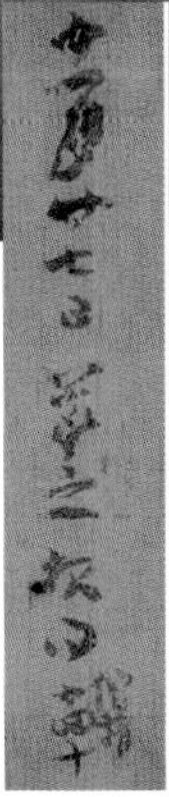

The present Tianjin Museum replaces an earlier museum established in 1918 that was ultimately housed in a French-style Art Deco mansion dating to the 1930s. Although quaint, space restrictions in the old building allowed only a small part of the collection to be exhibited. The new museum on a new site was designed by the Japanese architect Mamoru Kawaguchi to represent a swan with wings extended and ready to take flight, meant as an analogy to Tianjin's re-emergence as a city of major importance. The complex consists of the main building, a long walkway (the swan's neck) across a small lake and a garden surrounding the lake.

The ground floor is mainly a large atrium housing an information counter, ticket office, bookstore and so on. The two upper floors house an impressive collection of ceramics, paintings, calligraphy, jades, bronzes, ink stones and oracle bones. On the top floor are a number of historically important Shang dynasty oracle bones dating from the Reign of Wu Ding. One of them, along with a divination regarding the weather, records the sacrifice of 500 people to ensure success in battle.

While viewing the jade collection, do not miss the Neolithic Hongshan material, notably a yellow-jade pig dragon, *hongshan huangyu zhulong*, with the head of a pig and the coiled body of a dragon. The Hongshan Culture, which stretched from Inner Mongolia to Liaoning and Hebei and which dates to *c.* 4700–2900 BC, is renowned for its jade-carving techniques. Such items are related to Neolithic tombs and rituals.

Be sure to see the Qing dynasty jadeite leaf with two crickets and a mantis, *feicui guoguo baicai*. This beautifully carved object is made from a single piece of stone and varies in colour from yellow to bright green. The bronze collection also contains splendid items, including a Warring States *ding* known as the *Chu Wang Ding*. It has a loop and three stylized bird-shaped knots on the lid, with handles on each side. The three legs are in the shape of hooves at the bottom and animal masks at the top. A forty-six-character inscription near the rim records the story of producing this *ding*, which was made from the weapons seized by the Chu

Walkway leading to museum entrance

A section of a Tang copy of Wang Xizhi's *Hancie Tie*

Painting by Ming artist, Chen Hongshou (1598–1652), *Drinking Wine in the Garden*

Tianjin concession box: Tianjin had many European style buildings which are now disappearing

King to celebrate his victory in a particular battle. One of the great treasures of this museum is the *Tai Bao Ding* dating to the Reign of Emperor Zhou Kang. This *ding* is known for its fine casting and elaborate decoration consisting of crawling mythical animals and abstract designs on body and legs. Inside the *ding*, there is a three-character inscription recording its casting by Tai Bao.

The History Exhibition Hall has exhibits related to the foreign presence in Tianjin. There is the actual stone tablet erected in memory of an American captain serving with the US 9th Infantry Regiment who was killed fighting Chinese forces in the area, as well as weapons captured from the Eight Allied Army, made up of troops from eight countries whose citizens were under siege in the Beijing Legation Quarter by the Boxers. Other items include a Ming dynasty cannon, a model of the old city wall in Tianjin, China's first

Tianjin Concession District

Like many other Chinese cities, Tianjin is rapidly taking on a modern look. But explore the centre of the old city and you'll discover a walking museum of European, Russian, and Japanese architecture in its former foreign-concession area.

Tianjin, a special municipality some 90 km east of Beijing, allowed the British and French to establish concessions as a result of the Treaty of Tianjin (1858), which ended the Second Opium War. A number of other Western powers and Japan followed on their heels, building their own concessions along the waterfront. The former European and Japanese areas lay to the south of the Hai River. The Western-style buildings show the wishes of the city's former foreign residents to bring something of their home with them to China.

The former French Concession was established in 1861, and most of the buildings remain, including the consulate, the French Club and several cathedrals. Traditional chateaux sit in the French Concession along Jiefang Lu. Central Park, on Huayuan Lu, was a French park. Xi Kai Cathedral (*Xikai Jiaotang*) was erected in 1916; the edifice is a copy of Notre Dame de la Garde in Marseilles. Dedicated to St Vincent de Paul, it was originally run by missionary priests from the order he founded. The church's towers are topped by colourful green domes. Notre Dame des Victoires (*Shengmu Desheng Tang*) is Tianjin's oldest Catholic cathedral, having been built in 1869. Destroyed in 1900 during the Boxer Rebellion, it was rebuilt, destroyed again by the Tangshan earthquake in 1976 and rebuilt once more in 1983.

The British Concession, established in 1860, was the biggest in Tianjin. The area still boasts grand Edwardian structures. The New World Astor Hotel (*Lishunde Dafandian*), on the banks of the Hai, is worth a visit. The last Chinese Emperor, Puyi, came here regularly after he was forced out of the Forbidden City in 1924 and made Tianjin his home. Although a shadow of its former self, this is one of the best examples of European architecture in the city. Across the river is the former Russian Concession, established in 1900 but never completed; the land was returned to the Chinese government in 1920. The two structures of interest from the Japanese Concession, established in 1888, include Jing Garden and Zhang Garden, the homes of Puyi from 1924 until 1931. Other countries that had concessions included Germany, Italy, Belgium and the Austro-Hungarian Empire.

mini-submarine and 'The Rocket of China', China's first locomotive.

The museum has a fine ceramic collection that covers China's entire history. Of special interest is the Qing period *famille rose* enamel vase, *yu hu chun*. This marvellous pot, decorated with birds and peonies and inscribed with a poem, was made for the Qianlong Emperor and painted by the court painter at the imperial workshop. It is considered one of the museum's prized possessions. Also note the Southern Song *guan* ware brush washer (*guanyao longwenxi*), a perfect example with its pale greenish-grey glaze and fine brown crackles. The pot is rimmed with bronze, providing a beautiful contrast with the colour of the glaze.

The museum also houses a fine collection of folk art, including woodblock prints, kites and masks.

56

Tianjin Natural History Museum

天津自然博物馆 *Tianjin ziran bowuguan*

206 Machangdao, Hexi District, Tianjin
天津市河西区马场道206号

Tel: (022) 2335 9807 / 2334 7988
Open: 9.00–17.00 except Mon; ticket office closes at 15.30
www.tjnhm.org
Audio guides in three languages / disabled access and wheelchairs available
Kids

The museum was founded in 1914 by the French palaeontologist and Catholic priest, Émile Licent, who, together with his French Jesuit colleague Teilhard de Chardin (who participated on the Gobi Desert expedition with Roy Chapman Andrews), went to China during the early 1900s when it started to open to the West and a number of foreign-led expeditions – including those of Aurel Stein – fuelled interest in China's past. Although Licent went originally to work in China's educational institutions, during his twenty-five years in China from 1914 to 1939 he also began to train Chinese colleagues as archaeologists from his base in Tianjin. His grounding in palaeontology proved invaluable as he and Teilhard de Chardin conducted numerous expeditions across northern and central China, including at the important site of Salawusu in Inner Mongolia which contained early fragmentary human remains (*Ordos Man*) attributed to early modern humans or Neanderthals.

This museum is one of the oldest of its kind in China and Licent's accumulation of knowledge, specimens of plants and minerals, Quaternary mammal fossils, prehistoric human tools – not to mention his travelogues and scientific reports – firmly set the scientific foundations of this remarkable museum. Today it

Atrium space displaying dinosaurs

The aquarium

still prides itself on being home to several thousand of China's natural history treasures among its nearly 400,000 specimens and its reputation for continued research in the field collaborating with many of China's leading universities as well as those abroad.

The museum has moved several times during its long history and in 1997 a purpose-built structure was built to display this vast collection in an informative and creative way to enhance the visitor's experience. This has been achieved by using interactive displays and imaginative display within all the exhibition halls including those on palaeontology, amphibious reptiles, ecology, insects and tropical plants. A definite highlight is the triple-height glass atrium displaying a dozen skeletons of dinosaurs in a recreated Mesozoic landscape. Among the lush plants stands *Monolophosaurus jiungi*, a single-crested carnivorous lizard of the Middle Jurassic along with *Bellusauruus sui*, a herbivore from the same period, both found in China. Towering over them is the Middle Jurassic daddy, *Omeisaurus* which grew up to 20 metres in length, also discovered in China. Another joy for children is the crowd-pulling aquarium opened in 2004 on the ground floor.

57

Tianjin Science and Technology Museum

天津科学技术馆 *Tianjin kexuejishuguan*

94 Longchang Road, Hexi District, Tianjin
天津市河西区隆昌路94号

Tel: (022) 2832 0403
Open: 9.00–16.30 except Mon
www.tjstm.org
Kids

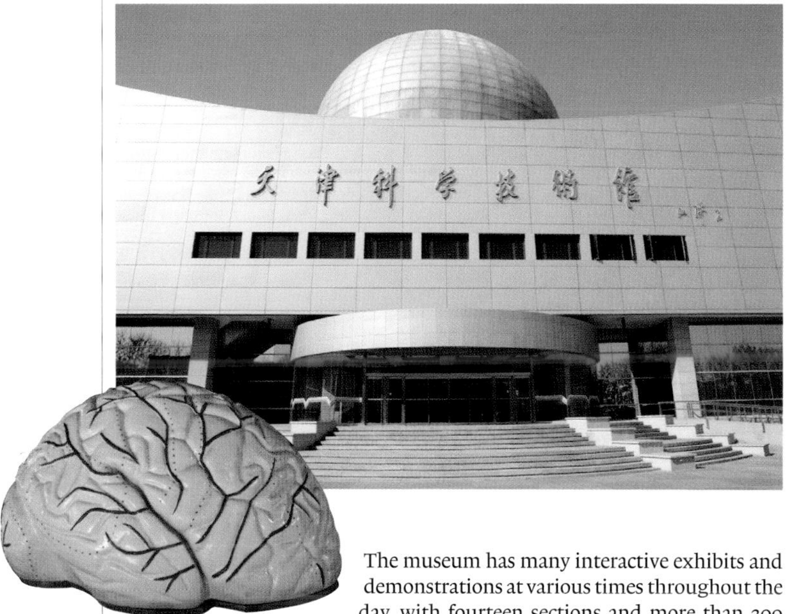

The museum has many interactive exhibits and demonstrations at various times throughout the day, with fourteen sections and more than 300 items on display.

The first floor has exhibits on energy, communications and astronomy, and an area dedicated to famous scientists. The second floor offers a look at the human body, life sciences, mathematics, acoustics, optics, machinery and robotics. The space theatre on the third floor serves as a cinema and planetarium.

Unfortunately, the museum has not been properly maintained. Lighting is poor, and some of the interactive exhibits don't work. There are some English captions but no explanations, as well as a simple English brochure. Photography is allowed.

58

Hebei Provincial Museum

河北省博物馆 *Hebeisheng bowuguan*

4 Dongda Street, Shijiazhuang, Hebei
石家庄市东大街4号

Tel: (0311) 8604 5642
Open: 9.00–17.00 except Mon
www.hebeimuseum.org/

This building, a copy of Beijing's Great Hall of the People, was constructed in 1968 for the purpose of displaying Chairman Mao's books, memorabilia and related artefacts. In 1986, the building became the Hebei Provincial Museum. The museum is now home to a superb collection of art, archaeological artefacts and documents from prehistory to modern times, and is well worth an admittedly long day trip to Shijiazhuang.

The imposing building, an excellent example of Stalinist architecture, is an artefact in its own right. Huge bronze friezes depicting labouring revolutionary soldiers, workers and peasants decorate either side of the façade.

Large sconces in the form of sunflowers adorn the outer walls as well as the interior halls. During the Cultural Revolution sunflowers facing the sun were a metaphor for the Chinese people who 'looked towards' the Great Helmsman, Mao Zedong. The ground-floor exhibition entitled 'Hebei Today' features crude displays of local industry and are not worth viewing; go directly to the second floor.

The objects in the Warring States and Han era galleries are the stars of the collection and some of the finest material from these periods to be seen in China. On view are objects excavated from the late fourth-century BC tombs of King Cheng and his son, King Cuo of the Zhongshan kingdom. The Zhongshan were non-Chinese nomads who assimilated into Chinese culture, as is evidenced by the artefacts and bronze inscriptions they left behind. Although the burial chamber of King Cuo was looted in antiquity, undisturbed material was discovered in associated rooms. Discovered in Tomb 1 and on exhibition here is a bronze 'map' (inlaid with gold and silver) of the tomb complex. Using this, archaeologists have reconstructed detailed plans of the royal tomb. This double-walled complex would have been built on a pounded-earth mound with the grave pit underneath. The mound would have had roofed wooden structures on top and probably looked very similar to the palace complex. According to the literature, these remains are the earliest evidence of monumental architecture in China. The bronze plan shows us that the King was meant to have two tombs built on either side of his own, housing his wives and consorts. There are also six more tombs presumably for retainers or family, as well as two horse-and-chariot pits. There were further pits for animals and a pit containing three boats and evidence of a canal which led out to the nearby Hutuo River.

The many bronzes found in the tombs include inscriptions describing historical events including a war in 312 BC against the Yan state to the north. There is a large tripod with cast-iron legs inscribed with 469 characters, and two bronze vessels listing the lineage of the Zhongshan kings. Don't miss the pair of bronze dragon-like beasts inlaid with silver from the tomb of King Cuo. These chimeras, known in traditional Chinese literature as *bixie*, meaning 'to ward off evil spirits', have claws, wings, horns, scaled skin and long forked tails. The purpose of these objects is not known, but they may have been weights to hold down mats for sitting on. It wasn't until the tenth century that chairs appeared in China.

Also not to be missed is the silver- and gold-inlaid bronze sculpture depicting a tiger trapping a deer in its jaws. Some scholars believe this illustrates the artistic traditions of the nomadic Di tribe which ruled the Zhongshan state. The Di may have brought with them the Animal Style art of the steppes. Again, what use these objects had can only be conjectured.

The objects found in the Zhongshan tombs differ from those of earlier periods in that they contain more objects of daily use. In addition, the tombs themselves are set up as a house for the dead with rooms for specific purposes, not just as a burial pit as in previous periods. Many scholars feel that at this time, people began

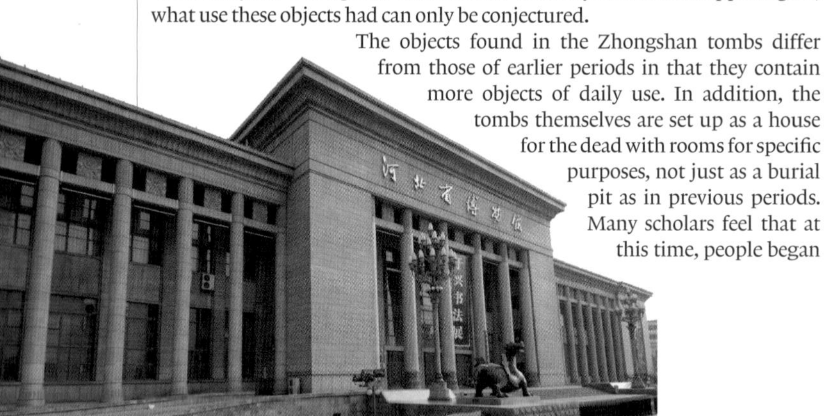

to think of themselves as having souls – and the soul needed a place to live, eat and enjoy life just as the living did.

The Hebei Provincial Museum is also known for its superb collection of objects from the tomb of the Western Han dynasty King Liu Sheng and his consort Dou Wan. These tombs, dug into a rocky hillside, contained an entrance room, a central room, two side rooms for storage and, in the rear, the room containing the coffin itself. More than 2,700 objects made of bronze, gold, silver, jade, iron, silk, lacquer and clay were found in Liu Sheng's tomb, ranging from the everyday to highly ornate and refined pieces. The most famous objects are the jade funeral shrouds, the finest examples, in terms of both quality and condition, ever found. These funerary suits are made up of jade plaques with small holes bored into the corners and sewn tightly together with gold wire. This tomb also yielded numerous smaller jade offerings, including the fine nephrite cicada (Western Han), probably placed in the mouth of the deceased. Jade was believed to have the power to preserve a corpse from decay, and besides being encased in jade suits, members of the royal family had their orifices plugged with small pieces of jade.

Don't leave the gallery without seeing the elegant gilt bronze lamp in the form of a young kneeling woman holding a lantern. Her robe and long, flowing sleeves are carefully tucked under her legs, the backs of her feet so realistically cast! The lamp comes apart for cleaning; the light could be directed and adjusted, the smoke disappearing into the woman's sleeve. Another exceptionally beautiful object from this tomb is a pedestalled bronze censer inlaid with gold, the shape of which is known as *boshanlu*, or 'universal mountain'. Rising from the bowl, the censer assumes the shape of a storm-battered mountain peak populated with animal and human-like creatures. The *boshanlu* made its first appearance in the Han dynasty and is thought to symbolize the home of the Immortals. When lit, the smoke from the incense drifted out of the crags, creating a numinous mist.

Besides the fabulous tomb finds, there are several thousand bronze and stone Buddhist stelae and statues, including white marble and sandstone ones excavated in the 1950s at the Xiude Temple in Xiudesi, Quyang. Notable is the early eighth-century headless standing bodhisattva exquisitely carved with scarves looping across the body and draped over the legs, as well as the Northern Wei seated Maitreya stele in sandstone.

Hebei is noted for its ceramics, including the white Tang dynasty porcelain from the Xing Kiln. Many fine examples of Cizhou ware are on display, including a white-glazed vase decorated with peonies and pillows, one with a boy playing cards, another with a young boy fishing. Characteristic of this type of porcelain is the use of bold, brownish-black pigment on a background of heavy white slip. The collection of paintings and calligraphy is also noteworthy and includes masterpieces by such distinguished painters as Wen Zhengming and Zhu Da.

Jade burial suit from the tomb of Liu Sheng, Western Han dynasty

Gilt bronze figure of a maidservant holding a lamp from the tomb of Dou Wan, Han dynasty

During the Japanese occupation, Hebei was a major area for Communist-led guerilla warfare. The museum has a large collection of material dealing with the War against Japan, and many photographs, objects and documents are on display. There is also a model of the tunnels by the locals to fight the Japanese from underground. The museum has an exhibition of Hebei revolutionary history from the Opium Wars through to the Communist takeover. Finally, there are exhibition halls displaying artefacts from prehistory though the Song period.

At the time of writing an expansion project is underway.

59

Yinxu Museum

殷墟博物馆 *Yinxu bowuguan*

Yinxu Site Garden, 1 Yinxu Road, North Section, Xiaotun Village, Anyang, Henan
河南省安阳市小屯村殷墟路殷墟遗址

Tel: (0372) 3686 809
Open: 8.00–18.30 Apr–Oct; 11.00–15.00 Nov–Mar
www.ayyx.com
English and Chinese tour guides

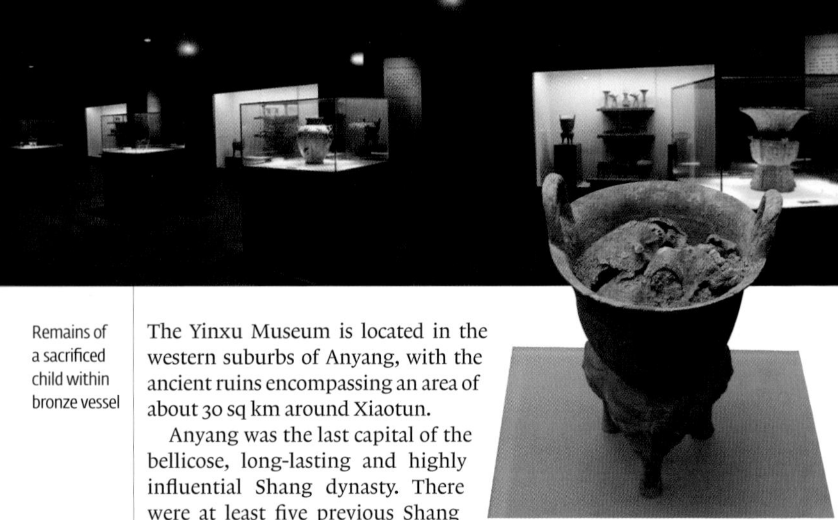

Remains of a sacrificed child within bronze vessel

The Yinxu Museum is located in the western suburbs of Anyang, with the ancient ruins encompassing an area of about 30 sq km around Xiaotun.

Anyang was the last capital of the bellicose, long-lasting and highly influential Shang dynasty. There were at least five previous Shang capitals, but in 1300 BC King Pan Geng moved it to Anyang, where it remained for 250 years.

Yinxu ('the ruins of Yin') is located on the southern bank of the River Huan and is called by some 'China's ancient Egypt' due to the splendid tombs of the Shang kings hidden underground and filled with valuable, extraordinarily beautiful objects, including famous bronzes. Aerial and satellite photos of the area displayed in the first gallery identify archaeological sites and royal tombs. Shang dynasty cities were complex and sophisticated. The streets were well planned, laid out on a north–south axis according

to the rules of feng shui and incorporated drainage pipes. They were built around royal palaces and cemeteries, but there were also smaller outlying kinship settlements, as well as what seem to be 'industrial areas' for pottery, bone-carving, stone-cutting workshops and the like. The excavated material culture is rich and varied, permitting archaeologists and historians to understand much of the social organization of the Shang period as well as its infrastructure, culture, art and religion.

The original finds at Yinxu were incised oracle bones. Up until the end of the nineteenth century, ancient incised animal bones and tortoise shells were thought to be dragons' bones. Highly prized, they were ground up and sold in apothecaries as a cure for many ailments. But at the beginning of the 1900s the markings on the bones were identified as an early form of writing. The oracle bones at Yinxu are unique in that they were often inscribed with questions, answers and results.

Oracle Bones and Divination

Shang Culture was driven by ritual, and the King was the intermediary between his people and the divine. The latter consisted of gods and nature spirits – the highest of whom was known as Di or Shang Di – as well as the King's ancestors. Both controlled all aspects of life and so required attention in the form of offerings and sacrifices, hence the large–scale use of human and animal oblations. Oracle bones made of ox scapulas and the bottom shells of turtles were used to ask specific questions – most often regarding rituals and sacrifice but also about weather forecasts, upcoming harvests, warfare, hunting and the like. Divinations were conducted by the King with the help of his diviner. Unique to Yinxu is that not only the question but also the answer was inscribed – and sometimes even the outcome.

After preparing the bone or shell to make a smooth surface, small hollows were carved in columns along the length of the bone, thus weakening its structure. A hot point was applied, causing cracks to appear. The angle, size and shape of the cracking all had meaning. These cracks were interpreted and the results inscribed and marked as favourable or unfavourable.

The inscriptions, which are the earliest form of Chinese writing we have, were created in logograms of which about 40 per cent have been identified. Some are pictographs and some paired symbols – one for meaning, the other for sound. This form of writing evolved into modern Chinese. The questions are written in a negative and positive manner – the harvest will be good; the harvest will be bad. Most of the inscriptions give the date of the divination, the name of the King doing the divining and the diviner. This amounts to a list of kings in chronological order, giving us a relative chronology which matches up to other historical sources, thus offering historians a wide range of information regarding Shang society.

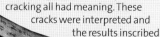

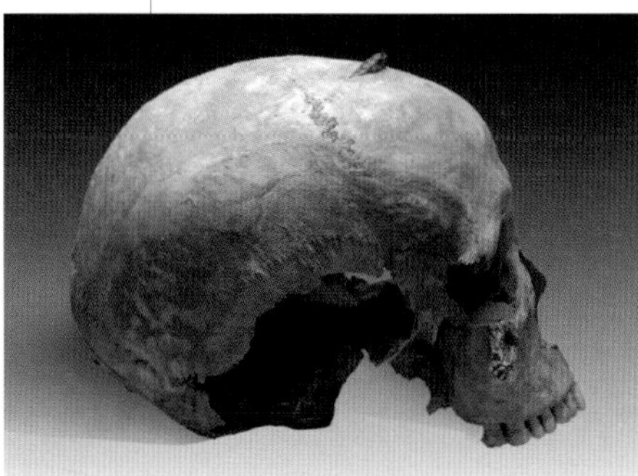

The museum at Yinxu, designed in 2005 by Cui Kai, one of China's leading modern architects, sits below ground level so that it merges into the surrounding landscape, thus evoking the underground tomb discovered on the site while maintaining its integrity. The proportions of the rooms mirror the ruins of the palace found nearby, with objects thoughtfully displayed to present a coherent sense of the city's life and culture. The cases are well lit, with information in Chinese and English.

The museum is divided into five major galleries: Exhibition Hall of the Great Capital, Exhibition Hall of Bronzes, Exhibition Hall of Jades, Exhibition Hall of Oracle Bones and the Special Exhibition Hall.

You first enter the Great Capital Hall, where aerial and satellite photos show the layout and plan of the archaeological sites of Yinxu. There is a model of a courtyard and simple dioramas which bring the aerial views to life. Pottery drainage pipes unearthed from the Baijiafen site are exhibited. Seeds and floral remains indicate that temperatures in Anyang were 2 to 3 degrees higher than today. The Huan often flooded, making the area very fertile. Millet and wheat seeds have been found, as well as boiled sheep and pig bones indicating the existence of animal husbandry. Bone ornaments, hairpins (both males and females had long hair), jewellery with turquoise inlay – even a ceramic loufa – are on exhibit. There are cowries used as currency originating from as far away as Taiwan and Hainan – indicating that the Shang people traded with other groups.

Fourteen large-scale tombs with a few thousand sacrificial pits have been found here. Skeletons are also found along the foundations of houses. Some were beheaded and their heads buried separately. Some of these people were the King's servants; others were slaves or vanquished in war. In the museum can be seen a mass burial of as many as seventy young girls approximately fifteen years old. There is a bronze *yan* containing the remains of the boiled head of an enemy King, as well as a pottery vessel containing the squashed skeleton of a small child. Human and animal sacrifices as well as grain, alcohol and meat were offered to the gods and the royal ancestors, who controlled the weather, harvest and childbirth, war and illness. The living King needed their guidance and received it daily via the oracle bones.

Shang dynasty soldier's skull with spearhead still embedded

The Oracle Bone Hall contains many examples of the incised ox bones and turtle shells used for divination. These are beautifully displayed with translations of the characters in both Chinese and English.

Chariot Pit I

Bronze production in the Shang dynasty represents the technological pinnacle of the age. At Yinxu fantastic examples have been excavated, including the largest and heaviest sacrificial bronze vessel ever found: the spectacular *si mu wu fangding* (its current home is the National Museum in Beijing). Intricately designed bronzes were cast using pottery moulds, a process which could be quite complex when the object was large and the decoration complicated. Bronze objects were used mainly for military and ritual purposes; for agricultural and utilitarian purposes wood and bone continued to be utilized. Many types of bronze vessels and weapons are on view here. Don't miss the fabulous bronze *yue* from Tomb M26 at Guojiazhuang or the skull of a Shang soldier with a spearhead through it.

One of the most spectacular finds at Yinxu was the undisturbed tomb of Princess Fu Hao. Discovered in 1976, this is the only intact Shang dynasty tomb excavated to date. Fu Hao was one of the consorts of King Wu Ding; oracle bones tell us she was a general who participated in military campaigns. This explains why her tomb, consisting of more than 1,500 objects, contains military bronzes as well as jades from the Liangzhu Culture, which would have been collected as antiques. Many of these objects can be seen in the Henan Museum in Zhengzhou.

The Shang are also known for their jade craftsmanship. Jade objects and ornaments were buried in many tombs. Many beautiful examples are on display.

Five excavated chariot pits are on display in a separate building within the park grounds. Each pit contains the skeletal remains of two horses ritually buried with their chariots. Many more chariots are known to exist but are yet to be excavated. A new chariot museum is planned.

This archaeological park was recently awarded inclusion on UNESCO's World Heritage List and is justly renowned for its archeological richness and presentation.

60

Kaifeng Museum

开封市博物馆 *Kaifengshi bowuguan*

26 Yingbin Road, Kaifeng, Henan
开封市迎宾路26号

Tel: (0393) 2178 8010
Open: 8.30–11.30 & 14.30–17.30
Tues–Sun
www.kfbwg.com/

This is a dreary museum of little appeal and on the whole, not recommended for a visit. However, the museum does have in its collection a limestone stele dated to 1489 which records the history of Kaifeng's Jews. Unfortunately the characters, are for the most part, worn and illegible, but rubbings made in the past are displayed alongside. On one side the stele recounts the rituals and stories of the Jews of Kaifeng. The inscription on the opposite side is dated

to 1512 and describes the life of the Jews at the time, comparing Judaism to Confucianism.

There was also a second stele, usually dated to 1663, which disappeared in 1912. Only a partial text had survived on the stone which honoured the Jews who were active in the community at the time and had restored the temple. Seeing the surviving stele is a disappointing experience as it is exhibited in a dusty, dirty top-floor gallery which is kept locked. Reservations must be made in advance to see this room by calling the Kaifeng Tourism Bureau at (0378) 398 9388 or CITS at (0378) 393 9032. There is a small cost.

Jews of Kaifeng

Jews have a long and interesting tradition in this city. It is thought the first Jews came to China as traders on the Silk Road in the early eighth century during the Kaiyuan period of Emperor Tang Xuanzong. By the time of the Northern Song, the Jewish community here was well established. A synagogue was built in 1163 and during the Ming dynasty, the Jews were given permission to use seven Chinese surnames: Li, Zhao, Shi, Ai, Zhang, Gao and Jin. Marco Polo mentions meeting Jews in Kaifeng during his travels there in 1286. The stele tell us that in 1421, the Kaifeng Jews were given permission to take the civil service exam and enter government service, which was, no doubt, a large factor in their assimilation as they began to travel away from the core community. In 1605, Ai Tian, a Kaifeng Jew who had travelled to Beijing for the exam, met Matteo Ricci, the well-known Jesuit missionary. The records of his and other Jesuit missionaries' contacts with the community contribute greatly to the available information regarding the Jews in the city.

As the Jews began to intermarry with the Chinese population, they gradually lost their their knowledge of Hebrew and the rituals and traditions of Judaism. The synagogue in Kaifeng was repeatedly damaged by Yellow River flooding and destroyed by an earthquake in 1840. The synagogue no longer had a Torah and finally there were no more rabbis in the city.

Today there are, by some accounts, approximately 600 people who identify themselves as Jews descended from this ancient community. Nowadays, however, they neither practise nor know much about the religion except that they abstain from eating pork.

As the Chinese pass their heritage on through the father, and Jewish tradition is matrilinear, there is a technical problem for some (but not all) Jews to consider these people Jewish. There is, however, great interest in the Jewish community regarding this history and many Jews come to Kaifeng looking for any vestiges that might remain.

Disappointingly, there is now almost nothing of 'Jewish Kaifeng' to be seen. The site of the synagogue is now the Number Four Hospital and there are no traces of the Jewish Quarter or the now extinct Jewish community of Kaifeng.

A Jewish family from Kaifeng, early 1900s

61

Longmen Grottoes

龙门石窟 *Longmen shiku*

Approximately 13 km south of Luoyang, on the west bank of the Yi River, Henan
洛阳南郊13公里 伊河西岸

Tel: (0379) 6598 0216
Open: 7.30–18.30 spring, summer and autumn; 17.30 winter (summer late-night opening until 22.00 with special lighting)
www.longmen.com/
Kids

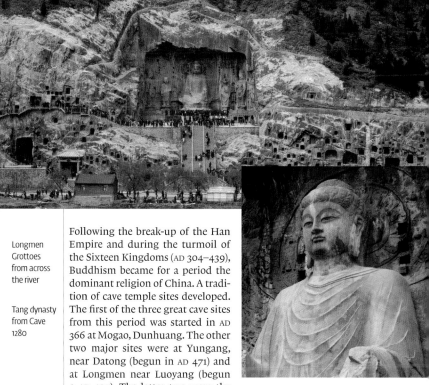

Longmen Grottoes from across the river

Tang dynasty from Cave 1280

Following the break-up of the Han Empire and during the turmoil of the Sixteen Kingdoms (AD 304–439), Buddhism became for a period the dominant religion of China. A tradition of cave temple sites developed. The first of the three great cave sites from this period was started in AD 366 at Mogao, Dunhuang. The other two major sites were at Yungang, near Datong (begun in AD 471) and at Longmen near Luoyang (begun *c.* AD 495). The latter two were the capital cities of the Northern Wei dynasty, Tuoba Turkic people who fiercely embraced Buddhism in opposition to Confucianism.

The Longmen site features more than 30,000 Buddha statues and 100,000 Buddha images in a series of caves hollowed out of the rock over a 1.5-km stretch of the river. Production continued there for more than 200 years. Sadly many of the caves have suffered damage from the weather, theft by European and American collectors, and wanton destruction during the Cultural Revolution.

The entrance is at the north end. Moving from north to south, the caves of particular interest are: the Three Binyang Caves with some fine Northern Wei, Sui and Tang figures; the Tang dynasty Ten Thousand Buddha Cave, with little Buddhas, a giant Buddha and celestial dancers; the Northern Wei Lotus Flower Cave, with graceful *apsaras* flying among lotus flowers on the ceiling; the Tang Ancestor Worshipping Temple, the largest at Longmen, with the best works of art, including a large seated Maitreya; the tiny Medical Prescription Cave, the entrance of which is filled with sixth-century stelae; and finally the Carved Cave, full of intricate carvings of processions of the Northern Wei.

62

Luoyang Ancient Tombs Museum

洛阳古墓博物馆 *Luoyang gumu bowuguan*

Zhongtou Village, Mangshan Town, near Luoyang, Henan
洛阳市北郊邙山镇塚头村

Tel: (0379) 6319 0737 / 0740
Open: 8.30–17.30 summer; 17.00 winter
Kids

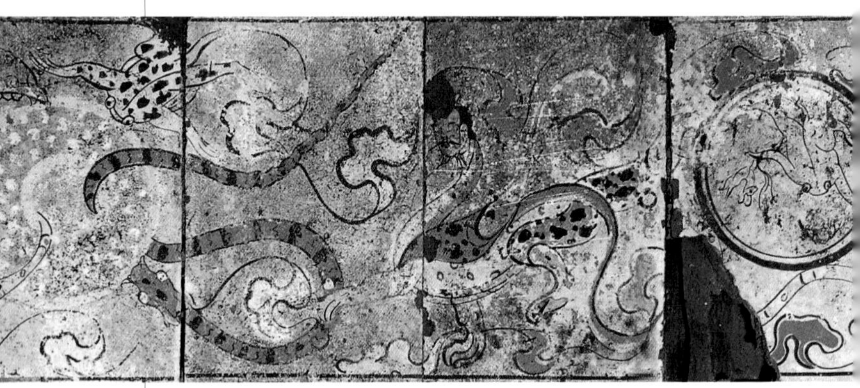

Wall paintings from ancient tombs now on exhibit

This museum was opened in 1987 and was the first of its kind in China. Its purpose is to exhibit and illustrate the evolution of tomb design over a period of more than a thousand years from the Han (206 BC – AD 220) to the Song dynasty (960–1279). At the time of the author's visit, the museum's lighting and climate control were being updated, some improvements were being made in the presentation and a separate museum was in construction due to open in 2009 which will house the museum's collection of ancient tomb murals and frescoes.

One's first impression when entering the museum is not positive. It appears dark, dank and mouldy but don't be put off – if you have the opportunity to visit with an informed guide you will find this to be a fascinating and rewarding experience.

Twenty-one of the twenty-five tombs in the museum are on public view along four underground passageways radiating out from a central atrium. Both sides of the passageway from the museum entrance to this central area

are lined with glass-fronted cases containing photos, pottery and other artefacts from the tombs. Some may be copies.

The halls are divided as follows: the Western and Eastern Han dynasties Hall, Wei and Jin dynasties Hall, the Tang and Song dynasties Hall and a separate hall to display artefacts.

The tombs, all from Luoyang excepting one from Jiaozuo, were taken apart brick by brick and reconstructed in the museum.

The tombs are organized in such a way to illustrate their development over time. For instance, the Western and Eastern Han tombs are contrasted. The early Western Han (206 BC – AD 9) tombs were quite simple and were built with hollow bricks. The ceilings are usually flat. In the Eastern Han (25–220), the bricks are often solid and much smaller than those of the Western Han, which allows for a vaulted ceiling. The tombs of the Eastern Han consist of four rooms, mirroring those in life: a sitting room, bedroom and two storage rooms. In both cases, the ceilings were painted to symbolize heaven. Clouds, divine celestial creatures and auspicious symbols are in abundance. Constellations and star charts can also be seen in the frescoes in many of the tombs here. Notably, on the ceiling of the tomb of Emperor Yuan and Emperor Cheng (49–7 BC) there is a star chart reputed to be the earliest ever found.

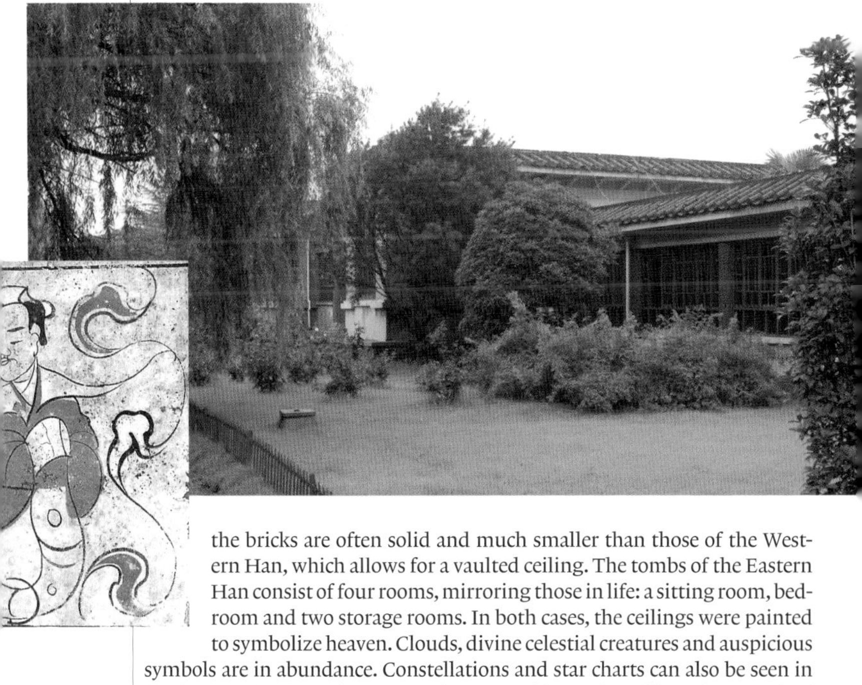

The museum's garden

The objects found in the tombs are also different. The Western Han tend to have fewer and simpler vessels. Some of the pottery from the Eastern Han is foreign in shape indicating that there was trade from abroad.

By visiting the fresco tomb of the Xinmang dynasty one can observe the transition from Western to Eastern Han. The subject matter and composition of the painting here is closer to that of the Western Han while the painting style is closer to that of the Eastern Han.

Contrasting the tombs of the Jin and Northern Wei dynasties with the Eastern and Western Han, the former tend to be much simpler and not so well ordered. The people of the Jin and Wei did not seem to spend so much money on their tombs probably because it was a period of continuous war. There are two especially interesting Jin dynasty tombs. One is for a single woman. This is quite mysterious as it is highly unusual to have a person buried alone – especially a single woman. Another tomb is that of a family: grandmother, mother, father and adult daughter. In true Confucian style, grandmother gets the biggest room, mother and father the middle-sized and daughter the smallest.

Progressing along the time-line, we see in the Tang and Song Halls the continued trend towards complexity in design and structural detail. Notable amongst the Tang dynasty tombs is that of Anpu – a local military man – and his wife. Built to imitate a wooden-structured house it contained 129 objects, including fifty *sancai* glazed pottery pieces, excavated unlooted from the eastern mountain of Longmen Grottoes. This tomb also has beautiful wall paintings open to view.

Some of the tombs are on view with their wall paintings removed as conditions in the tomb were not safe for the fresco. Such is the case with a tomb from the Northern Wei. It contained a fresco illustrating a warrior leaning on his sword – the sleeves are especially well painted. This is the best preserved painting of the Northern Wei, and no doubt will be on view in the new museum.

Once the new museum opens, the Luoyang Ancient Tombs Museum will be an enlightening experience on two fronts – the development of tomb architecture and the exhibition of rare wall tomb paintings.

Luoyang was the logical location for this museum as it was repeatedly a capital city from the Zhou to the Tang and more than ninety ancient emperors were buried here. The museum is built on the grounds of the tomb of Emperor Xuanwu, the second Emperor of the Northern Wei who ruled for sixteen years (from AD 499 to 515) and who died at age thirty-three. This tomb was excavated in 1991 as the second stage of the opening of this museum. The rammed earth mound had a paved passage leading down to a stone door and a single brick square chamber six metres below ground. All the brick surfaces in the tomb were painted black. This was a period of frugality, hence there were no paintings or carvings in the tomb. At the time of excavation a stone head was found at the entrance to the tomb passage indicating that originally there were guardians at the front of mausoleum. It is the only Emperor's tomb in Luoyang open to the public.

The lush and well-planned gardens surrounding the museum are an added pleasure. There is no restaurant, snack bar or drinks stand at the museum so take a boxed lunch with you and have a pleasant picnic there.

63

Luoyang Museum

洛阳博物馆 *Luoyang bowuguan*

298 Zhongzhou Zhong Road, Luoyang, Henan
洛阳市中州中路298号

Tel: (0379) 3937 107
Open: 8.30–17.00
www.luoyangmuseum.com
Personal guides

Luoyang sits in a key geographical position at the heart of western Henan on the southern side of the middle reaches of the Yellow River. It was the capital city of nine dynasties from the Western Zhou stretching over more than 1,500 years. It was also the easternmost city on the principal section of the Silk Road,

and during the Eastern Han, it was one of the most populated, flourishing cities in the ancient world. It continued to expand under the Northern Wei, who built the famous Buddhist caves at Longmen. As the eastern capital of the Tang, the western being Xi'an, it became one of the main production centres for tri-coloured glazed pottery *sancai*.

Although the museum is in need of refurbishment, it is certainly worth spending time to see this treasure house of finds unearthed in and around the city. Arranged over two floors are six galleries, including a temporary space that displays highlights from recently excavated sites and chance discoveries. All of the galleries have some English signage, though this too could be improved. It would be best to head first to the galleries showcasing ceramics, jade and bronzes and, if time permits, wander through the others.

One of the slightly better-lit galleries is devoted to Luoyang's pottery and porcelain.There are several simple, beautifully painted pots from the early Neolithic, including those from sites of the Yangshao Culture at Wangwan and Zhouli. Especially stunning are vessels from the Tumen site in Baiyuan with designs in black on a white ground. The apogee of pottery-making in the Xia is represented by finds from the Erlitou and Dongmagou sites located in the Yiluo basin. The Erlitou Culture built large palace sites with residential and workshop areas, and graves filled with bronzes, ceramics and jade have been found over a broad region.

During the Western and Eastern Han periods, pottery-making at Luoyang was highly developed, with rich, bright colours like red and green in geometric patterns, spiralling clouds, and human and animal shapes. The vivid figures included depictions of farmers, acrobats, dancers and the like, as well as of domestic animals, and were buried in tombs to create for the dead a microcosm of the universe in the afterlife.

Evidence of a flourishing porcelain-making industry in the Sui and Tang periods can be seen here in great abundance. It was a period of economic boom, in particular throughout the Tang, when products made in Luoyang were highly sought after and traded along the Silk Route. By far the most popular was *sancai*. It has been found at tomb sites clustered in the suburbs, at the foot of the Mangshan Mountains and elsewhere. Besides practical vessel shapes like wine- and food-storage vessels, there were figures, toys and the glorious horses for which this period is so famous, including a rare black-glazed horse from Guanlin some 66.5 cm in height. The tomb of

Turquoise inlaid bronze plaque, Xia dynasty

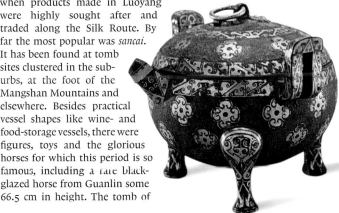

Ding inlaid with gold and silver, Warring States period

Tang dynasty horse and trainer from the tomb of Liukai in Yanshi

Anpu and his wife in Longmen yielded more than fifty masterful examples, included a *hu* foreign-faced rider on a horse; a figure leading a white-glazed horse with a green blanket; tomb guardians; and camels in life-like poses laden with bags full of silk and other items. There is also a rarely seen, beautifully shaped glazed lamp from Jilin. Many privately run kilns such as Gongxian existed in the city. Excellent Song ceramics are also on view, including the tri-coloured porcelain pillow with peony designs (the peony has been a decorative motif for centuries, and Luoyang continues to be a centre of peony cultivation).

Bronzes in the collection excel; hundreds upon hundreds have been unearthed in large groups at sites in Luoyang and nearby. Superb examples have been found in burials at Erlitou and are among the earliest bronze vessels discovered in China. Among these are bronze *jue*, some decorated with nipple patterns. They were cast using multiple-piece clay moulds, a technique central to production in the later Chinese Bronze Age. Astonishing are bronzes found at this site with gold inlays and a turquoise-inlaid bronze plaque in the shape of a shield with an abstract animal face, discovered in a tomb at Yanshi and among the earliest inlaid objects anywhere in China.

To date, bronze finds from the Shang are sparser in Luoyang, most coming from Yanshi (an early Shang capital) and others from Yinchuan and Jianxi. One stellar example is a large square vessel with a roof-shaped lid, in fact a wine-storage vessel, from Pangjiagou at Beiyao, decorated with *taotie* and dragon patterns.

The ultimate highlights of this collection are the bronzes from the Western and Eastern Zhou periods. Not only have large assemblages of bronzes been found in the hundreds of tombs which have been excavated; a large-scaled bronze foundry not far from Beiyao indicates that there was local production. The tombs revealed spectacular examples like the *fangding* (a rectangular food vessel with legs) decorated on all four sides with *taotie* designs with bulging eyes – a rare example from this period.

More than a thousand Eastern Zhou tombs have been unearthed in and around Luoyang, including those from the Spring and Autumn period whose bronzes are characterized by very bold designs. One example is a large *yu* – the largest bronze found to date in Luoyang – with four dragon-shaped handles; it is believed to have been made as part of the trousseau offered by the Marquis of Qi to his second daughter Zhongjiang, who married the King of the Zhou.

The glory of Western Han dynasty bronze work can be seen in the gilded examples. Most unusual is a winged immortal with large ears and pointed nose who holds a container. Found in a brick tomb under a mound, this was one of the few objects left by ancient robbers in what must have been a noble or high-ranking person's burial. Large numbers of mirrors too (more than a thousand to date) have been unearthed, including those from the late Eastern Han period covered with mythical figures and animals and cosmological symbols, and Tang ones burnished with gold and silver foil. Originally hung by a cord slotted through the central knob, mirrors were cast from bronze alloyed with a high percentage of tin, silver or lead to increase their reflectivity.

Although significant gold and silver objects have been found in Luoyang and nearby areas such as Yanshi, Yinchan and Mengjin, very few are on display. Among them are some from the Tang period: plates, bowls and pots favoured by the high-ranking officials and elite living there.

Jade work from many of the tomb sites mentioned is also unsurpassed. Excellent examples have been found from the Xia and Shang periods at the Erlitou site, including knives like the one with seven holes in the shape of a trapezoid with double edges. Each side of the handle has toothed projections, and both are decorated with geometric patterns. At 65 cm in length it is one of the longest jade knives ever found. Spectacular too is the *zhang* blade also discovered there and similar to those found at Sanxingdui in Sichuan and other parts of China, suggesting communication between the Xia and other regional cultures at the time. Western Zhou jades from Beiyao include weapons and ornaments such as sheep, cicadas, fish and birds, while those from the Warring States period reflect the gradual decline of ritual jades in favour of garment hooks, spoons and beads. More jewels of the collection are found among the Han dynasty jades in the form of pendants with openwork designs. The Three Kingdom jade cup found in a tomb in the Jianxi district is a masterpiece. The inspiration for its tall, elegant shape no doubt came from glass imports from western Asia as trade between China and the West continued to expand.

This quality collection deserves better display facilities, and one can only hope that soon it will have them. Meanwhile, the best way to learn more about the full extent of the museum's exquisite holdings is to purchase the excellent *Ancient Treasures from Luoyang* (published in 2001 and available in the museum), as well as several other more specialized guides.

A bronze with a four-piped base and double-faced figurines, Western Zhou dynasty

64

Luoyang Museum of Ancient Arts

洛阳古代艺术馆 *Luoyang gudai yishu bowuguan*

Guanlin Temple, Guanlin Town (approximately 7 km south of Luoyang), Henan
洛阳市南郊7公里 关林镇关林庙

Tel: (0379) 6597 5746
Open 8.00–18.30 summer; 17.30 winter

Tucked away in the peaceful setting of the Guanlin Temple is not a museum as such but rather displays of stone stelae set out in the cypress-filled gardens and exhibition halls with a rather jumbled display of stone sculpture, stelae and copies of inscriptions from the Han to the Ming dynasties. There are several impressive winged, horned feline creatures, *bixie*, and other stone guardian figures which would have lined the paths, known as 'spirit roads', up to important tombs. But these displays play second fiddle to the temple itself, where, legend states, the head of the famous general of the state of Shu, Guan Yu, is buried. The protagonist of the ancient tale from *Romance of the Three Kingdoms*, Guan Yu became a symbol of loyalty after he was beheaded in battle and continued to be worshipped as the god of war by emperors in succeeding dynasties.

65

Museum of Zhou Capital and Royal Six-Horse Chariot

周王城天子驾六博物馆 *Zhouwangcheng tianzi jialiu bowuguan*

Wangcheng Plaza, Xigong District, Luoyang, Henan
洛阳市西工区王城广场

Tel: (0379) 6391 2366
Open: 8.00–22.00 summer; 21.00 winter

Horse and chariot sacrificial pit

A tussle between archaeologists and developers resulted in saving at least part of this site from being entombed forever under a shopping mall in the centre of Luoyang.Thankfully, visitors can now marvel at the large burial of Eastern Zhou dynasty horses, chariots and dog and human skeletons in the museum built above the site. It consists of two exhibition areas. The first displays ritual bronzes, jade and pottery found at the site and presents a potted history of the Luoyang region when it served as an imperial capital over five dynasties. The second hall displays two of the seventeen unearthed horse-and-chariot sacrificial pits, including the unique six-horse, two-wheeled chariot interred with its six skeletons and bronze axle pin. Ancient texts record 'the Son of Heaven (the ruler) riding six', suggesting that this chariot belonged to the ruler of the Eastern Zhou.

66 Henan Museum

河南博物院 *Henan bowuyuan*

8 Nongye Road, Zhengzhou, Henan
河南省郑州市农业路8号

Tel: (0371) 6351 1237
Open: 8.30–18.00 summer; 17.30 winter
www.chnmus.net/Template/home/chnmuse/index.html
English & Japanese audio guides
Personal guides available – phone one day ahead to reserve an English-speaking guide

Dancers on a Han tomb brick

The Henan Museum was first established in 1927 in Kaifeng City which was then the capital of Henan Province. Due to its excellent collection it became one of the premier museums in the country and remains so to this day. In 1961, the provincial capital was moved to Zhengzhou and the Henan Museum followed. In May of 1998, a new and modern facility was built which is the present day Henan Museum.

The museum, built in a pyramidal shape, is on four floors. The entire museum collection contains approximately 130–140,000 objects, of which about 4,000 are on display at any one time. Every object in the museum is from Henan Province. The first and second floors comprise a chronologically displayed exhibition called 'The Most Brilliant Cultural Achievements in Ancient Henan'. The first hall contains an excellent selection of Palaeolithic and Neolithic artefacts. Of special interest are items of the Neolithic Peiligang Culture stone tools and pottery, including red pottery bowls, a *ding* with nipple pattern and a bone flute from Jiahu Village which is the earliest musical instrument ever found in China and the earliest musical instrument ever found with a complete scale of seven descending tones. Also displayed in this hall are objects from the Yangshao Culture, among the artefacts to be noted is a pottery funeral urn from Zhengzhou which has been the subject of discussion as to whether it is a funeral urn or large drum. The exhibit moves on to objects of the Longshan Culture. Among the objects displayed are pottery drainage pipes from Pingliangtai City ruins and bits of copper slag, evidence of the transition from the Stone to the Bronze Age.

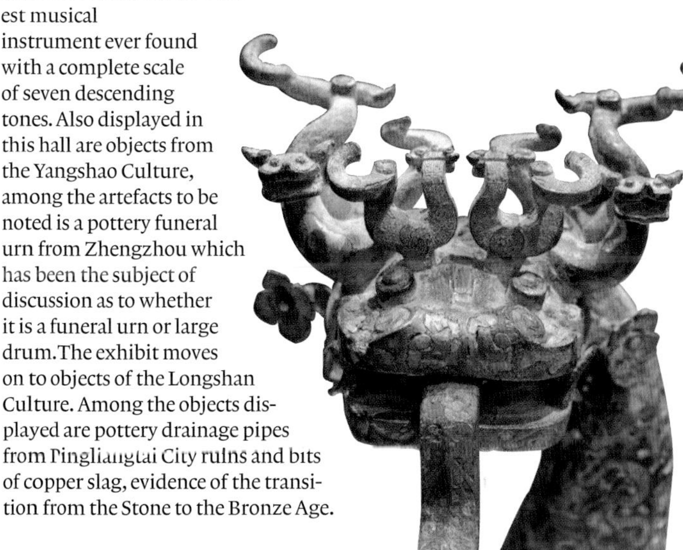

Chu state mythological animal, bronze with hardstone inlay

The second hall is entitled 'Three Splendid, Three Dynasties' and exhibits artefacts from the Xia, Shang and Zhou periods. Here we see in addition to an impressive collection of pottery and bronze vessels, a beautiful lead architectural piece decorated with an abstracted *taotie* (fierce animal) design, as well as Shang dynasty inscribed oracle bones. Take note of an especially important piece in this gallery, as it is the earliest porcelain in the museum – a proto-porcelain *zun* (wine vessel) from Zhengzhou, although, in fact, the museum does have an even earlier example which was not on display. There is also a selection of objects from the burial site of Queen Fuhao, known as Houmuxin. She was the Shang dynasty consort of King Wu Ding and, incredibly, a general who took part in several successful campaigns. This tomb, dated *c.* 1250 BC is the only unlooted Shang tomb that has been found to date and contained 468 bronze objects as well as jade, stone, ivory, bone, pottery, cowry shells and many weapons and war implements.

Tang dynasty 'fat ladies'

A Tang maiden

Throughout the galleries, there are signs in English as well as Chinese explaining the transitions between periods and explanations of how and why the material culture differs and evolved.

The next room is Eastern Zhou, Spring and Autumn period and Warring States displays. Here are wonderful bronzes of all sorts, including nine large *dings* (bowls for meat) and *you* (wine vessels) excavated in 1997 from Xinzheng and a most elegant gilt bronze lamp in the form of a kneeling woman. Pride of place here and one of the jewels of the museum is an enormous bronze rectangular ewer (*fanghu*) with lotus and crane design. This was excavated from the tomb of Duke Zheng at Lijiayuan in Xinzheng County in 1923. This is one of a pair – the other, which is damaged, is in the basement of the Forbidden City. This piece is noteworthy, not only due to its beauty and complicated decoration, but because it has so much historical and spiritual meaning. The ewer rests on the backs of two dragons, ferocious animals inhabit its centre, writhing dragons are its handles and on the lotus petal lid stands a crane not in the traditional stance, but just about to take off with its wings spread for flight. This is a political analogy of strength, ferocity and finally at the top of the vessel, a sense of spirituality and hopefulness symbolized by the bird. There is also a visual demonstration of lost-wax casting and other various manufacturing techniques popular in the Warring States period such as stamping and inlaying with gold wire and stones.

'Incorporating the Diverse' is the title of the next hall. This includes the Western and Eastern Han, Wei, Jin and Southern and Northern dynasties and contains many large pottery funerary architectural models of houses and buildings of the Han period. These houses are thought to be actual representations of the houses of the dead. There is an especially impressive six-storey mansion found in Jiaozuo. Also here are smaller objects:

tomb bricks, some with the original paint and a large mural painting of the Western Han depicting a blue dragon, white tiger, red bird and clouds. This painting is older than those at the Mogao Grottoes and is in superb condition.

The exhibition moves upstairs to the Han, Tang and Song Halls where the first gallery showcases objects from the Western and Eastern Han, Wei, Jin and Southern and Northern dynasties. Here there is a selection of ceramics, tomb bricks and models of buildings as well as Buddhist artefacts from the Gong Yi Grottoes. Of note here, Northern dynasty green ware and white-glazed pottery which is the precursor of Tang dynasty ceramics. The next hall is Sui–Tang where there is a large model of the imperial palace in Luoyang during the Tang dynasty along with pottery tiles and Tang dynasty guardians, horses and grooms, and camels. To be noted is a silver coin from the kingdom of Persia found at Luoyang and painted pottery seated musicians (*zuobuji*) and a lovely group of Tang 'fat ladies'. Also displayed are bronze mirrors, white wares, tri-colour pottery and of special note a white-glazed porcelain *weiqi* chessboard. Displays of Tang dynasty Buddhist stone heads and sculptures are worth seeing, as Henan was the major region in China for the diffusion of Buddhism during this period. Following is the hall displaying Northern Song, Jin and Yuan objects including copper coinage, Yuan dynasty ceramics, blue and white ware, Jun ware of various shapes, Song dynasty ceramics and descriptions of major scientific contributions of this period such as gunpowder, moveable type and the compass.

Yuan dynasty whistling man

Tang dynasty guardian

The Third Floor galleries include the 'Ming and Qing Dynasties Handicraft Articles Hall' consisting of gold and silver jewellery, Qing enamel ware, ivory, porcelain, bronze, lacquer ware, and embroidery. Most impressive is the 'Chu State Bronzes Art Hall'. These are bronzes from tombs of the Spring and Autumn period Chu State found in Longcheng. Of special note is a set of twenty-six very large Yong bells buried with royalty and aristocrats indicating their high social status. There are also Han dynasty ceramic architectural ancient jades from the Neolithic to the Qing, examples of Shang halberds (*ge*), battle-axes (*yue*), spears, knives. Note a jade *huang* or pendant from the Shang tomb of Fuhao, a Warring States *bi* and some lovely Western Zhou jade jewellery and a pair of jade ornaments from the Spring and Autumn period found at the Baoxiang Temple, Guangshan carved with a face looking like an indigenous Central American. The fourth floor contains a natural history exhibition.

This museum is one of the finest museums in the country. It is full of gorgeous artefacts sensitively displayed with adequate English signage. A visit to this unforgettable museum will be one of the highlights of your visit to China.

67 Linzi Funerary Horse Pit Museum of the Eastern Zhou

东周殉马馆 *Dongzhou xunmaguan*

One side of the rectangular pit lined with horse skeletons

Impression of a chariot wheel recorded in clay, Museum of Chinese Ancient Chariots

Heyatou Village, Qidu Town, Linzi District, Zibo City, Shandong
淄博市临淄区齐都镇河崖头村

Tel: (0533) 783 0229 / 1008
Open: 8.00–17.00 (call to check opening hours and for directions)
Chinese guides only
Kids

This extraordinary site museum is located down a dirt road in a small farming village near Linzi. Measuring 26 by 23 m, the partially excavated tomb is probably that of Jing Gong, ruler of the Qi dynasty. In the centre, still unexcavated, is the burial place of the King himself; surrounding him on three sides is a rectangular pit lined with the skeletons of 600 horses. Only 228 of these have been excavated – one side of the pit – as the museum currently does not have the resources to properly protect the site if it were fully excavated. Jing Gong is believed to have been a great lover of horses, so he was buried with this enormous number of animals to serve and protect him in the next life. The horses show no sign of struggle, and it is likely that they were given some type of herbal medicine to drug them before being buried alive.

This excavation pit is an astonishing sight and should not be missed if you are in the area. According to the curator, a new museum has been designed, but no date had been set for commencement of the project.

68 Linzi Museum of Chinese Ancient Chariots

临淄中国古车博物馆 *Linzi zhongguo guche bowuguan*

Houli Village, Qilin Town, Linzi District, Zibo City, Shandong
淄博市临淄区齐临镇后李村

Tel: (0533) 708 3310
Open: 8.30–17.00
Kids

Two-horse war chariot

This beautifully preserved sacrificial horse pit dating to the middle of the Spring and Autumn period was discovered while excavating for the road. Indeed, cars on the motorway rattle the roof of the excavation site conserved just below it. The museum was completed in 1994 and is presented in two sections: the burial-pit area and a hall of chariot reproductions.

Two pits have been excavated. The first is 32 by 5 m and contains the remains of ten chariots and thirty-two horses; six of the chariots are associated with four horses, and four chariots were buried with two horses. The second pit is 8 by 3 m and contains three chariots and six horses. The wood of the chariot frame has decayed, but its impression remains in the loess. Traces of bronze beads, large bronze buttons and cowrie shells sewn on to fabric in a circular pattern can still be seen on the horses' skulls, along with some of the surviving tack, permit the whole arrangement to be revealed. The chariots are mostly about 3 m long and between 2.5 and 2.7 m wide. They are all single-axle. The wheels have a diameter of between 50 cm and 1.4 m. The chariots are of two types: smaller two-horse ones (war chariots) and larger four-horse ones (for transportation of goods). In the first pit, the horses and chariots are lined up in an orderly fashion. In the second pit, three chariots are buried beneath and the six horses above.

This museum also has a large collection of ancient Chinese chariot reproductions on display along with an exhibition case devoted to the development of the stirrup in China. To the north of the chariot museum lie the ancient walls of the Qi state, while to the south are the striking pyramid-shaped tombs of four Qi kings from which the museum borrowed its pyramidal design.

69 Qi State History Museum

齐国历史博物馆 *Qiguo lishi bowuguan*

Qi State Museum, Qidu Town, Linzi District, Zibo City, Shandong
淄博市临淄区齐都镇

Tel: (0533) 7830 229
Open: 8.30–17.0

Qi State period bronze zun

The Qi State Museum in Linzi, a district of the modern city of Zibo, and the nearby sites of the Ancient Chariot Museum and the Funerary Horse Pit of Eastern Zhou dynasty can all be seen in one day and make a neat unit. Ancient Linzi was the capital of the Qi State of the Eastern Zhou (770–221 BC). This period is divided by historians into two separate subdivisions, namely the Spring and Autumn period (770–450 BC) and the Warring States period (450–221 BC). Although an era of instability, war and confusion it was, conversely, also an age of great developments in culture and civilization.

At the end of the period preceding this, the Western Zhou, smaller vassal states began to gain in power and confidence and desiring autonomy, broke off from the centralized Zhou State. In addition, nomadic groups were invading from the West causing the Zhou King to move his capital eastwards to Luoyang.

From this point, the military power of the Zhou kings continued to diminish and the smaller states – now in effect independent – began fighting amongst themselves for influence and hegemony. This period of decentralization, violence and unstable alliances is known as the Eastern Zhou, which continued until 221 BC with the complete victory of the Qin.

From the Spring and Autumn period the Qi state, with its capital in Linzi, gained in prominence mainly due to the successful leadership of Duke Huan of Qi in the mid fifth century BC. The Qi State became very prosperous and powerful – so much so that they were able to keep the formidable Chu and Qin states at bay but ultimately they could not resist domination

by the Qin in 221 BC. The walled city, believed to have been highly populated, was built on a north–south axis and was surrounded by a moat. It had a functioning water and drainage system, a royal palace, roads, market places and workshops. Iron tools and pottery were produced in large scale, bronze- casting technology advanced, coins were cast, textiles such as silk, hemp and linen were produced and salt production was a local industry.

The muscum, built in 1990, displays over 300 objects in a modern museum environment. Oracle bones, bronzes, silver, ceramics and royal burial material from the Han Qi tomb of Dawu, are displayed. There is also an ancient technology hall, exhibition hall of musical instruments and an exhibit about the Qi State's invention of football.

The specific highlights of the collection include:

- Western Zhou incised oracle bones and turtle shells.
- A very large bronze *yu* with two handles in the shape of dragons.
- A wonderful bronze *zun* in the shape of a stocky ox-like mythical animal with its head facing upward expressively, its ears erect and a delicately formed tail. It is inlaid with gold and silver in an abstract cloud pattern.

Another prized object in the museum is a very large bronze mirror with a dragon-incised pattern excavated from the Han Qi tomb at Dawu.

There is a set of fourteen bronze bells exhibited. The music of these bells can be heard playing in the background in this gallery.

Many Qi pottery roof tiles from tombs decorated with patterns and characters are presented. Each of the several hundred roof tiles found is different. They are often decorated with trees accompanied by wild animals, birds, eyes, circles and other decorative motifs. Some are inscribed with inscriptions such as '10,000 autumns, 10,000 years' meaning 'long life'.

The Ancient Technology Exhibit shows how pottery-making in the Qi went from handicraft to production line. There is also a display of the development of bronze-casting technology in the Qi State as well as a presentation on the casting of coinage including the inscribed knife-shaped currency of the Warring States period.

The ancient game of *cuju*

The game of football has been officially recognized as originating in Linzi. In 2004, FIFA acknowledged that the ancient game called *cuju*, played as early as the Spring and Autumn period and depicted on a Song dynasty mirror displayed in the museum, is the origin of the modern game. The museum also exhibits FIFA's certificate attesting to this assertion.

70 **Shandong Provincial Museum**

山东省博物馆 *Shandongsheng bowuguan*

At time of publication: 14 Jin 11 Road, Jinan; new location: north of Jingshidong Road and east of Yanshan Viaduct in the new Culture and Museum Centre

济南市经十一路14号
新馆地址：十东路以北，
燕山立交桥以东

Tel: (0531) 8296 7179
Open: 8.30–12.00 & 14.30–18.00 except Mon
www.sdmuseum.com
The museum will be closing and plans to re-open in 2009 when the new museum is completed; check local listings or website for opening date
Many useful publications are available, including *Introduction to Cultural Relics*, *History of Ancient Coins in China* and *Insect Fossils in Shandong*

This museum has undergone several incarnations – not surprisingly, as it was among the earliest museums in China. It was established in two parts, the first part by the British Baptist missionary J S Whitewright in 1904, with natural-history specimens which he used to attract crowds to hear his Christian sermons; the second part in 1942 by a religious society. The two were amalgamated in 1954 to form the kernel of today's museum and expanded with donations from the city library, the Committee of Cultural Relics, private donors from the 1950s onwards, and the vast number of archaeological excavations in the province. When they moved again in 1992 to their purpose-built home at the foot of Qianfo Mountain, the collections numbered more than 200,000 items, a true amalgam of natural and man-made artefacts.

Its recent move is to yet another newly designed building in a new location which at the time of writing had not yet opened. The winning design combines a square and circle, reflecting the ancient Chinese conception of the earth as square and the circle symbolizing heaven. Set out over 80,000 sq m will be eight galleries and four halls. The galleries will encompass all the aspects expected of a provincial museum, from the history of Shandong to folklore, ancient transportation, archaeology and natural history. The four halls will consist of spaces for temporary loans, a conference hall, an education centre and a special exhibition gallery.

Bronze *dou* with designs in turquoise and copper inlays, early phase of the Warring States period

Yue, with Yachou emblems (besides mouth), late Shang from Tomb M1 at Sufutun site

Shandong is one of China's political, economic and cultural hubs, situated east of the Taihang Mountains on the lower reaches of the Yellow River. A large, agricultural province, it is rich in natural resources including coal and oil, and with its large eastern coastline reaches out to countries over the sea. It is known for its numerous early Neolithic sites and was ruled by the Shang and, later, the powerful Zhou until the Eastern Zhou period, when the rulers fled eastwards and it was split between the Qi and the Lu. The Qin defeated the Qi, and during the Han dynasty the region was split between areas north and south of the Yellow River. Jinan, the present-day capital, was a military outpost and trading centre in the fourth century, and during the Ming became a walled city (no longer visible; its original position is defined by the remaining moats).

The museum's core holdings range from the important Neolithic sites of the Dawenkou and Longshan Cultures, to bronzes from the Shang and Zhou, to bamboo slips from the Han, to Buddhist and other stone carvings and tablets, and finally to natural-history material from the Palaeolithic to the more recent past.

Neolithic food container, early phase of Dawenkou Culture

Grave deposits from the early to the middle Neolithic Dawenkou Culture site of Tai'an on the lower reaches of the Yellow River were excavated by the museum and yielded a vast array of goods, including jades, painted pots and inscribed turtle shells (plastrons), indicating that the inhabitants were skilled craftsmen and that the materials they used pointed to interactions with outlying communities. Holdings include a stemmed food container decorated with octagonal designs (possibly symbolizing a cosmological system); a red-clay zoomorphic jar with holes at both the tail and head end, the back one for water coming into the container and front for it to pour out; and distinctive white-clay tripod vessels for heating food. A rare item is the *hu* jar painted with black and white net designs. Jade comes in a bewildering range of shapes and colours from a light yellow shovel to a necklace consisting of eleven pieces including rings and a turquoise pendant. Special funerary objects on display include a hook made from roe-deer teeth with a bone handle found in the hands of the deceased and a bone tube with turquoise inlays. Artefacts from Longshan sites yielded distinctly different pottery, black with incised designs – like the spectacular 'egg-shell' *bei* cup with a long stem.

The collection of ceramics continues with superb examples from the Shang right through to the Qing. Visitors can select from a green-glazed Eastern Han figure chopping food at a table (likely to be a chef); a double-fish-shaped tricoloured vase from the Tang; a Song celadon covered vase with six tubes extending from the neck and decorated with flowers; a Ming gourd-shaped vase with its lower belly decorated with auspicious animals; and another in the same shape from the Qianlong period decorated with red bats, green leaves and yellow gourds. Double gourds were associated with abundance and fertility and also the double structure of the universe – heaven and earth – while the red bats are a rebus, or visual pun, signifying good fortune.

Not to be missed is one of the defining objects of the museum: a *yue*, or ceremonial axe, with a vicious human face with bulging eyes and clenched teeth pierced into the bronze. Unearthed at the Shang site of Yidu, Sufutun in Qingzhou, it was used to behead humans and animals for sacrifices. It is similar to a *taotie*, though all parts of the face are human. Another stunning object from this site is the bronze *he* with a tubular spout and animal-head handle. Unearthed at the Xiaotun site in Changqing is a square *ding* with *kui*-dragon

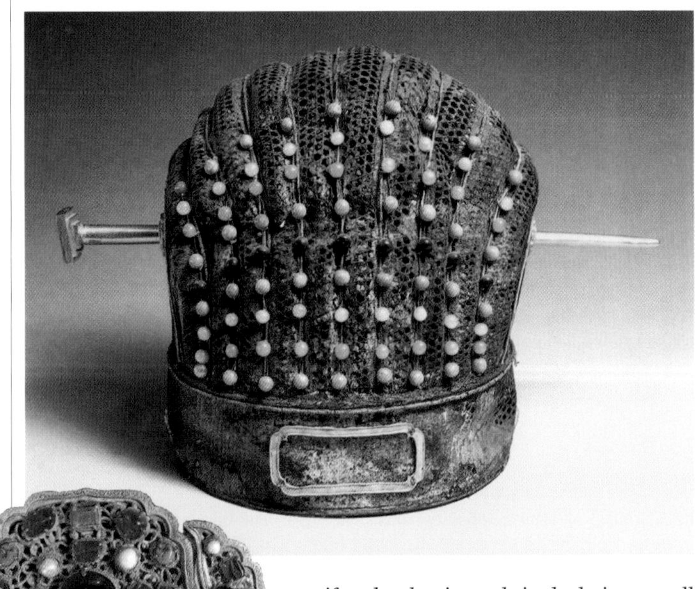

motif under the rim and cicada designs on all four legs. Remarkable are several bronzes from the Xiaowangshuang site, including a bronze *hu* with a rope design, handles in the shape of an elephant's trunk, and a thirteen-character inscription stating that it is from the Chen state (today's eastern Henan). Several splendid mirrors and plates from the Warring States period are inlaid with turquoise, gold and silver.

Ming dynasty leather hat from Duke Lu Zhu Tan's tomb

Ming dynasty gold buckle from Duke Lu Zhu Tan's tomb

Objects excavated from the tomb of Zhu Tan, Prince of Lu in the fourteenth century and the tenth son of the founding Emperor of the Ming, yielded around 400 painted wooden figures of musicians, attendants and military figures along with other personal possessions like his crown of wood and jade beads, gold buckle, several jade blades wrapped in gold, a wooden zither and a red-lacquer box with gold-inlaid clouds and dragons.

The holdings of stone sculpture here are outstanding. Among them are Eastern Han stone pictorial carvings with intricately carved scenes of everyday life or life imagined after death. One from Xihukou has seven bands carved with various scenes, among them animals with human faces, men holding weapons, and carriages with servants. Another from the Longyangdian site, carved in relief, shows people spinning and weaving as well as travelling in horse-drawn chariots. Scenes of merriment with musician, dancers and acrobats occupy one side of another carving found in Jiaxiang County while on the other side the audience is shown eating and drinking.

Among scores of other objects is the Yuan warship (20 m in length) uncovered at the site of the Ming naval base in Penglai (former Dengzhou). The Emperors of the Yuan were keen to strengthen their sea power and ordered thousands of warships to be built. The collections also excel in their holdings of paintings, hand scrolls and calligraphy, as well as fossil, dinosaurs and other natural-history specimens. The province has several major fossil sites, including the Laiyang Formation (Lower Cretaceous) in the Shandong Peninsula, which have revealed numerous fossil insects, while the coal mines

of the Wutu Basin east of Jinan, dating from the Early Eocene, have revealed numerous mammal and plant fossils. One of the richest assemblages of plant and animal remains in the province is located in the Shanwang National Geological Park. During the Middle Miocene the humid and warm climate was host to hundreds of species. Remains from here include beautifully preserved skeletons of deer and mice, as well as fish, insects, amphibians, birds, mammals and fossil pollens.

71

Qingdao Municipal Museum

青岛市博物馆 *Qingdaoshi bowuguan*

Hi-Tech Industrial Park, 27 Meiling Road, Laoshan, Old Stone Man Beach Area (west of Wushan), Qingdao, Shandong
青岛市崂山区梅岭路27号

Tel: (0532) 8889 6286
Open: 9.00–17.30 except Mon, Apr–Sept; 16.30 except Mon, Oct–Mar
www.qingdaomuseum.com
Bookshop / coffee shop

Knife-shaped *jincuodao* coin inlaid with gold

A modern semi-circular complex built in 1997 provides the space for this science museum and conference facility sponsored by Haier, China's largest white goods company. The six permanent galleries have recently had a makeover to take advantage of the waves of visitors attending the 2008 Olympic sailing competitions at the city's new facility. To accommodate foreign visitors, the museum has introduced new English audio guides and English- and Chinese-speaking guides, along with signage in these two languages and Japanese.

The collection is a real mixed bag of treasures; among the best galleries are those of Ming and Qing dynasties porcelain, numismatics from the Xia and Shang dynasties to the Republican period, and calligraphy and paintings ranging from works by the well-known Ming painter Xie Shichen to the Qing dynasty Buddhist monk Zhu Da and Qingdao-born painter Gao

Detail from frieze on museum façade

Fenghan, one of the 'Eight Eccentrics of Yangzhou' known for his paintings of flowers and landscapes. There is also a gallery of ancient Chinese crafts containing lacquer wares, bamboo and ivory carvings, enamels and implements such as brushes and ink slabs. Another room offers a chronological overview of Qingdao's development up to its establishment as a municipality in 1891. The climax of the collection is the four large, elegantly carved Buddhist limestone statues from the Northern Qi dynasty which the Japanese attempted to remove during the occupation of Shandong.

72

Qingdao Naval Museum

青岛海军博物馆 *Qingdao haijun bowuguan*

8 Laiyang Road, Qingdao, Shandong
青岛市莱阳路8号

Tel: (0532) 8286 6784 / 8287 4786
Open: 7.30–18.30 Apr–Oct; 8.00–17.00 Nov–Mar
Extensive shop offers a mixed selection of gifts
Kids

502 Nanchong 'Jiangnan' Class (Type 065) Frigate

This specialist museum founded by the Chinese People's Liberation Army Navy (PLAN) faces the sea at the now defunct naval base on the edge of scenic Lu Xun Park. Opened in 1989 to showcase China's naval history, it consists of two parts: an enclosed exhibition space and a sprawling open-air area which extends to an assortment of piers.

A Yuchai class landing craft armed with two machine guns

A brief wander through the hall provides visitors with an overview of the PLAN's history told through exhibits of uniforms, historic images and insignia from 1949, the year PLAN was founded, to the present day. Among the highlights is the dress uniform of the first commander of PLAN, Gen. Xiao Jingguang. More than 300 gifts given by foreign armies to PLAN are also displayed, including a sword presented by the Soviet Vice National Defence Minister to Gen. Xiao in 1957.

A rare treat is in store outside, where open access allows visitors to get up close to all sorts of weapons and equipment, including aircraft, missiles, artillery, torpedoes, radar and submarines. The accelerated development of China's naval radar and electronic-warfare systems came in 1953, when Russia agreed to assist with aid and licenses to manufacture this equipment; therefore much of what is seen was either directly purchased from the Soviets or bears a close resemblance to Russian counterparts. Highlights include the wooden-hulled torpedo boat that carried Chairman Mao and Zhou Enlai in 1957 when they reviewed PLAN in Qingdao; a Y-14 aircraft which was a make favoured by Mao; a Chinese-developed Hongqi-2 surface-to-air missile based on the Russian S-75; and a row of MiGs or Soviet fighter airplanes and their Chinese variants, F-5 etc. In the port you can enter many decommissioned vessels, including an Anshan-class destroyer – the first destroyers of China which were modified ex-Soviet destroyers from WWII; a Romeo-class 229 submarine copied by the Chinese with six torpedo tubes at the front and the 90-m long Chinese-built Nanchong launched in 1968. At the time of writing the museum complex was undergoing modernization and expansion, so parts of it were closed to visitors.

Tank landing ship, No. 926 formerly a US WWII-era LST

73

Qingzhou Municipal Museum

青州博物馆 *Qingzhoushi bowuguan*

No. 1 Fangongting West Road, Qingzhou City, Liaoning
青州市范公亭西路1号

Tel: (0536) 3261 736, 3266 255
Open: 9.00–17.00
www.qzbowuguan.com
Personal guides: call (0536) 3266 219 to arrange in advance. Shop with reproductions and publications
NOTE: A new extension is being built to house the Buddhist statues

Bodhisatva, Eastern Wei period, painted stone

Qingzhou is the poor cousin to other cities in the province and, as such, its museum does not appear particularly inviting at first glance. Do stop, however, for within the museum's galleries, which are set around a courtyard, is one of the most astounding collections of Buddhist statues ever to be unearthed in China. Startled construction workers making way for a sports complex chanced upon this cache of nearly 400 Buddhist sculptures in 1996. Several years ago they went on a world tour, which was hailed as one of the great Asian shows of recent years and resulted in a wonderful catalogue entitled *Return of the Buddha: The Qingzhou Discoveries.*

The poorly lit gallery, with its sparse English labels detailing only the date, leaves you with little to read but here that is a bonus, for each and every piece resonates with a spiritual aura and beauty which is seductive. Found near the former site of the city's Longxing Temple in a bare earth rectangular pit, the fragmented figures of Buddha and his attendants (*bodhisattvas*) were arranged in three layers with their heads around the pit walls, with the most complete ones in the centre. Most are carved from local bluish-grey limestone and date from a period which spans 600 years, from the late Northern Wei dynasty (386–534) to the Northern Song (960–1126), with the core dating from the sixth century, providing scholars with a unique historical continuum of Buddhist sculpture in China. Some are gilded and painted in a range of natural blue, green and black pigments, the majority are incomplete and noticeably restored with their jigsaw-puzzle pieces stuck together. Why they were buried and left, no one really knows. Perhaps they were buried during a period when rulers persecuted followers of Buddhism and they were in danger of confiscation.

Central to this collection is the fifty-year period between 529 and 577, when two main stylistic differences were evident as Buddhism spread along the trade routes and blended with Chinese qualities. Those from the Northern (386–534) and Eastern (534–550) Wei dynasties embraced all things Chinese and so designed their figures in typical Chinese monastic robes concealing the body, with stiff faces bearing benign smiles, elongated earlobes and Buddhas with prominent *usnisa* (protuberances on the head representing wisdom). The Northern Qi (550–577), on the other hand, whose dislike of all things Chinese, turned to Gupta India, adopting close-fitting, light garments revealing the body's contours, with fuller faces bearing perfectly formed sensuous lips. These, along with other recently unearthed hoards, add greatly to our knowledge of Chinese Buddhist art. In 2005, 400 Ming dynasty stone Buddha statues were uncovered in Chongqing during a survey of a ruined

Ming temple in Liangping county, and a cache of Buddhist statuary consisting of 324 pieces was discovered in 2006 in Houdigecun village, Nangong, Hebei, dating from the Northern dynasties through to the Tang.

Besides these wondrous sculptures, there are galleries on the Neolithic Cultures of Longshan and Dawenkou, displays of Warring States period bronzes and Eastern Han dynasty pottery, including, among other pieces, a wonderful glazed model of a pottery store. Painting and calligraphy are displayed in rather drab galleries with no English signage, and important silver pieces unearthed in the city languish in poor conditions.

At the time of writing a new display was in the making, which will contain a selection of the brightly painted pottery figurines from the recently discovered Xiangshan Han tomb site, believed to have belonged to a nobleman. It is similar to the well-known Han tomb site of Weishan, discovered in 2003 in Shangdong near the Weishan Mountains, where foot-tall terracotta warriors, horses and chariots were found, some of which were brightly painted.

Bodhisattva, Northern Wei period

Triad with mandorla, Eastern Wei (534–550) or Northern Qi dynasty (550–577)

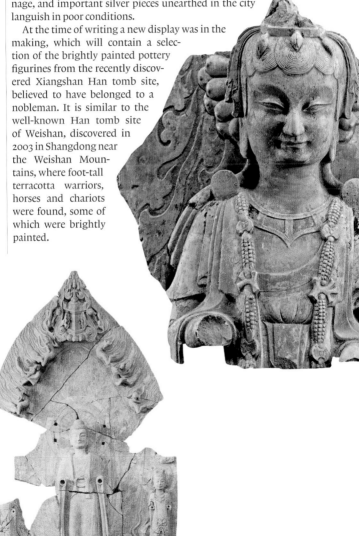

74

Yungang Grottoes

云冈石窟 *Yungang shiku*

Wuzhou Mountain, 16 km west of Datong City, Shanxi
山西省大同市西16公里 武周山麓

Tel: (0352) 302 6230
Open: 8.30–17.30, 15 Apr–31 Oct; 17.00, 1 Nov–14 Apr
www.yungang.org

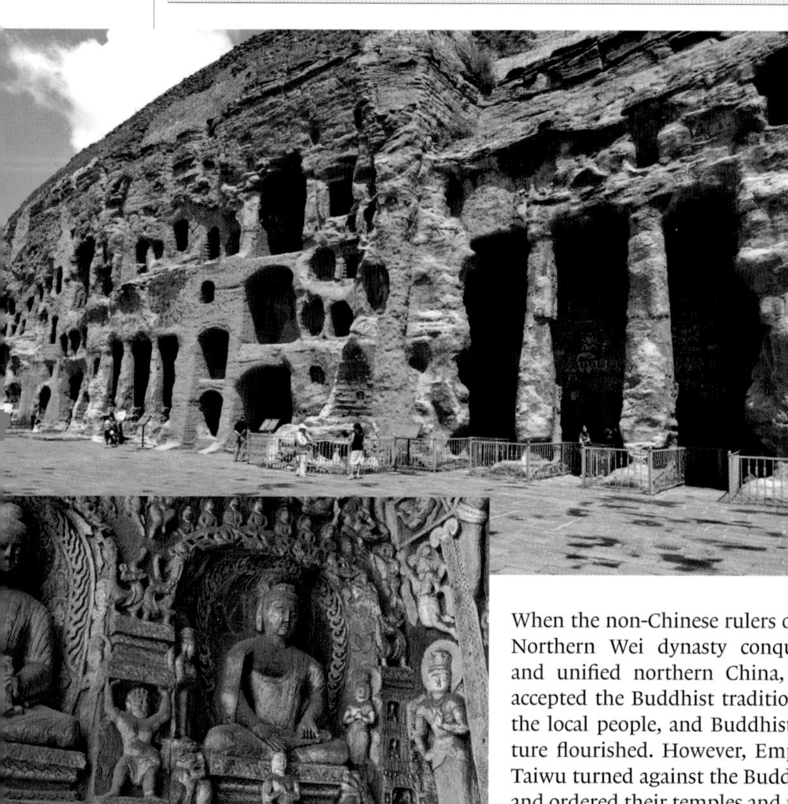

View of grottoes from Caves 9 and 10

Cave 10

When the non-Chinese rulers of the Northern Wei dynasty conquered and unified northern China, they accepted the Buddhist traditions of the local people, and Buddhist culture flourished. However, Emperor Taiwu turned against the Buddhists and ordered their temples and monasteries destroyed. The building of the Yungang Grottoes began after Taiwu's death under the Emperor Wencheng, his grandson and successor, in contrition for the violent persecution of Buddhists wrought by Taiwu.

Work on the earliest caves was supervised by the monk Tan Yao, a native of Gansu. The grottoes took forty years to complete with the help of up to 40,000 workers, and reveal the international influences resulting from trade along the Silk Road. Although the caves were built for the most part between AD 460 and the early 490s, restoration and repairs continued throughout the succeeding dynasties as they still do today. Fifty-three grottoes are carved into the sandstone cliffs at the southern end of the Wuzhou Mountains, stretching out in an east–west line for about 1 km. Many of the sculptures placed in and outside the caves are huge. The tallest is a seated Buddha measuring 17 m in height; in contrast, some of the tiny figures lining the grotto walls in their

Cave 20

hundreds are as small as 2 cm high. Some figures are painted; others no longer are. There are wall paintings, bas-reliefs and carved pillars. The material here is marvellous – literally. In fact, in 2001, the Yungang Grottoes became a UNESCO World Heritage Site.

The caves are divided into three sections – East, Centre and West – and have been given numbers which are not connected to their chronology. The earliest ones, built by Tan Yao, are Nos 16–20, where colossal statues of the Buddha are said to represent the first five Emperors of the Wei dunasty. In Cave 5 there are beautiful wall paintings and the 17-m-high Buddha. Caves 13 and 20 house equally impressive, slightly smaller giants. Huge sandstone pillars eroded by time and weather dominate Caves 9 and 10.

Due to conservation work, some of the grottoes may be closed during your visit.

75

Former Residence of Lei Lutai

雷履泰故居 *Lei Lutai guju*

11 Shuyuan Street, Pingyao, Shanxi
山西省平遥城书院街11号

Tel: (0354) 5627 660 (Pingyao Tourism Bureau)
Open: 8.00–19.30 summer; 18.00 winter

Lei Lutai (1770–1849) was the founder of the Rishengchang in Ping Yao. This system of credit and currency conversion revolutionized the banking business in China and made Lei very wealthy indeed. His Qing dynasty courtyard home is now open to the public and provides a peek into the life of this illustrious nineteenth-century personality.

76

Pingyao International Photography Museum (Confucius Temple)

平遥文庙 *Pingyao wenmiao*

North of Yunlu Street, Pingyao, Shanxi
山西省平遥县城东南隅云路街北侧

Tel: (0354) 5758 444
Open: 8.00–19.00

The main building of this temple, Dacheng Hall, was built in 1163, much earlier than the Confucius Temple in Beijing or even that in Qufu, the hometown of Confucius. In the temple are eighty-seven sculptures of Confucius and his disciples, and an exhibition surveying the history of the ancient imperial examination system.

Also in the complex is the Pingyao International Photography Museum. Picturesque Pingyao, with the best-preserved city walls in China, is an outstanding example of a Han Chinese city of the Ming and Qing dynasties and

Pingyao's Confucius Temple during the Photography Festival

is always buzzing with shutterbugs. Since 2001, it has hosted an annual international photography festival, providing a window onto China's burgeoning photography scene. The collection includes photos by the well-known documentarians of the revolution, Sha Fei and Wu Yinxian, as well some work by Western photographers.

77

Pingyao Museum (Qingxu Temple)

平遥县博物馆，清虚观 *Pingyaoxian bowuguan, qingxuguan*

Dong Dajie, Pingyao, Shanxi
山西省平遥县城东大街

Tel: (0354) 5685 851
Open: 8.00–19.00

This Tang dynasty Daoist temple is also home to the Pingyao Museum in which there are exhibits of Daoist civilization, the history of Pingyao and a small collection of local artefacts.

Qingxu Temple

78 Rishengchang Financial House Museum

日昇昌 票号 *Rishengchang piaohao*

West Street, Pingyao, Shanxi
山西省平遥县城西大街

Advisable to buy a tourist museum ticket which will get you into most of the museums in town in addition to the city wall
Tel: (0354) 5685 364
Open: 8.00–19.00

The Ancient Han town of Pingyao, like other UNESCO World Heritage cultural properties, is in itself, a museum. Just walking through the massive gate on the cobblestone road, circumnavigating the ramparts of its defensive wall or exploring the architecture of its many classic courtyard houses open to the public, is a 'museum experience'. What the city has to offer – its wall, its shops, temples, streets and houses famous for their vaulted ceilings and intricate carvings – constitutes a wonderfully preserved antique. Originally constructed in the Western Zhou (eleventh century BC to 771 BC), the town was enlarged and developed in the Ming dynasty (1368–1644). The wall, made of pounded earth covered with bricks and stones stretches 6 km in length around the ancient town and includes seventy-two watch towers, six city gates and 3,000 embrasures. These features are said to reflect the area's strong Confucian values by representing his 3,000 disciples and seventy-two top disciples.

Outside the wall lies the far from beautiful modern town of Pingyao, but most tourists do not venture out of the old town and spend their time wandering the poetically beautiful streets of old Pingyao while staying in one of its many courtyard-style inns. Do avoid visiting during the major Chinese holidays, however, as it gets unbearably crowded and the charm of the place will be hard to appreciate.

A typical Pingyao building

Pingyao was a famous banking centre during the nineteenth and early twentieth centuries. The Rishengchang (Prosperity with the Rising Sun) Exchange Shop – now a museum – was one of the earliest and most successful 'exchange shops' in China. Established in 1823 it had branches in almost all of China's major cities as well as abroad. These exchange shops or 'remittance draft banks' dealt with 'bills of exchange'. At this time, China was using silver coin as its currency. Obviously, this was inconvenient in terms of security and long-distance transactions. Using these remittance drafts in such exchange shops, cash deposited at one branch could be payable at another branch allowing transfers of funds for business purposes. This system, in use for over a century, had a great impact on the Chinese economy and banking system.

The Rishengchang Exchange Shop can be identified by the traditional wooden sign board over the thick wooden gate at its entrance. The building consists of three courtyards in which were offices, accommodation for staff and rest areas for important clients. For security, a net made of metal thread enclosed the entire compound. Hung onto the net, small bells would sound the alarm should a robbery be attempted.

In the building are models of scenes from the bank as it would have been in the nineteenth century as well as furniture and artefacts of the period including examples of remittance drafts.

79

Shanxi Museum

山西博物院 *Shanxi bowuguan*

13 North Section, West Binhe Road, Taiyuan
山西省滨河西路北段13号

Tel: (0351) 8789 222 / 555
Open: 9.00–17.00; last entry 16.00; closed on the 15th and 30th of every month
www.shanximuseum.com.cn
English guides – ring ahead to book / audio guides are in Chinese only, though English ones are planned
Excellent publications, including *Rare Treasures in Shanxi Museum* (published by the Cultural Relics bureau)

Museum façade

This remarkably shaped museum looming large on the bank of the Fen River emerges between nests of high-rise buildings like a spaceship that has just landed on some alien planet. Its central rhomboid is the result of combining two shapes, that of a *dou* – a measure for dry grain – and that of a *ding* – a round-bodied three-legged vessel for food – the former symbolizing a healthy harvest, the latter, stability. Added to this are four smaller buildings resembling outstretched wings, so embodying the ancient Chinese association of the free spirit with flying birds. Walk inside and you enter a double-height

Bronze lamp bearer riding an ox, Warring States period

Jade disc with dragon designs, Western Zhou dynasty

atrium mimicking the unique shape of the wooden Sakyamuni pagoda, built 950 years ago. Walk further in and the granite-and-glass interiors open up to reveal twelve exhibition halls over four floors, seven devoted to ancient history, the remaining five a combination of fine art and themed galleries.

As the main repository of cultural relics from this rich province, it is the largest and most prestigious, housing research and conservation facilities, temporary exhibition spaces, conference halls, a library and all the usual services including a canteen. Like so many museums, a small percentage of its massive collection of more than 200,000 items is displayed; the majority are authentic. All the displays are beautifully lit with comprehensive labels in English augmented by excellent images, dioramas, maps and interactive computer displays. The collections have been amassed since 1919, originally as part of the Shanxi library, then moved to two locations (a Confucian monastery and a former palace) until being reincarnated in their latest form. It opened in 2005.

A panel in the entrance atrium illustrates numerous ways of depicting the character for the word *jin* – the shortened name for Shanxi. Located in the centre of the county, it is embraced by the nurturing Yellow River as well as the Fen, which runs across the loess plateau. To east and west it is bounded by mountains which protected it from the invading minorities of the north. Over the centuries, though, cultural interactions and exchanges took place to create this rich cradle of civilization. As you weave your way through the chronologically laid-out galleries, you start on the ground floor with numerous dioramas and a selection of artefacts discovered from the hundreds of Palaeolithic sites located in Shanxi. Interactive models, didactic explanations and comparisons with finds of similar dates in other parts of the world put the finds in context.

The second floor is home to the museum's teahouse, as well as exhibits on the later Neolithic Cultures of north-central China, including the site of Taosi (2300 BC) in the southern part of the province (an offshoot of the Central Plain Longshan Culture). This extensive site with houses and kilns is defined by its large cemetery containing thousands of burials, several with outstanding contents indicating social stratification. Besides brown earthenware with red painting

Relief carving on the white marble stone outer coffin in the tomb of Yu Hong, Sui dynasty

on a black ground, the site also contained wooden furniture and jade objects. Laid out in the centre of the gallery is a female skeleton of high rank (judging by the outstanding quality of the jade found with her, much of which is jewellery). Surrounding cases display superb examples of jade artefacts including axes, rings and a single-tiered jade *cong* with a hole through the middle.

Displays continue with the rich seam of finds from the Xia and Shang dynasties in Shanxi, including outstanding examples of Xia period pottery such as the large steamer (*yan*) excavated at the Erlitou site in Dongxiafeng. Objects that will blow your socks off include the high-quality ritual bronzes from the Shang; many unusual shapes are on display. Among these is the owl-shaped *you* excavated from Erlangpo in Shilou County and, from nearby, a dragon-shaped *gong* excavated from Taohuazhe, as well as one of the museum's national treasures: an imaginary animal-shaped *gong* excavated at Jinjie in Lingshi County. All are elaborately decorated and likely to have been used to make wine offerings. Superb here too are the three-dimensional animal- and bird-shaped carved jades.

Gallery 3 highlights the achievements of the Jin kingdom and the splendour of the bronzes of the Western Zhou. When the Zhou overthrew the Shang and established their capital near present-day Xi'an, relatives of their kings ruled small city-states. One of these was the vassal state of Jin. Among their most stellar objects are their ritual bronzes, including a *zun* and *you* with animal faces (*taotie*) – a decorative element they borrowed from

the Shang – as well as inscribed pig and bird-shaped *zuns*. Other bronzes are displayed from the royal cemeteries of the marquises of Jin discovered in the 1990s. Tombs M63 and M31 revealed exotic bronzes including a *hu* with a bird-shaped lid and human feet. Besides the stunning *dings* and other bronzes there are a large number of jades of the highest class. Among the most spectacular of these are sets used as facial coverings during burials and as ornaments. Body ornaments consisted of *huangs* (arch-shaped ornaments) and beads; the longer they were, the higher the wearer's status.

The collections are so varied that it's worth spending time admiring the workmanship and their whimsical forms. A bronze worth special mention was found in the Jin cemetery site at Shangguo in Wenxi: a miniature carriage or chariot box with a hinged cover. Rectangular and decorated on top and sides with birds, lions, monkeys and tigers, it has six wheels. At the door stands a guardian or slave with his left foot amputated for having committed a serious crime; his job was to guard the royal zoo.

Dazzling bronzes from the Jin tombs of the Spring and Autumn period should not be missed, as the quality is astounding. Many were probably produced at the large foundry site at Houma, where refined, complex bronzes have been found along with the clay moulds and models used to produce them. Among these are a *ding* with openwork interlace designs, a bird-shaped *zun* with a tiger handle, and a set of bells with handles in the shape of creatures with wings and claws like Central Asian griffins – illustrating the outside influences on this local industry. Also found at several sites around Houma were tablets of jade and stone with brush-written red-ink inscriptions recording rituals of covenant and curses buried in sacrificial pits. From the Warring States period are bronzes including a *hu* with scenes of people picking mulberries, and a highly decorated ox with a man springing from its back holding a circular plate stand.

Collections of stone carving also stand out and cover more than 2,000 years from the Western Han dynasty onwards. Among the highlights is the Han dynasty crouching tiger from Yuncheng and the finely modelled stone coffin found in the tomb of Emperor Shaozu of the Song dynasty. Composed of hundreds of pieces, the coffin provides a rare insight into the architecture of the Northern Wei period. Another jewel is the marble outer coffin from the 1,400-year-old tomb of Yu Hong of the Sui dynasty (uncovered in Taiyuan) with exquisite relief carvings of people with European traits such as straight noses and deep-set eyes. Evidence points to Yu Hong having been of European origin (his DNA has been analyzed). He probably married a local woman and became leader of the Central Asian people who settled here at that time. He belongs to one of the oldest known genetic groups from western Eurasia.

Bronze, animal-shaped *gong*, Shang dynasty

The richness of Buddhist statues from the province is brought home not only by those on display but also by a diagram listing and illustrating those which have been lost to leading overseas museums. Shanxi is famous for it numerous temples, and of course for the Han dynasty Buddhist

Jade human figure, Shang dynasty

caves at Yungang. At the museum there is a wide range of examples dating from the Northern dynasties to the Tang and found at sites in Qinxian and elsewhere. Among the beauties on display is a white-marble head of Buddha Sakyamuni from the sixth century found in Huata in Taiyuan.

The collections of pottery are equally noteworthy, from the early Yangshao Cultures, to the dancing figures of the Northern Qi, to the amazing brick carvings illustrating festive performances and figures of eight immortals from the Jin period tombs of southern Shanxi. The most distinctive pieces of porcelain are those made in the north. From the Song onwards, Shanxi entered a golden age of porcelain-making with numerous kilns all over the province characterized by superb workmanship.

The gallery displaying a selection of the thousands of paintings and calligraphy scrolls housed in the museum dating from the Yuan to the Qing dynasties should not be missed, nor should that devoted to ancient currency. There's so much to see that you won't be able to take it all in on one visit.

80

Taiyuan Art Museum

太原美术馆 *Taiyuan meishuguan*

Chang Feng Culture and Business District, Taiyuan
太原市长风文化商务区

Open: Scheduled for 2011

The architect's renderings of the exterior and interiors of the museum

Construction of this museum began in 2009 and it promises to be a worthwhile destination with displays of ancient and modern folk art, sculpture, painting, photography and calligraphy. Architecturally innovative, the building's form is inspired by the traditional cultures of this early centre of civilization and the extraordinary agricultural landscapes of the province. The international competition for the design was won by the American firm Preston Scott Cohen, Inc. and will be part of a group of cultural centres on an island adjacent to the Fen River. The other proposed projects for the complex include a theatre, library, science and technology museum, and geography museum.

81 Harbin Building Art Centre

哈尔滨市建筑艺术馆 *Haerbinshi jianzhu yishuguan*

88 Toulong Street, Daoli District,
Harbin, Heilongjiang
哈尔滨市道里区透笼街88号

Tel: (0451) 8468 4170 / 8469 0304
Open: 8.30–17.00
www.sofia.com.cn/Enmain.Asp

The Centre is situated inside the impressive and unmistakable former Orthodox Church of St Sophia, constructed from 1923 to 1935 on the site of an earlier church built in 1907. Located in the heart of Harbin's historic district, this institution forms the centrepiece of the city's world-renowned architectural ensemble, largely designed and constructed by the Russians in the early twentieth century. The museum's inception formed an integral part of the regeneration of Harbin's architectural heritage by the Municipality in the 1990s and included the complete renovation of St Sophia itself, which had been used as a warehouse for many years. Exhibits include audio-visual displays of the city's architectural history, which boasts a rich and diverse character influenced heavily by Art Nouveau.

Heilongjiang Provincial Museum, formerly the Moscow Shopping Hall (1906) (right, no. 82)

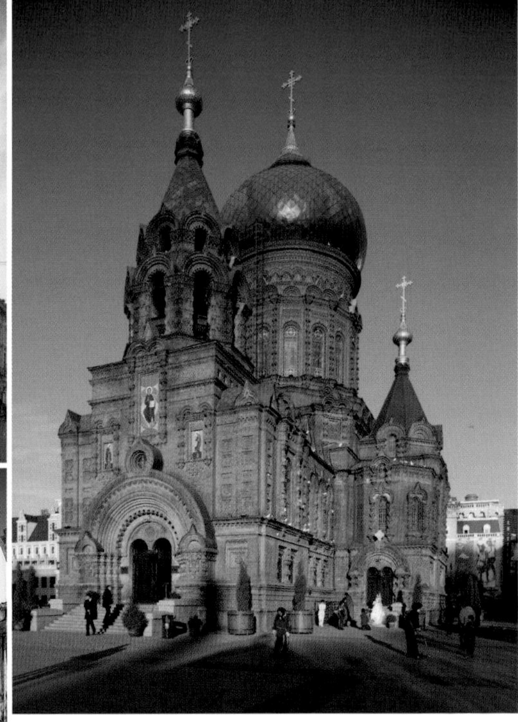

Church of St Sophia (right) and other Harbin historic buildings

82 Heilongjiang Provincial Museum

黑龙江省博物馆 *Heilongjiangsheng bowuguan*

50 Hongjun Street, Harbin, Heilongjiang
哈尔滨市红军街50号

Tel: (0451) 5364 4151
Open: 9.00–16.00

The museum is housed in the old 'Moscow Emporium', built in 1904 near the centre of Harbin. The site is one of the large open civic spaces that form a key component of the city's original urban plan as laid out by the Russians at the turn of the early twentieth century. The building became a museum in 1922 and officially the Heilongjiang Provincial Museum in 1954.

The uninspiring collection numbers over 100,000 objects including stuffed animals and dinosaur fossils, and there is an aquarium in the basement. Perhaps of greatest interest is the archaeological and ethnographic material displayed upstairs, including silks and jade from the Jin dynasty (1115–1234), which had its first capital just outside of Harbin, as well as textiles and artefacts from the Hezhen minority of Heilongjiang. Among highlights of the several thousand historical documents are the 'Painting of Silk Weaving' and a historical map of the west of China from the Qing dynasty. English signage is sparse.

83 Japanese Germ Warfare Museum Unit 731

侵华日军第731部队罪证陈列馆 *Qinhua rijun diqisanyaobudui zuizheng chenlieguan*

Xinjiang Street No. 25, Pingfang District, Harbin, Heilongjiang
哈尔滨市平房区新疆大街25号

Open: 9.00–11.30 (tickets not sold after 11.00) & 13.00–16.00 (tickets not sold after 15.00) except Mon

This infamous establishment, Unit 731, located in the village of Pingfang, 30 km from central Harbin, was where Japan conducted extensive research and testing of biological warfare agents and established the biological warfare command during World War II. Between 1939 and 1945, the Japanese performed unspeakably horrific acts on mainly Chinese prisoners of war and civilians but also on Soviet, Korean, British and Mongolian prisoners. More than 3,000 souls perished as victims of grisly experiments including vivisection. These people, whom the Japanese referred to as 'logs', were injected with viruses and diseases, left out in the cold to freeze, cut open and dissected – and on and on. There is a long list of unimaginable acts of barbarity.

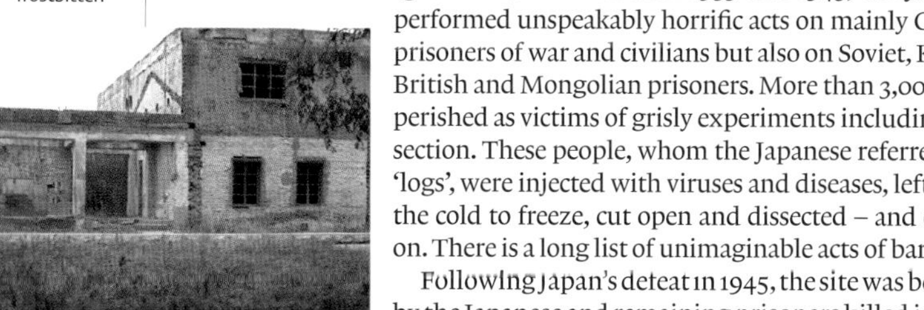

'Frostbite Lab' – from holes in the walls (circles in photo) prisoners had to stick out their arms till frostbitten

Following Japan's defeat in 1945, the site was bombed by the Japanese and remaining prisoners killed in an effort to hide what went on there. Today, only a few origi-

The main building, Unit 731

nal structures survive, all of which are incorporated into the museum, which remains a pertinent reminder of the most gruesome aspects of the Japanese occupation of China during World War II.

The museum itself is located in Unit 731's only fully intact structure, the former main office. Actual historical artefacts are sparse but there are photographs and tableaux with wax figures illustrating the site's gruesome past. At the end of the tour, and most affecting, is a video showing former Japanese soldiers, now repentant, speaking bluntly about their work here and the events that took place. The video includes English subtitles.

84 American POW Memorial Museum – Mukden Prison Camp

沈阳二战盟军战俘营旧址纪念馆

Shenyang erzhan mengjun zhanfuying jinzhi jinianguan

7 Qingguang Street, Dadong District, Shenyang, Liaoning

辽宁省 沈阳市大东区青光街7号

Tel: (024) 8832 6828

Open: Spring/Summer 2009

As many as 1,500 allied troops – mainly Americans and British – were held at any one time as slave labourers at Mukden Camp from 1942 to 1945. The total number throughout the war totalled 2,027, many of whom had survived the Battles of Bataan and Corregidor, as well as the infamous 'Bataan Death March'. They were then shipped by the Japanese to China in the holds of 'Hell Ships', named for

the horrendous conditions in which the prisoners were kept. At first they were taken to a camp in Shenyang, then a few months later moved to this site, about 3 km away, which became a Japanese showcase camp as it had barracks made of bricks. When visitors and UN inspectors came, the prisoners' conditions were temporarily improved, in a masquerade of adherence to the Geneva Convention. In fact, the men were used as slaves at a heavy machinery plant (which they continuously sabotaged), a tannery, a canvas-weaving factory and other work places. While in detention they were routinely beaten, tortured and starved. Between November 1942 and March 1943 alone – the first winter at Mukden Camp – 206 prisoners of war died.

Perhaps most egregiously, many have also testified that they were used as guinea pigs for medical and germ warfare experiments.

Scheduled to open in Spring 2009, the museum is located in the old prisoner-of-war camp. Displays include photos, uniforms, dog tags, letters and other documentation, as well as DVDs of ex-prisoners recounting their experiences here. The museum continues to actively seek contact with and donations from survivors and their families.

85

Liaoning Provincial Museum

辽宁省博物馆 *Liaoningsheng bowuguan*

363 Shifu Da Road, Shenhe District, Shenyang, Liaoning
辽宁省沈阳市沈河区市府大路363号

Tel: (024) 2274 1193
Open: 9.00–17.00 except Mon
English guidebook & audio guide

Liao dynasty gilt silver death masks, male and female

The Liaoning Provincial Museum was one of only three major national museums planned by the Republican government between the end of the war in 1945 and the establishment of the People's Republic in 1949 – the others being the Palace Museum and the Nanjing Museum. It was originally called the Dongbei Museum (the Northeast Museum), and was planned as the national museum of Manchuria, the northeastern provinces of China that had recently been liberated from the Japanese.

The original collections were based on the art and archaeology of the northeast. The archaeological collections have been hugely expanded by nearly fifty years of excavation in the region. However, many of the finest of the other treasures come from the old imperial collections housed in the Forbidden City – in common with the Palace Museum in the Forbidden City, which houses the parts of the original collection that never left Beijing, and the Nanjing Museum and the National Museum in Taipei. However, unlike Nanjing and Taipei, which owe their collections to the wanderings, and eventual flight and defeat of Chiang Kai-shek and the Nationalist army, the story of the Liaoning collection goes back earlier to the Reign of

Liao dynasty attendant with crossed hands

Puyi, the last Qing Emperor. On the founding of the Republic in 1911, Puyi was allowed to live on in the Forbidden City – until his eventual expulsion in 1924, after which he first lived in Tianjin and eventually moved to the northeast where in 1932 he became the puppet Emperor of the Japan-established Manchukuo. He probably started selling works from the collection shortly after 1911, and, on his final departure from Beijing, he took with him a number of important works to sell, or to barter with the Japanese. These treasures had been gradually dispersed throughout Manchuria by 1949, and it is to the huge credit of the Liaoning Museum that so many were tracked down and have come to be housed in Shenyang. Only some of these had been fully documented, and it is possible that yet more may still come to light. Even as they stand, they represent one of the finest collections of Tang and Song calligraphy and painting in the world, making the collection of this museum one of the key destinations for the visitor to China.

The museum was renamed the Liaoning Provincial Museum in 1959. In 2004, a new three-storey 10,000 sq m purpose-built museum was opened to house the collections. It is an imposing building constructed to international museum standards, which provides a base not only for exhibition and storage but also as a centre for the continuing province-wide programme of excavation.

The centre of the archaeological exhibit is a permanent display of Liaoning's ancient history, in particular of the distinctive regional cultures found along the Daling River and the Liao River, and along the shores of the Yellow and the Bohai seas. Other galleries, radiating off a central well area near the entrance to the building, show well-displayed and instructively arranged collections of historical artefacts, and of the major Liaoning archaeological sites. There are impressive tableaux of the life of the early peoples of the province, and a gallery devoted to Chinese history. The most important and impressive of the excavated objects are the bronzes from the sites at Kazuomachanggou, Beidong and Shanwanzi.

The calligraphy collection contains masterpieces such as a Tang dynasty copy of a work by Wang Xi Zhi, and works by Ouyang Xun and Zhang Xu, amongst many others. The painting collection contains works by Zhou Fang, Dong Yuan and the Song dynasty Emperor, Huizong.

Poem by Du Fu, calligraphy by Song dynasty artist, Zhang Jizhi

There is a spectacular collection of tapestry and embroidery beginning with a Five Dynasties embroidered Buddhist sutra, and exam-

Details from a Tang dynasty painting

Liao dynasty gilt silver ornaments

ples of *kesi* work from the Northern Song, the Southern Song and the Ming dynasties. The most impressive of the Northern Song examples come from the private collection of Zhang Xue Liang, one of the most powerful of the warlords who carved little kingdoms for themselves in the northeast during the Republican and the Civil War periods.

There is also a fine exhibition of the history and achievement of Liao ware ceramics, and a collection of maps and topographical studies including very rare works by Xu Lun and the Jesuit priest, Matteo Ricci.

Zhongshan Square

中山广场 *Zhongshan guangchang*

Junction of Nanjing Street and Zhongshan Road, Heping District, Shenyang, Liaoning
沈阳市和平区 南京街和中山路交叉口

This is not a museum but it should not be missed if you are in Shenyang. Many of the once ubiquitous statues of Mao Zedong have been torn down recently, as the cult of Mao has subsided, but this work of art will hopefully remain. It is a massive fibreglass statue of Mao in his usual pose – right arm raised in salute to the masses, body standing to attention. Built in 1969 at the height of the Cultural Revolution, it forms an island in the middle of a busy roundabout in central Shenyang. At the base of Mao's pedestal and surrounding the great helmsman are proportionately huge and meticulously detailed sculptures of earnest workers, soldiers, peasants and students gripping their weapons, tools and little red books and surging forward with earnest faces as they seize power and embrace Mao's directive to destroy the 'Four Olds': old ideology, old thought, old habits and old customs. This sculptural group is an archetypal example of civic art of the Cultural Revolution and is an extraordinary sight in China's current climate.

86 September 18 History Museum

918事变纪念馆 *Jiuyibashibian jinianguan*

46 Wanghua Nan Street, Shenyang, Liaoning

辽宁省沈阳市望花南街46号

Open: 8.30–16.30

Gift and bookshop / museum guide in English

This memorial museum is built on the actual site of the September 18th Incident, known in the West as the Manchurian Incident, or the Mukden Incident (Mukden being the Manchu name for Shenyang). This date in 1931 marked one of the key events leading to the total Japanese occupation of Manchuria and the foundation of the puppet state of Manchukuo in February 1932.

Museum façade

The Japanese had occupied part of Manchuria since the war of 1894–95, and it was alleged that Chinese forces had carried out a bombing raid on September 18 on a Japanese-operated bridge and railway crossing just north of Shenyang. This gave the Japanese army the excuse to capture Shenyang, to occupy Liaoning, Jilin and Heilongjiang, and to create the puppet state of Manchukuo in 1932.

The date of 18 September 1931, even more than that of the Nanjing Massacre, has come to be regarded as one of the defining moments of modern Chinese history – known to every twenty-first-century Chinese schoolchild. The museum memorializes the brutality of the attack on Shenyang and the savage oppression of the Chinese population of the whole of Manchuria until 1945. Opened in 1999, the museum, set on a huge 35,000 sq m site, is housed in dramatic and unusual buildings resonating with symbolism. The exhibition area shows reconstructions – some life-size, some models – of scenes of destruction and acts of heroism. The total impact is horrifyingly impressive. There are also instruments of torture on display and a life-size reconstruc-

Battlefield reconstruction of the War Against the Japanese

tion of a medical team shown dissecting patients (who would have been still alive), and experimenting with bacteriological weapons – with the claim that 2.7 million Chinese soldiers were killed in this way.

Many of the captions are in Chinese, but there is enough English information for the visitor to get the point of this monument to a particularly nasty and brutish war of occupation.

The Eastern Wing of the palace complex with its distinctive Manchu-style architecture

87 Shenyang Palace Museum

沈阳故宫博物院 *Shenyang gugong bowuyuan*

171 Shenyang Road, Shenyang, Liaoning
沈阳市沈阳路171号

Tel: (024) 2485 2012
Open: 9.00–16.00 Nov–Apr; 8.30–17.00 May–June & Sept–Oct; 8.30–17.30 July–Aug
Bookshop / café / English-speaking guides

The octagonal Dazheng Hall, The Hall of Great Affairs housing an elaborate throne where Emperor Shunzhi was crowned

Qing imperial robe

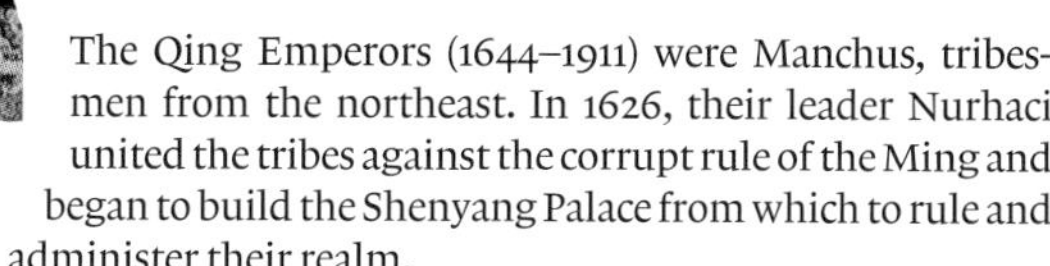

The Qing Emperors (1644–1911) were Manchus, tribesmen from the northeast. In 1626, their leader Nurhaci united the tribes against the corrupt rule of the Ming and began to build the Shenyang Palace from which to rule and administer their realm.

The Manchu were horsemen, who, as a result of years of gripping their stirrups, evolved to grow a second little toe.

The palace was modelled on the Forbidden City in Beijing – partly because it was the imperial palace model to hand, and partly to reflect growing ambitions of China itself. Partially completed by 1636, it was laid out in three sections and based on Ming style, with colour and decoration subtly altered to reflect Manchu taste. The earliest and most interesting section was the Eastern Wing, a rectangular open space with the Dazheng Hall of the Emperor at the north point and eight pavilions, four ranged on either side, for his kings – who became his banner men, his elite regiments of fearsome cavalry.

The layout of these pavilions was like a military camp, reflecting the power and structure of Manchu rule. It was from here that the Emperor Shunzhi ordered his troops to sweep across the plains, capture Beijing and overthrow the Ming Empire in 1644.

After the transfer of government to Beijing in 1644, the Shenyang Palace remained the centre of Manchu power in their homeland, and thereafter both their cultural and their power base. It was embellished and enlarged by Qianlong (1736–1795), and now has 300 halls and covers 60,000 sq m.

Any visitor interested in Chinese history, or in Qing art and architecture, must visit this well-preserved and intact site. It is interesting to see it after a visit to the Forbidden City in Beijing.

88 China Textile History Museum at Donghua University

中国纺织史博物馆 东华大学 *Zhongguo fangzhishi bowuguan Donghuadaxue*

1882 Yan'an West Road, Shanghai (4th floor of the teaching block)

上海市长宁区延安西路1882号

（东华大学教学大楼4楼）

Tel: (021) 6237 3678
(University phone 学校电话)
Open: 9.00–17.00

This museum was opened in November 2004, both as a public museum as well as a resource for the students of the university to study the development of Chinese clothing design.

The collection's main focus is on the less expensive and less elaborate dress of the common woman and man from the Qing dynasty (although there are some items made earlier than the Qing) rather than the extravagant and elegant clothing of the distant past.

Much of the collection is gathered from the university archives, but other pieces have been donated by individuals. In addition, a large clothing manufacturer based in Ningbo donated the museum's most valuable item – a dragon robe dating to the Reign of Emperor Guangxu (1871–1908) in the Qing dynasty, woven in the intricate *kesi* technique. These dragon robes could be worn only by the Emperor and by senior officials and the royal family. The iconography of royal dragons required that the dragons woven into the Emperor's robe should have five claws, those on the robes of lesser mortals only four.

One of the major themes of the museum's collection is the contrast between the clothing of the end of the Manchu Qing dynasty and that of the Republican period, i.e. between traditional Chinese women's clothing and 'modern' clothing, which was a blend of Chinese and Western styles, designs and manufacturing techniques.

During the Qing dynasty, the two main traditions in women's clothing were based on those of the Manchu elite and the Han groups, mainly from southern China. By the latter part of the dynasty, these two traditions were merging, although some differences remained. Manchu women stuck to their traditional colours and tight, long-sleeved designs. Han women bound their feet (unlike Manchu women) and so developed a tradition of narrowly embroidered delicate shoes, of which the museum has a collection on display.

Qing dynasty silk robe

Qing dynasty *kesi* embroidered dragon robe

After the establishment of the Republic in 1911, new fabrics, designs and colours were introduced as a result of Western influences and

Silk jacket from the collection

technologies. The museum presents the history of the *qipao*, the form-fitting dress so often associated with Chinese women's clothing and which actually originated from a Manchu style. They became very popular in the 1920s, although at that time they were usually worn over trousers. The trousers faded out by the 1930s and '40s, which was, according to the museum's catalogue, 'the golden period of the *qipao*'. At this time, there was a truly modern Chinese fashion style, especially notable in Shanghai.

Many wonderful examples of these *qipaos* are displayed, along with trousers, blouses, coats, jackets, collars, waistcoats and headdresses. There are also collections of shoes, buttons, fans, trimmings, fastenings, handbags, cotton thread, socks and stockings.

In addition to the assemblage of clothing, the museum also has a collection of early twentieth-century objects that would have been used in the manufacture of the clothes – sewing machines, irons and other artefacts from the USA, Europe and Japan, along with a collection of photographs of people wearing the outfits.

The enthusiasm and loving attention of the curators and of the students associated with this museum is clearly evident here. Viewing this unusual collection of modern Chinese fashion, especially in this city, is very evocative of the Shanghai pre-war period familiar from so many photographs.

The exhibits are well displayed and well lit.

89 China Tobacco Museum

（上海）中国烟草博物馆 *Zhongguo yancao bowuguan*

728 Changyang Rd, Shanghai

上海市长阳路728号

Tel: (021) 6547 1135

Open: 9.00–16.00

www.tobaccomuseum.com.cn

English audio guide / gift shop

This is the largest tobacco museum in the world (appropriately enough, as China is the world's largest tobacco producer), housing over 150,000 artefacts tracing the history of tobacco agricul-

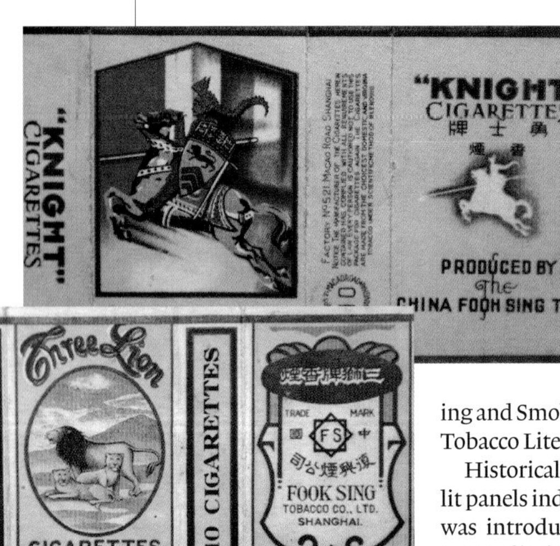

Old cigarette packet labels

ture, industry, economy and trade in China over the past 400 years. The museum is state owned and situated in a purpose-built modern edifice in the Yangpu District. The collection is divided into eight sections: Development Course of Tobacco, Tobacco Agriculture, Tobacco Industry, Tobacco Economy and Trade, Tobacco Administration, Smoking and Smoking Control, Tobacco Culture and Tobacco Literature.

Historical information is presented on well-lit panels indicating the route by which tobacco was introduced to China, the rapid development of its influence through the Qing dynasty, the industry's prosperity during the anti-imperialism movement and the subsequent struggle against the imperial tobacco monopoly. There is also documentation on the tobacco workers' movement, with information about the Shanghai Tobacco Trade Union, established in 1921 in the wake of the cigarette workers' anti-imperialism strike of 1919. Smoking-related paraphernalia is also on display, including ornate water pipes from the 1800s, snuff containers, matchboxes and agricultural tools. The collection includes smoking equipment belonging to famous Chinese people, such as an ashtray of Mao Zedong and a cigarette case used by Mao's friend, Madame Soong Ching Ling. The museum also houses tobacco processing machines and several engaging, life-size dioramas of tobacco farmers and cigarette factory workers. The sixth section presents information on the detrimental effects of smoking on health. This is particularly relevant in China, where the death rates due to smoking-related diseases are very high.

90 Jewish Refugee Museum / Ohel Moishe Synagogue

上海犹太难民遗址 摩西会堂 *Shanghai youtai nanmin yizhi / moxi huitang*

62 Changyang Lu, Shanghai
上海市虹口区长阳路62号

Tel: (021) 6541 5008 / 3511 0215
Open: 9.00–16.30 Mon–Fri

The Jewish community of Shanghai once supported seven synagogues but today only two still stand. The first built was the Ohel Rachel Synagogue constructed by Sir Jacob Sassoon in 1920 to support the thriving community of Baghdadi Jews who had emigrated to China. Although the building still exists it is not open to the public. You can take a look at it through the closed gate at 500 North Shaanxi Road.

Ohel Moishe Synagogue, or the Jewish Refugee Memorial Hall, was built in 1907. No longer a functioning synagogue it is now a museum of the Jew-

ish experience in Shanghai and is open to the public. Its official name is the Jewish Refugee Memorial Hall and it is located in the centre of Hongkou – the old Jewish ghetto. The subject of the Jews in China and in the Shanghai community is a popular one. Many Jews have strong feelings of gratitude to the Shanghainese for their role as hosts and in some cases even saviours to the Jews at a difficult time. It is not unusual that visitors have had some connection to Jewish Shanghai and are searching for traces of their relations who have passed on stories of their life in these streets.

The museum has recently undergone renovation and expansion. The temple itself has been refurbished – the brick restored and sanded, the shutters repaired and repainted. Inside, the women's balcony and the bima (altar), both of which had been removed in the past, have now been reconstructed. Two new exhibition halls have been added; one relates the history of the Jewish community in Shanghai with photographs and multimedia displays and the other is dedicated to the story of Feng Shan Ho, the Chinese diplomat who saved many Jewish lives during the war (see box).

View of former Jewish ghetto from synagogue window; buildings now demolished

The restored synagogue (right, top and bottom)

For those who are interested in the history of Shanghai's Jews it is also possible to contact Mr Dvir Bal-Gal. He is an Israeli living in Shanghai who has set up 'The Shanghai Jewish Memorial Project'. He is working on collecting and cataloguing Jewish tombstones, most of which were lost and dispersed when the four Jewish graveyards of Shanghai were destroyed during the Cultural Revolution. Mr Bal-Gal gives tours of Jewish Shanghai including the neighbourhood of Hangkou. Traces of Jewish life in Shanghai do still exist.

There is also a memorial tablet in the nearby Huosha Park to the memory of the Jewish refugees of Hangkou. If you would like to see it, ask the guard at the entrance to the museum the way.

Jews in Shanghai

There have been three major waves of Jewish migration into Shanghai in modern times. The first group, Sephardic Jews from Baghdad and Bombay, arrived in the mid nineteenth century. The well-known Sassoon family were businessmen from Bombay who rose to prominence during this period. Along with the Hardoon and Kadoorie families, they led a community that became highly successful in the world of business and finance.

The 1920s to the mid 1930s saw a second wave of Jewish immigration to Shanghai – this time by Ashkenazi Jews fleeing Russian pogroms. They first came into northeast China to Harbin, Tianjin and Dalian, but after the Japanese invasion of Manchuria they moved further south to the flourishing Jewish community in Shanghai. They became the middle classes of the community – the bakers, tailors, teachers and shopkeepers. With their arrival, the population of the community swelled to about 5,000.

During World War II, the Chinese actively helped German, Austrian and Polish Jews to escape from the Nazis. Feng Shan Ho was the Chinese consul general in Vienna from 1938 to 1940. He issued hundreds, some say thousands, of visas to Jews fleeing Germany. When the Japanese invaded China in 1937, all Jewish refugees in Shanghai were labelled 'stateless' and forced by the Japanese occupiers to live in a ghetto; by the time of the bombing of Pearl Harbour 30,000 Jews lived in the neighbourhood of Hongkou. There, Jews continued their traditions and built cafés, delicatessens, schools and businesses. By all accounts, the community lived in harmony with its Chinese hosts but by 1949 almost all the Jews in China had dispersed to other countries.

Feng Shan Ho

91

MoCA Shanghai

上海当代艺术馆 *Shanghai dangdai yishuguan*

People's Park, 231 Nanjing West Road, Shanghai
上海南京西路231号，人民公园7号

Tel: (021) 6327 9900
Open: 10.00–18.00, Wed until 22.00
www.mocashanghai.org
Kids

Set in Shanghai's central park, a stone's throw from the Shanghai Art Museum and close to the Shanghai Museum, is this greenhouse-turned-contemporary art space. The brainchild of Samuel Kung, a Hong Kong jewellery designer, it must have been the most innovative proposal put to Shanghai's officials when they were looking for an alternative use for this largely glass-walled space. Add a sweeping ramp, several enclosed exhibition spaces and a roof-top café and you have an impressive contemporary museum with an income stream attached.

Groundbreaking when it opened in 2005, it was hailed, along with the city's other privately funded contemporary space, the Zendai Museum of Modern Art , as Shanghai's answer to New York's MOMA, or at least a smaller version of it. Hiring Victoria Lu, the funky, energetic founding board member of the Taipei Contemporary Art Museum as its creative director, launched the mu-

seum on its mission to promote Chinese contemporary art and bring quality international contemporary art and design to China. This was achieved with great aplomb, with Ms Lu hosting a variety of powerful, adventurous shows at the moment when China was positioning itself as a world centre for contemporary art and riding the wave of success set by the establishment of the Shanghai Biennale in 1994.

Ms Lu has departed – although she still curates the odd show – and adequate funding is now a problem. A re-think of the space has resulted in a smaller café and a new area which will host installations, performance art and lectures by well-known artists and photographers. In this way, it hopes to draw in visitors on a more regular basis. Check local listings for exhibition schedules, special events and lectures.

92

Moganshan M50 Contemporary Art District

莫干山M50艺术区 *Moganshan wushi yishuqu*

50 Moganshan Road, Shanghai

上海市莫干山路50号

With the global frenzy over Chinese contemporary art, many of China's major cities are developing art neighbourhoods, usually in old factory areas, which contain galleries, studios, trendy restaurants, bars and galleries. Moganshan is Shanghai's contemporary art district. As is the case with all such neighbourhoods, galleries and spaces come and go and there is always something

Island 6 Gallery in Moganshan

new, so it is necessary to check local listings for the most up-to-date information.

Just as in Beijing's 798 or Caochangdi art districts, it is great fun to stroll through the streets and alleys here, climbing the stairs of warehouses and discovering which studios are open and which artists are in and receiving visitors. There are galleries worth seeking out in other areas of the city too. As the scene is in constant flux, talk to gallery staff at Moganshan and consult Shanghai's weekly event magazines for the latest openings and events.

93 Museum of Oriental Musical Instruments at Shanghai Conservatory of Music

东方乐器博物馆，上海音乐学院 *Dongfang yueqi bowuguan, Shanghai yinyue xueyuan*

20 Fenyang Road, Shanghai
上海市汾阳路20号

Tel: (021) 6437 0137 ex 2134 / 2132
Open: 9.00–16.00

Tang funerary pottery figurines from a tomb in Xi'an

This museum, previously housed in the Shanghai Conservatory of Music, was closed at the time of writing, but was due to re-open imminently in this new location. The collection numbers over 400 instruments, including a selection of unusual examples from China's ethnic minorities. Ancient instruments are displayed, some of them very rare, such as an 8,000-year-old Neolithic flute found near Shanghai and a Tang dynasty five-stringed *pipa*. Also known as the Chinese lute, the *pipa* is played by plucking and has a pear-shaped wooden body. Modern Chinese pieces are on view, as well as folk instruments from foreign countries.

94

Shanghai Art Museum

上海美术馆 *Shanghai meishuguan*

325 Nanjing West Road, Shanghai

上海市南京西路325号

Tel: (021) 6327 2829
Open: 9.00–17.00
Terrace restaurant on the top floor

The Shanghai Art Museum is an exhibition centre which places particular emphasis on contemporary and international art. It was founded in 1956, and subsequently moved to its present site in the old Shanghai Race Club building, one of the social centres of the old international Shanghai of the 1920s and 1930s. Built of granite with a tinge of purple, the building once featured an impressive clock tower and had a grandstand overlooking the old race course, now the site of People's Park, People's Square and all the major new municipal buildings of Shanghai including City Hall, the Opera House and the Shanghai Museum. The terrace restaurant on the top floor offers magnificent views of all these buildings. The architectural detailing and decoration is of a high standard, and its original function is evident in the magnificent wrought iron horses' heads on the stair rails in the entrance hall.

The interior, consisting of twelve exhibition halls over four levels, and a basement, has been completely modernized. There is usually something of interest among the temporary exhibitions, and the original building is worth a visit in itself. There is also a lecture theatre, conference room, library, multimedia reading room and artists' workshop.

The museum is particularly active in the international contemporary art arena, and has been hosting various exchange events and programmes with Chinese and international art museums. The Shanghai Biennale is the most renowned international show the museum has hosted since 1996; it is considered one of the most influential contemporary art exhibitions in Asia. The concept of the Shanghai Biennale is intended to reflect the international, cosmopolitan and creative nature of Shanghai City itself.

The clock tower and main entrance

95 Shanghai Astronomical Museum

上海天文台佘山站 *Shanghai tianwen sheshan zhan*

West Sheshan Hill, Sheshan National Forest Park, Songjiang District, Shanghai

上海市松江区佘山国家森林公园西佘山顶

Tel: (021) 5765 1723
Open: 8.00–16.00
Bilingual podcast: www.shanghaidaily.com/sciencepod/sheshan.asp

The Chinese have, since at least the second century BC, taken a serious interest in the cosmos. The Emperor was fit to rule only if he performed the correct round of ritual sacrifices to the sun, moon, earth and heaven. Maintaining cosmic order in this way was believed to enable him to keep order in his political realm, as disorderly phenomena in the skies were a warning of impending political doom. Today, China continues to take heed of the heavens, not only with its ambitious space programme but also by studying historical astronomical records as a way to enhance modern astronomy.

Besides the museum there was, until recently, an optical astronomy laboratory (not open to the public) housing the country's second largest optical telescope, but light pollution has forced it to move to Zhejiang Province. What remains in the old observatory buildings are the museum's clearly delineated galleries covering topics such as time, the history of Chinese astronomy, the founding of the observatory and its role, both past and present. The Time Gallery includes models of early observatories, and incorporates video games to entertain children. There are also photographs explaining the founding of the museum in the 1890s by the Jesuit missionaries who, with their knowledge across a range of subjects including astronomy and meteorology, were key in establishing and developing this and other important scientific institutions in China. Highlights include displays of telescopes, from the one housed in the original observing room used to measure sidereal time (the measurement of time using the stars), to the prized refracting telescope that still functions for demonstrations and is accompanied by displays of photographs it has taken of comets (it observed Halley's comet in 1910 and 1986) and nebulas, among other cosmic phenomena. There are no English explanations, so you might want to admire the highlights armed with the bilingual podcast tour (link provided above) produced by the *Shanghai Daily*, which gives you basic information about some of the displays, or you may simply want to admire the view from the highest point of the city.

Portrait of the Jesuit, Fr Johann Adam Schall von Bell who reformed the Chinese calendar

96

Shanghai Auto Museum

上海汽车博物馆 *Shanghai qiche bowuguan*

7565 Boyuan Rd, Anting Town, Jiading District, Shanghai

上海市安亭博园路7565号

Tel: (021) 6955 0055
Open: 9.30–16.30, last entry 15.30 except Mon; Tues–Fri groups only; Sat & Sun open to public
www.shautomuseum.gov.cn/
English audio guide
Kids

Deng Xiaoping on parade in a Red Flag (*Hongqi*) automobile

A Red Flag on display in the museum

Next to the USA, China has the world's largest car market – more than ten million cars made and sold in 2008 alone. Despite horrific pollution levels and gridlocked traffic, the Chinese public is mad for cars and car culture. This museum, only partially opened at the time of writing, is a vehicle lover's dream.

Located in the Auto Expo Park of the Shanghai International Automobile City the innovative museum design by Stuttgart's Atelier Brückner is based on the concept of an urban landscape. The layout of the exhibition is arranged as a street, complete with road markings that guide you through a time line of automobile history and innovation. The galleries and cases are sleek and smooth, mimicking an atmosphere of speed and aerodynamic design.

At the time of writing two of the five planned pavilions were open: the Antique Car Pavilion and the History Pavilion. Still to be opened were the Technology, Brand and Temporary Exhibition Pavilions.

In the Antique Car Pavilion are cars from France, Germany, Italy, Britain and the USA dating from 1904 to 1972 and including elegant classics such as a 1967 Jaguar XKE convertible, a 1923 Rolls Royce Ghost Phaeton and a 1936 BMW Cabriolet.

The galleries in the History Pavilion are divided by subject (mass production, racing and speed, energy saving etc.) and the design of each gallery reflects its subject. Appropriate cars are on display, so you will see a 1913 Model T Ford in the mass production gallery and a 1939 Lincoln Zephyr in the aerodynamic gallery.

There is also an exhibition of the fifty year history of the Chinese auto industry. There you will see some of China's classics, including a 1959 Red Flag (*Hongqi*) CA72 and a 1964 Shanghai SH760.

97

Shanghai Bank Museum

上海市银行博物馆 *Shanghaishi yinhang bowuguan*

7F, 9 Pudong Avenue, Shanghai
上海市浦东大道9号7楼

Tel: (021) 5878 8743
Open: 9.00–11.30 & 13.00–16.00, Mon–Fri, by appointment only to groups; open to individual visitors 13.00–16.00; best to ring ahead to confirm opening hours
www.icbcmuseum.com

A script note issued in Beijing; the financial hub of the north during the Qing

Coin tree with minted coins not yet cut from the stalk, Guangxu Reign of the Qing dynasty

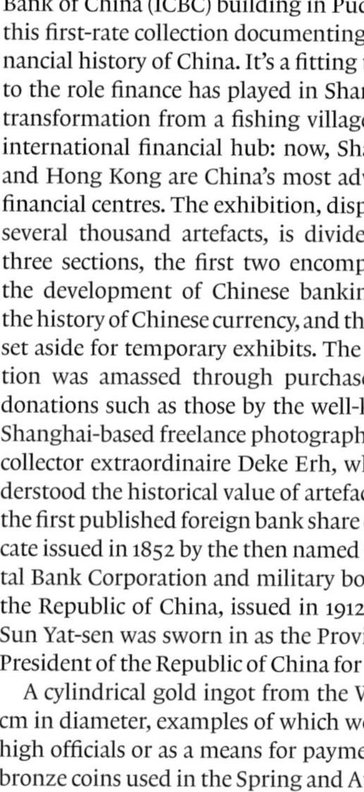

Housed in the Industrial and Commercial Bank of China (ICBC) building in Pudong is this first-rate collection documenting the financial history of China. It's a fitting tribute to the role finance has played in Shanghai's transformation from a fishing village to an international financial hub: now, Shanghai and Hong Kong are China's most advanced financial centres. The exhibition, displaying several thousand artefacts, is divided into three sections, the first two encompassing the development of Chinese banking and the history of Chinese currency, and the third set aside for temporary exhibits. The collection was amassed through purchases and donations such as those by the well-known Shanghai-based freelance photographer and collector extraordinaire Deke Erh, who understood the historical value of artefacts like the first published foreign bank share certificate issued in 1852 by the then named Oriental Bank Corporation and military bonds of the Republic of China, issued in 1912 when Sun Yat-sen was sworn in as the Provisional President of the Republic of China for the purpose of raising capital.

A cylindrical gold ingot from the Western Han dynasty measuring just 6 cm in diameter, examples of which would have been used as royal awards to high officials or as a means for payment, are shown alongside spade-shaped bronze coins used in the Spring and Autumn period, a knife-shaped *jincuodao* coin inlaid with gold from the Xin dynasty and a coin tree of the Qing dynasty showing the coins minted but not yet cut from the stalk; the twenty-one coins flanking both sides were not for general circulation but served as commemorative awards to high officials. Several hundred examples of paper money are on view, along with documents and photographs tracing the opening of Shanghai to foreign trade in 1843, accompanied by the establishment of British-funded banks, the first of which was the Oriental Bank Corporation in 1847. Major events in China's financial history are highlighted, such as the gold certificate issued in 1911 by Sun Yat-sen who sought to raise funds

in San Francisco for his campaign to overthrow the Manchu government. Issued in three denominations of 10, 100 and 1,000 yuan, after the Revolution he redeemed most of them, and others were either destroyed in public or kept as mementoes – hence today they are extremely rare.

Among the museum's treasures is the only volume in existence of Chinese specimens of bank notes published by the American Bank Note Company, recording successive issues of Chinese paper currencies between 1905 and 1949. It includes 1,113 specimens as ordered by fifty-four financial institutions, including Chinese banks, foreign banks and joint ventures, documenting each, with details such as the issuing bank, par value and printing date of each note. Associated equipment and instruments, such as a first-generation note-packaging machine dating from the 1950s, reminds us of the former time-consuming and demanding task of manual packaging of paper notes, while the first auto-teller machine installed in Shanghai in 1988 demonstrates how far the industry had come by then.

A 1,000-yuan gold certificate issued in 1911 by Sun Yat-sen to raise funds in San Francisco to overthrow the Manchu government

98

Shanghai Bund Museum

上海外滩历史博物馆 *Shanghai Waitan lishibowuguan*

1A Zhongshan East Road, Wai Tan (The Bund), Shanghai

上海市外滩中山东路1号

Tel: (021) 6321 6542; 5308 8987
Open: 9.00–16.30

No visitor to Shanghai misses a walk along the Bund – the iconic riverside strip of mostly 1920s and 1930s monumental edifices that was once known as the 'Wall Street of Asia' and gave this city its cosmopolitan hub. A visit to this museum located at the southern tip of the Bund is a good place to start your walk. A former signal tower and meteorological station built in 1884 and later remodelled, it is home to a modest selection of old photographs and maps showing scenes of the Bund dating back to the nineteenth century.

Take a look at the Ground Plan of the Foreign Settlement produced from a survey conducted by Mr F B Youel of the Royal Navy in May 1855. It illustrates the extent of the settlement of foreign nationals – here mostly under the British or American consulates – listing the names of the families, their companies, the ships and even the rents paid by the property owners. This was done just thirteen years after the signing of the Treaty of Nanking in 1842, which gave British residents the rights to reside and trade in the city. Jump ahead to 1923 and the panoramic photograph illustrating how quickly the city had developed by then and how years of frantic building work had transformed the

The Bund, c. 1920s

Bund and the surrounding area. The Bund now had a proper esplanade with an inner section for vehicles (complete with traffic jams) and a fine promenade with gardens. Foreign architects were numerous, and despite the problems of building on the Bund (there is no bedrock so building high was a real problem), the construction of Sassoon House, The Great Northern Telegraph Company Building and the Hongkong and Shanghai Bank, among others, was possible using concrete rafts underpinned by wooden piles.

Also on display is a series of individual photos of the key buildings along the Bund, with their sponsors and architects listed, and information on whether they are still standing. However, a walk along the Bund armed with a good map or guide is the best way to take in the opulence of the remaining buildings that represent the domination of foreign businesses in Shanghai before World War II. Although many are still home to prominent banks, these are now largely Chinese. Many of the main foreign banking and financial institutions are now found opposite the Bund in Lujiazui.

Do take a moment to visit the second floor, which sometimes shows films of early Shanghai, as well as the observation deck (not always open) on the third floor for an excellent view of the comings and goings along the Huangpu River.

99 Shanghai Duolun Cultural Street

上海市多伦路文化街 *Shanghaishi duolunlu wenhuajie*

Duolun Road, Shanghai
上海市多伦路
Office: 145 Duolun Road, Shanghai
上海市多伦路145号

Tel: (021) 5696 0178

Only a short walk south from Lu Xun Park, Duolun Road winds through a historic area of the Hongkou District. This area was originally part of the American Concession which eventually merged with the British Concession. By the

time the writer Lu Xun moved into the neighbourhood in the 1930s, Duolun Road was a popular enclave for progressive artists and writers (Mao Dun, Guo Moruo, Ding Ling), many of whom were part of the League of Leftist Writers, and was known as the cultural and literary centre of the city. The street has since been transformed into a pedestrian mall of galleries, bookshops, teahouses and historic homes. The Duolun Art Gallery (no. 27 Duolun Road, closed Mon), a museum of contemporary art, hosts travelling exhibitions and has a core collection of contemporary art across all media. The Old Film Café shows Chinese films from the 1920s and 1930s; and at Lane 201, no. 2, is the League of Leftist Writers Museum (daily 9.30–16.30; in Chinese only).

100 Shanghai Earthquake Museum

上海地震科普馆 *Shanghai dizhen kepuguan*

Sheshan Earthquake Observation Station, Sheshan Town, Songjiang District, Shanghai

上海市松江区佘山镇西佘山，佘山地震基准台内

Tel: (021) 5765 2473
Open: 8.30–16.00
www.shdzkp.cn (Chinese only)
Bilingual podcast: www.shanghaidaily.com/sciencepod/shEarthquakeMus.asp
Kids

China hardly needs reminding of the devastating effect of earthquakes. At the time of writing, only months have passed since it suffered one of the most powerful in modern times – along the Longmenshan belt in Sichuan Province, and with a magnitude of 7.9. The displays in this museum clearly illustrate the importance of and difficulties associated with the early prediction and detection of these formidable natural occurrences caused by movement of the earth's tectonic plates. Over the last hundred years China has suffered the highest number of quakes in the world. A map on display confirms that this is because China's landmass contains several major fault lines – the points at which earthquakes occur. Panels and accompanying images emphasize that preparation is crucial and, similar to other earthquake-prone cities, quake-

Scenes from the tragic 2008 Sichuan earthquake

proof buildings are being built in Shanghai and elsewhere in the country.

Old scientific instruments rub shoulders with more modern devices. There are those which were brought by the Jesuit missionaries when they founded the original monitoring station in 1873 in Xujiahui and installed the first telescope in China, located in the south of Shanghai. (Besides seismology the station also included astronomy, meteorology and magnetic science.) Then there is a working seismometer used to measure the intensity of an earthquake. Among the highlights of the collection is an instrument known as an electromagnetic field detector (or galvanometer), used for measuring current, manufactured in the 1870s by one of London's leading scientific instrument makers, Elliott Bros. Together with a selection of seismographs made in the last sixty years from countries across the globe are related documents recording earthquakes which made history, from Tokyo to San Francisco. There are also computers allowing you to watch documentaries on earthquakes and then to test your knowledge on what you have learnt. Do stop to examine a replica of what is the world's first seismograph, devised in AD 132 by Zhang Heng, a scholar who also held the post of Grand Astrologer. Having a method of predicting

such natural occurrences as earthquakes made him more effective in his role, for it was believed that there was a correlation between forces of nature and political events. This rather odd, egg-shaped contraption, originally 2 m in diameter, has eight dragons positioned around its middle, each with a bronze ball in its mouth. Below each dragon is a bronze toad, its mouth wide open. Allegedly, a tremor would cause the pendulum hanging in the centre to strike one of the dragons causing a ball to drop into the mouth of the toad below. Sceptical officials were proved wrong when several days after a ball fell from the mouth of one of the dragons, an earthquake hit.

101 Shanghai Jiangnan Shipbuilding Museum

江南造船博物馆 *Jiangnan zaochuan bowuguan*

2F and 3F Jiangnan Zaochuan Building,
600 Luban Road, Luwan District,
Shanghai
上海市卢湾区鲁班路600号江南造
船大厦2,3楼

Tel: (021) 6313 2500
Open: 9.00–17.00
www.jnmuseum.cn/ (Chinese only)
Kids

China's loss to the British navy's technological superiority during the First Opium War of 1839–42 clearly pointed to their need to modernize their army and navy. But it was not until after the Taiping rebellion of the 1850s and the foreign occupation of Beijing in 1860 that the humiliated Qing dynasty officials set their course, embracing Western technologies focused on improving its navy and military might. A champion of what became known as China's 'Self Strengthening Movement' was Li Hongzhang, a general and leading statesman. In 1864 he purchased a defunct American shipyard in Shanghai and amalgamated it with his already established cannon factory to establish the Jiangnan Arsenal. Fitting it out with machinery bought from America it was the first factory in China to implement mass production and is regarded as 'the cradle' of China's industry. Its subsequent success required a move to its present site on the Huangpu River where modern machinery turned out guns and ship armaments. It produced China's first steam warship in 1868 which was the beginning of the Jiangnan Shipyard. China's continued success in shipbuilding has recently necessitated yet another move to Changxing Island, on the mouth of the Yangtze River. This allows the shipyard to more than double its capacity to become among the largest in the world and the current site to be redeveloped for the 2010 World Expo. The company's technical centre, where the current museum is located, will remain and plans are in place to build an industry-themed museum in the old workshop of the shipyard.

Li Hongzhang, one of China's first industrialists

Using technical drawings and designs, models, images and replicas interspersed with interactive displays and English signage, the exhibitions provide visitors with a chronological synopsis of China's shipbuilding history and related technological developments. The space is divided into two parts, the first from the point of its establishment through to 1949 when the Communists took command of Shanghai from the

KMT who retreated destroying the entire facility in their wake. The second celebrates China's achievements post 1949 up to the present. Highlights focus on the ground-breaking accomplishments of the facility, from the production in 1888 of the country's earliest wrought-iron Armstrong breech-loading cannon invented by the English engineer, Sir William Armstrong, to pictures of China's first lathe, a crucial machine tool used to perform precision machining operations and key to mass production. More modern 'firsts' for China include a model of the Minzhong, the largest and fastest passenger ship of her time. Built in 1954 she was capable of carrying up to 968 passengers and had installed the country's first designed and made electro-hydraulic steering gear. Additional photos explain China's history of submarine development with the Soviet Union playing a crucial role. Not only did they train a team of Chinese submariners in 1951, but sold them several old submarines in 1954, which were the beginnings of their force, and later in 1956 supplied parts for the first type-03 sub which was assembled at this shipyard and deployed to the People's Liberation Navy under the name New China 15. A visit to the yard by Mao Zedong during its assembly underscored his keenness to develop a submarine force as a national priority.

Children will enjoy the interactive software which allows you to build a virtual ship and customize it by painting it with a colour of your choice, as well as the replica of a submarine command centre which visitors can enter to get a feel for life down under.

102

Shanghai Kids' Museum

上海儿童博物馆 *Shanghai ertong bowuguan*

61 Songyuan Road, Changning District, Shanghai

上海市长宁区宋园路61号

Tel: (021) 6278 3127 / 3130
Open: 8.30–17.00 Tues–Sun; last entry 15.45
www.shetbwg.com (Chinese only)
Shop / publications / brochure in Chinese with a map of the museum with main points of interest identified in English
Kids

The Shanghai Kids' Museum has a hands-on approach to learning that encourages children to not only look but also to touch just about everything in sight. There are few explanations in English, but the museum's focus on interactive exhibits means language is not really a problem.

The first floor includes the Space Hall, Nautical Hall and Planetarium, which has a ceiling video screen. The Nautical Hall has a toy submarine for children to play in, a large

screen that allows users to choose a boat – from a selection of old Chinese sampans to modern-day container ships – which they can then steer through large waves that break against the ship. There is also a good collection of model boats from different periods of history. The Space Hall contains a series of Chinese space ships, training equipment for astronauts and other exhibits.

On the second floor is the Interactive Exploration Area, with interactive screens and a robotic arm children can play with. The costume room and stage allows children to dress up and perform, and they can record themselves with a camera as well as control the lighting and sound effects. There is also a mock grocery shop, doctor's office, beauty salon and dentist's office to play in. In addition to a computer room there is a reading room with weekly storytelling in Chinese and English. The museum has astronomy and satellite demonstrations five times a day.

103

Shanghai Lu Xun Memorial Hall and Final Residence

上海鲁迅纪念馆（鲁迅故居）*Shanghai Lu Xun jinianguan (Lu Xun guju)*

Museum: 200 Tian'ai Road, Hongkou District, Shanghai

上海市虹口区甜爱路200号

Residence: Shanyin Road, No. 9, Lane 2, Hongkou District, Shanghai

山阴陆2弄9号

Tel: (021) 6540 2288; 5666 2608 (residence)
Open: 9.00–17.00; last entry 16.00
www.shcrm.com.cn/SHCRM/luxun/default.htm (Chinese only)
Bookshop / English-speaking guide available at the house only

Lu Xun (1881–1936) was a famous left-wing Chinese writer of the first half of the twentieth century. In October 1927, he left Beijing for Shanghai, where he spent the last decade of his life.

The museum was originally housed in Lu Xun's final home in Shanyin Road, where he lived from 1933 until his death – in a very interesting new–style experimental housing development called Continental Terrace, which was completed in 1932. Now, the house contains little more than some simple furniture, a few objects and the respirator that he used during his final illness, but it has a certain charm which, combined with its literary associations and the unusual building, definitely makes it worth a visit.

The museum was moved in 1956 to the nearby park, now named after Lu Xun, which also contains his monumental tomb. A new building was opened in 1999, which is rather too grand and appears somewhat overblown in comparison with the simplicity of the house. It contains a thorough pictorial record of Lu Xun's life, his studies in Japan, his role in the New Culture Movement and his membership of the League of Leftist Writers. It is revealing that he insisted on the translation and publication of Western writers in Chinese. There is also a good collection of woodcut illustrations, contemporary magazines and books, and historic photographs – and some rather startling waxwork recreations of Lu Xun and his colleagues. The English signage is unreliable and the visitor should preferably have an interest in twentieth-

Lu Xun in 1933

century Chinese writing.

The introduction states that 'The Museum is the National Exemplary Base for Patriotism Education, and is one of the dedicated places for the Red Tour of Shanghai which is to help travellers learn about our history and understand patriotism education.' More prosaically, however, the New Culture Movement, which is well documented in the museum, made a great contribution to Chinese communist culture, introducing the thoughts of the early German philosophers, and the likes of John Dewey and Bertrand Russell, as well as the Russians and the Marxists.

104 Shanghai Museum

上海博物馆 *Shanghai bowuguan*

201 Renmin Avenue (Renmin Square), Shanghai

上海市人民大道201号 (人民广场)

Tel: (021) 9696 8686 / 6372 3500
Open: 9.00–17.00; last entry 16.00
www.shanghaimuseum.net/
Bookshop / gift shop / restaurant

The Shanghai Museum was the first museum of modern China of outstanding international quality – in terms of wealth of collection, display and architecture.

Originally built in 1952 on the site of the old racecourse, it re-opened in 1993 in a startling new building in People's Square in the heart of central Shanghai. Designed by the architect Xing Tonghe, the building has a circular top on a square base, reflecting the Chinese cosmological belief in a square earth under a round sky. It also resembles a *ding*, one of the most important forms of the ancient funerary bronzes that are among the glories of the collection. The design of the building is thus a wholly modern exercise on an ancient Chinese form, with a cosmological reference tying it to one of the fundamentals of Chinese philosophy.

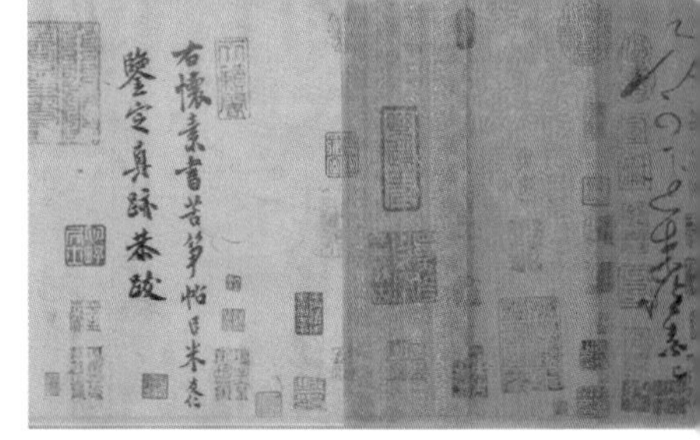

The museum is situated opposite the new City Hall and the new Opera House. It provides an iconic symbol of the staggering new wealth, power and taste of the city of Shanghai, which

Gold-plated stone statue of Buddha, Liang dynasty (546)

was, already by the early 1990s, as it has remained, the most potent engine driving the startling recent economic renaissance of China today.

The building was financed largely by the Shanghai City government. The collections have been hugely enhanced by a large number of gifts from outside China, many from prominent overseas Chinese collectors.

There are nine major collections, all important and representative, with items of the highest quality: the ancient Bronze Collection is unique. The Ceramics Collection and the Painting and Calligraphy Collection are also of outstanding national importance. Other galleries are devoted to seals, jades, Ming and Qing furniture, coins, and the arts and crafts of the minority nationalities.

On the ground floor, the first gallery is devoted to the whole of the history and art of the ancient Chinese bronze from the eighteenth to the seventh century BC.

Early bronzes were intimately linked with the religious and political structures of their time as, aside from weapons, they were designed and made for sacrificial and other ritual ceremonies. They are cast in bronze to an astonishing degree of skill; their colours, shapes and very presence give an air of ancient mystery which in this display is perfectly brought out by the presentation and lighting. A visit to the bronzes in the Shanghai Museum is one of the great experiences to be enjoyed by the visitor to the museums of China. There are many national treasures, such as the famous *Da Ke Ding*.

Also on the ground floor is the sculpture collection, filled with masterpieces of all types and periods. From tomb figurines and carved stones, to Buddhist cave and temple sculptures, the collection also contains representational pieces from all periods from the Warring States period to the Qing.

The first floor is entirely devoted to porcelain and ceramics, with masterpieces from all the major kilns – from the exquisitely carved earthenware of Liangzhu Neolithic Culture, through stoneware and then porcelain from the Tang and Song periods, to the products of Jingdezhen imperial kiln in the Ming and Qing periods. The collection covers the complete history of Chinese ceramics.

The *Kusun Letter*, Tang dynasty (737–799)

The calligraphy and painting collections exhibited on the second floor are said to comprise half the total collection from southern China. The calligraphic masterpieces include the *Yatouwan Letter* by Wang Xianzhi; the *Kusun Letter* by Huaisu; the Tang period *Thousand Character Classic*, in cursive script, by Gao Xian; and the Song period *Landscape after a Poem by Du Fu*, by Zhao Kui.

The Ming and Qing painting and calligraphy collections represent a comprehensive history of this period. Paintings such as Sun Wei's *Hermits* and Liang Kai's *Eight Eminent Monks* are world treasures, while the Ming and Qing painting collection is unsurpassed. There are earlier works such as *Retreat in the Blue Bian Mountains* by Wang Meng of the Yuan. The Shanghai Museum also has more works than any other Chinese museum of the so-called 'The Ming Masters' and 'The Four Wangs of the Qing'.

There is also a fascinating collection of the oldest writing discovered in China, which was found inscribed on oracle bones from the Shang period site of Yinxu. These inscriptions were carved on tortoise plastrons and animal bones and provide a record of the history of the Shang dynasty 3,000 years ago. And there is a collection of early pre-Han books made from wooden or bamboo strips inscribed with one or more lines of writing and strung together to form a continuous text.

Also on the second floor is the Chinese seal gallery. Chinese seals combine the arts of calligraphy and carving, and are praised in Chinese as showing 'thousands of variations within a square inch'. Shanghai Museum's seal collection, comprising around 13,000 items, is special as it is comprehensive and representative of Chinese seal history.

On the third floor there are galleries dedicated to jades, Ming and Qing furniture, the art of the minority peoples and to Chinese coins.

Jade plays a key role in Chinese civilization. China was not only the first culture in the world to carve jade, and the stone was also linked from the earliest times with religious, ritual and political influence. Not only did it have a decorative function, it was also used as a symbol of wealth and power, for talismans by rulers making offerings to heaven and earth, for instruments of communication with the ancestors and for charms for the dead to fend off evil spirits.

Square mirror with inlaid geometric pattern, Warring States period

Bronze *you*, Early Western Zhou

The furniture gallery contains pieces from two great masters, Wang Shixiang and Chen Mengjia.

The exhibition of the art of the minority cultures of China includes works of art, religious art, folk art and items for everyday use, including jewellery, clothes and textiles.

The Shanghai Museum coin collection has one million items, and is renowned for its quality.

In addition to all of the above, the museum has a fine collection of lacquer ware, tapestry and embroidery, and bamboo, wood, ivory and rhinoceros horn carvings.

105 Shanghai Museum of Arts and Crafts

上海工艺美术博物馆 *Shanghai gongyi meishu bowuguan*

79 Fengyang Road, Xuhui District,
Shanghai

上海市 徐汇区汾阳路79号

Tel: (021) 6431 4074 / 6437 3454
Open: 9.00–16.30
Kids

A range of folk crafts are demonstrated, displayed and sold

This museum was established by the Shanghai Arts and Crafts Research Institute to promote traditional arts and crafts and the work of new artisans. There is a small collection of arts and crafts displayed in glass cases on the first floor, some with good English descriptions. The tiny pieces of ivory carved with several thousand Chinese characters visible only through a magnifying glass are especially interesting. Many of the items on display, as well as some antiques in the basement, are for sale.

A special feature of the museum is that it has a number of artisans working on site who can be observed as they work at their crafts: embroidery, woollen needlepoint, paper-cutting, lacquer ware, ivory and wood carving, dough modelling and the making of snuff bottles and opera costumes.

The museum building, a late French Renaissance mansion built in 1905, is worth visiting in itself. Set in a beautiful garden it was originally built for a high-ranking French official working in the French settlement. The structure was restored in 2002 and is today a protected historical site.

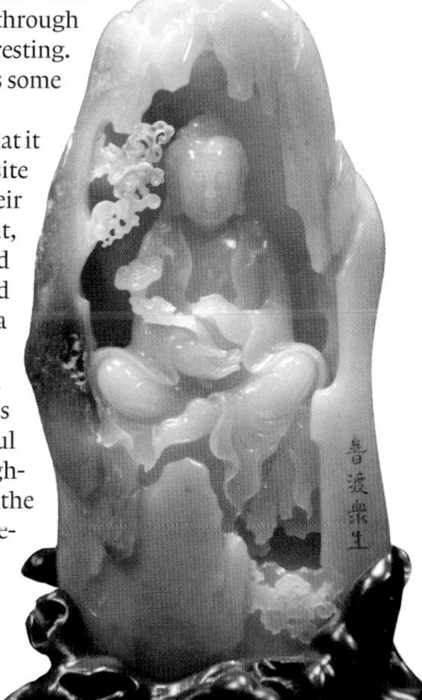

106

Shanghai Museum of Public Security

上海公安博物馆 *Shanghai gongan bowuguan*

518 Ruijin South Road, Shanghai
上海市瑞金南路518号

Tel: (021) 6472 0256
Open: 9.00–16.30 Mon–Sat; last entry 16.00
www.policemuseum.com.cn/

This museum traces the history of the police force in Shanghai, from the establishment of the city's first police department in 1854 to the People's Republic of China. The collection of 3,000 items is arranged over the second, third and fourth floors. There is a description in English at the entrance to each floor but unfortunately none of the items on display have English descriptions. In fact, many speak for themselves and need no introduction.

The old city of Shanghai had an infamous reputation as a centre for drug selling, gambling and prostitution, populated with gangsters such as Pockmarked Huang and Big-eared Du (he sent coffins to the establishments of potential clients), and this museum provides some interesting illustrations of the bad old days.

The second floor of the museum draws you immediately into the past. The first exhibit is a reconstructed old Shanghai Street, complete with cobblestones and antique iron manhole covers emblazoned with the word 'England' and the cryptic letters 'S.M.C.' and 'P.W.D.'. There are life-sized wax statues of red-turbaned, bearded Sikh policemen standing beside pith-helmeted British police officers, part of the international force that once patrolled the old International Settlement. Nearby, an old fire hydrant stands along the sidewalk. According to the sign, the Kuomintang (KMT), or Nationalist, police used water from the fire hydrant to 'suppress mass protests' before liberation in 1949.

There is also a beautiful selection of pistols on display: a small one neatly hidden away in a musical instrument box in true gangster style, an elaborately engraved pistol once owned by Sun Yat-sen and a small pistol with a folding gold handle that was once deftly hidden up the sleeve of 1930s crime boss Pockmocked Huang. Huang had little to worry about in any case: he also served as the chief detective for the French Sûreté.

A display case exhibits a book with the centre of its pages neatly cut out to hide secret documents or paraphernalia. Two stuffed pigeons, used for secret communication in the 1950s, sit in another glass case. A Minox spy camera, no longer than an index finger, was used by an unnamed Chinese operative; no details are provided.

Jiang Qing, the difficult wife of the Great Helmsman, and Lin Biao, former heir apparent to the Chairman until he allegedly attempted a coup in 1971, are vilified in another exhibit for the harm they did to the city's police system during the chaotic days of the Cultural Revolution.

Other displays include antique police equipment: a protective vest made of bamboo tubes, antique handcuffs, leg irons and thumb rings.

There are also confiscated 'evil' artefacts: an old roulette wheel from the city's wild past, drug paraphernalia including an opium pipe, name cards for some of the city's former ladies of the night, and 'pornographic' material, including a porcelain vase displaying erotic scenes.

The third floor introduces criminology, including gruesome photos and

descriptions of some of the most famous crimes in the city. There is the bloody *'chaotou an'* or 'knock on the head case' in which a serial killer terrified Shanghai's female population by beating women on the head with an axe. Rumour had it that the murderer had a penchant for women with long hair, a rumour that is said to have given the local hair-cutting business a significant economic boost.

The museum offers a detailed description of the city's first bank robbery, which was carried out by a modern-day Bonnie and Clyde in the early 1980s. The police killed him, and she served a prison term, later becoming a popular singer after her release. And there is the 1996 case of best-selling author Dai Houying, who was mysteriously murdered in her home along with her niece by a robber.

There is a model prison cell and an authentic day-by-day prison menu, which included green peppers and shredded meat, pickled vegetable and egg drop soup.There's even a special chair used for police interrogations, which has a wooden plank running across the lap to keep suspects securely in place during questioning, and the actual form used by Shanghai university students to apply for permission to hold demonstrations following the NATO bombing of the Chinese Embassy in Belgrade in 1999.

The fourth floor is dedicated to firefighters and firefighting equipment, hero police officers, police uniforms and equipment, and a large selection of guns and rifles.

The display of old firefighting equipment includes an antiquated manual pumping tank, complete with hoses and wooden buckets, much like the ones seen in films set at the turn of the twentieth century. In addition, there are straw conical hats once worn by firefighters, and more modern metal firemen's helmets with the city districts written on them in Chinese. There is also a wonderful collection of replicas of classic old fire trucks. The collection of captured weapons includes pistols, rifles, shot guns and machine guns.

107

Shanghai Natural History Museum

上海科技馆自然博物分馆 *Shanghai kejiguan ziran bowufenguan*

260 Yan'an East Road, near Henan Road, Shanghai

上海市延安东路260号

Tel: (021) 6321 3548

Open: 9.00–17.00 Tues–Sun; last entry 15.30

Note: A new museum is scheduled to open in 2010 in Jingan Sculpture Park, west of Chengdu North Road, north of Beijing East Road, east of Shimen Er Road, south of Shanhaiguan Road

位于静安雕塑公园内成都北路以西，北京东路以北，石门二路以东，山海关路以南

Kids

Plans are afoot to inaugurate a new museum in time for the 2010 World Expo in Shanghai, but for now visitors have to be content with the rather charming presentations of dated exhibits here, which include sections on human evolution and primitive civilizations (unfortunately, with very little English signage). Cases brimming with taxidermy, fossils, plants, several

Displays of animal skulls overseen by its founder, Heude, in the Siccawei Museum

notable mummies (including ones from the Tarim Basin in Xinjiang) and a collection of dinosaur skeletons are well worth a look, as are the mosaic floors and stained-glass windows in the building that was formerly the Cotton Exchange (from the late nineteenth to the early twentieth centuries cotton production was a major industry in Shanghai).

The new museum is planned to be state-of-the-art – both architecturally, as well as in the way it communicates its contents – using modern museum techniques to optimize the collection. Ecologically designed with geothermal heating and other energy-saving technologies, it will consist of four floors (two underground). Exhibits will include a collection of rare and endangered mammals from across the globe donated by the American, Kenneth Behring.

The origins of this collection can largely be credited to the French Jesuit missionary-cum-naturalist, Pierre Heude (1836–1902), who arrived in Shanghai in 1868. He was more interested in collecting than converting and until just before his death, organized numerous expeditions, not only in China, but also the Philippines, French Indo-China (now Vietnam), Japan and other nearby countries, assembling specimens of plants, fish, birds, mammals and molluscs (he published several volumes which identified many new species of molluscs in China). Passionate about zoology, he focused on the systematic collecting and studying of mammals. Heude, along with other fellow missionaries, set up the precursor to this museum in 1868 in the Xujiahui District of Shanghai (also as Zikawei) in what was then the French Concession District. Known as the Xujiahui Museum (also as Siccawei Museum or Musée de Zikawei), its English name was the Museum of Natural History. It was the first museum built by a Westerner and the earliest museum in China. It predates the Nantong Museum, established in 1905, regarded by many as China's first museum. In 1874, it was integrated with the Shanghai Museum, a museum founded by the North China Branch of the Royal Asiatic Society, and after being relocated several times, became the Shanghai Natural History Museum in 1956.

An international team of zoologists has recently rediscovered crates containing over 100 lost type specimens (original skeletal material used to identify a species) collected by Heude. Uncatalogued and languishing in the bowels of this museum and the Beijing Institute of Zoology, they included a rare dwarf species of a buffalo (*Bubalus mindorernsis*) native to the Philippines and now almost extinct, as well as a species of pig (*Sus cebifrons*), also from the Philippines and first identified by Heude.

108

Shanghai Postal Museum

上海邮政博物馆 *Shanghai youzheng bowuguan*

250 North Suzhou Road, Hongkou District, Shanghai

上海市虹口区北苏州路250号

Tel: (021) 6306 0798
Open: 9.00–17.00 Wed, Thurs, Sat & Sun; last entry 16.00; groups must make an appointment
English guides available upon request in advance

Very rare stamp (only nine examples known) of 1897 '2 cents' surcharge in green on '3 cents' red

Shanghai's Central Post Office houses on its second floor a museum on the history of postal services in China, along with an outstanding collection of mostly Chinese stamps, from the rare to the beautiful. The 1924 classical building, by the architects Stewardson & Spence, is among the finest of its type in Shanghai, with its Ionic colonnades and 150-foot clock tower featuring Hermes and two maidens.

The rather majestic staircase leads to the first floor, where you can visit the business area of what continues to be the most comprehensive postal service in Shanghai. Its tasteful interior is a mixture of original fittings, including the black and white tiled floors, light fittings and decorative plaster ceilings, while the brass tellers' screens and marble counter tops are new additions. To the far right of this expansive space is the entrance to the museum's exhibition halls, well signposted and with almost all labels and signage in both Chinese and English. The outstanding collection of postal objects, uniforms, post boxes, letters and general postal memorabilia was donated by past and present postal staff and amassed from acquisitions made by the China Philatelic Association. Many of the objects associated with particular individuals were donated by the people themselves or their relatives, from around 1896 when the postal services began.

Displays are chronological, starting with cases of objects, illustrations and dioramas depicting the origins and development of the postal service. Zhu Xuefan, who was the People's Republic of China's first Minister of Post and Communications from 1949 until 1969 and the onset of the Cultural Revolution, is honoured in a display of personal objects, including his inkwell and brush pot. There are copies of oracle bones inscribed with records of the delivery of military information by beating drums during the Shang dynasty, which evolved into a more sophisticated means of communication during the Zhou dynasty, when messages were relayed by couriers on foot or horseback between the various states via station posts. During the Song dynasty, beacon fires set up along the Great Wall warned of impending attacks and this is illustrated in a large diorama. During this dynasty, official documents were delivered exclusively by soldiers. During the Yongle period (1403–1424) in the Ming dynasty, the first private mail service in China began in Zhejiang province. Later, during the Qianlong to the Jiaqing periods (1736–1820), the private mail services became chaotic and were used for smuggling goods, including

Stewardson & Spence's Shanghai Central Post Office, 1924

drugs. Notices, including the one issued in 1922 ordering all private services to close, are on display, as is the final mandate issued by the State Postal Bureau.

One of the leading lights of China's customs service was the Briton Robert Hart (1835–1911), who spent from 1868 to 1907 in Peking fostering China's naval development and schools, and setting up the country's Western-style postal service in 1896. A portrait of Hart is on display, with a model of the customs house where he worked. There are also displays of the first stamps issued in China in 1878, when the post office of the Qing dynasty produced the Giant Dragon stamps, along with the first commemorative stamps from 1884 celebrating the sixtieth birthday of the Empress Dowager Cixi. Designs submitted for the Central Post Office competition, including the winning ones, are on display; postal labour movements and strikes are documented; distinctively coloured post boxes from across the globe are on display, with scales and an automatic parcel sorting machine from the 1950s, shown working at the press of a button. Cases crammed with personal letters written by famous people remind us of a now largely forgotten means of communication, while large displays of stamps from every corner of the world vie for space alongside commemorative stamps including those issued in 2000 to mark China's first unmanned spaceship. Others incorporate the latest technology, such as the Swiss stamps which smell of chocolate!

The last gallery, or Treasure Room, with its state-of-the-art lighting and humidity control, is a stamp collector's dream, with rotating exhibits of outstanding examples of both Chinese and foreign stamps, from Britain's Penny Black to one of only ten known examples of a faulty stamp produced in the Qing dynasty.

A courtyard space shows off replica mail vehicles and a carriage used for delivering post in the Qing dynasty, while a nearby elevator waits to take you to the roof garden for the most spectacular view of the city and a chance to examine the figures at the base of the clock tower, including Hermes with his staff, his *kerykeion*.

109

Shanghai Propaganda Poster Art Centre

上海宣传画艺术中心 *Shanghai xuanchuanhua yishuzhongxin*

Room OC, Building B, 868 Huashan Road, Shanghai

上海市华山路*868* 号*B* 座*OC*室

Open: 10.00–16.30
Tel: (021) 6211 1845

In 1966 Mao Zedong launched his 'Cultural Revolution' to claw back political power after the failure of the Great Leap Forward and in the process purged Liu Shaoqi, then Chairman of the PRC. Mao was

Situated in a basement flat in an apartment block on Huashan Road, in the former French Concession, this place is not easy to find. There are two rooms, one a shop and one housing an exhibition showing many of the 5,000 posters, cards and printed memorabilia collected by Mr Yang Peiming. Many originals and reproductions are on sale in the shop, at fairly stiff prices.

The poster art, covering the history of the Revolution from 1949 to the death of Mao in 1976, is displayed in chronological order. Certain themes emerge: the early pride in the Revolution: the promotion of hatred towards intellectuals and 'rightists'; the cult of personality and

Chairman of the Party. The first poster shows, left to right, the four top leaders of China during the 1950s: Zhu De, Zhou Enlai, Mao Zedong and Liu Shaoqi. The second poster, published later, shows the same scene with Liu Shaoqi removed, reflecting his downfall

the apotheosis of the Great Helmsman himself and the rhetoric and destruction of the Cultural Revolution.

The best of this art reflected either German expressionist graphics of the 1920s or the poster art of the Russian revolution. These were mingled with various sentimental representations of happy peasants and workers.

Chinese propaganda art of this period was not amongst the greatest, but it certainly gives a vivid picture of the changing aspirations of political leadership during the lifetime of Mao.

110

Shanghai Science and Technology Museum

上海科技馆 *Shanghai kejiguan*

2000 Shiji Avenue, Pudong New Area, Shanghai

上海市浦东新区世纪大道2000号

Tel: (021) 6854 3044
Open: 9.00–17.15 except Mon
www.sstm.org.cn
Cafés / movie theatres: IMAX Dome; IWERKS 4D; IMAX 3D / gift shops throughout
Kids

It would not be difficult to spend the entire day at this goliath of a museum, which features twelve exhibition halls and four movie theatres. A must-see for anyone travelling with children, there is something for every budding scientist. The Spectrum of Life has exhibits on animal species from all the continents; a selection of Yunnan habitats including the Stone Forest (with a bat cave) and a rainforest; and a labyrinthine exhibit on insects, amphibians and microscopic creatures. Earth Exploration uncovers geological mysteries, with engaging displays on natural phenomena such as earthquakes and volcanoes; understanding tectonic processes; and the make-up and uses of minerals, including a particularly good exhibit on coal. The Home on Earth exhibit focuses on sustainable development and protecting our ecological resources.

There are hands-on activities and a play area for the youngest visitors in Children's Science Land. For older children and their parents there are a number of interactive modules in the Light of Wisdom, AV Paradise and Cradle of Design areas, where you can create your own audiovisual products or or design items using lasers and CAD (computer-assisted design) programs, which may be purchased separately on admission. Technology is also a significant component of the Space Navigation, Information Era and World of Robots sections, all of which have a variety of demonstrations, short films and educational modules. The Hall on Human Health features interactive modules, with (free) health and exercise testing. The one exhibit found to be lacking was Light of Exploration, which explores scientific exploration and the history of science and which inexplicably did not contain many opportunities to experience basic hands-on experiments in gravity, electricity and force that are common in most science museums.

111 Shanghai Urban Planning Exhibition Centre

上海市城市规划展览馆 *Shanghaishi chengshiguihua zhanlanguan*

100 Renmin Avenue, Huangpu District, Shanghai

上海市黄埔区人民大道*100*号

Tel: (021) 6372 2077 / 6318 4477

Open: 9.00–17.00 Mon–Thurs; 9.00–18.00 Fri–Sun

Scale model of Shanghai 2020

Depending on your interest in either Shanghai or urban planning issues, this recently opened (2006) modern museum should have something to offer, with a large detailed scale model of 2020 Shanghai on the third floor, exhibits on proposed future transportation systems, including the magnetic levitation train (the Maglev), subway and light-rail trains, and plans to replace ageing housing (hovels) with modern apartment blocks. If your interests lie more in historic

preservation, there are some photographs of old Shanghai and a small exhibit on preserving Shanghai's architectural legacy. There are exhibition spaces for rotating exhibitions and a café on the fifth floor with a good view of the park. The underground level that connects to the Metro has 1930s-style restaurants and shops.

112

Shanghai Zendai Museum of Modern Art

上海证大现代艺术馆 *Shanghai zhengda xiandaiyishuguan*

No. 199 Lane, No. 28 Fangdian Road,
Pudong New Area, Shanghai

上海市浦东新区芳甸路199弄28号

Tel: (021) 5033 9801
Open: 10.00–18.00 Tues–Sun; until 21.00 Wed & free entry
www.zendaiart.com

You will know you are approaching the entrance to Pudong's Zendai MoMA when you see Robert Indiana's sculpture, *LOVE*, and Cesar Baldaccini's *THUMB*, standing proud in the pedestrian mall, called Thumb Plaza. Sandwiched between several uninspiring modernist buildings, this gallery has an ambitious and energetic mission to bring cutting-edge contemporary art – painting, sculpture, video and performance – to the attention of the public and to challenge conventional methods of doing it. Recently, the museum curated a work called 'Intrude: Art and Life 366 Project', which consisted of 366 art events all over the city in locations public and private, one for each day of the year. It featured many well-known artists and curators in China and showcased all manner of arts, from the visual to performance. The aim was to engage the whole country in a particular piece thereby capturing and hopefully cultivating its interest in avant-garde artistic output.

The museum aims to hold five major exhibitions a year focusing on emerging Asian artists. It has inaugurated an 'art bank', giving space and exposure to many young artists. In addition, it attaches great importance to the education department and has a library open to the public. A stated mission of the museum is to not only exhibit art but also to establish an 'art platform' in China – in other words, an increased awareness and appreciation of the contempo-

Avant–garde art on display

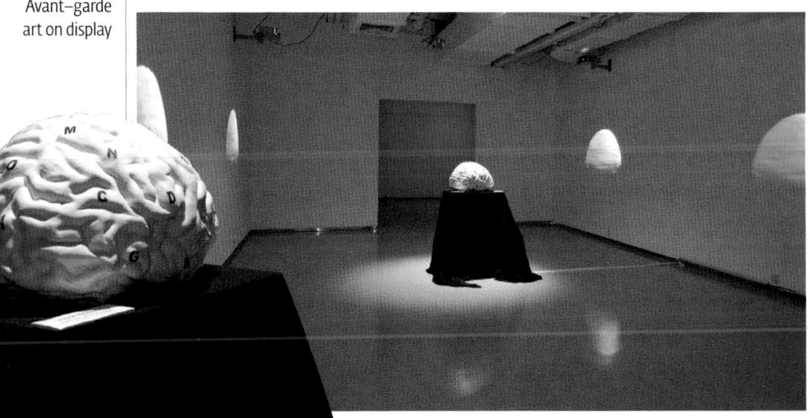

rary scene. The exhibitions it holds often push the envelope in terms of government acceptability; several shows have been deemed offensive and shut down.

A former warehouse, the museum's expansive white spaces, with exposed ducting, provide a very contemporary backdrop for both visiting exhibitions and the permanent collection of sculpture, paintings, videos and multimedia currently numbered at 200 and growing. This non-profit museum, founded in 2005, is sponsored by the Zendai Group, a privately owned security investment and real estate development enterprise based in Shanghai and known for its support of Chinese contemporary art.

In its efforts to expand its educational mission regarding contemporary art, and to keep Chinese contemporary art in China, the Zendai Group plans to open in 2010 the largest museum in Shanghai, The Zendai Museum of Modern Art, which will be the centrepiece of the Zendai Himalayas Centre – a cultural centre that will also include a performance hall, office space for designers and an 'art hotel' (see Stop Press).

Check local listings for temporary exhibitions at the Zendai MoMA.

113

Shikumen Open House Museum

石库门博物馆（屋里厢）*Shikumen bowuguan (wulixiang)*

No. 25 Lane, 181 Taicang Road, Shanghai
上海市太仓路181弄25号

Tel: (021) 3307 0337
Open: 10.30–22.30 Sun–Thurs; 11.00–23.00 Fri & Sat

The *tingzijian* – a small room often rented out to artists and writers

Located in the heart of Shanghai's Xintiandi District – a complex of reconfigured heritage buildings redeveloped into luxury boutiques, bars and restaurants – is a museum of the city's unique and once ubiquitous Shikumen or lane houses.

The origin of Shikumen buildings can be traced to the 1860s, when the Taiping Rebellion led to a surge in the refugee population in Shanghai and an increased need for housing. Due to the scarcity of available land, many of the houses were constructed close together in rows of the Shikumen style, which was a mixture of Chinese and foreign styles of architecture. At their peak, Shikumen-style housing accounted for 60 per cent of the total housing in Shanghai. This remained the case until the city's economic resurgence, beginning in the 1990s, which resulted in the demolition of tens of thousands of these houses. As with the destruction of the *hutongs* in Beijing, the whole character of Shanghai has changed with the destruction of the Shikumen neigbourhoods.

This museum offers an opportunity to see how the Shanghainese lived when the Shikumen was in its prime in the early twentieth century. Arranged over two floors, the museum comprises two separate parts: a restored Shi Ku Men unit sumptuously furnished with authentic period pieces from the 1920s and 1930s, and a modern exhibition space. Entry into the museum is not through the original stone doorway (or Shikumen, from which the building type derives its name), but via a side entrance. Beyond the small ticket hall visitors pass through the reception hall, living room, downstairs bedroom and rear kitchen before climbing the stairs to the second floor and passing the celebrated *tingzijian* – a small and inhospitable room often rented to artists and writers. Mao Dun, Lu Xun, Ding Ling and others lived in such rooms, and their writings of this period are known as '*tingzijian* literature'. Upstairs is the study and two master bedrooms. Next to the study, which overlooks the small courtyard at the front of the building, is an exhibition space illustrating the history of the Shikumen and the development of Xintiandi.

114 Soong Ching Ling Mausoleum

宋庆龄陵园 *Song Qingling lingyuan*

21 Songyuan Road, Changning District, Shanghai

上海市长宁区宋园路21号

Tel: (021) 6278 3104
Open: 8.30–17.00

Soong Ching Ling (Song Qingling), the wife of Sun Yat-sen, passed away in Beijing in 1981 at the age of ninety. In front of her tomb, where she is buried alongside her parents and a former maid, is a white marble statue of her surrounded by her favourite camphor trees. The adjoining International Cemetery contains the graves of some 600 famous foreigners who lived in the city prior to 1949, including members of the well-known Kadoorie and Sassoon families.

A small museum beside the tomb houses a collection of hundreds of black and white photographs documenting Mme Soong's life, as well as some of her personal effects, including memorabilia from Wesleyan Female College where she studied in the USA.

Soong Mei Ling ('loved power') and her husband, Chiang Kai-shek

The Soong Sisters

The three Soong sisters, Ching Ling, Mei Ling and Ai Ling played an enormous role in the Chinese Republic (1911–1949) as influential and charismatic wives of its leaders. Born to a wealthy banker called Charlie Soong, who was a Christian, their life paths were to lead in very diverse directions. There is a glib saying (which feeds the Communist view on the three women), which nonetheless sheds light on their roles and their marriages: Mei Ling 'loved power'. She married Nationalist Party (KMT) strong man Chiang Kai-shek, who converted to Christianity. She was very much the power behind the throne in the National Government and even after the KMT's flight to Taiwan she continued to espouse the anti-Communist cause in Washington.

Ai Ling 'loved money'. She married H H Kung, the enormously wealthy Minister of Finance at the heart of the party's business interests.

'But Ching Ling loved China' (this is the Communist punch-line to this saying). She married Sun Yat-sen, first President of the Republic. After her husband's death in 1925, her politics took a leftist, pro-Soviet direction, with her leading a split in the KMT and ultimately aligning herself with the Communist Party and becoming a prominent 'non-Communist' figure in the post-1949 government.

Today, with the mainland trying to get Taiwan back in the fold, the fierce Communist polemics against Mei Ling have subsided, and tourists can visit her wartime home in Chongqing. The story of these three sisters remains one of great significance and fascination.

115

Sun Yat-sen's Former Residence and Museum

孙中山故居纪念馆 *Sun Zhongshan guju jinianguan*

No. 7 Xiangshan Road, Shanghai
上海市香山路7号

Tel: (021) 6437 2954
Open: 9.00–16.00
www.sunyat-sen.org/

Sun Yat-sen is considered the father of Republican China and, as such, is one of the most important figures in modern Chinese history. He and his wife, Soong Ching Ling, a prominent Chinese stateswoman in her own right, lived in this well-preserved European building in the old French Concession from 1918 to 1924 (Ching Ling continued to live here after her husband's death until the Japanese occupation of Shanghai in 1937). It was while he was here that Sun Yat-sen wrote some of his most important political works. It is also where the Suns entertained the famous people of their day, including George Bernard Shaw, Lu Xun and Ho Chi Minh. This complex contains two British-style structures that date back close to a century, one their former residence and another building which was turned into a museum in 2006.

On arrival, you will see a large statue of a seated Sun Yat-sen at the front of the two buildings. The structure on the right is the museum, where the exhibits all have good English descriptions. On the first floor is an old sword and various pistols 'used by foreign invaders'. Some of Sun Yat-sen's personal effects are also on display: his medical tools in a leather case, a faded Republican flag used during an uprising and daily items used by the Suns. On the second floor there are TV screens in each room showing archival footage from the turn of the twentieth century. There is also a Chinese suit worn by Sun Yat-sen, his cane, a fur-lined jacket, a stethoscope, a sphygmomanometer and a blue polka dot *qipao* worn by his wife. The third floor is devoted to a collection of calligraphy seals.

Proceed next door through the charming garden to the former home of the Suns, where the rooms still contain original furniture. When you enter here you must put plastic bags over your shoes to protect the floor. The first item on view is an old black, heavy metal oven, *c.* 1920s. On the first floor is the dining room where it is explained that the Suns lived a simple life, spending just 2 yuan a day on food. On the second floor is a small sitting room, a bedroom and a large number of books neatly stacked in a glass-covered bookcase – a closer look reveals that they are actually photocopies of the bookbindings.

Sun Yat-sen (1866–1925)

Sun Yat-sen is celebrated in China today as the 'father of the nation', revered in equal measure in Beijing and in Taipei as a great nationalist revolutionary and the first President of the Republic after the overthrow of the Qing dynasty. It is difficult to get an idea of the real person through the mythology that has grown up around him; the historical view of him has been generous and tends to gloss over his deficiencies as a leader and a thinker.

In the face of what was seen as China's impending dismemberment by the great powers, Sun threw himself into revolutionary politics, organizing a series of uprisings against the Manchus, all of which failed. Having spent time as a teenager with relatives in Honolulu, he now engaged in fundraising and organization among Chinese communities from Hawaii to Japan to England. In 1896 his kidnap by the Chinese embassy in London, and his eventual release before he could be shipped back to China for execution, gave him instant fame overseas, which contrasted with his low profile in China. Having established a unified coalition of anti-Qing dynasty groups in Japan in 1905, the 1911 revolution was actually triggered, ironically, by an uprising by troops in Wuchang, working independently of Sun. However, he returned to form the first government of the Republic of China, which can be seen as the high point of his career. The Republic soon fell victim to warlords who seized power and broke up China. Sun's Nationalist Party eventually came to learn from Soviet advisors and created its own military force to reunite the country. But it was left to Sun's successor, Chiang Kai-shek, to complete that reunification process.

116 Yang Shaorong's Collection of 3-inch Women's Shoes

百履堂古鞋博物馆 *Bailutang guxie bowuguan*

Room 903C, Building 3, Lane 786, Ao Sen Apartment, Hongzhong Road, Shanghai

上海市虹中路786弄3号楼903室，奥森公寓

Tel: (021) 6446 0977;
Mobile: 0136 0189 9451
Open: By appointment only
(只对外宾开放)

This private museum, located in the tiny living room of Mr Yang Shaorong, contains more than 1,000 pairs of antique embroidered shoes that were worn by women with bound feet. Foot-binding first appeared in China in 961, when the breaking and binding of feet to make them into the shape of a pointed lotus first began. Mr Yang explains that the foot was considered the most erotic

Embroidered shoes for bound feet with a central panel of ivory silk also embroidered; the back tab enabled the wearer to pull on the shoe, it was then tucked inside out of sight

The curved, shaped soles of bound feet shoes are padded with cotton and covered with embroidered silk

of three parts of the body that should not be seen; the foot fetish was common throughout China. However, the custom of binding women's feet did not become widespread until several hundred years later during the Ming and Qing dynasties. The practice generally died out after the fall of the Qing dynasty in 1911, but elderly women can still be seen tottering on their 'three-inch lotus feet' in some rural villages.

The shoes, collected by Mr Yang over the past three decades, are works of art, displaying wonderful embroidery, appliqué techniques and quilted stitching. The motifs on the shoes are highly symbolic, revealing much about Chinese society and culture of the past. Mr Yang, wearing white gloves when handling the shoes, shows them to visitors and offers explanations in Chinese. A pair of embroidered phoenixes is a symbol for a wedding, and a squirrel eating grapes is a play on the Chinese words for giving birth to many children. Some shoes have soles shaped like a gourd, an auspicious Chinese symbol; children embroidered onto them were to ensure the wearer would give birth; and a fish represented 'abundance'. There were a variety of colourful shoes for everyday wear, a soft shoe worn for sleeping (the foot had to be covered at all times), a white and black model with a minimalist design that was worn during mourning, and a shoe with a ladder on the bottom so that deceased women could climb up to heaven. There was even a shoe that was made to hold a small porcelain wine cup that a man could drink from. 'The smell was part of the fun,' says Mr Yang. Some shoes have drawings of sexual positions inside, and Mr Yang explains that the drawings served as a sex education of sorts.

In addition to the shoes themselves, the museum exhibits related accessories such as leggings, bindings and tools that were used to make the shoes: embroidery needles, wooden shoe blocks and a tiny iron for ironing the cloth. A glass case in the centre of the small room displays porcelain items related to the tradition, including porcelain statues of women with bound feet.

Zhang Daqian's *Green Mountain with a Fall*

117

Changfengtang Museum

长风堂博物馆 *Changfengtang bowuguan*

16 F, Heping Plaza, 22 Beijing East Street, Nanjing, Jiangsu

南京市北京东路22号
和平大厦16楼

Tel: (025) 8688 2760
Open: 9.30–16.30 Mon–Fri

This private collection was the brainchild of Mr Yang Xiu, a Nanjing property developer with deep pockets, a love of history and an appreciation of classical Chinese painting and calligraphy. He made headline news in 2004 when he paid 69.3 million yuan (US$8.35 million) for an album of landscape paintings by Shanghai-born artist, Lu Yanshao (1909–1993), at the time the highest price ever paid in the world for a single Chinese art lot. Naturally, the highlight of the museum, which opened in the same year, is this prize lot of paintings from the hundred-leaf landscape album the artist produced in 1962, inspired by the poems of the great Chinese poet, Du Fu. Each masterfully realized leaf has a slightly different composition and whilst they are clearly influenced by the late seventeenth-century landscape painter, Shitao (1642–1707), they are distinct for Lu Yanshao's unique use of colour and manipulation of space.

Other gems include a painting from the Sui dynasty of a Buddha from Dunhuang, works by masters from the Ming and Qing dynasties and calligraphy by artists both ancient and modern, such as Xu Wei from the Ming and Qi Gong (1912–2005). Rubbing shoulders with the Zhang Daqian work entitled *Green Mountain with a Fall* are paintings by Ren Bonian and Fu Baoshi. There is also a commercial gallery attached to the museum, selling modern Chinese paintings.

118 Fu Baoshi Museum

傅抱石纪念馆 *Fubaoshi jinianguan*

132 Hankou West Road, Gulou District, Nanjing, Jiangsu

南京市鼓楼区汉口西路132号

Tel: (025) 8372 0987
Open: 8.30–11.30 & 14.00–17.00 except Mon

Fu Baoshi (1904–1965) was a famous twentieth-century Chinese painter. Born into a poor family in Jiangsu Province, he was apprenticed to a chinaware shop and taught himself the art of seal carving. Helped by Xu Beihong (1895–1953), also from Jiangsu, Fu Baoshi received an art education and became a prominent landscape and figure artist, seal engraver and educator. As with all the modern Chinese artists, he tried to reconcile the conflicting approaches of Chinese and Western art. His most powerful landscapes were painted during his exile in Chengdu during the Japanese War, when the grandeur of the Sichuan scenery and the unrest of the times inspired him to create new definitions of foreground, middle ground and distance in Chinese landscape. He did this through a technique that alternated parallel and horizontal brushstrokes interspersed with clear space.

Fu Baoshi's *The Great Capital of Coal*

The Fu Baoshi Museum is housed in what was the artist's home for the last two years of his life. It is a Western-style villa on a wooded slope – a comment on the lifestyle of artists praised by the regime. Unfortunately, although the house is a research centre, most of the works on view are reproductions, and a visit is only worthwhile for those especially interested in twentieth-century Chinese painting.

119 The Memorial Hall to the Victims in the Nanjing Massacre by Japanese Invaders

侵华日军南京大屠杀遇难同胞纪念馆 *Qinhua rijun Nanjingdatusha yunantongbao jinianguan*

418 Shuiximen Street, Nanjing, Jiangsu
南京市水西门大街418号

Tel: (025) 8661 2230
Open: 8.30–16.30 except Mon
www.nj1937.org/

Atrocities committed against the Chinese are still not fully acknowledged by the Japanese government

The Nanjing Massacre was one of the most appalling events of the brutally cruel Japanese War. Nanjing, capital of the Republic of China, fell to the Japanese invading forces on 13 December 1937, the start of two months of murder, rape and looting. Chinese estimates put the death toll at 300,000 – with 20,000 rapes. The Japanese, who have never fully accepted the scale of the atrocity, put it as low as 40,000. A wartime tribunal gave a figure of 142,000.

Whatever the truth of the numbers, there is no argument, attested by Westerners as well as Chinese, that a third of the city was destroyed, shops and private homes were looted, and for weeks corpses littered the streets. It is also accepted that the Japanese have never fully acknowledged or taken clear responsibility for the scale of the atrocity. Japanese history books have played the event down, souring relations between the two countries still today.

The memorial is a moving tribute to relatives, friends and fellow citizens. One need only see the faces of some of the elderly people here, or the schoolchildren writing and leaving cards, to comprehend the nature of the loss and sorrow.

The new memorial hall, opened on 13 December 2007 – the seventieth anniversary of the start of the massacre – is on a par with the holocaust museums of Europe, and with Hiroshima and Nagasaki.

The hall stands on the site of the Jiandong Gate, on a mass grave of 10,000 corpses. It is designed like a ship, with a huge prow rising to the heavens. The approach along a sloping wall is reminiscent of Washington's Vietnam Memorial. Inside, a room shows, behind glass, corpses packed into the burial pit. In the next room, the public can leave mementoes, tokens and cards with messages. Following this are darkened rooms with memorial lights, multimedia exhibits, survivors' accounts, dioramas of bombed-out buildings, and accounts of the history of Sino-Japanese conflict dating back to the 1890s.

120

Nanjing Cloud Brocade Museum and Research Institute

南京云锦博物馆，南京市云锦研究所 *Nanjing yunjin bowuguan, Nanjingshi yunjin yanjiusuo*

240 East Chating Road, Nanjing, Jiangsu

南京市茶亭东街240号

Tel: (025) 8651 8580 / 8661 1377
Open: 9.00–17.00
www.njyunjin.com
Kids

Detail from a cloud-pattern brocade (*yunjin*) dragon robe

The historical importance of Nanjing (it served as the capital of China during several earlier periods) is reflected in the richness of the collections showcased in the city's museums and this one, focusing on *yunjin* – or cloud-pattern brocade – is no exception. During the Yuan, Ming and Qing dynasties, tens of thousands of looms wove this highly prized, exquisite textile exclusively to make dragon robes (*longpao*) and official garments for the Emperor, other members of the imperial household and his courtiers. Official fabric bureaus were set up by the rulers to administer and control its production in the city. By 1949, however, only four looms remained, and this uniquc handicraft was dying out. Today, this 'living museum' and its associated research institute are working hard to revive this unparalleled textile tradition, with teams of expert artisans weaving away on over a dozen reproduction wooden looms, producing traditional silk brocades for sale here and elsewhere in the city.

The institute and the museum displays are located in a rather institutional-looking building reached via a gate in the parking lot of the Memorial Hall of the Victims of the Nanjing Massacre. By far the most fascinating part of the visit is watching the weavers in action on the first floor. The process requires two weavers; the one at the top of the loom controls the pattern and the bottom weaver manipulates vertical frames of thread with a series of pedals, while feeding numerous shuttles of various coloured silk strands under and over these threads. In the past, these might also have included gold or silver supplementary weft threads, interwoven to produce shimmering pattern silks with designs of brightly coloured peacocks, dragons, flowers and clouds for exclusive use by thc Emperor.

The other three floors are devoted to displays of imperial garments (the best examples of Nanjing cloud-pattern brocades are housed in the Palace Museum, where the largest number of them ended up) and textile samples produced in Nanjing dating from the Warring States period to the Qing. There are also various types of looms, Chinese minority textiles, additional weaving tools and a shop selling examples of brocade and other garments made of silk. Besides those on display, the institute houses hundreds of additional brocade samples, patterns of cloud designs (the first step in producing brocade is to draw its pattern) and thousands of books relating to the production of brocade both in Nanjing as well as the other two imperial brocade- and silk-weaving cities, Suzhou and Hangzhou.

121 **Nanjing Museum**

南京博物院 *Nanjing bowuyuan*

321 Zhongshan East Road, Nanjing, Jiangsu

南京市中山东路321号

Tel: (025) 8480 2119 ex 2320
Open: 9.00–16.30
www.njmuseum.com/
Book and gift shop / English audio guide / delightful tea shop under the main staircase

The Nanjing Museum is one of the most beautiful modern museums in China and its collection is rivalled only by those at the museums of Beijing and Taipei. It is on no account to be missed.

It is both the provincial museum of Jiangsu Province, as well as a national museum. It was founded in 1933 (making it one of the oldest museums in China) by Cai Yuanpei (1868–1940), the educator and prominent scholar who had been Minister of Education in Sun Yat-sen's government. Cai was also the founding director.

Built in the form of a Liao dynasty palace, the museum is sited on a fine 83,000 sq m estate, near the Zhongshan Gate to the east of the city. From its foundation it was dedicated to achieving the highest international standards in conservation, research, pedagogy and display.

From the outset it showed not only the arts, but also the crafts, both of the Han as well as the minority cultures of China; and aimed to show these within the context of the natural world.

The Civil War between the Kuomintang and the Communists on the Chinese side, and the invading Japanese on the other, had a profound effect on the city and, in turn, the fortunes of the museum.

Nanjing had been the capital city of China from the third to the sixth centuries, and again briefly during the Ming dynasty. It was in Nanjing that the new republic was officially proclaimed on 1 January 1912. After Chiang Kai-shek abandoned Beijing to the Japanese, it again became the Chinese capital during the 'Nanjing Decade', from 1928 to 1937. Then, it too fell to the Japanese

Gilded bronze Buddhist triad, Qing dynasty with wooden screen behind inscribed in Manchu, Chinese and Tibetan giving presentation details including that it was presented to the Qianlong Emperor in 1778 (top left)

Carved lacquer imperial box with the character *chun* (spring) carved on its lid, Qing dynasty (bottom left)

Gold Bodhisattva in the Tibetan style and made in the Imperial Palace Workshops, Qing dynasty (top right)

Chased gold quatrefoil dish hammered and pressed out of a single piece of gold, Yuan dynasty (bottom right)

and suffered the appalling Nanjing Massacre in December 1937, during which some 300,000 of its people were murdered. Although the Kuomintang had to move their headquarters to Chongqing until the end of the War against Japan, they were back in 1945. Nanjing remained the capital until 1949.

Therefore, at the time of its foundation, the museum was a leading institution of the Chinese capital, active in scholarship, publication and excavation. It is telling that, during this period, the Beijing History Museum was a branch of the museum at Nanjing. Some 300,000 pieces, including six of national importance, had been collected by 1949, despite the turbulent history that accompanied the early years of its growth.

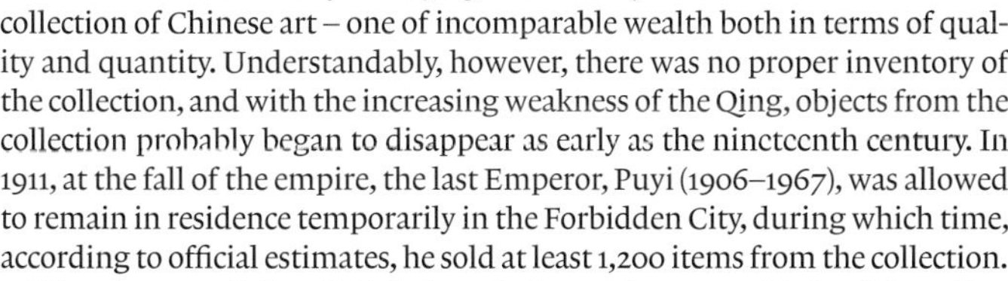

When the Ming Emperor, Yongle, moved the capital northwards to Beijing in 1420, he took the whole of the great imperial art collection with him, which continued to grow during the rest of the Ming dynasty, and again, spectacularly, during the Qing. Until 1949, the imperial collection in the Forbidden City in Beijing was the only national collection of Chinese art – one of incomparable wealth both in terms of quality and quantity. Understandably, however, there was no proper inventory of the collection, and with the increasing weakness of the Qing, objects from the collection probably began to disappear as early as the nineteenth century. In 1911, at the fall of the empire, the last Emperor, Puyi (1906–1967), was allowed to remain in residence temporarily in the Forbidden City, during which time, according to official estimates, he sold at least 1,200 items from the collection.

Then, in 1927, Chiang Kai-shek packed up at least two-thirds of the collection rather than leave it to the Japanese. These objects were transported first to Nanjing, then to Chongqing, and in 1945 back to Nanjing again. In 1949, when it was evident that Kuomintang power was on the brink of collapse, the nationalists collected up works of art from all over China and intended to take all of it, including the entire imperial collection, with them to Taipei. The speed of their demise was such, however, that at least half of the objects were left in Nanjing where they now form the cream of the collection. The imperial collection is therefore shared between the Palace Museum in Beijing, the National Museum in Taipei and the Nanjing Museum. It is even possible that some items still remain hidden in Nanjing.

Thus, the Nanjing Museum now holds some 420,000 items, of which more than 2,000 are national treasures. Many are acquisitions made after 1949, and there are many stupendous, recently excavated treasures. The museum has over 300,000 manuscripts and books.

A second and beautifully appointed building, in the same Liao style as the original, was opened in 1999, the same year in which the museum was upgraded to the rank of national museum.

The collection in the newer building is laid out over two floors, ground and lower, with galleries devoted to Folk Art, Bronzes, Porcelain, Treasure, Pottery, Textiles and Embroideries, Jades, Calligraphy and Painting, Lacquer, and Costumes and Accessories. It also has a gallery for temporary exhibitions of modern art. The objects are beautifully presented, and there are instructive and attractive reconstructions of pottery kilns and factories, and of weaving and embroidery techniques.

With a collection of such wealth it is almost invidious to single out individual items for the visitor's attention, but the following pieces will guarantee satisfaction, ensure that all the main galleries are visited and hence lead to a host of other treasures:

- Small Bronze Seated Deer with the most elegant antlers, from the Warring States period (excavated at Lianshui, Jiangsu)
- Qing Gold Boddhisattva made in the Imperial Palace Workshops
- Jade *Pei* Pectoral – fourteen pierced jade plaques from a Dawenkou Culture tomb (*c.* 2500 BC) excavated in Jiangsu
- Grey Pottery Brick with a Design of a Winged Immortal, Southern dynasties (317–589), from Xinyi, Jiangsu
- Peach Bloom Water Pot with Incised Dragon Design, Qing dynasty
- Carved Lacquer Barbed Dish, Qing dynasty, illustrating the story of 'The Cowherd and the Weaving Maid'
- Bamboo Carving of a Fisherman, Ming dynasty
- Imperial Painting of Birds by the Song Huizhong Emperor (r. 1101–1125)
- Embroidered Portrait of Guanyin by Guan Zhongji (1261–1319), Yuan dynasty. Guan Zhongji was the wife of Zhao Mengfu, a famous Yuan dynasty artist

Apart from its permanent exhibitions, the museum organizes frequent special events, including international exhibitions and exchange projects with foreign museums, including Japan, Germany, Egypt, Mexico, Spain, Russia, Belgium, South Korea and Australia.

The Nanjing Museum is the only Chinese museum with developed ethnic and folklore research, most recently on the Han ethnic group of the Tai Lake region.

A stroll in the sculpture garden after your visit will be an added pleasure.

122 Taiping Heavenly Kingdom Historical Museum

太平天国历史博物馆 *Taiping tianguo lishi bowuguan*

128 Zhanyuan Road, Nanjing, Jiangsu
南京市瞻园路128号

Tel: (025) 8662 3024
Open: 8.00–18.00
www.njtptglsbwg.com/home.html
Café in garden

The Museum is situated in the Zhanyuan Garden, a Ming garden of 18,000 sq m – one of the finest of the Suzhou-style gardens in China. In 1853, the garden was made the seat of the East kingdom of the Taiping rebels, but was destroyed in 1864 when the rebel regime was crushed. It has subsequently been recreated and is worth a visit in its own right.

The Taiping Rebellion was the greatest of the popular uprisings against the Manchu Qing dynasty in the nineteenth century. Led predominantly

by the Hakka and Zhuang minority peoples, it was driven by the unorthodox Christianity of its leader, Hong Xiuquan, who believed he was the younger brother of Jesus.

From 1850 to 1864, the Taiping kingdom ruled a large portion of southern China, with a population of some thirty million and its capital in Nanjing. This fascinating museum gives a full picture of this extraordinary regime – its organization based on imperial China; its revolutionary social ideas on the one hand, and its obscurantism on the other. For instance, women played a role in public life for the first time in Chinese society, even becoming generals in the army. Foot binding, one of the great social evils, was abolished (although it has to be said that few working women bound their feet, and this was a predominantly working-class movement). There was strict segregation of the sexes – even amongst married couples. Land was socialized and, in theory, dispossessed. Private trade was also, in theory, suppressed. Confucianism as the dominant philosophy and regulator of Chinese life was replaced by a form of Christianity. Simplified Chinese characters were introduced by the regime a century earlier than their eventual acceptance. Poetry books were written for the education and edification of peasant children. Examples of all of these can be seen in the museum.

Museum buildings set in the Ming dynasty Zhanyuan Garden

Displays inside the museum

Unsurprisingly, all this radical and inflammatory policy drew the condemnation of landowners, merchants and foreign powers, who helped the Qing government to destroy it. Probably 30 million people died, many of starvation. Mao viewed the Taiping as early anti-feudal revolutionaries. Today, the verdict on their temporary success and the destruction they wrought may be more open. See for yourself in this fascinating museum who they were, what they achieved and why they failed. The English signage is not particularly good – but the graphics are fine.

123

Nantong Blue Calico Museum

南通蓝印花布博物馆 *Nantong lanyinhuabu bowuguan*

No. 81, Haodong Road, Nantong, Jiangsu
江苏省南通市濠东路81号

Tel: (0513) 8510 8771
Open: 8.00–17.00

After a final wash, long lengths of died fabric are thrown high into the air to dry on poles

If you have an interest in ethnic textiles or textile technology and it is a sunny day, a trip to Nantong makes a worthwhile day's outing from Shanghai. This city, famous for thousands of years for its cotton and textile industry, has a tradition of producing the national craft of 'blue calico', as it is usually translated. Largely handmade and produced by family companies as a cottage industry, the fabric is made either by block printing or more often by a process of paste (not wax) resist. The process involves stencils, originally made of wood but now

more commonly of heavy paper. The stencil is placed on top of locally handwoven white cotton, then a paste made of soy bean flour and lime is spread on top. When this has dried, the fabric is repeatedly dipped into a succession of vats of indigo dye to achieve a rich blue colour. When the dyeing process is completed satisfactorily and the fabric has dried, the bean and lime paste are scraped off. The areas protected by the paste remain white. The long sheets of dyed material are then washed again and hung high on lines to dry in the sun.

In a charming pavilion surrounded by bamboo groves and rich greenery in the Hao He Park is the Nantong Blue Calico Museum, a private museum managed by Wu Yuanxin, whose family has been producing blue calico for five generations. His collection contains over 10,000 examples of calico-printed cloth and related objects. His research has resulted in two published volumes illustrating his vast collection, with more books planned. He is often at his museum and is happy to speak to visitors and demonstrate his craft. Several looms are set up in the museum and there are demonstrations of cotton weaving and the stencilling stage of the wax-resist process.

At the time of writing, only a limited number of pieces from this huge collection were on display. Tantalizing chests in the hallways of the building held many examples but these were not available for examination. However, a new and larger museum is planned, where many more textiles will be displayed. The most exciting part of a visit here, however, is a trip to the dyeing workshop, which the staff are pleased to show anyone who asks. The new museum, which will imminently be finished, will combine the collection and the 'factory', although at the time of the author's visit the factory was about 1 km away. If the new museum is not yet open, the staff will be happy to escort you down the road to see this fascinating and photogenic production process – the only caveat being that the sun must be out.

124

Nantong Abacus Museum

南通中国珠算博物馆 *Nantong zhongguo zhusuan bowuguan*

58 Haobei Road, Nantong, Jiangsu
江苏省南通市濠北路58号

Tel: (0513) 8505 3103
Open: 9.00–11.30 & 14.00–16.30
Wed–Sun, closed Mon & Tues
Shop and leaflets in Chinese, English, Japanese & South Korean

The yin-yang symbol decorates the centre of a circular shaped abacus

Believed to have been invented in China, the abacus (*suan pan*), as most of us know it, is a wooden-framed counting device with beads sliding freely on

An educational manual for the abacus, 1946

A classic Chinese abacus with two beads on the upper deck and five on the lower deck

fixed rods. A visit to this museum, however, will confirm that abaci have been made from many other materials too: gold, silver, brass, agate, ivory and even ceramic (which requires that it is made all in one piece when fired). They come in a myriad of shapes and sizes, and in Chinese banks they are still the preferred tool for calculation, often placed next to the tellers. In fact, Chinese bank employees and certified accountants are required to pass an exam using only an abacus, and many claim they can calculate faster with one than with a calculator.

The sweeping galleries on the ground floor take visitors through the instrument's history. On display is a whole range of simple counting devices such as calculating sticks and boards with moveable counters that were in use as early as the Spring and Autumn period, according to an early work on the subject. Diagrams, pictures of important books on calculations and the men who wrote them attempt to take you through the complicated history of Chinese mathematics, which, unlike other forms of mathematics, developed out of the need to solve problems to do with land measurement, architecture and the like. Few early documents have been found which offer any real insights; however, it is clear that early astronomy texts showing how to measure the positions of the heavenly bodies played an important role in the development of the subject. The most famous is the Han dynasty book, *Nine Chapters on the Mathematical Art,* which solves 246 practical problems over nine chapters and which dominated Chinese mathematics for hundreds of years. Several of these ancient texts, including Sun Zi's manual on mathematics (*c.* 460) also includes instructions on how to use counting rods to add, subtract, multiply, divide and perform square roots. When the abacus finally came into use in China is debatable; however, it seems that it may have appeared as early as the eleventh century.

Other galleries highlight the role abaci have played in modern Chinese history. On display is a replica of an abacus used by Chinese physicists at the secret department at Peking University, where they were studying the theory of nuclear reactors later used to produce the plutonium isotope for China's first atomic bomb in the 1960s. The physicists' biggest problem was a numerical calculation for which they lacked any kind of computer device and which they used abaci to solve instead. A bronze bust of Cheng Dawei, the influential sixteenth-century Chinese mathematician who published the *Suanfa tong zong* (General source of computational methods), takes pride of place. His treatise contained 600 computational problems, many applicable to everyday business and commerce. Displayed at the end of the gallery is a bust of Hua Yinchun (1896–1990), who spent most of his life on the systematic study of the abacus, producing the definitive text on the subject at the age of ninety, entitled *1000 Years of Abacus History*.

The second floor showcases dozens of abaci collected by the Chinese Association of Abacuses since their formation in 1979. Many have been purchased; others are donated often after visitors have been to the museum. Most on

show are original, or are labelled when reproductions. They range from a 4-m-long abacus from 1949, which was used in a medical herbal factory, to a modern ivory one measuring 6 x 4 mm, which you view through a magnifying lens. The reproduction Qing dynasty abacus made for officers building the first iron warship in China is equally remarkable. Called the Zi Yu Abacus, it was needed for large number calculations and had forty-nine crosspieces with two beads on the upper deck and five on the lower (referred to as a 2/5 abacus). The last cases feature the ubiquitous plastic abaci, which can still be found throughout Asia, and the various combinations of calculators and abaci still being produced.

125

Nantong Kite Museum

南通风筝博物馆 *Nantong fengzheng bowuguan*

No. 1 Huanxi Road, Nantong, Jiangsu

南通市环西路*1*号

Tel: (0513) 8558 0858
Open 8.30–17.00
www.cn-kite.com (Chinese only)
Note: Planning to move to a new location along the Haohe River
Kids

A kite decorated with a spider web design

This one-room museum is plastered from top to bottom with kites of all shapes, sizes and colours; even the ceiling is draped with distinctive examples. Display panels divide the space into sections, with diagrams, images and maps used to celebrate the origins and artistic achievements of this remarkable folk craft in China. The collection focuses on the whimsical creations known as whistle kites, made exclusively in Nantong for hundred of years.

The art of making these unique kites still thrives in Nantong and you can visit workshops in the area and view generations of kite makers producing these works of art. The process consists of three steps, each executed by an artisan who specializes in a particular stage. Only very few makers are considered 'perfect masters' – able to do all three. Using thin strips of bamboo (different types are used depending on the size of the kite), the pieces are flexed into various shapes to produce the frame of the kite. Unique to these kites is the use of squares and rectangles, which are placed on top of one another to produce a hexagonal shape. The most basic kite is the 'one-star form', with one large square turned at an angle and laid over a similarly sized rectangle to form a star or semi-hexangular shape. One of the largest on display has 271 'stars' sewn together. The frame is covered with either ordinary or specially prepared paper and then painted with vivid geometric designs, animals or with images from legends, often with auspicious meanings. Lashed to the bamboo frame in various formations are rows of whistles of various sizes and either cylindrical or orb shaped. The cylindrical ones are fashioned out of very thin bamboo and are paper-thin to reduce weight and increase their vibration capacity in the wind. The orbs are made from dried, hollowed-out gourds with slotted tops carved from wood, which allow the wind to enter. Each of these 'whistles' is painted, usually in red and green, and lacquered. The whistles can also be made from other hollow shapes, from silkworm cocoons to the egg shells of chickens or quail. A large late Qing dynasty whistle, made from a gourd and beautifully painted, is on display. Acquired by the museum from a local family, the top is carved from a special tree native to the area. Some of the kites on display have dozens of whistles attached (the largest has over one hundred), but even larger ones have been known to have up to 300. The smallest whistles are at the top of the kite in rows of descending sizes, ending with the largest at the back so that the 'wind is not stolen'. When flown, each whistle produces a musical tone which together creates a 'symphony in the sky'. By slackening the line and pulling it in, the flier can generate a variety of rhythms and sounds.

The invention and early history of kites can only be surmised from legends, which suggest they were in existence 3,000 years ago in China and perhaps Malaysia. There is, however, evidence which points to them being flown in China back in 200 BC, used as a tool during the Chu–Han War and later spreading west to Japan and Korea and then eastwards via the South China Sea and overland via the Silk Route. Other uses through the ages have been to scare birds from crops and to lift fireworks into the air. During World War II, whistle kites were used in Nantong to warn locals that the Japanese were invading, and in ancient times to predict the weather. Strong winds would mean rain and storms were on their way and the resulting louder whistling sound would warn fishermen and those drying salt.

Besides Nantong, there are other areas in China famous for kites, including Beijing, Weifang in Shandong Province, and Tianjin. Weifang is famous for its annual International Kite Festival, when the air swarms with ingeniously designed examples, and there is also a kite museum there (www.wfkitemuseum.com). There are numerous other kite festivals, clubs and kite competitions throughout the country and, besides being a popular pastime for families, the Chinese believe that flying a kite is very therapeutic and allowing it to fly away even healthier, as it will take your illness away with it.

Large whistling kites with rows of whistles attached, the smallest ones at the top

126

Nantong Textile Museum

南通纺织博物馆 *Nantong fangzhi bowuguan*

4 Wenfeng Road, Nantong, Jiangsu
南通市文峰路4号

Tel: (0513) 8551 7697
Open: 9.00–5.00 except Mon (call ahead as they are sometimes closed unexpectedly)

The semi-tropical monsoon climate in eastern Jiangsu Province is perfect for growing cotton, which has been a thriving industry here since the Song dynasty. It is not surprising, therefore, that the area has a rich tradition of textile design.

This old-fashioned but charming museum displays examples of a variety of ethnic textiles besides the local Nantong blue calico. In addition to the large collection of woven fabrics and clothing, other aspects of traditional life are illustrated, for example through demonstrations showing the old techniques such as hand weaving on traditional looms and basket weaving. There are also reconstructions of an old-fashioned kitchen and shop, making this as much a folk museum as a textile gallery. All sorts of paraphernalia and tools involved in textile production, from ancient to modern times, is exhibited. Historical contracts, bills and paperwork regarding transactions of local textile mills are also on view.

A detailed understanding of a number of the displays may be difficult as English signage is quite limited but the collection is well worth seeing, and the spacious rooms and pleasant gardens make for an enjoyable visit.

Woven silk with drinkers, tomb 507, Astana, Turfan, Xinjiang Uighur Autonomous Region, sixth to early seventh century

Zhang Jian and Dasheng Cotton Mills

The prosperity enjoyed by the inhabitants of Nantong is often credited to the solid foundation built by the town's local hero, Zhang Jian (1853–1910), 'The King of Nantong'. This entrepreneur, starting with the Dasheng Cotton mills, developed an astounding breadth of enterprises – cotton, silk, a distillery, flour mill and more, transforming the city from a sleepy backwater to China's best example of modernization in industry within a period of fifteen years.

In 1899 he founded Nantong's famous Dasheng Cotton mills, and used his wealth to encourage education by building various technical colleges such as a teacher training institute, a medical school, an industrial college and an agricultural institute, among many others. All have flourished and, today, form Nantong University. In his commitment to philanthropy, Zhang also built the Nantong Museum, a school for the blind and deaf, libraries and theatres. The town has built a memorial park and hall to Zhang in Zhuanyuan Street, Nantong.

127

Suzhou Museum

苏州博物馆 *Suzhou bowuguan*

204 Dongbei Street, Suzhou, Jiangsu
苏州市东北街204号

Tel: (0512) 6757 5666
Open: 9.00–17.00 (last entry 16.00) except Mon
www.szmuseum.com/szbwgen/index.html

The new museum in Suzhou looks set to become an iconic building that will do for Suzhou what the Guggenheim has done for Bilbao, the difference here being that the collection itself is of more intrinsic interest than Bilbao. Suzhou is one of the most famous and beautiful cities in China, and the building is the last work of one of the city's most internationally famous native sons.

I M Pei's ancestors were of a noble Suzhou family. As a child, he lived in the Pei family house in the Lion Forest Garden, one of the great gardens of Suzhou, close to the site of the new museum. He emigrated in the 1930s and studied architecture at MIT and Harvard. He has undertaken many high-profile building commissions world-wide, including the Louvre pyramid, the Miho Museum near Kyoto and the Museum of Islamic Art in Doha. In 1999, he was commissioned to build this new museum for Suzhou, which opened in 2006.

Suzhou must not be missed. Situated on the lower Yangtze and the shores of Lake Taihu, its garden and water culture are one of the great achievements of China. It is the capital of a land of tea, rice, fish and silk, with a recorded history of 2,500 years. In the Warring States period, it was the cradle of Wu culture, a highpoint of early Chinese civilization. Marco Polo called it 'the Venice of the East'; the Chinese called it 'Heaven on earth' (with Hangzhou).

Since 1949, the economy of the city has grown steadily, and it has sought to blend its new commercial wealth with the historic and pivotal role it has played in the taste and culture of southern China.

The original Suzhou Museum was opened in 1960 and housed in the Palace of Zhong Wangfu – a memorial to the history of the Taiping Rebellion. The new museum, of 10,700 sq m, is attached to Zhong Wangfu. It abuts the Humble Administrator's Garden, a high point of Suzhou's garden design. Situated on the corner of Dong Da Jie, it is thus at the heart of old Suzhou.

The building combines Pei's distinctive modern style with classical Suzhou style. Pei uses modern materials to recreate traditional structures; the steel and glass roof recreates the character of the seemingly random mixture of movement and structure found in traditional Suzhou building. The traditional pattern of white walls with black tiles is recreated in the white walls with grey-black granite.

I.M. Pei

Innovative design melds with traditional architecture

The traditional wooden roof is replaced by steel and glass with metal louvers with wooden covers, allowing daylight to permeate the building and thereby minimizing the need for artificial lighting. Breaking with the tradition of large sloped roofs, Pei has created a complex of carefully integrated directional lines in harmony with the slopes of surrounding buildings.

The museum is centred on a garden with several smaller courtyards. The trees of the Humble Administrator's Garden provide the backdrop; there are staggered white walls, and a range of miniature mountains of slabs of sheet stone. There is a large water area with a cobbled bottom, a rockery, a zigzag bridge, an octagonal pavilion, bamboo groves and a stunning selection of trees. This modern Suzhou garden is worth a visit in itself.

The collections are housed in galleries which encircle the central garden, each one having its own shape and character appropriate to the nature of its contents – with a logical layout combined with constant glimpses of water, white walls, grey granite and a pattern of sloping roofs.

The treasures range from the Neolithic to the Qing. The tomb of King Helu of Wu has yielded agricultural implements, weapons and ritual bronzes. Another Wu tomb at Zhenshan has revealed a set of splendid jade objects with specifically local features from the Warring States period. Two excavations from the Five Dynasties and the Northern Song have enriched the collection; the former with an exquisite olive-green celadon lotus-shaped bowl and saucer; the latter with a pearl shrine for Buddhist relics, 122 cm tall, uniquely designed and superbly made.

The collection contains many treasures from the Tang and the Song dynasties, and a collection of painting and calligraphy from the Ming and the Qing.

A visit to the Suzhou Museum combines the pleasures of a most beautiful city, a landmark modern museum with a beautiful garden, and an interesting and varied collection.

128

Kunqu Opera Museum

中国昆曲博物馆 *Zhongguo kunqu bowuguan*

14 Zhongzhangjia Lane, Pingjiang District, Suzhou, Jiangsu

苏州市平江区中张家巷14号

Tel: (0512) 6727 5338 / 3334
Open: 8.30–16.30
www.kunopera.net/
Tea house decorated with scenes from famous operas

This is a place no opera buff should miss, for Kunqu opera is a cultural institution like no other. One of the oldest surviving operas in China, along with the famed Peking Opera, it is one of the best known forms among over 300 varieties. It originated in Kunshan, near Suzhou, during the Yuan and early Ming dynasties and is characterized by a classical form that focuses more on music and poetic wording than acrobatics. Librettos cover a range of topics and themes, including the intrigues of emperors and gods, love stories and comedies. The stories combine Chinese folklore, symbolism and drama, and include dancers, clowns and acrobats, as well as singers. The result is an extremely stylized spectacle that attempts to portray the full spectrum of life and beauty through crystallized choreography, make-up and costumes. Common actions such as laughing, crying, sleeping and opening doors are all precisely choreographed. The accompaniment usually consists of six instrumentalists led by the clapper, and includes the vertical flute and the *pipa* (lute) players, as well as other percussion players. Kunqu opera is a remarkable sight, but can be an acquired taste on account of its guttural, high-pitched singing style that differs so drastically from that of Western opera.

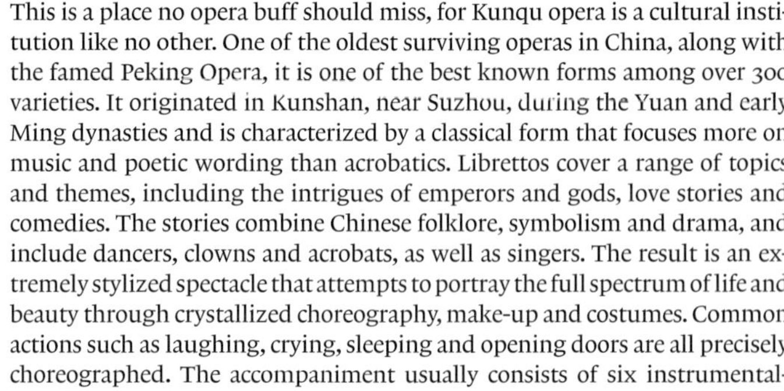

The theatre in the museum

Actors in the Kunqu opera *Tie Long Shan* (Tielong Mountain)

Model theatre in the gallery

Being listed by UNESCO in 2001 as one of the Masterpieces of Oral and Intangible Cultural Heritage has led to government funding for the collection of traditional librettos, to support public performances and to train professionals. As a result, performances of updated versions of classic operas have been playing to large audiences around China, as well as abroad, with the Suzhou Kunqu Opera Company touring Europe and the USA with one of the classic plays of the Kunqu opera, *The Peony Pavilion,* written during the Ming dynasty and first performed in 1598.

Beautiful wooden doors flank the entrance of this recently restored venue, built by a Shanxi businessman during the Qing dynasty and opened as a museum in 2003. Visitors are greeted by a wooden sculpture of Wei Liangfu, a Ming musician who worked on developing southern opera to bring it up to par with that from the north, eventually producing rules for the singing of Kunqu. Music fills the air in the courtyard, giving a flavour of the artistic and dramatic power of watching a performance in the main building with its classical stage covered by a saddle-shaped roof and decorative well-shaped ceiling (caisson). Collections of costumes, scripts, masks, instruments, photographs, historical documents and miniature models are displayed in the exhibition areas offering a concise introduction to Kunqu, although with limited English explanations.

Very few historic Kunqu stages survive, so the displays of scaled wooden models of reconstructed stages are the best way to learn about the de-

velopment and variety of opera venues. Performances took place in playhouses in the city, but also in private gardens (including Suzhou's Humble Administrator's Garden) and residences, guildhalls, government offices, teahouses and even in fields and temples. The Kangxi and Qianlong Emperors, on their tours south to the city, had their provisional palaces fitted out with stages and make-up rooms. Performances were played out on red carpets, hence the association of the phrase 'red carpet' with centre stage. Suzhou's profusion of waterways meant performances were also often staged on the bow of boats, with the cabins used as make-up rooms, while spectators watched seated on the boat or from boats nearby. Impromptu venues were replaced by more permanent playhouses, many of them refurbished old teahouses equipped with stages, pits and electric lighting. Besides a 1:25 scale model of the first lit stage in Suzhou, fashioned from stone and wood, there is a model of a mobile stage which originally would have been made of wood and bamboo so that it could easily be disassembled and moved to another venue. A replica stage boat is also on display.

Several traditionally dressed characters from celebrated Kunqu operas give visitors some idea of the complexity and sophistication of the headpieces and costumes, many richly embroidered and all with long sleeves extending well beyond the hands, used to great effect when executing a movement. A range of musical instruments used in Kunqu are displayed, along with an assortment of books about Chinese opera (all in Chinese) and works by the famous painter of Kunqu characters, Gao Made. This is a research venue for Kunqu opera, although performances for small groups can be arranged if booked in advance. A DVD (in Chinese and English) is also available, providing information on the history and practice of Kunqu opera.

Erotic stone sculptures and reliefs decorate the museum's garden

129 Ancient Chinese Sex Culture Museum

中国古代性文化博物馆（同里）*Zhongguo gudai xingwenhua bowuguan (Tongli)*

Tongli Township, Wujiang County, Jiangsu

江苏省吴江县同里镇

Tel: (0512) 6332 2973 / 2972

Open: 9.00–18.00

Note: You must pay to get into the mock village; park first and there is an additional entrance fee for the museum

Leaflet available in Chinese and English

This museum, originally located in Shanghai, is now housed in a former private girl's school built during the late Qing dynasty in the water town of Tongli. Established by the sex-guru duo, Professor Liu Dalin and Dr Hu Hongxia

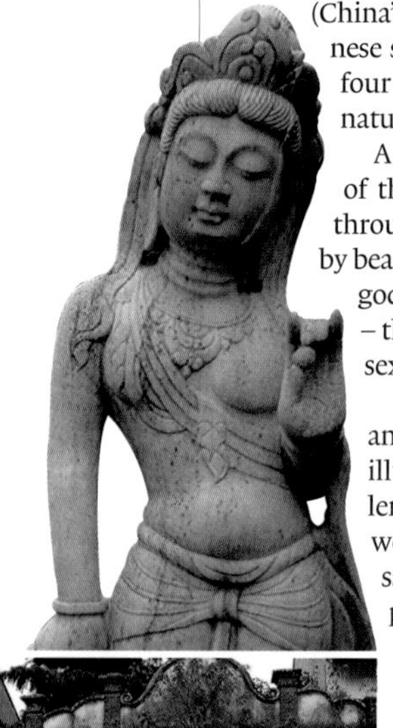

(China's answer to Alfred Kinsey), the museum showcases ancient Chinese sex objects from over 9,000 years ago to the present day, over four exhibition halls. The objective is to educate and to encourage a natural and healthy attitude towards sex.

A large stone phallus takes centre stage at the entrance to one of the newly built sections of the museum. To the right of here, through an arched gate, are the original school buildings surrounded by beautiful gardens dotted with erotic stone sculptures, from Indian goddesses in evocative poses to figures of the gods of wind and rain – the connection being pleasant weather equates to a harmonious sexual life.

The first gallery – Sex in a Primitive Society – informs that food and sex are two basic needs of even the most primitive of societies, illustrated by numerous penis worship objects. The second gallery – Marriage and Woman – explores how, throughout history, women have been exploited by men and used as tools for sexual satisfaction and for procreation. Crude ceramic figures in sexual poses greet you in the gallery called Sex in Daily Life. Here, dildos from different centuries, including a gilt bronze one, are shown next to tea trays and porcelain cups painted with erotic scenes. Slightly more informative, that is if you know little about the sexual fortunes of Chinese women, is that during the Tang dynasty women were able to initiate divorce, and in the early twentieth century it was common for prostitutes to be registered in the cities where they worked, with records documenting their age, education and past employment. No museum of this type would be complete without artefacts relating to the male fetish for foot binding, including a stool used for winding the binding tightly around the foot, or artefacts relating to eunuchs, such as the porcelain penis used by them on girls in the imperial palaces.

130

Huaihai Campaign Martyrs Memorial Tower and Park

淮海战役烈士纪念塔 纪念馆 *Huaihai zhanyi lieshi jiniananta jinianguan*

2 Jiefang South Road, Xuzhou, Jiangsu
江苏省徐州市解放南路2号

Tel: (0516) 8384 0397
Open: Tower 7.00–17.30 summer; 7.30–17.00 winter
English audio guide
Gift shop / refreshments available in the park

The park is rated a major memorial site, a base for patriotic education, a National Red Tour area and contains a statue purported to be 'the largest group sculpture of important personages' (notable in that Mao is not among those represented) of Deng Xiaoping, Su Yu, Liu Bocheng, Chen Yi and Tan Zhenlin, constituting the General Front Committee during the Campaign. Both museums are located in the rear of the park.

The Patriotic Education Museum is an older building surrounded by artillery batteries, tanks and planes and the single floor of the collection, with

limited English signs, spans the history of weapons and warfare, including a collection of spears and martial arts weapons.

The Huaihai Martyrs Memorial Museum fills a unique niche in the spectrum of Chinese museums, as it is not located on a special site, nor is the primary feature a collection of artefacts. It is a new breed of history museum, built in 2007, whose main purpose is education – some might say propaganda – but this is thus far the best of them, providing insights not only into a critical period in China's history, but the fluid nature of Chinese perspectives on relatively recent events and a still evolving evaluation of history for the next generation. The exhibit details and commemorates one of the greatest battles of modern Chinese history, considered by many military historians to be one of the key battles of the twentieth century.

The museum begins with a brief history leading up to the Civil War and ends with a review of the final events leading up to the formation of the People's Republic of China. Most of the exhibits concern the campaign itself and go step by step through the events beginning 6 November 1948 and ending 10 January 1949 as the Communist East China Field Army and Central Plains Field Army decisively defeated the field armies of the Kuomintang, or Nationalist Party, in a series of three battles centred on Xuzhou. The Communist victory in Huaihai paved the way for a final march to Nanjing and Chiang Kai-shek's resignation as leader of the Nationalists on 20 January 1949.

This newly built museum employs state-of-the-art curatorship to bring history to life, with extensive photographs, artefacts such as weapons and communication equipment, original documents, vignettes and interactive touch screens (Chinese only) to access historical and statistical details. The informative English audio is highly recommended, as despite good English signage, historical details are more fully elaborated upon. There was horrendous loss of life during the Huaihai Campaign, with 550,000 Nationalist troops killed or captured and the loss of 124,000 Communist soldiers, but the museum is dedicated to the 30,000 'Martyrs', ordinary citizens whose lives were lost while ferrying food or helping the wounded. Displayed on the third floor is a 360-degree painted panorama of the battle, but the real drama unfolds on the two floors below.

131

Xuzhou Cultural Site of the Han Dynasty

徐州汉文化景区 *Xuzhou hanwenhua jingqu*

No. 1 Bingmayong Road, Xuzhou, Jiangsu

徐州市兵马俑路1号

Tel: (0516) 8316 7053 / 8315 7205
Open: 8.30–17.30 summer; 16.30 winter; box office closes at 16.30
www.hwhjq.com
Gift shops / refreshments

Xuzhou is an industrial city in the northwest of the province and is primarily a destination for the business traveller, but during the Western Han dynasty it was home to a succession of Chu kings who ruled and were buried here in a complex of tombs cut into the rocky hillsides in the eastern part of the city. Located along the Grand Canal and approximately midway between Beijing and Nanjing, Xuzhou is rarely included in travel guides. However, the intrepid traveller will be pleasantly rewarded by visiting this complex containing the Han dynasty tomb built for the third king of the Chu kingdom, Liu Wu, and its associated museums, for among the hundreds of Han tombs scattered throughout the city and surrounding areas, this is the most significant. It is the only tomb site outside of the more famous one of the first Emperor of the Qin dynasty at Xi'an and those of the Han unearthed at Yangjiawan of Xianyang, to contain significant numbers of terracotta warriors and horses.

The complex, located at the foot of the Lion Mountains, consists of a whole array of buildings, three of which are especially worth visiting. They are the Han Terracotta Warriors and Horses Museum, the Aquatic Terracotta Warrior Museum, and the Chu Prince Mausoleum (Tomb). There is also the Cultural Exchange Museum, which displays decorative elements of the tombs, including stone relief carvings and rubbings; however, no English descriptions are provided and at the time of writing, half of the exhibition space was not utilized.

Aquatic Terracotta Warriors Museum

Cavalry figurines from the Western Han Chu King's tomb

The Chu Prince Mausoleum was created for Liu Wu, who reigned from 174 to 154 BC, and his wife. Excavated in 1994–95, this massive vaulted space consists of an outer passage, an inner passage, a courtyard and chamber, covering an area of over 850 sq m. The tomb's entrance is immediately visible upon entering the large display hall. Steps lead down into the deep, narrow rock cave tomb built along the mountain, where thousands of funerary objects made of gold, silver, bronze, iron, jade, stone and lacquer were unearthed. Representative pieces are on display, but the most impressive, such as Liu Wu's jade burial suit are displayed in the Xuzhou Museum.

Built as an annex to the tomb, and on the original site of its discovery, is the Han Terracotta Warriors and Horses Museum, displaying a good portion of more than 4,000 warriors and horses arranged in battle formation. Found in six pits, several hundred metres west of the tomb, are rows of infantry (both soldiers and officers) and cavalry in battle formation, as well as chariots drawn by terracotta horses, providing Liu Wu with military servants in his afterlife. There are English signs throughout, consisting of simple descriptions. Objects found in the tomb are on display, along with supplementary weapons from the Western Han dynasty, typical battle equipment and single figurines. Although standing only around 40 cm in height – compared to the life-size figures found

at Xi'an – these warriors are crafted with wonderful attention to detail, their different functions clearly distinguished by their poses or the weapons they hold, including crossbows. Some are painted, and they have a range of facial characteristics and expressions.

The recently completed Aquatic Terracotta Warrior Museum (2006) presents two of the most northern terracotta warrior pits in galleries built underwater near the Lion Pond. These pits became submerged underwater several years after they were first discovered. The museum comprises two exhibition halls. The West Hall displays Pit no. 5 as it was originally discovered, the warriors and horses scattered across the barren earth in disarray, while the East Hall displays finds from Pit no. 6, showing multiple ranks of hundreds of cavalry – or men on horseback – displayed as they were likely to have been placed originally to guard the tomb of Liu Wu.

132

Xuzhou Museum

徐州博物馆 *Xuzhou bowuguan*

101 Heping Road, Xuzhou, Jiangsu

江苏省徐州市和平路101号

Tel: (0516) 8380 4400 / 4409
Open: 9.00–17.00, last entry 16.30; closed on Chinese New Year's Eve
www.xzmuseum.com/

Although not considered a tourist hot spot, Xuzhou (previously known as Pengcheng) was the capital of the vassal state of Chu in the early periods of the Western Han dynasty (206 BC – AD 9) and in recent years has demonstrated how significant a place it was by the astounding finds excavated from a number of tombs among hundreds scattered throughout the eastern part of the city and in nearby locations. Many of the tombs are open for viewing, including the rock cut tomb at Shizishan (Lion Hill) built for the King of the Western Han dynasty Chu state, Liu Wu (174–154 BC), that of the third Prince of Chu and the Guishan (Turtle Hill) tomb of Liu Zhu (128–116 BC), the sixth Prince of Chu.

The tomb and mausoleum of Liu Wu and his wife were excavated in 1994–1995 and, besides the numerous miniature terracotta warriors and horses (25–60 cm in height) buried in pits around the tomb, it yielded thousands of stunning finds. A selection of these, plus several items from the other tombs are on display in the second floor galleries. They include finely fashioned jades, gold plaques, bronzes, seals, gilt belt buckles, coins and lutes, giving visitors an idea of the lavish lifestyle of the princes and an insight into their burial practices. Liu Wu's tomb, cut deep into the rock face of the mountain, includes a 117-m long vaulted passage connecting to a burial chamber with a nearby courtyard. That of Liu Zhu and his wife was rather more elaborate, with two connected coffin chambers and ancillary rooms including a stable, two chariot and horse rooms, an armoury and even a lavatory. They had complicated bathing rituals which included using silver

Jade burial suit sewn with gold wire from tomb of Chu state prince

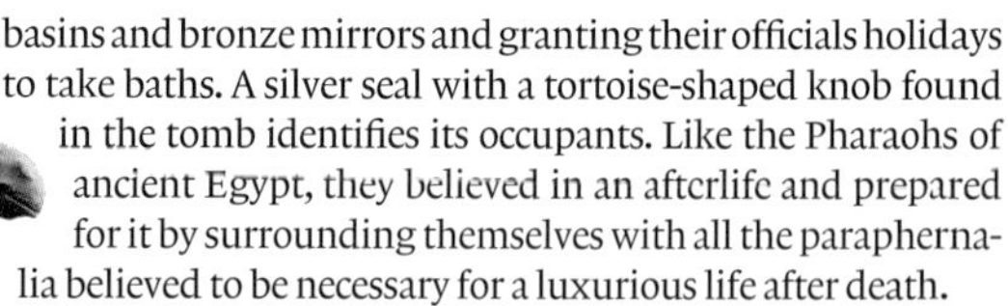

Pottery cavalry man on horse inscribed 'flying horse', Western Han

basins and bronze mirrors and granting their officials holidays to take baths. A silver seal with a tortoise-shaped knob found in the tomb identifies its occupants. Like the Pharaohs of ancient Egypt, they believed in an afterlife and prepared for it by surrounding themselves with all the paraphernalia believed to be necessary for a luxurious life after death.

Liu Wu was entombed within a coffin consisting of three layers: the outer rock mausoleum, a jade and red lacquered wooden coffin and a jade burial suit stitched together with gold thread (which has been replaced because the thread was stolen by ancient grave robbers). The exceptional burial suit, a national treasure, is also on display. Constructed of over 4,200 pieces, it covered every part of the body, including the head and feet. There was even a jade mask for his face made from some twenty-eight geometrically shaped pieces. The ancient Chinese believed jade would help preserve the body and therefore also their spirits.

Other highlights among the finds from the Western Han tombs are some lovely terracotta figurines, in particular a collection of dancers and musicians, as well as a selection of notable jade artefacts including a jade dragon and ceremonial *bi* that exemplify the skills of the ancient craftsmen who fashioned such quality objects. The first floor contains a collection of pottery and jade pieces dating from the Neolithic Qingliangang Culture to the Qin dynasty. The third floor focuses on porcelain, with representative examples from the Tang to the Qing dynasties, including a large selection of Tang *sancai*-glazed pottery and figurines. There are English labels on most of the exhibits and some introductory signs are in English, but little else in the way of supplementary information. However, the beauty of many of the items on display speaks for itself.

133 **China Grand Canal Museum**

中国京杭大运河博物馆 *Zhongguo jinghang dayunhe bowuguan*

1 Grand Canal Culture Square, Gongshu District, Hangzhou, Zhejiang

杭州市拱墅区运河文化广场1号

Tel: (0571) 8816 2058

Open: 9.00–16.30 Wed–Sun

www.canal-museum.cn/index_en.html

English audio guide and brochure

Completed in the Sui dynasty (581–618), the Grand Canal laid the foundation for the economic development of the Tang and subsequent dynasties. This major engineering feat, which stretches 1,800 km from south to north, was designed to serve as a transport channel, providing an economic and cultural conduit through the heart of China.

Teams of men and often horses attached by long harnesses pulled the boats up and down the canal

Canal boat replica

Little more than half of the original Grand Canal is still a functional transport channel, but it's still a bustling and important channel and a historical site. Triple the amount of goods is transported along the canal each year than is moved by railways between Beijing and Shanghai. Furthermore, the industrial output of the eighteen key cities straddling the canal accounts for one-fifth of the country's total industrial output. Unfortunately, parts of the canal, primarily in the north, have gone dry, making it impossible for boats to pass through.

This interesting and well-organized museum is divided into five halls, each dedicated to a different topic, and with limited English explanations. The Introductory Hall focuses on canals around the world and China's own Grand Canal. The First Hall and Second Hall are devoted to technical issues regarding the Grand Canal, the Third Hall tells the story of cities along the canal, and the Fourth Hall describes canal culture.

The exhibits are quite interesting, and include the following: a 3D movie theater, cartoons, interactive screens, boat replicas, a mock canal dock, old black and white photos of towns and life on the canal, and artefacts discovered along the canal, from buckets to pottery. In one large room, a glass-covered replica of the Grand Canal runs underfoot from Hangzhou to Beijing, winding its way along the floor past houses, bridges and other recognizable landmarks.

One of the highlights of the Grand Canal Museum is that just to the west of the entrance is the ancient Gongchen Bridge, which spans the Grand Canal. Walk out the entrance and turn left and walk through the square until you reach the sharply arched bridge. When you get to the top, you can sit there and watch the barges going up and down the canal as they have for centuries.

134

China National Silk Museum

中国丝绸博物馆 *Zhongguo sichou bowuguan*

73-1 Yuhuangshan Road, Hangzhou, Zhejiang

杭州市玉皇山路73-1号

Tel: (0571) 8703 5150 / 2060
Open: 8.30–16.30 daily
www.chinasilkmuseum.com
English and Chinese audio guide / small guide book / gift shop / shop selling silk items / tea house
Kids

No textile enthusiast would miss this superlative storehouse of cultural wonders covering all aspects of silk history, from sericulture (silk production) and the origins of silk weaving and trade, to displays of twentieth-century fashion. Known as the 'queen of fibres', silk has been produced in China from around 2700 BC and since it became a major commodity in the Western Han under the reign of Emperor Wu-ti (140–87 BC), it has played a significant part in the economic and social development of the country. Located near the city's scenic West Lake, the museum opened in 1992 and is one of the largest showcases for silk history in China. Daily fashion shows, as well as educational activities and a textile conservation, research and identification facility make this a truly vibrant museum.

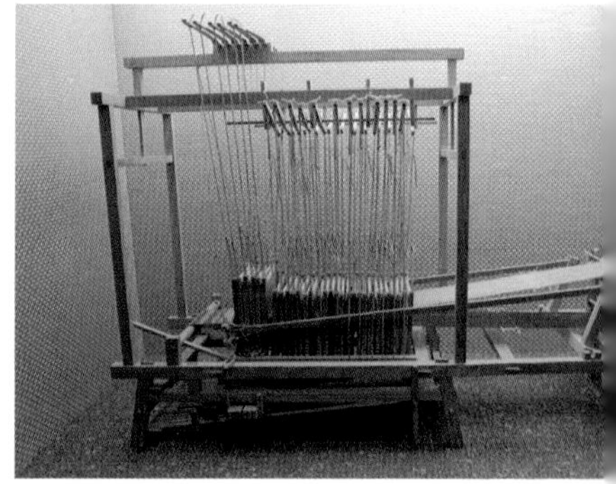

Model looms (left to right) include: a minor drawloom for intricate patterning, Warring States and Qin periods, a slanted loom as seen on Han dynasty relief stone carvings and the Greater Drawloom used for large patterns such as those on dragon robes – it requires two people to operate and was already in use by the late Tang dynasty

Over three floors there are eight galleries with displays in well-lit, modern showcases augmented with excellent and more than adequate English and Chinese signage. Although the lighting may seem dim in some galleries this is because textiles are highly sensitive to light and explains why they are also regularly rotated. Besides drawing from the museum's core collection, much of which has been donated by private collectors, some objects are on loan from the Palace Museum and other institutions.

A good place to start is in the entry hall on the first floor, where an illustrated, comprehensive time-line on the history of silk sweeps across a curved wall. In another hall, a large map shows the three major Silk Roads: the one through the grasslands of the north, the one via the desert to the west and the maritime route. For those interested in weaving technology, head to the ground floor's Dyeing and Weaving Gallery and Weaving Workshop. The first section uses objects and reproduction images of Chinese women processing silk to demonstrate the steps required in silk dyeing and thread production. Unwinding the cocoons is done by 'reeling' women. Once the pupae in the cocoon are killed by heating, they are placed in hot water to soften the gum that binds the filaments together. The reeling women find the loose end of the cocoon and, with great skill, several filaments at a time are reeled onto a bobbin to make one long thread. The more filaments wound together the thicker the

thread and, when woven, the heavier the cloth. Two large model looms illustrate the processes of shedding and patterning in weaving. Shedding is one of several complex steps used in loom weaving and is the point where the warp (or vertical) yarn is raised to form a 'shed' through which the shuttle carrying the filler yarn is passed. Models of ancient looms from China and elsewhere are on display. Particularly fascinating are the numerous replica working looms manned by first-rate weavers producing an array of silk cloths. They range from a drawloom operated by two people and used to weave complicated figured fabrics like brocade and samite, to a balance treadle loom popular in the Qing and a multi-heddle loom developed in the Han for the production of *jin* silk (complex warp-faced polychrome woven silks).

The first floor includes the Textile Gallery, which explores the origins, production and trade of silk, and features displays of different types of woven silks, and dyed and printed textiles. There is also the Costume Gallery and a delightful gallery devoted to sericulture, which children will enjoy.

Understanding the lifecycle of the silk moth is crucial to appreciating the mystery of silk and its considerable value in China and elsewhere for centuries. Interactive displays and enlarged models of the silk worms and cocoons bring to life the four stages of the blind, flightless moth, *Bombyx mori*. The moth lays hundreds of eggs (approx 500 eggs will produce 10 kg of silk) which hatch into worms (larva) that munch away on a diet of mulberry leaves until they are bursting and ready to spin their cocoon of silk filaments from a substance in their silk glands. Several days later they produce a white fluffy cocoon – home

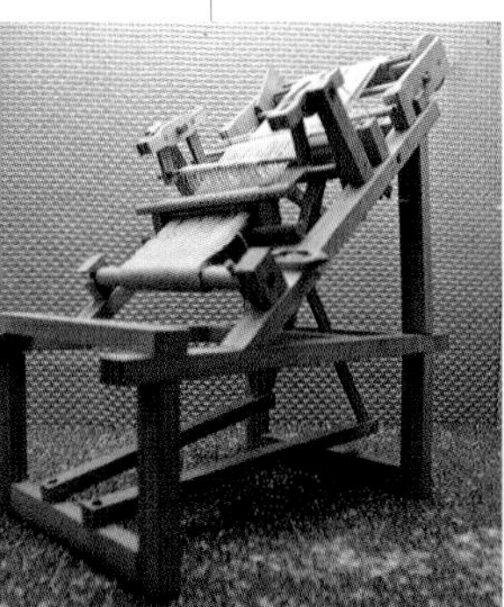

for the pupa. Eight days after that, they are baked to kill the pupas, placed in hot water and the silk filaments unwound.

The textile galleries are the highlight of the museum, displaying samples of rare silks discovered in tomb sites and along the Silk Road; decorative textiles – woven, printed, tie-dyed, clamp-resist dyed and embroidered – imperial robes and accoutrements, and garments such as the delicate gauze pants and coat dating from the Southern Song. Here, not only does it start to become clear how important a role silk has played in China on many levels, including economically and politically, but also the sheer artistic magnificence of the creations on display is breathtaking in itself. These galleries offer a wealth of information on this fascinating art form, including the technological advances that made possible the weaving of symbols and complicated designs into colourful, patterned fabrics to make garments which had deep meaning and were visually stunning. One of the items is a silk ribbon dating from 2750 BC, which was discovered in 1958 at the Qianshanyang site of the Neolithic

Silk worm cocoons

Liangzhu Culture. One of the earliest silk finds in the Yangtze River basin, this small, seemingly insignificant group of threads represented a historical milestone. It was here, from this small beginning in the Yangtze Delta, that silk production originated and where later, in the Ming dynasty, ten major weaving and dyeing workshops were established. By the Qing dynasty, there were three official imperial silk workshops located here, in Jiangning (present day Nanjing), Suzhou and Hangzhou. During the Qing, passports were issued for the silks produced by these private imperial looms, allowing them permission to travel to the imperial workshops for fashioning into garments, or as gifts for the Emperor to bestow on dignitaries or high-ranking officials.

An entire gallery is dedicated to the various classifications that categorize woven textiles, from silk tabby, plan gauze and twill damask to *kesi* or tapestry weave. Magnified sections of samples illustrate the complexity of their construction. Starting during the Shang dynasty we learn that the dominant stitch of Chinese embroidery was the chain stitch, which was later replaced in the Tang dynasty by the plain and coaching stitches. The Han and Tang silks from the Silk Road and the Liao and Yuan examples from the northern grasslands are especially beautiful. Samples of *jin*-silk, with dragon and phoenix designs dating from the Warring States period are a must see, as are later examples woven with musicians, hunters and animals from the Northern dynasties (AD 386–581). The Liao (916–1125) examples include brocaded twills with designs of birds and flowers, and gauze embroidered with animals. Among the rows of cases displaying costumes are marvellous Yuan robes punctuated with thick waistbands, looking like contemporary garments with their simple designs and muted colours; and the Qing brocade four-clawed dragon robes, some of which are decorated with Taoist emblems and clouds, reflect the importance of ceremony and ritual.

The second floor displays more recent textiles from the late Qing dynasty to the present day, and although there are no English labels, there are excellent examples of *qipaos*, and Western-style jackets and shirts dating from 1912 to 1949, some fur lined, others quilted. The *qipaos* from the 1930s reveal how Western influences transformed these once loose garments into closer-fitting dresses with side slits. Using imported and Shanghai Art Deco designed fabrics made them fashionable even abroad.

135

China National Tea Museum

中国茶叶博物馆 *Zhongguo chaye bowuguan*

No. 88, Longjing Road, Hangzhou, Zhejiang
浙江省杭州市龙井路88号

Tel: (0571) 8796 4221
Open: 8.30–16.30 except Mon
Tea house / shop

The museum is set amongst the fields of tea plants

It's worth being dropped off at the end of the road which leads up to the museum and walking up, as the surrounding sea of green leaves being plucked from the low lying tea plants by women young and old wearing cone-shaped straw-hats, each with a basket strapped to their backs, is well worth savouring. Nestled amongst these rolling mounds covered with Hangzhou's famous Longjing (or Dragon Well) green tea, are four separate buildings comprising this complex. The main two-storey building contains six halls covering every aspect of tea, from its cultural significance and its bewildering varieties, to tea customs, the art of the tea ceremony and the role tea has played in the world's economy. The other buildings are used for educational purposes, tea ceremonies, receptions and academic conferences and there is a tea house, restaurant and shop where you can sip infusions of steely coloured balls of Gunflower tea, or the flat leaves of the local Dragon Well tea or else purchase a tea pot from a dizzying selection.

Statues of Lu Yu, the Tang scholar cum tea sage, greet you both inside and outside the main exhibition building. Revered as a saint in China, he wrote the *cha jing* or 'Classic of Tea', a three-volume discourse covering every aspect of tea, from growing and brewing it to a description of a formal tea ceremony using dozens of tea utensils. During the Song tea tasting became an intellectual enjoyment and a means of cultivating one's moral character. It was seen to be in harmony with other arts such as poetry and painting.

Artefacts such as a Han dynasty model pottery stove and tea cups and saucers from the Southern dynasty among other items in the first galleries attempt to shed some light on the question of where tea-drinking began or how the wild tea bush, *Camellia sinensis* (a strain of camellia, but with duller flowers) arrived in China. It is thought that it was first brought in the Han dynasty from India with Buddhism via Sichuan, which today remains a main tea-growing region. Then it was most probably used for medicinal purposes. Certainly by the Tang, tea was being drunk for pleasure and had become a popular activity in the imperial court. At this time tea also started being traded for horses along the ancient 'tea-horse road' stretching from Sichuan and Yunnan provinces to the Tibetan Plateau. *Pu-erh* tea named after the area in Yunnan where it is produced became sought after by the Tibetans (they mixed it with yak butter) and for ease of transport was steamed and compressed into various shapes, including square blocks or bricks. Examples of those displayed include ones imprinted with patterns or designs and which were also used as a form of currency in China and Central Asia.

Tea-processing methods, which produce an intricate variety of specialities from black tea, white tea, green tea and Oolong tea etc. are demonstrated through images, diagrams and models. Green tea remains the most popular tea in China. Around 70 per cent of the world's trade is produced here made from unfermented leaves that are heated or steamed, rubbed, dried and rolled into a variety of shapes. Black tea is allowed to wither in the sun, then kneaded and allow to oxidize and finally dry roasted to stop the oxidation. The process of preparing infusions is also explained. Making a cup of Longjing tea is not a matter of just pouring boiling water on the leaves. Instead, two grams are placed in a transparent glass and infused with around a quarter of a cup of 80-degree centigrade water and left for 40 seconds before more hot water is poured in with three nods of the kettle until it is 70 per cent full. The filling action helps the leaves to 'dance' up and down and evens out the concentration between the layers, while filling it to just 70 per cent leaves 30 per cent for affection!

The second floor is split into two galleries and shows several hundred top class tea implements, including kettles, cups, trays and bowls from the glazed ceramic beauties of the Song dynasty, to an underglazed blue tea vase from the Qing. Objects include imperial pieces on loan from the Palace Museum and others from Korea and Japan. The Customs Hall describes the five main tea-drinking regions of China and their variations through recreated displays of their furnishings and sets of tea implements. Included is a bamboo pavilion from an area called the Xishuangbanna in southern Yunnan where the Dai and other ethnic groups grow the well-known *Pu-erh* tea in the tropical forests of this region, to the serene setting of Sichuan where green tea infused with jasmine blossoms is sipped from porcelain tea bowls complete with a lid and saucer.

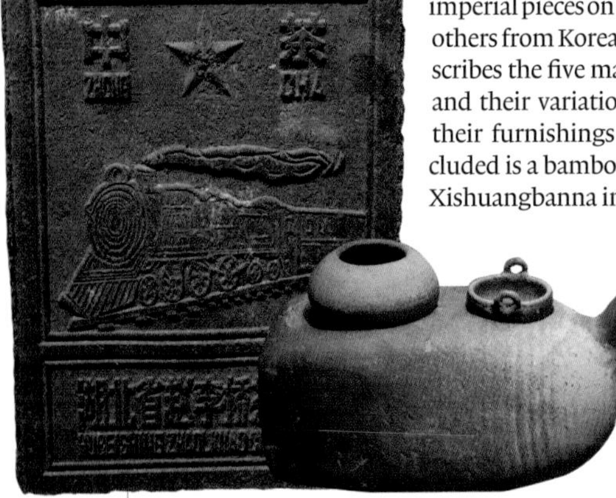

Mid twentieth century tea brick

Han dynasty ceramic tea kettle

136

Hu Qingyu Tang Traditional Chinese Medicine Museum

胡庆余堂中药博物馆 *Huqingyutang zhongyao bowuguan*

95 Daijing Lane, Hangzhou, Zhejiang
浙江省杭州市大井巷95号

Tel: (0571) 8781 5209
Open: 8.30–17.30
Chinese medicine pharmacy

The working Qing period pharmacy

Handheld balance scales are used to weigh the Chinese herbs

'Collect bulging caterpillar fungi... dry them in the dark... take five *bai* (grain-like plant), two *mendong* (drug from plants in the genus *Liriope*), and one *fuling* (pine truffle). Pestle them together... soak in water... press to obtain liquid ... drink a three-fingered pinch in one half cup of...' Although this sounds like the witches' brew from Shakespeare's Macbeth, it was written 1800 years earlier in a medical manual, entitled 'Recipes for Nurturing Life' unearthed in Tomb 3 at the famous Western Han dynasty site of Mawangdui in Hunan Province. It was one of eighty-seven detailed concoctions recorded in medical manuscripts written on silk. Today this 'curative' and other traditional Chinese herbal medical literature and plants are being screened for new drugs by the powerful Western drug companies in the hope of discovering new cures for cancers, malaria (extracted from the Chinese plant sweet wormwood and used for malaria since the second century BC) and other ailments. Step through the austere entrance of this museum cum working pharmacy and you'll be staring in awe at a rare original Qing period pharmacy and come face to face with jars and cabinets piled high with all kinds of weird and wonderful substances, from dried geckos to *Hippocampus* (sea horses) and behind the polished wooden counters, row upon row of small wooden drawers and mounds of paper-wrapped parcels filled with remedies. The only hint of the present are the dispensing

The herbs are mixed according to a prescription

A selection of desiccated herbs, lizards and sea horses

staff dressed in white lab coats. Even if you don't buy into traditional Chinese medicine (TCM), this place is a must, and you will come away with a broad sense of its philosophy; the desire to treat the body, mind and spirit as one system using a combination of herbs, diet and exercise.

The pharmacy was established in 1874 by the well-known Qing businessman, Hu Xueyan who besides dealing in silk and tea became known for his astute running of this successful medical dispensary. Since 1991 it also opened as a museum with displays presenting a general overview on the history and development of TCM with good English signage throughout. Included is an area demonstrating how pills were shaped and coated with wax and herbs were cut. There is a separate building where medicines were prepared and behind it what was once a deer farm. Their antlers were a common ingredient in many preparations and it was necessary to have a fresh supply always on hand. Ground up and mixed together with tortoise shell and ginseng they produced a remedy to replenish the *yin*, tone the *qi* (the body's energy) and strengthen the *yang* (the opposite of the *yin* and in Chinese medicine the two must be in balance for a healthy body). They were also widely used in a tonic produced in pill form – one to nourish the right kidney (*yang*), the other the left (*yin*).

Further displays consist of tools used for external treatments, such as bell-shaped cupping jars used in cupping, which treats pain in various ailments, mortars and pestles in all shapes and sizes for mixing, numerous books on concocting medicines, methods of processing, including stewing and fermenting, copper ladles, brushes, and a mussel shell cutter for slicing pills. There are sections describing medicines used by the various minorities. Fascinating is the current obsession and collecting methods of the parasitic fungus that grows on a caterpillar mentioned in the recipe above. Native to the Tibetan plateau, this rare and very expensive fungi (£19,000 a kilo) known as *Cordyceps* is considered a wonder drug, curing a whole range of ailments from hepatitis to sexual dysfunction and today can be found served at select restaurants in China and in Western skin creams and energy drinks.

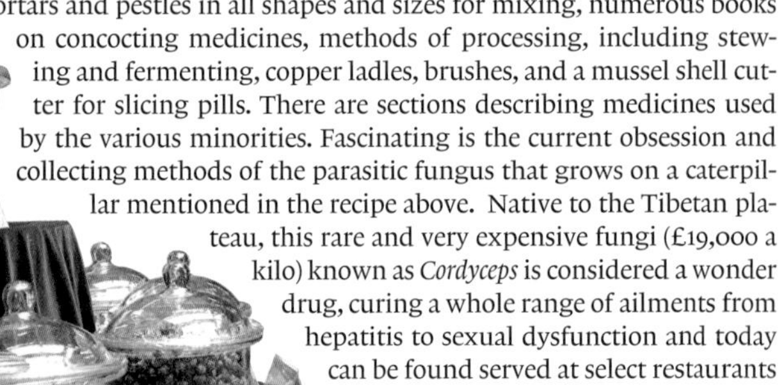

137 **Pan Tianshou Memorial Hall**

潘天寿纪念馆 *Pantianshou jinianguan*

212 Nanshan Road, Hangzhou, Zhejiang

杭州市南山路212号

(中国美术学院内)

Tel: (0571) 8791 2845

Open: 9.00–11.00, 13.30–16.30; except Mon & Fri afternoons

Shop with books on the artist, mostly in Chinese

Pan's desk and painting table

Pan Tianshou (1897–1971), one of the most important traditional Chinese painters of the twentieth century, is admired for his landscape, bird-and-flower and occasional figure painting and his calligraphy. Although he came from a small mountain village, his father sent him to a private village school as a young boy, where he studied literature, painting and calligraphy. When he was nineteen, he enrolled in the Zhejiang Provincial Teachers' College in Hangzhou, where he began to formally study painting. In 1923, Pan moved to Shanghai, where he was greatly influenced by the powerful calligraphy and fruit-and-flower painting style of the eighty-year-old master Wu Changshuo. In 1928, he was appointed to teach Chinese painting at the newly established National Academy of Art in Hangzhou, later becoming the president of the academy. It was not until the 1940s, however, that Pan began to develop his own unique style, but he did not fully mature as an artist for at least another decade. Pan came under harsh attack at the start of the Cultural Revolution (1966–1976), and continued to be persecuted right up until his death in 1971.

The Pan Tianshou Memorial Museum is divided into two parts, a residence and a gallery. Only the first floor of Pan's former home, where he spent his last years, is open to the public. Visitors can see his furnished studio and study and a limited display of his personal effects. The gallery, in an adjoining building in this complex, exhibits a collection of some of his finest works.

138 Southern Song Dynasty Guan Kiln Museum

南宋官窑博物馆 *Hangzhou nansong guanyao bowuguan*

42 Shijiashan Nanfu Road, Shangcheng District, Hangzhou, Zhejiang
浙江省杭州市南复路施家山42号

Tel: (0571) 8608 2071
Open: 8.30–16.30 except Mon & official holidays
www.ssikiln.com/doce/zs.htm

The word 'guan' means 'official', and guan kilns were set up to make porcelain exclusively for imperial use in both the Northern and Southern Song dynasties. The Song dynasty originally had its capital in Kaifeng (Henan Province) until Tartar invaders from the north forced them to flee southwards in 1127. Emperor Gaozhong established a new capital in present day Hangzhou, then known as Lin'an, where it remained until the end of the dynasty in 1279. Thus, the Song is divided into the Northern and Southern Song periods.

Two guan kilns were set up at Hangzhou, one near the Xiuneisi (the government department in charge of maintenance of imperial buildings, including kilns) and one at Jiaotan (the Altar of Heaven). The location of the Xiuneisi Kiln was a great mystery until it was finally discovered in excavations undertaken between 1996 and 2001 at the Tiger Cave Kiln site located near the north wall of the imperial city. The Jiaotanxia Kiln (the site of this museum) was first excavated in 1930 and then again in the 1980s and is located at the foot of Tortoise Hill on the south edge of West Lake.

Remains of the ancient kiln workshop

The dragon kiln is more than 40-m long

Guan ware of the Southern Song is considered one of the finest of the period and is famous for its celadon glaze which is light green, grey or yellow in colour. The body of the vessels is thin, with either a thick or thin glaze, but the best pieces are those with the thickest glaze – applied in many layers often thicker than the body itself. The rich, smooth and bright glaze is deliberately crackled, with names such as 'iron thread' for the black cracks and 'silk thread' for the yellow. Another characteristic is what is known as 'violet mouth and iron foot' which refers to a purplish colour on the upper rim caused by a separation of the glaze with the iron-rich clay left unglazed and exposed on the foot.

The modern museum galleries include ceramic examples in well-designed cases from the Neolithic to the Qing dynasty, as well as displays and signage in Chinese and English explaining the history and development of the Southern Song guan kiln.

During the Southern Song, guan kiln celadon was used for ritual ware, replacing shapes used in earlier Shang and Zhou dynasties bronze vessels. This is effectively illustrated in using photo-

Fragment of Southern Song celadon from the Guan Kiln; note the fine celadon glaze (below inset)

Western Jin dynasty (265–317) Yue Kiln lamp on display in the museum table

graphs of the earlier bronzes which hang above the porcelain objects on display.

Another part of the museum is the ancient kiln workshop site, with reproduction architectural features. It is hard to get a sense of the production process they attempt to describe from the sanitized and strangely bare excavation area, even though each feature is labelled. There is also a resident potter here and it is possible to try your hand at the craft, something particularly popular with visiting schoolchildren.

The highlight here, however, is the remains of the dragon kiln itself, which stretches upwards for over 40 m. Stairs have been added along the sides so you can walk along the length of the kiln, with the remnants of the firebox at the lower end visible. There were two main benefits to this type of kiln. Firstly, thousands of pots could be fired at once and secondly, the length and slope of the design, along with side stoking, allowed for a rapid rise to extremely high temperatures, followed by a quick fall. This was particularly advantageous in terms of the chemistry of the clay and glazes in use here, as the clay could be prevented from distorting or cracking during firing, allowing for a bright, clear finish to the glaze.

139

Zhang Xiaoquan Scissors Museum

张小泉剪刀博物馆 *Zhangxiaoquan jiandao bowuguan*

33 Daguan Road, Hangzhou, Zhejiang (inside the Zhang Xiaoquan Scissors Factory)

浙江省杭州市大关路33号 杭州张小泉剪刀厂内

Tel: (0571) 8882 3065
Open: 8.30–15.30 weekdays only
www.zxq2.mountor.net/e_index.asp

This small, but quirky collection of countless varieties of scissors is displayed within the Zhang Xiaoquan Scissors factory. The main factory areas are off limits; however, visitors are encouraged to view the three poorly lit rooms lined with cases displaying scissors that tell the story of their production in China dating from as far back as the late Eastern Han dynasty.

Since the Tang dynasty, the regions around Suzhou and Hangzhou south of the Yangtze River have been famous for silk production. Little wonder then to find Hangzhou home to this 300-year-old scissors-making company. Dating back to the Qing Dynasty (AD 1663), it was established by the city's celebrated scissors producer, Zhang Xiaoquan. By 1953 there were five scissors factories in Hangzhou bearing his name, each producing a specific type of scissor. Later, they were integrated under one roof and today manufacture scissors under a company which still bears the founder's name. It is one of the most famous scissor brands in China, producing a quality product which has been acknowledged by numerous awards won at international trade fairs now proudly on display. The make became a symbol of patriotism during the Cultural Revolution when Chairman Mao announced that one should 'never lose the scissors of Zhang Xiaoquan, even after ten thousand years'.

The three exhibition rooms are divided into The History of Scissors, the Art of Scissors and the Scissors Collection. There is no English signage; however, in the first gallery one can follow the history of the development of scissors by examining old documents, pictures and a selection scissors from the early Han and Tang dynasties. The oldest pairs are rather chunky curved blades of iron with crude-shaped holes at the ends for one's fingers, which later developed into more sophisticated cutting implements made in a variety of metals, shapes and sizes. Here you can also learn more about the history of the company through numerous objects, photographs and a portrait of Zhang Xiaoquan. A selection of scissors produced in the 1950s when the company was most productive can be seen in the second room, including the biggest scissors in China which measure 1.15 m in length and weigh 28.5 kg, as well as the smallest pair, measuring just 5.7 cm. Displays of original equipment and photographs illustrate the seventy-two steps once required to produce a pair of scissors compared to the less labour-intensive automated technology used today. More than 700 scissors line the cases of the last room with examples from countries including Germany, Japan, Korea, England, Hong Kong and Taiwan. The largest numbers are award-winning designs produced in China since 1960, and not surprisingly a majority are those manufactured by Zhang Xiaoquan ranging from a multi-purpose travelling pair, to fish scissors.

Right: Song dynasty scissors

Left: Tang dynasty scissors

The History of Scissors in China

Archaeological evidence suggests that scissors first appeared in China during the late Eastern Han dynasty, roughly 1,500 years after they were invented in Egypt. These first examples were made of two knives bound together with a loop in the shape of a figure eight. Later, the form altered slightly, as evidenced by both a bronze and an iron pair unearthed in Tang dynasty tombs. Both have two intersecting loops. Evidence points to scissors having been used as burial objects since the Jin dynasty, especially in female tombs. They were also considered excellent wedding presents, to endow the bride with good needlework skills. Scissor design appears to have remained the same during the Song dynasty and it was not until the Yuan dynasty that imported scissors as we know them today – with two separate finger holes – were introduced. This type then became widely used during the Ming. The renowned brand, Wang Mazi, was established during the Ming and remains popular today, along with those produced by the Zhang Xiaoquan factory.

140 Zhejiang Provincial Museum

浙江省博物馆 *Zhejiangsheng bowuguan*

25 Gushan Road, Hangzhou, Zhejiang

浙江省杭州市孤山路25号

Tel: (0517) 8797 1177 / 0017
Open: 12.00–17.00 Mon; 9.00–17.00 Tues–Sun
www.zhejiangmuseum.com/
Gift shop

This museum is set on the shore of Hangzhou's sublimely picturesque West Lake. The design of the museum is characteristic of Southern Yangtze River construction in that the building and its gardens seamlessly flow into one another. The serene lake in front and the green hills behind the building complete its perfect 'feng shui'.

In 1993 the museum was reconstructed and expanded. The complex consists of a main building with three floors and numerous additional gallery spaces – some of which are connected to the main building by covered walkways meandering through landscaped gardens.

The collection of over 100,000 objects come mainly from Zhejiang Province and exhibited objects are regularly rotated. Most of the galleries have labelling in both Chinese and English.

On the ground floor of the main building are two galleries dedicated to the Neolithic Hemudu and Liangzhu Cultures. This museum, like many in China, sometimes displays replicas of particularly valuable pieces which may not be labelled as copies. Note the (unmarked) replica of a lacquer beaker believed to be the earliest known example of Chinese lacquer ware from the Neolithic Hemudu Culture. From the third millennium BC Liangzhu Culture, be sure to see the jade battle axe excavated at Jaoshan, the jade *cong* (ritual object) with *taotie* decoration and an exceptional black pottery *ding* excavated in Huzhou. Also significant is a large stone plow head indicating the beginnings of agriculture and the possible of the use of animal labour. The second floor exhibits many artefacts from the Yue kingdom of the Spring and Autumn period. From Tomb no. 306 of the Yue kingdom Cemetery near Shaoxing

The galleries are named as follows:

- Historical Relics Gallery
- Celadon Gallery
- Gem Gallery
- Painting and Calligraphy Gallery
- Arts and Crafts Gallery
- Ming and Qing Furniture Gallery
- Coin Gallery
- Souvenir Gallery
- Wenlan Pavilion
- Zhejiang West Lake Gallery

Northern Song bodhisattva

Self-portrait of Chang Shuhong and family (right)

there are many fine examples of pottery, bronzes and weaponry. Don't miss the exceptional bronze tripod vessel with dragon spout, hoof-shaped feet and a lid adorned with animals.

In another room on this floor objects from the kingdoms of Wu and Yue are on view. During this time, known as the Five Dynasties and Ten Kingdoms period, the Wu and Yue kingdoms were united under the Emperor Qian Liu. This was a prosperous period in which there was much patronage of Buddhist art and architecture, hence the preponderance of Buddhist art in these galleries. Note the silver tablets inscribed with a prayer for good weather, which was thrown into the West Lake by King Qian Liu and found at the bottom of the lake, the white porcelain ware for use by the Emperor alone and a small bronze pagoda from the tomb of Qian Liu's parents.

Finally on this floor is the Northern Song Gallery. As Hangzhou was a capital during this period there are many fine Buddhist pieces in the collection including a model for the rebuilding of a pagoda. During the Song, models were often made of buildings before construction.

Also note a lovely small blue *sarira* glass vase with engraved decoration. Although glass was imported into China from the Han period, it was first made in China during the Song dynasty. *Sarira* are bead-like relics found in the ashes from the cremation of the Buddha. The *sarira* is placed in reliquaries which in turn are placed in a pagoda along with other offerings.

The third floor of the main building is dedicated to Zhejiang's history from the Opium War to 1949. Artefacts, photos and documents are presented.

One of the historical figures featured is Qiu Jin (1875–1907), a poet, orator and early leader of the Chinese women's movement. She was a collegue of many of the forward-thinking intellectuals of the time, including Cai Yuanpei and Sun Yat-sen. An ardent feminist, she fought for women's rights including the abolishment of foot binding and forced marriage and was co-founder of the 1906 journal 'Chinese Women'. Because of her revolutionary activity and following her involvement in an uprising in Shaoxing, she was tortured and then executed in July 1907.

As noted above there are many adjacent buildings in the museum. The gallery known as the Gem Gallery is not for viewing valuable stones, but rather to exhibit the very best, 'the gems' of the collection and of visiting collections. At the time of the author's visit this gallery had an exceptionally fine exhibition which was presented in a contemporary manner with well-lit cases but no English signage.

There are several galleries dedicated to individual Zhejiang painters. One of them is devoted to the paintings and drawings of the modern painter, Chang Shuhong (1904–1994) who was born in Hangzhou. Returning from France in 1936 where he was studying painting, Chang became very worried about the possible fate of the Mogao Grottoes (see no. 200) in Dunhuang during the Japanese invasion. Taking his family with him, he moved to the site in order to protect and conserve this world treasure. He spent the rest of his life dedicated to the preservation of these incomparable wall paintings and was appointed Director of the Dunhuang Cultural Relics Research Institute in 1950.

The Ming and Qing furniture gallery is sparse. At the time of writing, the display was dusty and poorly lit with no English signage.

The Celadon Gallery exhibits examples of ceramics from

the famous kilns of Zhejiang – the Yue, Wuzhou, Ou, Deqing, Southern Song Guan and the Longquan. The objects are displayed to illustrate the evolution of pottery to porcelain and the rise and fall of the various kilns.

The museum also has galleries dedicated to the exhibition of currency, gifts presented to the Province of Zhejiang by foreign countries, specialty crafts of the province such as lacquer ware, bamboo ware and ivory work and a painting and calligraphy gallery.

A new branch of the museum, located in downtown Hangzhou is scheduled to open imminently. We are told its galleries are entitled History and Culture of Zhejiang, Modern History of Revolutions in Zhejiang, Folk Art, and Paintings.

141

Ningbo Museum of Art

宁波美术馆 *Ningbo meishuguan*

122 Renmin Road, Laowaitan, Ningbo, Zhejiang

宁波市人民路122号

Tel: (0574) 8764 3222 (group booking); 8766 1709
Open: 9.00–17.00, last entry at 16.30 except Mon & during installations
www.nma.org.cn/
Gift shop / rooftop café

As a port city, Ningbo has a long history of prosperity dating back to the Tang dynasty, which was only recently overshadowed in the twentieth century by the development of Shanghai, just to its north.

This modern gallery (2005) was designed by Wang Shu of the Chinese Academy of Art. It is located on the site of the old port, and the building is a renovated passenger terminal. The museum is host to rotating domestic and international exhibits and is part of a planned 'Culture Corridor' along the river front, which includes the Exhibition Hall next door and the refurbished Bund, with galleries and restaurants, and additional museums under construction or still in planning stages.

142

The Museum of Hemudu Site

河姆渡遗址博物馆 *Hemudu yizhi bowuguan*

Hemudu Township, Yuyao, Zhejiang

浙江省余姚市河姆渡镇

Tel: (0574) 6296 3731 / 3732
Open: 8.30–17.00, last entry 16.20 Apr–Oct; 8.30–16.30, last entry 16.00 Nov–Mar
www.hemudusite.com/
A 20-minute video in Chinese, English or Japanese is available for viewing
English guide available / gift shop / restaurant

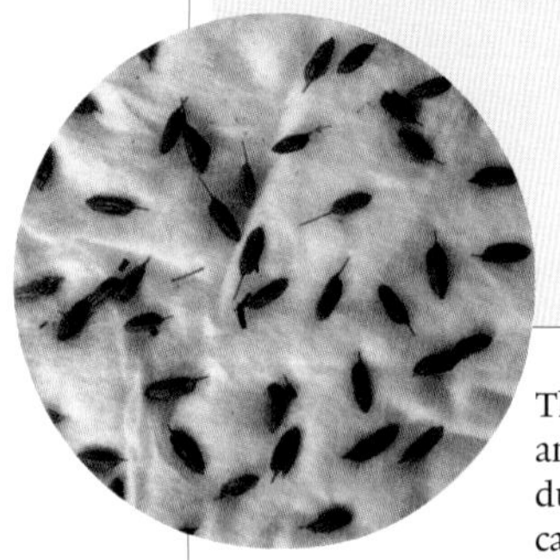

Preserved grains of rice found in paddy accumulation on site

The site contains a museum, an open excavation site, and a model village representing local life and customs during the Neolithic period. The Hemudu site has been carbon dated to between 7,000 and 4,700 years ago. The exhibits are from local excavations and tombs and include many items of daily use, including pottery and bone and wood tools such as needles and knives. In addition there are toys and decorative objects such as carved stone animals and ivory, jade and shell jewellry. Important information about the local Neolithic Culture can be gleaned from the artefacts unearthed at Hemudu, including the content of their diet and the centrality of rice, which is evidenced in pottery with rice designs and vessels that were found containing remnants of the grain. The model village contains buildings constructed using Hemudu architectural styles and materials, and has various scenes of typical Neolithic life, including clothing, weaving and cooking methods.

143

Tiantai County Museum

天台县博物馆 *Tiantaixian bowuguan*

Tiansi Village, Dongsheng Xingzheng Village, Tiantai County, Zhejiang

浙江省天台县东升行政村田思村

Tel: (0576) 8395 8799
Open: 8.00–17.00, closed for lunch 11.00–14.00
The museum is located along the road to Tiantai Mountain (Temple and Monastery), an important Buddhist site 200 km from Ningbo, 218 km from Hangzhou. Most tourists travel to Tiantai for the Buddhist monastery and attendant obligatory climbing of Mt Tiantai.

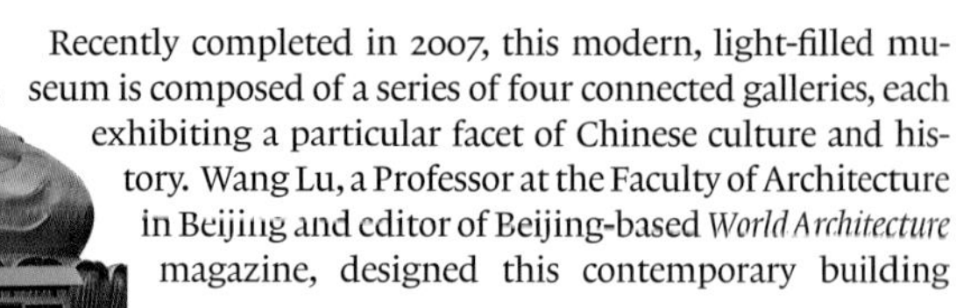

Buddha Workshop and Gallery

Recently completed in 2007, this modern, light-filled museum is composed of a series of four connected galleries, each exhibiting a particular facet of Chinese culture and history. Wang Lu, a Professor at the Faculty of Architecture in Beijing and editor of Beijing-based *World Architecture* magazine, designed this contemporary building

Combining local granite with traditional building techniques, Wang Lu has created a museum which sits serenely against the backdrop of the Zhejiang Mountains

using traditional building techniques, the four exhibition halls and internal patio referencing traditional courtyard houses, and the rough granite combine natural, yet weathered façade in keeping with the Buddhist traditions so central to the surrounding area. Two of the galleries are devoted to traditional Chinese paintings, the first featuring exhibits by local Zhejiang artists and the second devoted to building up a permanent collection, which is still in progress. Another gallery focuses on folk handicrafts, including embroidery and architectural and carved wood screens and furniture. Neolithic pottery, bronzes, porcelain and local historical photographs are well displayed with English signage, and there is even a fine exhibit of local fossils and dinosaurs for the young-at-heart Buddhists among you. Located next door is also the Buddha Workshop and Gallery which has a collection of Arhats and Buddhas and an enormous golden Buddha in the interior courtyard. If you are contemplating a Buddha purchase, this is the place to go.

144

Xikou Fenghaofang Chiang Kai-shek's Former Residence

溪口丰镐房 蒋介石故居 *Xikou Fenghaofang Jiang Jieshi guju*

Xikou Township, Fenghua, Zhejiang
浙江省奉化市溪口镇

Tel: (0574) 8885 0410
Open: 7.45–17.30

A popular tourist attraction or scam, depending upon which way you look at it, Chiang Kai-shek's hometown, 35 km from Ningbo is constantly bustling with sightseers and pedicabs, curious about one of modern China's more notorious sons. In 1949 Mao Zedong himself gave explicit orders that Chiang Kai-shek's (Jiang Jieshi) home was to be protected. The four primary sites included in the basic admission price are all connected to Chiang Kai-shek and his family. The Yutai Salt Shop was owned by Chiang's grandfather and where he was born in an upstairs room. Fenghao House was a later family home, and where Chiang's mother lived until her death during a Japanese bombing raid. The Jiang Ancestral Hall contains a record of Chiang's lineage and few captioned photos entitled 'A Photo Exhibit of Taiwan Issue'. The Wenchang

Pavilion is a Western-style home built by Chiang and was where Chiang and Soong Mei Ling lived for a time after their wedding in 1927. Adjacent to the house is the Wuling School, founded by Chiang in 1927 to be a model school. Chiang served as its first headmaster and remained involved in subsequent years. There is limited English signage and pictures of Chiang and his family throughout the four buildings, but some of the more interesting artefacts are found in Wenchang Pavilion and Wuling School, where Chiang's interest in education and desire to give something back to his hometown is evident. The museum is located on the old site of Wushan Temple, exhibiting locally found pottery, handicrafts and furniture.

Chiang Kai-shek (Jiang Jieshi, 1887–1975)

Whether reviled or revered, it is indisputable that Chiang Kai-shek, as he is more familiarly known, was an important figure in China's modern history. The son of a wine merchant, Chiang was born in Xikou, located near Ningbo. His father died when Chiang was a child, leaving his family impoverished so Chiang was sent to live with relatives. He soon ran off to join the provincial army and later attended the Military College in Tokyo. Chiang returned to China and supported Sun Yat-sen during the 1911 revolution, his regiment capturing Shanghai for the Nationalists. In 1924 Chiang was appointed head of the Whampoa Military Academy and after Sun Yat-sen's death in 1925, Chiang emerged as the leader of the Nationalist forces or Kuomintang (KMT), and proceeded to wage war against the Communists. When the Japanese invaded China in 1937, Chiang was forced to move his capital from Nanjing to Chongqing, and grudgingly agreed to collaborate with the Communists in order to fight the common enemy. After the Japanese defeat, the KMT and Communists resumed fighting. With the Communist victory in 1949, Chiang retreated to Taiwan, where he established a government in exile.

145

Liangzhu Culture Museum

良渚文化博物馆 *Liangzhu wenhua bowuguan*

Liangzhu Township, northern suburbs of Hangzhou, Zhejiang

浙江省杭州市北郊良渚镇

Tel: (0571) 8877 0700 / 8900
Open: 8.30–16.00 except Mon
www.liangzhuculturemuseum.com/index.asp

This is the first museum in China by one of England's celebrated architects, David Chipperfield. Built of cream and tan Iranian travertine, inspired by the colour of the jade artefacts for which the Liangzhu Culture is so famous, the glorious structure surrounded on three sides by water is set in charming new cultural parkland. Composed of four rectangular volumes of different heights, it rises out of the landscape like a sculptural form. A bridge leads to the en-

The museum created from four rectangular volumes of Iranian travertine was designed by David Chipperfield

trance where visitors can choose to view either the permanent collection or the temporary exhibitions. Internal courtyards link the indoor galleries, allowing natural light to enter and provide visitors with the experience of taking a journey through time. A second bridge in the rear of the building brings you to an island and the museum's outdoor exhibition area, as well as a view of the surrounding rolling landscape under which the artefacts from this Neolithic Culture emerged. Recently opened, it replaces the original Liangzhu Culture Museum built in 1994. It not only has more excavated objects on display, but also engages visitors through the use of interactive displays that explore the material and spiritual life of the Liangzhu.

The Liangzhu Culture (*c.* 3500–2500 BC), named after one of China's most important archaeological sites, is defined by its well-developed rice and silk agriculture (sections of silk looms were found), black-burnished pottery, lacquer ware and most of all by its quantity of stupendous jade artefacts found at sites located northwest of Hangzhou embraced by the Tianmu Mountains and two rivers. Several of this Culture's best-known sites, among more than 135 scattered across the area, are those of Fanshan, Yaoshan, Huiguanshan, Mojiaoshan and Tangshan. The site of Fanshan revealed burial grounds with graves for people of high rank, at Yaoshan there was a cemetery as well as earthen altar, while at the other sites defensive works and workshops were discovered. Among the objects displayed is a selection from the many thousands of jade objects found in the graves; at Fanshan alone around 3,200 were recovered. The jades are of outstanding craftsmanship and include the distinctive *cong* cylinder, *bi* disc and *yue* battle-axe shapes, as well as plaques incised with human-like faces with large bulging eyes often found alongside beads, indicating that they may have been personal adornments or associated with shamans. Certain shapes probably indicated status, power and sex of their owners, therefore indicating a stratified society. The *cong* (square in shape with a circular bore in the centre) found at Fanshan is the largest and most distinctive found to date in China. Milky-white in colour, it is decorated with pairs of faces, bird-like figures and human figures with large headdresses and must have belonged to someone important; however, their use remains a mystery. Visitors will leave having not only seen an amazing collection of artefacts, but knowing more about the possible uses and significance of the jade objects in the life of this Culture, as well as the methods of production.

Besides the display areas, there is an educational space where children can reconstruct a Liangzhu house, produce pottery, or enjoy multimedia programmes.

146 Anhui Provincial Museum

安徽省博物馆 *Anhuisheng bowuguan*

268 Anqing Rd, Hefei, Anhui
安徽省合肥市安庆路268号

Tel: (0551) 2823 465
Open: 9.00–17.00 except Mon
www.ahm.cn
English audio guide
Gift shops
Kids

Located in Yixian County in southern Anhui are houses typically laid out symmetrically with halls flanked by wing rooms and decorated with wood carvings and stone

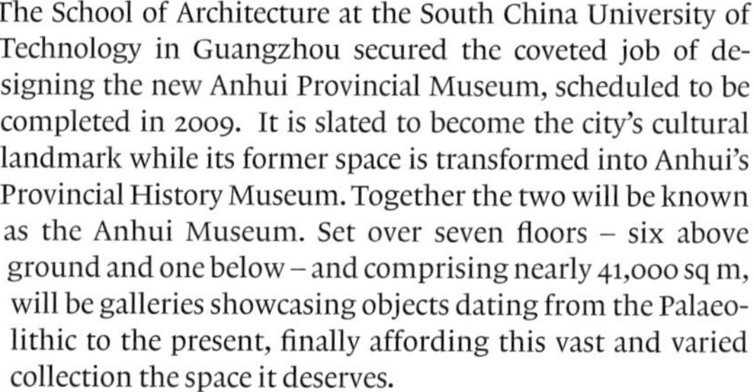

Buddhist stele, Northern Qi dynasty

The School of Architecture at the South China University of Technology in Guangzhou secured the coveted job of designing the new Anhui Provincial Museum, scheduled to be completed in 2009. It is slated to become the city's cultural landmark while its former space is transformed into Anhui's Provincial History Museum. Together the two will be known as the Anhui Museum. Set over seven floors – six above ground and one below – and comprising nearly 41,000 sq m, will be galleries showcasing objects dating from the Palaeolithic to the present, finally affording this vast and varied collection the space it deserves.

The exhibitions currently on view are well worth seeing should you happen to be in Hefei. There are superb collections of bronzes, pottery, porcelain, jade, ancient coins, paintings, fossils and natural history specimens, as well as displays of architecture and the 'Four Treasures of the Scholar's Study': writing brushes, ink sticks, ink slabs and paper. Highlights include the Anhui bronze treasures, with a number of exceptional ritual bronzes from the Shang dynasty, the vassal state of Cai (Spring and Autumn period) and the state of Chu (Warring States period). These include the most admired artefact in the museum: a large bronze *ding* from Chu weighing 400 kg, the largest extant one of its kind. On seeing it, Chairman Mao was said to have remarked that 'it was big enough to cook an ox in'. Equally exceptional are the Spring and Autumn period bronze vessels from the tomb of the Marquis of Cai, discovered in 1955 during a major construction project to harness the power of the Huaihe River.

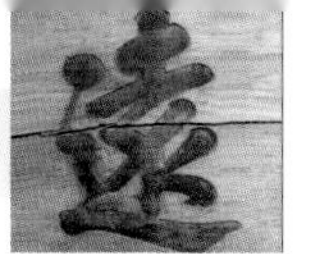

Scenic villages in the surrounding countryside are a popular tourist attraction and the basis for an award-winning exhibit on Huizhou vernacular architecture. The audio accompanying the exhibit is excellent, providing commentary on cultural history and beliefs. Such architecture is admired for it beauty and elegance, embodying as it does the aesthetic values of the region such as harmony and symmetry.

The museum's fine collection of ceramics extends from the Western Zhou to the Qing dynasties, and contains many unusual pieces, especially dating from the Western Zhou, Jin, Tang and Song periods. Notable among these are the Song dynasty celadon, including the rare bowl unearthed from a tomb of the Northern Song dynasty.

Currently, all the first-floor galleries are devoted to travelling exhibitions, from contemporary Chinese paintings to documentary photography. The museum is quite prolific when it comes to publishing collection catalogues; these include (among others) *Selected Masters' Paintings* and *Excavations from the Marquis of Cai Tomb in Shou County.*

147 Tonglushan Ancient Metallurgy Museum

铜绿山古铜矿遗址博物馆 *Tonglushan gutongkuangyizhi bowuguan*

30 km southwest of Tonglushan, Daye County, Huangshi, Hubei

湖北省黄石市西南30公里 铜绿山矿区

Open: The museum has been closed to visitors since 2007 due to subsidence from illicit mining in the area; call the Hubei Provincial Museum (Tel: (027) 8679 4127) to check if it has reopened

This is the largest and most important ancient copper-mining site in China; it was in use in ancient China for more than a thousand years, from the early Western Zhou to the Han dynasties. Discovered in 1965, later excavations revealed a number of techniques from drift mines (tunnels dug horizontally into the side of the mountain) to mines that slanted upwards. Wooden tunnel supports were constructed to prevent the walls from collapsing, and wooden lifting devices were used in the Warring States period and perhaps earlier to send baskets full of material up and, once emptied, back down again to be refilled. Tools used to process the ore – bronze, iron, bamboo and stone axes, adzes and picks – have been found along with tons of slag left over from the production of what is estimated to have been around 40,000 or more tons of copper.

Woodcut illustrating the smelting of tin with lead, which, combined with copper, produced bronze for casting artefacts

The museum is built over part of the site so that numerous shafts can be viewed from the large central hall. Displays along the surrounding walls illustrate the techniques used to mine copper, which, when alloyed with tin and lead, produced the bronze used to cast the magnificent ritual vessels that can be seen in collections in China and elsewhere. The site has been on the UNESCO World Heritage list since 1996.

148 Hubei Provincial Museum

湖北省博物馆 *Hubeisheng bowuguan*

156 Wuchang Donghu Road, Wuhan City, Hubei

湖北省武汉市武昌东湖路156号

Tel: (027) 8679 4127
Open: 9.00–17.00 except Mon; last entry 15.30
www.hubeimuseum.net
English audio guide

The Hubei Provincial Museum, which houses more than 200,000 cultural relics, is located on the banks of the beautiful East Lake. Some 1,000 items are considered to be national treasures. The museum is divided into three sections: the Chu Culture Exhibition Hall, the newly opened Comprehensive Exhibition Building, and the Chime Bells Exhibition Hall. It is one of the best provincial museums in China. There are good English descriptions on the displays.

The Chu Culture Exhibition Hall, the first building on your left after you enter the grounds, features the regional culture of the state of Chu, which dates back to the Spring and Autumn period (770–476 BC). The cultural relics exhibited in this hall are primarily bronze vessels, lacquer ware, bamboo and wooden artefacts, and silk products. Some of the highlights include ancient weapons such as the sword of Gou Jian (King of the Yue state in the Spring and Autumn period) and the shaft of Fu Chai (King of the Wu state), both still in excellent condition. The sword is as legendary in China as King Arthur's sword is in the West. On the blade near the handle are eight seal characters that proclaim: 'This sword belongs to Goujian, the King of the Yue State'. Other ancient weapons include a crossbow, a bronze dagger axe and a lacquer shield, all from the Warring States period. There is also a large model of the ancient capital of Chu, later known as Ji'nancheng, and exhibits showing smelting and casting.

In 2002, archaeologists discovered the remains of chariots and horses from the Chu era. Some of the chariots and skeletons were painstakingly excavated and are displayed in this hall. There are two pits here, one real, the other a replica. This room also displays chariot parts, including fittings for bridles and decorative bronze axle caps.

Bell stand hung with sixty-five bronze chimes on three tiers from the tomb of the Marquis Yi of Zeng; the bells are ornamented with knots and held in place with clasps in the shape of tigers

The museum's central structure, the Comprehensive Exhibition Building, opened in September 2007. On the second floor are exhibits of lacquer ware, including ear bowls (so named because they look like ears) and jade, as well as displays explaining ancient customs such as hairstyles, clothing, headgear styles and forms of recreation.

The third floor has several exhibits. 'The Art of Earth and Fire' displays ancient porcelain such as celadon, blue and white and official kiln porcelain. The Lacquer Hall exhibits bowls, ear cups, pitchers and wine vessels. There's also a section on the history of writing on bamboo. One of the main items of interest is Prince Liang Zhuang's tomb. This room

Bronze food container of the *dui* type, Spring and Autumn period

has a selection of beautiful items made from gold: teapots, buttons, ear picks, coins, belts, hair pins, head ornaments, bracelets and so on. In the Yunxian Man Exhibition Hall there are examples of fossils from the Palaeolithic period. Archaeologists say that two skulls on exhibit are fossils of *Homo erectus* dating back a million years. Their facial features are similar to that of palaeoanthropological fossils that have been excavated in other parts of China.

The fourth floor features exhibits of modern paintings and photos of Hubei's favourite sons from the past century. There's also a gift shop, a café and an area outside from which you can see the city.

The Chinese Bells Exhibition Hall is on your left as you walk back towards the gate. In 1978, 15,000 items were excavated from the tomb of Marquis Zeng, King of the Zeng state in the Warring States period. Discovered in Suizhou, these included bronze ritual vessels and weapons, horses and carts, items made of bamboo, lacquer, gold and jade, coffins and musical instruments. The highlight of the excavation is the sixty-five bronze chimes hanging on a three-tiered rack weighing more than 2,000 kg. Although the bells date back more than a thousand years, their tone quality is still excellent. The chimes are believed to be the biggest and oldest bells in existence. Of various sizes, they play a range of tones on the musical scale. Some 3,000 ancient gilt Chinese characters are inscribed on the bells and hooks, providing us with the oldest known details about musicology. Several times a day, musicians dress up in ancient costumes and perform on a replica set. Bell performances last twenty minutes.

149

Dayi Liu Family Estate Museum / Rent Collection Courtyard

大邑刘氏莊园博物馆 *Dayiliu shizhuangyuan bowuguan*

Anren Township, Dayi County, Sichuan
四川大邑县安仁镇

Tel: (028) 8831 5113
Open: 9.00–17.00

A tour of the typical Qing dynasty home of the landlord Liu Wencai is only of moderate interest. The complex, home to Liu's extended family, was originally built in 1931. It had twenty-seven courtyards, three gardens decorated in both Western and Chinese style, and about 180 rooms. An addition was completed in 1938 with a further 170 rooms and three courtyards. Besides an opium warehouse and tennis court, there are various outbuildings. Visitors led by a guide can peek into some of the living quarters fitted out with fusty furniture and accoutrements. Liu's old car is displayed behind glass, and exhibition halls feature rosewood furniture, wedding paraphernalia and other Qing artefacts. The most pleasant part of the visit, though, is wandering through the gardens.

Dayi Liu Family Estate Museum / Rent Collection Courtyard

The Qing dynasty home of the landlord Liu Wencai served as the backdrop to one of the most emblematic works of Mao era art – *The Rent Collection Courtyard*. Still in situ, it is a collection of 114 life-sized clay figures in a series of scenes depicting the heinous deeds of a pre-revolutionary landlord. These figures, combined with props such as brooms, hoes, baskets and other agrarian implements, form twenty-six tableaux of misery and despair. Starving, beaten and abused peasants are exploited and assaulted as they come to pay their rent, the grain is measured and so on.

This political work, meant to stir the emotions, instil revolutionary fervour and highlight class struggle, was created a year before the beginning of the Cultural Revolution by a group from the Sichuan Art Academy whose names were kept anonymous in keeping with the revolution's collective ideals. The piece soon became famous, a model sculpture and favourite of Jiang Qing, Mao's wife. Adaptations and revisions were made, and it travelled around the country and abroad.

In 1999, at the Venice Biennale, the celebrated artist Cai Guo-Qiang won a prize for a work entitled *Venice's Rent Collection Courtyard* which re-created some of the original figures. As they were fired, the sculptures cracked and then disintegrated, revealing the armatures around which they'd been constructed. This work of part conceptual part performance art caused outrage in China and started a huge debate about the place and value of contemporary art. Cai, the Biennale and its director were threatened by a lawsuit brought by the Sichuan Academy of Fine Arts and some of the original artists for copyright infringement – an irony considering that when the original work was created, it would have been unthinkable for individuals to take credit for it. Cai has since made another version, *New York Rent Collection Courtyard*, which was shown at the Guggenheim Museum in New York in 2008.

150 Jianchuan Museum Cluster

建川博物馆聚落 *Jianchuan bowuguan juluo*

Anren Township, Dayi County, Sichuan
四川省大邑县安仁镇

Tel: (028) 8831 8000
Open: 9.00–17.30 except Chinese New Year's Eve
www.jc-museum.cn
English and Chinese audio guides
Hotel / restaurant on the premises

Hold on to your hats – this is one of the most impressive museum experiences you will ever have. Fan Jianchuan, the owner of this private complex, has personally built it, with his own money, a half billion RMB at last count, to house his collection of more than 8,000,000 (yes, EIGHT MILLION) artefacts dealing primarily with the Cultural Revolution and the War against Japan. This charismatic powerhouse of a man is not a materialist gone mad; his museums are an expression of his wish to expose man's inhumanity to man, and to show that although the Japanese behaved savagely to the Chinese during the war, the Chinese did the same to their own people during the Cultural Revolution. He wants us to remember, to learn, to honour the heroes of these struggles and to admit to the many shameful acts of the times. The fact that this museum even exists in China is reason enough to visit. As one walks through the exhibitions, the message is clear: Never forget.

What is displayed is only the tiny tip of the iceberg – much is stored away, still too sensitive to be safely exhibited. Documents, photos, diaries and letters must wait for their creators to die before they go on view. Twenty-five museums are planned for the site – ten had been completed and opened at the time of writing. Each building has been designed by a well-known contemporary architect, whether Chinese or foreign. These are not tiny galleries but full-size buildings, each meticulously designed to reflect its content. The cases and exhibits are creative, imaginative and innovative with signage in both Chinese and English.

The grounds are set round a lake, and you travel from museum to museum either by walking down the tree-shaded lanes or by hitching a ride from one of the golf carts cruising the complex. All of the museums have a social or political aspect – even the two 'folk art' museums (the Gallery of Furniture from Private Houses, which features a set of furniture from the Sichuan State Guest House used by China's leaders from the 1960s through the 1980s, and the Three-Inch Shoe Museum). The experience in each one is unique. For instance, when one enters the Three-Inch Shoe Museum (Bound Feet Shoe Museum), at first it seems as if you're entering a brothel – the walls are pink, beaded curtains divide the space, the lights are low. Looking up, you are faced with big posters showing photographs of unwrapped 'lotus feet' and a description of the mutilation young girls were forced to undergo. As you walk through the gallery looking at all the paraphernalia of female repression, humiliation and sexual exploitation, you find yourself tripping and losing your balance on the uneven floor – and you realize the intention: this is what it is like to walk when your feet have been broken and bound.

The POW museum is built as a prison – a razor of light streaming in from the high window above, bleak grey walls, bars and cells all are deeply affecting, as are the accompanying

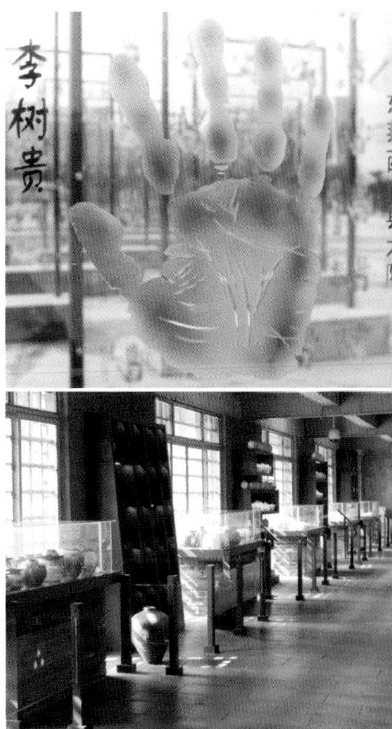

Handprint on the Veterans of the Anti-Japanese War Handprints Plaza.

The Porcelain Gallery

Chinese Heroes Statue Plaza

Flying Tigers Museum

period letters, artefacts and uniforms. Lining the walls are stark images of the Japanese committing atrocities against Chinese prisoners. As the Japanese have still not acknowledged the full extent of their barbarism, this gallery is deeply moving. Rather shaken, you pass out of the gallery through the barred gates and find yourself walking alongside a peaceful pond. On the wall is a plaque with the smiling photo of one POW, Cheng Penghua, reminding us that war is all about the sacrifice of individuals.

Each of the anti-Japanese-war museums focuses on a single theme. Open so far are the Hall of the Resistance, Hall of the Conventional Battlefront, Hall of the Sichuan Army, Chinese Prisoner of War Museum and Flying Tiger Museum. As well as the galleries above, there are two open-air exhibits: the Chinese Heroes Statue Plaza and Veterans of the Anti-Japanese War Handprints Plaza.

The collection of Cultural Revolution material, which for political reasons is referred to as 'Red Age', is exhibited in the Porcelain Gallery; the Daily Necessities Gallery; and the Badge, Clock and Seal Hall. The galleries are filled to the gills, and the message is presented in a subtler fashion than that about the War against Japan for obvious reasons. At the time of writing this is the only museum displaying such a comprehensive collection of Cultural Revolution artefacts in the country. Galleries planned for the future include, for the Anti-Japanese War: Chinese People Against the Invaders Hall, Japanese Invaders Hall, Traitors Hall; for the 'Red Age': Food Coupon and Daily Necessity Hall, Mirror Hall, Poster Hall, Music and Images Hall, Hall of Educated Youth, and the Square of Memory; and finally for Folk Art: Hall of Old Images, Hall of the 'Shuang Di'(double happiness) Culture, Hall of Brush Pots, Hall of Wooden Signs, and Hall of Smoking and Gambling Equipment.

One of the outdoor plazas is filled with life-size bronze statues of historical figures from the Civil War – both KMT and Communists – standing side by side. The arrangement invites you to walk between and around each one contemplating their past acts. Set in another plaza nearby is a display of large vertically mounted sheets of glass covered with orange handprints of Chinese veterans from the Anti-Japanese War inscribed with their names. It is a moving memorial, a combination of history and memory. At the time of our visit, the handprints of 3,000 soldiers were displayed – they hope to get 8,000.

To see the entire museum complex and leave time for contemplation you'll need at least two days. It's possible to stay in one of the two small guesthouses on the site or in the larger hotel. Reservations are essential.

Cultural Revolution

The origins of the chaotic and bloody Cultural Revolution (1966–76) go back to a rift in the Chinese Communist Party over the failure of the Great Leap Forward, which discredited Mao's economic plans and forced him to take a back seat in policy making. The 'Great Cultural Proletarian Revolution' began as a campaign by Mao to win back his power in the party.

Called 'Cultural' because initially Mao picked off his enemies through criticism of writings which had been a veiled attack on him, the revolution exploded into life in the summer of 1966 as he encouraged Red Guards (high school and university students) to verbally and physically attack people in authority ranging from professors and intellectuals to Party chiefs. Countless individuals were murdered or driven to suicide.

Though the Cultural Revolution did espouse 'radical' economic and social policies aimed at stopping China slipping into Soviet-style 'revisionism', in many cases these issues were inextricably linked to the power struggle that unfolded.

Having achieved the goal of purging the Chairman of the People's Republic, Liu Shaoqi, as well as Deng Xiaoping and other leaders who opposed him, in 1969 Mao sent the army in to take control of the country and rebuild the Communist Party.

The second phase, from 1969 to 1976, saw an uneasy calm return to the country. As Mao became increasingly senile, the 'Left', including his wife Jiang Qing, continued to instigate campaigns against Premier Zhou Enlai and other remaining moderates. The prisons, farms and labour camps held numerous officials and intellectuals.

In 1976, shortly after Mao's death, the 'Gang of Four' (including his wife) was arrested, and the Cultural Revolution ended. Deng Xiaoping soon took power, intellectuals returned from exile in the countryside, and economic reforms, including the dismantling of the People's Communes, were launched.

Today, the Chinese authorities widely acknowledge the 'serious mistakes' of Mao and the Cultural Revolution but stop short of acknowledging the complete truth for fear of undermining their own legitimacy and that of the Party.

151

Chengdu City Museum

成都市博物馆 *Chengdushi bowuguan*

Tianfu Square, Chengdu
四川省成都市天府广场

Scheduled to open in 2010/11

The Edinburgh-based architects Sutherland Hussey won first prize in the international competition to design this new museum in the heart of Chengdu. It will sit along one edge of Tianfu Square as part of a plan to create pedestrian routes through the site. These 'shortcuts' will allow people respite from the

Architect's rendering of the museum exterior

hustle and bustle of the square and the surrounding road traffic. It will also give them the opportunity to engage momentarily with the displays or events taking place in the museum. A monumental opening through the south-western part of the building will become a covered outdoor space where people can mingle, events can be held, or market stalls can be installed.

Collaborating with Pansolution International Design, the architects designed a dramatic structure with a glazed south façade and a large roof light which allows natural light to pour into and through the interior. The exterior will be covered in patinated brass-alloyed panels wrapped around a perforated mesh, resulting in a structure which has an intense gold colour by day and a golden glow at night, alluding to the gold artefacts of the province's ancient Shu Culture and to the Sichuan tradition of the shadow-play.

Over six storeys of exhibition space, natural history objects, folk art, history collections and shadow puppets will be displayed.

152 Chengdu Shu Brocade and Embroidery Museum

成都蜀锦织绣博物馆 *Chengdu shujinzhixiu bowuguan*

268 South Huanhua Road, Chengdu
成都市浣花南路268号

Tel: (028) 8738 3668 / 3891
Open: 8.00–18.00
www.cdbem.cn
English guides available upon request
Gift shop

Shu embroidery characterized by bright colours and detailed designs

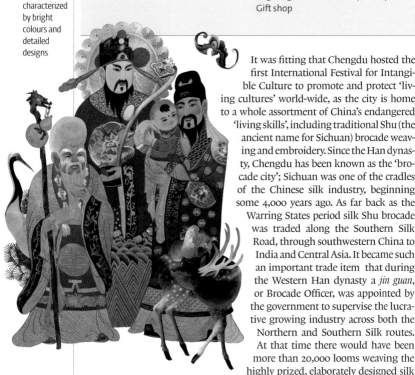

It was fitting that Chengdu hosted the first International Festival for Intangible Culture to promote and protect 'living cultures' world-wide, as the city is home to a whole assortment of China's endangered 'living skills', including traditional Shu (the ancient name for Sichuan) brocade weaving and embroidery. Since the Han dynasty, Chengdu has been known as the 'brocade city'; Sichuan was one of the cradles of the Chinese silk industry, beginning some 4,000 years ago. As far back as the Warring States period silk Shu brocade was traded along the Southern Silk Road, through southwestern China to India and Central Asia. It became such an important trade item that during the Western Han dynasty a *jin guan*, or Brocade Officer, was appointed by the government to supervise the lucrative growing industry across both the Northern and Southern Silk routes. At that time there would have been more than 20,000 looms weaving the highly prized, elaborately designed silk

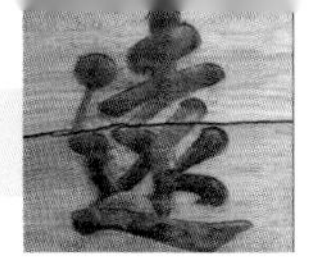

brocade. Today there are at most twenty people capable of operating the looms.

Recently relocated from its original site at the now defunct Shu Brocade Factory, this brand-new space is home to both the Shu Brocade Institute and the museum. Positioned near the River Huanhua, it was designed by one of China's leading architects (and local boy) Liu Jiakun, who is been celebrated world-wide for his imaginative creations, among them the stunning Luyeyuan Stone Sculpture Museum, also located in Sichuan. Over two floors the Shu brocade museum presents all facets of its subject, from its ancient history and the role it played in trade, to the development of the wooden looms used to weave it. Besides displaying examples of Shu brocade, silk embroidery and silk tapestry from the Tang dynasty to the present day, photographs, books illustrating the craft, and Qing dynasty brocade costumes, the Institute has enrolled the services of several retired master weavers from the Shu Brocade Factory to teach young interns with the aim of saving the ancient craft from extinction.

Weaving demonstrated on a replica Qing Shu brocade platform jacquard loom

At the museum's heart is an exhibition hall with five Shu brocade platform jacquard looms (known as *dahualou*) from the Qing dynasty (one is original, the others replicas) at which visitors can watch weavers at work. A complicated and highly skilled craft, Shu brocade requires more than a dozen preparation steps before weaving can begin, and these take up to six months for each motif. They include pattern designing, colour matching, basic weaving and pattern transfer. A loom, 6 m long by 5 m high and 1.5 m wide, requires two people to operate, a task undertaken more frequently by men than women, although there are woman weavers. Weavers train for more than two years just to learn the basic skills, and several more to become proficient and earn the title of 'master weaver'.

Watching the weavers in action is like seeing a well-choreographed dance. As the top weaver is pulling up the silk warps and separating them, the weaver seated at the bottom pushes the shuttles with the silk weft through them while controlling the shafts by a series of peddles called treadles. To produce brocade you have the addition of a supplementary weft, usually of a material different to that of the ground weft. These supplementary weft threads are often gold or silver, which catch the light and add a subtle shimmer to the final fabric. It takes good rhythm and perfect timing, with the top weaver controlling the pattern and the one below the colours and the speed at which it is woven. To produce 1 cm of brocade it takes 160 shuttle movements, producing on average only 7 cm of fabric per day depending upon the design.

The heyday of Shu brocade production lasted for about a thousand years from the Western Han dynasty through to the Song. It was particularly prized by the imperial family of the Northern Song dynasty because of its elaborate patterns and colours. Borrowing from the techniques of Shu brocade, three other schools of brocades were established, including Song brocade of Suzhou in Jiangsu Province; *Yun* (or Cloud) brocade of Nanjing, also in Jiangsu Province; and Zhuang brocade in Guangxi Zhuang Autonomous Region.

In an effort to keep this craft alive, the museum complex has a large shop specializing in fashionably designed products produced using old methods of embroidery. In 2006, Shu brocade weaving was listed as one of 'China's Intangible Cultural Heritages' by the Ministry of Culture.

153 Jinsha Archaeological Site Museum

金沙遗址博物馆 *Jinsha yizhi bowuguan*

2 Jinshayizhi Road, Chengdu
成都市 金沙遗址路 2号

Tel: (028) 8730 3522
Open: 8.00–17.30
www.jinshasitemuseum.com
English and other language guides / English and Chinese audio guides
Book / gift shops

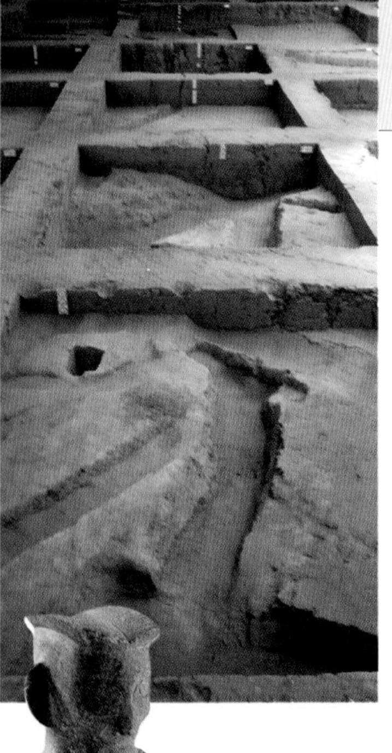

The excavation at the sacrificial zone

Sacrificial stone sculpture of kneeling man

In February 2001 construction for new housing in the village of Jinsha near Chengdu was halted as a trove of gold, bronze, jade, stone and ivory artefacts was unearthed. This site became known as one of the most exciting archaeological discoveries in Chinese history. Many of the objects bear a close relationship to those found at nearby Sanxingdui, helping to create a timeline for the mysterious ancient Shu kingdom.

Archaeologists then realized that a site discovered in a village near Jinsha was a part of that ancient city. So the two were combined into what is now a single site covering 5 sq km. Within it, archaeologists have identified a large building or palace zone, a residential zone, a graveyard and a sacrificial zone along the banks of an ancient river. Other smaller sites nearby have been identified as Shu kingdom sites, but Jinsha is by far the largest and has the most valuable artefacts and largest structures and so is believed to have been the capital city. It is now thought that when Sanxingdui was abandoned, the Shu capital moved to Jinsha until its mysterious decline around 600 BC.

The museum, opened in 2006, is set within beautiful landscaping and includes exhibits, open trenches in which there are walkways, a conservation studio and a visitor centre.

The archaeology tells us that the history of Jinsha can be broken into three distinct phases. Phase I dates to the late Shang period. The objects found in this phase are mainly ivory and stone. One sacrificial pit included fifteen ivory tusks in addition to other ivory objects. The longest one, on display in the museum encased in silicon, measures a whopping 8.5 m! Whether or not this ivory comes from wild elephants living in the area has been debated. Scientists now think they did live here as inscriptions from the Shang in the central plains speak of kings hunting them and of their use in battle. As the climate at the time was warmer than today and the Chengdu Plain was forested, it is not unlikely that elephants thrived here.

Phase II is equivalent to the late Shang to mid Western Zhou and marks the high point of Jinsha Culture. This is when we find beautiful bronzes, gold and jade, as well as some ivory. Phase III (late Western Zhou and early Spring and Autumn period) was a time of decline. Many fewer bronze and ivory artefacts have been found, though tortoise shells used for divination

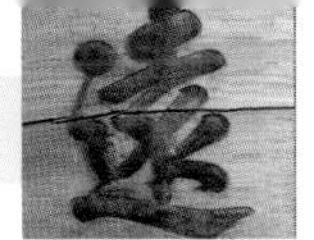

feature in this era. They were burned and cracked but carry no inscriptions. It is hard to believe that a culture as advanced as the Shu had no system of writing.

More than 2,000 graves have been discovered at Jinsha, all with a chamber running northwest to southeast. The bodies lie face up with their hands on their chests. There are single, group and couple burials. Some contain funerary objects; most are humble, but a few contain jade and bronze artefacts.

The finest objects at Jinsha were found in the sacrificial pits, and these trenches are open to public view. The quality and quantity of the gold and gilt objects here exceed any other pre-Qin site in China. So far, more than 200 gold artefacts have been unearthed, mostly gold foils attached to bronze objects. Now famous and the symbol of China Cultural Heritage is the circular 'Sun and Bird Gold Foil'. Cut out from the foil is the image of the sun with its rays swirling out in curves. Encircling the rays are four stylized divine birds. This iconography, not unusual in ancient China, was connected with sun worship.

Sun and bird gold foil, cut-out diameter 12.5 cm

Bi (disc) diameter: 10.6 cm, originally grey jade; however, now multi-coloured due to minerals in the soil

Bronze objects at Jinsha also show a close similarity to those at Sanxingdui. More than 1,200 bronze items have been excavated. It is interesting to see how our knowledge of the Shu kingdom is enhanced by comparing and contrasting the material culture of Sanxingdui and the Jinsha. For example, a small standing bronze figure was excavated at Jinsha which looks very much like the very large figure at Sanxingdui that originally held something in its cupped hands. Exactly what was being held is debated – a stick, a jade blade, something ceremonial? The hands of the small Jinsha figure are curved and look as if they could have been holding an ivory tusk. This theory is backed up by another object on display, a jade blade, finely and delicately etched, showing a man carrying a tusk over his shoulder.

Jade objects were also made with excellent craftsmanship and plentifully; more than 2,000 had been excavated by 2007. These include vessels, chisels, dagger-axes and other items. Most of the stone was locally sourced and includes hopfnerite, nefrite and marble. Be sure to see the ten-section jade *cong* identified as a 'national treasure'. It was brought into Jinsha from outside as it predates the Culture by a thousand years. Perhaps it came from the Liangzhu Culture in Zhejiang.

A tremendous amount of pottery has been found at Jinsha. Many typical forms are found; however, there are some unique shapes including certain types of cups and jars with pointed bottoms. These are all displayed in the museum.

This site should be visited in conjunction with a visit to Sanxingdui to give you an understanding of the Shu kingdom and ancient Sichuan. The basement gallery at Jinsha offers a lot of comparative material and posters explaining the history of the place and its relationship to other cultures in Sichuan, China and the rest of the ancient world.

154 Luyeyuan Stone Sculpture Museum

鹿野苑石刻艺术博物馆 *Luyeyuan shikeyishu bowuguan*

Yunqiao Village, Xinminchang Township, Pixian County, Chengdu

成都郫县新民场镇云桥村

Tel: (028) 8797 6166 / 6266
Open: 9.00–17.00
Ring at least one day in advance for an English guide

Sui dynasty standing Buddha

A drive of less than an hour from Chengdu brings you to a small farming village in Pixian County. Nestled against the banks of the Fu River is this delightful museum of primarily Buddhist stone sculpture designed by Liu Jiakun (one of China's leading architectural lights), who was born in Chengdu. Using a contemporary repertoire of grey reinforced concrete, shale, blue stone, glass and steel, he has created a remarkable modern structure that sits effortlessly in its traditional setting. Commissioned by a private client with connections to the Xiangcai Stock Company, the exhibition space is joined by a restaurant, meeting room and hotel for use by the company and others wanting conference facilities in an unusual and tranquil setting.

Upon arrival, you are greeted by a guard posted in the parking lot, but once you express your interest in viewing the collection you are directed to a meandering path hidden between magnificently groomed screens of bamboo which leads to the museum's entrance. A short walk along the stone-lined trail past the odd sculpture hidden between the bamboo groves brings you to a ramp that bridges a small lotus pond and deposits you on the second storey of the museum. Walk up towards the building, and the architect's desire for the visitor to experience a journey and leave their troubles behind – as on a pilgrimage to Mt Emei, the province's most holy Buddhist site – is achieved in spades. An entire wall in the dramatic double-height space bathed in light displays a large map showing the spread of Buddhism from India to all parts of Asia. While Indian Buddhist monks gradually travelled northwards across the mountain passes into China, Chinese pilgrims travelled in the opposite direction seeking information and opportunities to worship the 'Enlightened One'. Buddhism eventually reached China by the first century AD and by the end of the fourth century was well established. During the Northern Wei dynasty, a host of temples transformed the landscape, and sacred icons and sculpture were commissioned and produced in large numbers.

Displayed against the rough interior concrete walls, in spaces and voids delineated by large planes of glass, is a selection from more than 2,000 stone figures and works of art, the majority of which are Buddhist sculptures. The collections, dating from the Han, Southern and Northern dynasties, Tang, Song and Ming, are rotated regularly. The anonymous owner has a personal interest in Buddhist and other stone sculpture, and was instrumental in amassing this company-owned collection. A large number of the artworks come from areas along the Southern Silk Road, which extended from India through present-day Myanmar to Yunnan and across to Sichuan. Together with the Northern Silk Road through the Taklamakan Desert, this route formed a vast network along which tea, horses and silks were

Song dynasty Buddha head

traded, and Buddhism and (later) Nestorian Christianity and Islam were introduced to China. Along with these religious beliefs came a stream of sculpture, stelae and icons.

You encounter some of the first sculptures as you make your way round the second-storey gallery, which wraps around a roofed court dating from the Eastern Han dynasty. They include sandstone human figures, stone tomb gates carved with whimsical humans and animals, Buddha figures and pottery tomb figurines, all perfectly mounted on purpose-built black metal mounts. Labels and signage are in Chinese and English. There is a sign stating that all objects are original and authenticated by the Sichuan Institute of Social Science. However, ancient Chinese sculpture is extremely difficult to date, and it is well known that designs have been repeated using the same stones up to modern times.

A long table displays more than thirty samples illustrating the various stones used to produce the sculptures; these range from brown sandstone to dark green marble. Look over the balustrade down into a space brimming with Buddhist sculptures and long, thin windows opening out onto the manicured landscape and open-air exhibition spaces. A line of Sui dynasty standing disciples set in small lit alcoves leads to a narrow stairwell and into another large masonry volume filled with an enormous display of Song dynasty Buddhist heads, bodhisattvas (attendants of the Buddha) and figural triads in which the Buddha is flanked by bodhisattvas against an almond-shaped mandorla. Further along is a Tang green stone tablet illustrating a preaching Sakyamuni (the founder of Buddhism) with an arched top decorated with dragons. Here evidence of the sculptural styles that developed as Buddhism spread along the trade routes across Central Asia and then mixed with Chinese qualities is obvious.

A stone-lined path leads to other partially connected spaces including one entitled 'The Gallery of Three Lives'. A white and grey space with one wall painted Tibetan red, it exudes a Zen-like atmosphere and houses a range of monumental sculptures. Central are three large heads representing the Buddhas of the past, present and future. To one side are two pairs of stone lions; such sculptures were used extensively during the Southern dynasty to guard the entrances of tombs. Outside, water spills from an elevated platform dressed with a standing Buddha, creating a hypnotic sound that echoes off the hard surfaces of the surrounding buildings. Ahead is a partially submerged pavilion within which are displays of Tibetan art, but it will open to the public only after it has been blessed by a senior Tibetan monk.

155

Sichuan Cuisine Museum

川菜博物馆 *Chuancai bowuguan*

Gucheng Township, Pixian County
郫县古城镇

Tel: (028) 8791 9398; for restaurant reservation: 8791 8008
Open: 9.00–20.00
Chinese-speaking guide only
Kids

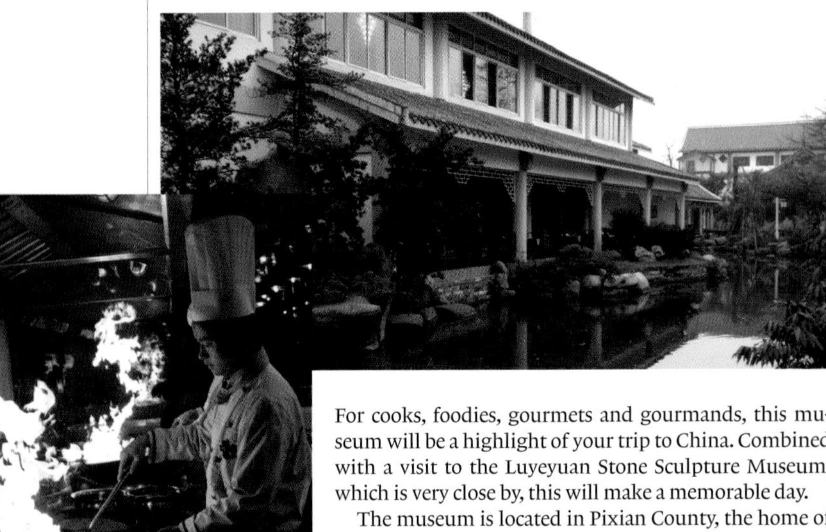

For cooks, foodies, gourmets and gourmands, this museum will be a highlight of your trip to China. Combined with a visit to the Luyeyuan Stone Sculpture Museum, which is very close by, this will make a memorable day.

The museum is located in Pixian County, the home of the eponymous chilli-bean paste, an indispensable element in Sichuan cooking. Until recently, Sichuan cuisine was not well known or appreciated outside of China. Indeed, Westerners tend to speak about 'Chinese food', but no such thing actually exists. Food in China is firmly regional; flavours and ingredients vary hugely. The cuisine that Westerners are most familiar with is very loosely based on the mild flavours of Canton.

Learn Sichuan cooking with the chefs

Happily, the situation is changing, and people are becoming more aware of the regional personality of Chinese cuisine. Among these, Sichuan cooking is considered one of the greatest. Although it is often described by the uninitiated as hot and spicy, the truth is much more subtle. Experts classify the cuisine according to different categories of flavours, textures, and slicing and cooking methods. Sour, sweet, salty, fish-flavoured, wine-flavoured, even 'strange-flavoured' – the variations are into the thousands. Not all Sichuan dishes are hot, although the Sichuanese do love their chillies and the flavour and experience of the Sichuan peppercorn. This distinctive ingredient comes from the berry of the prickly ash (*hua jiao*) – it is not actually a peppercorn. The best *hua jiao* comes from the mountains of Hanyuan County. Along with the flavour of Sichuan pepper, which could be described as smoky, woody or citrusy, comes a numbing sensation of the tongue and lip. In Chinese, this is called '*ma*'. At first offputting, it adds a thrill which to some diners soon becomes irresistible. The combination of hot (*la*) from the chilli pepper and numbing (*ma*) from the Sichuan pepper is known as *ma-la*, a common term used to describe this particular Sichuan flavour.

Salt – in particular well salt from Zigong – is another element in true Sichuan cooking. This salt has an especially intense flavour and has been mined since the Han dynasty. You can still visit the mines, as well as the Salt History Museum in Zigong.

The chilli pepper arrived in China from the New World in the sixteenth century, but ancient sources tell us that from even earlier days, the Sichuanese had a predilection for hot food which they satisfied using ginger, pepper and other spicy elements. This appreciation of the hot and spicy is due to the fact that the Chinese believe that a humid climate such as exists in much of

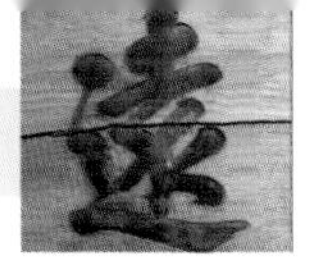

Kangqi Qing dynasty pickling jar

Sichuan is very unhealthy. The way to allay this is by sweating it out in both summer and winter.

Sichuan cuisine has a rich history and tradition and is a complex and sophisticated combination of flavour, texture, colour and heat. Foreigners who visit the province often pass up the adventure of eating local dishes because they are afraid of the heat, the *ma* or the strange ingredients. Be brave, be adventurous – give this renowned cuisine a try! The museum celebrates Sichuanese traditions and aims to educate those who wish to learn more.

The museum was a labour of love, taking ten years to create. Every brick, stone and roof tile is from the Qing dynasty. The goal is to experience Sichuan cuisine with both your mind and your taste buds. To that end you should start your visit in the galleries. Posters detail the history of Sichuan cooking and its early influences through travellers on the Southern Silk Road. Artefacts relating to cookery from antiquity to the present are displayed. The collection consists of more than 3,000 bronze, pottery, porcelain and wood objects, as well as books, menus and photos. Notable are a pair of terracotta Han dynasty chefs – male and female, Tang and Song wine vessels, Ming blue and white ware, Qing chopstick holders and an imperial lidded pickle pot. These are all authentic – not reproductions – and well displayed in modern, well-designed cases with clear, consistent English signage. The last two rooms are replicas of the dining room and kitchen of a wealthy Qing dynasty individual. There is also an open-air display of large stone and wooden tools, among them round wooden barrels used for hulling rice and other grains.

You can follow your museum visit with a stop at the teahouse; a cup of tea should be drunk before and after meals. The teahouse is set within the lovely grounds of the reconstructed Qing dynasty courtyard buildings. After your tea, continue on for a Sichuan meal in the restaurant. The dining room has an open-plan kitchen so you can see the chefs preparing the meal. For a small extra fee you can don a chef's apron, enter the kitchen and the learn how to prepare a dish of your choice.

156

Sichuan Provincial Museum

四川省博物馆 *Sichuansheng bowuguan*

No. 3, Section 4, Renmin South Road, Chengdu

成都市人民南路四段3号

Tel: (028) 8522 6723

Open: In 2009

Audio guides in all major languages and personal guides

Restaurant / fast-food café / bookshop / hotel

Set adjacent to the splendid Huanhuaxi Park a couple of kilometres west of Qingyang on the edge of Chengdu near Du Fu's Thatched Cottage, this new museum designed by the Chinese architect Zheng Guoying is a real jewel. It is the largest provincial museum in southwest China. Spread over 90,000 ha, the main building contains not only ten galleries but also four auxiliary centres: a conservation laboratory, an international cultural-exchange office, a

Eastern Han brick with chariot and horsemen crossing a bridge

Bronze *lei* (wine jar), late eleventh to early tenth century BC

cultural relics examination unit for authentication and another for training personnel for Sichuan's various museums (a hundred at the latest count and growing). Additionally, the museum has cleverly tapped into the growing tourism boom and opened a hotel nearby, providing an additional revenue stream. Although the museum keeps standard opening hours, the restaurant, as well as the Academic Hall, which seats close to 400 and can be used either as a conference centre or a performance space, stays open into the evening.

Started in 1941, the collection has grown exponentially as dozens of new sites have been discovered and excavated, and is now home to more than 260,000 cultural relics. Combine one of the seven best collections of artefacts in China with some of the most advanced multimedia tools in the museum tool box and a large investment from the city, and you get an intoxicating experience symbolic of the Sichuan Basin's rich cultural past. Exhibition areas feature: bronzes from the Ba and Shu Cultures; sculpture and tomb bricks from the Han dynasty; porcelain from the primitive to the Qing dynasty (in two parts: material from Sichuan and material from Song dynasty sites); ancient calligraphy; a gallery dedicated to Zhang Daqian, the renowned twentieth-century artist (400 paintings); cultural relics from the fourteen minorities in the province, including textiles; Southern dynasty Buddhist sculpture and costumes; Tibetan and Buddhist objects; arts and crafts, such as bamboo-carving, Shu textiles and lacquer; a modern history gallery covering events including the Red Army's Long March, most of which took place here; and two galleries for travelling exhibitions. Exhibits will be updated periodically, enabling the museum's massive collection to be seen in turns.

The holdings are particularly strong in Ba and Shu Warring States period bronzes, in particular vessels, weapons and ritual objects unearthed from the tomb at Xindu Majiaxiang in the territory of the ancient Shu kingdom; Han pottery figures and bricks; Liang and Tang dynasties Buddhist sculpture, including magnificent stele; Song dynasty Shu brocade; a large number of Tibetan objects and embroidery; Longquan celadon porcelain and a dizzying array of material culture from the fourteen ethic minorities in Sichuan.

The superb Warring States bronzes clearly show that although several distinct cultures originated in Sichuan they did not develop in isolation. Exchanges occurred not only among them but also with neighbouring cultures and even beyond. The tomb at Xindu Majiaxiang is the richest burial known to be from later Bronze Age Sichuan, possibly belonging to the King of Shu. More than sixty bronze weapons were found in the *yaokeng*, or waste pit, of the tomb, among them five rare swords of two types, which, at the beginning of the fifth century, became the classic forms most widely used in the Yangtze region and beyond. When they were excavated several were found in their original black-lacquered wooden scabbards. Most likely they were made in the state of Chu.

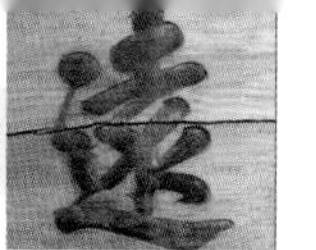

Equally delightful are the pictorial decorations carved on tomb bricks from the Eastern Han, the most impressive of which came from rock-cut tombs in cliff faces, the tomb type most commonly found in Sichuan. These pictures, along with pottery figurines and models also found in the tombs, provided the deceased with everything they needed in the afterlife. The tombs in Sichuan are famous for their depiction of farming scenes, salt production and entertainers, including one excavated from Peng Xian Taipingchang showing acrobats and jugglers. These along with the pottery figures of a squatting drummer, seated musician, dancing lady, kneeling woman and peasant soldier protected and entertained rich landowners and merchants in the afterlife.

Buddhist sculptures in Sichuan tended to be of the 'southern' as distinct from the 'northern' style and were mostly freestanding stone images and stele. A large body of Liang dynasty examples from Wanfosi, Chengdu and, more recently, the Xi'an Road in Chengdu are wonderful examples of this style, which favours realism and often includes exotic elements from India or Southeast Asia. The Wanfosi Shakyamuni is an example of such an indianized style. Particularly handsome is a fragmentary stele with bodhisattvas standing on lotuses on the front and landscape scenes on the back exhibiting distinctly Sichuanese innovations including spatial perspective.

157

Sichuan Science and Technology Museum

四川科技馆 *Sichuan kejiguan*

Renmin zhonglu Section 1, No. 16, Chengdu
成都市人民中路1段16号

Tel: (028) 8660 9999
Open: 9.30–16.30
www.scstm.com
Kids

Opened in 2006 in the city centre, this massive building is easily identifiable by the vast statue of Chairman Mao in front. Formerly the Sichuan Provincial Exhibition Hall, the newly refurbished space displays all things science-based, from aviation, space, robots and evolution to information about Nobel Prize winners, paintings with scientific themes and 'crazy science' shows for kids. Don't miss the three-dimensional rolling hoop, used by astronauts and pilots during training. Also worth noting is the only aircraft on display, a Chengdu Jian-7, a variant of the MiG-21, one of the most remarkable aircraft of the Cold War period. The interactive exhibits are plentiful. An added bonus is the English explanations, devoid of any reference to scientific socialism.

Statue of Mao stands in front of the museum

158 Sichuan University Museum

四川大学博物馆 *Sichuan daxue bowuguan*

29 Wangjiang Road, Chengdu
(entrance on the right side of the East Gate of Sichuan University)
成都市望江路29号

Tel: (028) 8541 2451 / 2543
Open: 9.00–17.00
www.scudm.cn/bwg/
Guides are available but must be arranged in advance
Shop sells craft items from ethnic minorities.

Qing dynasty leather shadow puppets

This museum is one of the earliest established in the southwest of China. Originally known as the West China Union University Museum, it was founded by the American Daniel S Dye, who taught there from 1910 to 1949, serving under the American Baptist Foreign Missionary Society. During his spare time he documented the designs used in West China window latticework, woven belts and pottery. Dye, like so many of his colleagues, contributed much of what they collected to the museum. During the war archaeologists from the east also came here and added to the collection. The University offers degrees in archaeology. Many of the country's famous sites have been excavated by scholars trained here, including Sanxingdui. The University also has a Centre for Tibetan Studies and for South Asian Studies.

Today the collection stands at some 40,000 items and ranges from folk art, embroideries, porcelain and bronzes to ethnography and traditional arts. At any one time there is a selection of objects displayed in one of the seven halls arranged over four floors. Good lighting, proper display cases and labels in

Han brick depicting hunting and gathering

Detail of Han brick illustrating a departure and an arrival

English and Chinese make this a pleasurable place to visit. The Tibetan collection and those of other minorities such as the Yi are considered among the best in China, with an impressive collection of ethnic costumes, and shaman's tools and exceptional painted *thangkas*. Equally outstanding are the Eastern Han dynasty tomb tiles, including one depicting Xiwangmu, the goddess of immortality, flanked by a tiger (east) and a dragon (west) and others illustrating an afterlife of fishing and harvesting.

There is a new room devoted to shadow puppets dating from the Qing dynasty (1644–1911) cut from paper-thin leather hide of donkey, cow or sheep delightfully painted on both sides with vegetable dyes in a kaleidoscope of colours. Made in sections, those depicting humans were usually composed of at least eleven parts with silk or cotton string holding the parts together. The heads were usually not attached permanently allowing the character to change persona during the performance. The application of tung oil made from the seeds of a fruit grown in China was applied to the leather to add to its translucency. Wires with bamboo handles were attached to manipulate the figures in front of a light source projecting their stained-glass coloured shadows onto a translucent screen. A selection of specialized chisels and knives used to cut the intricate designs into the leather are also displayed. (Note: A museum devoted to shadow puppetry is scheduled to open in Chengdu in 2009.)

159

501 Art Space

501艺术基地 Wulingyi yishujidi

126 Zheng Street, Huangjueping, Jiulongpo District, Chongqing
中国重庆市九龙坡区黄桷坪正街126号

Tel: (023) 6200 2919
www.501artspace.org

The brightly painted neighbourhood around the Art Space and Art Academy

Located in an old cigarette factory directly across from the Sichuan Fine Arts Institute, 501 Art Space is an independent organization run by artists and curators. Its mission is to advocate and support contemporary multicultural arts in visual arts and new media. Towards that end, the organization provides sixty studio spaces for over seventy artists as well as three separate galleries and a bar. The space, concept and name are reminiscent of 798 Gallery in Beijing. Sculptors, video artists, photographers, filmmakers, fashion designers, performance artists and architects work here. The project has welcomed artists-in-residence from abroad, sponsored art festivals and has worked with the British Council. As 501 was experiencing some growing pains at the time of our visit, the galleries on the street level were closed; however, the doors to the building do remain open and one can walk around exploring the building and peeking into studios. Everyone we met was friendly and most willing to show us his or her work. No doubt, purchasing would not be a problem. When we visited in late 2007, 501 was just getting off the ground with the expected hiccups, but this space and its associated galleries promises to be centre-stage in the developing Chongqing avant-garde art scene.

Contemporary Art Scene in Sichuan and Chongqing

Sichuan and Chonqing are emerging as burgeoning centres for contemporary art in China. The area, since ancient times, has had an individualistic reputation and its vibrant contemporary art scene maintains the tradition.

Chongqing The Sichuan Art Academy in Chongqing is known as one of the best art schools in the country and has produced some of China's most prominent contemporary painters including Zhang Xiaogang, Chen Wenbo, Feng Zhengjie and others. The Institute is now building two museums: the Sichuan Fine Arts Institute Museum and the Luo Zhongli Museum. In addition, the Art Academy maintains a contemporary art exhibition facility called Tank Loft – located in an ex-tank factory near the Institute. Directly across the street from the Sichuan Art Academy is '501' – a former cigarette factory, now an artists' community which is described in more detail on these pages.

Chengdu Chengdu has its own dynamic avant-garde scene first originally centred at the Blue Roof Art Centre located at Shouzhang Road in the Cuqiao district of Chengdu. This former warehouse area contains the studios of forty to fifty local artists, the majority of whom are painters. Most of the workshops are open to the public.

In 2001 Chengdu hosted its first Biennale – and these have been repeated sporadically throughout the years. In addition, Chengdu will soon have its own purpose-built Contemporary Art Museum – until recently this was a museum without a permanent home. However, funds and a site have now been allocated to begin construction.

Dujiangyan The government of Sichuan, realizing the financial and cultural benefits of a thriving art scene has taken an unusual step. Eight of China's most respected and well-known artists have each been given a museum, each with a separate architect, located an hour from Chengdu in Dujiangyan. It is not clear at this time whether they will show their own art, curate the works of others or indeed how they will run the museums at all. The eight artists are: Zhang Xiaogang, Wang Guangyi, Fang Lijun, Yue Minjun, Zhou Chunya, He Duoling, Zhang Peili and Wu Shanzhuan. Additionally, a public art museum and research archive will be built. These museums are scheduled to open in the spring of 2009, however, the devastating earthquake in May 2008 may have delayed progress (see Stop Press).

160 Baiheliang Underwater Museum

白鹤梁水下博物馆 *Baiheliang shuixia bowuguan*

Fuling District, Chongqing (located in the middle of the Changjiang (Yangtze River)

重庆市涪陵区（长江之中）

Open: Scheduled to open in 2009

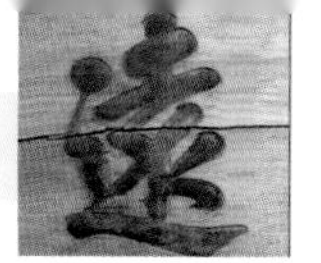

When the Three Gorges Dam project was announced, not only were the environmentalists up in arms along with the 1.5 million people who had to be relocated, but so were the archaeologists. The flooding of the Yangtze valley meant the loss of thousands of important sites, many related to the ancient Ba people. Archaeologists scrambled to save and record as many sites as they could before they were submerged forever. Baiheliang, although it will eventually lie under around 40 m of water, has had a reprieve, and when this new museum opens part of this unique site will be accessible.

Located along the river north of the Fuling District, Baiheliang, or White Crane Ridge, is covered with carp-shaped carvings and inscriptions dating back to the Tang dynasty. This ledge, 1,600 m long and 15 m wide, is an ancient record of changes in the river's water levels, knowledge essential for predicting availability for a good harvest. Only during the winter and early spring when the water table was low would the ledge have been visible; then it also was useful as a marker to navigators. What remains is 1,200 years of hydrological data enlivened by poetic descriptions of the landscape carved in the rock faces over various dynasties. The most impressive section of the ridge, including a pair of spectacularly carved carp, will be covered by a glass dome. This, together with two underwater channels extending out from the riverbank, will allow visitors to view the inscriptions and carvings lit with underwater lighting.

161

Chongqing Three Gorges Museum

重庆中国三峡博物馆 *Chongqing zhongguo sanxia bowuguan*

236 People's Avenue, Yuzhong, Chongqing

重庆市渝中区人民路236号

Tel: (023) 6367 9010 / 9226 / 9065
Open: 9.00–17.00 summer; 9.30 winter; ticket office closes at 16.00
www.3gmuseum.cn

It promised to provide hydro-electric power, flood control and enhanced navigation, but the world's largest dam, known as the Three Gorges project, has also displaced millions, flooded some of the best agricultural land in the area, destroyed natural wonders and lost to the world thousands of important ancient sites. Hundreds of archaeologists scrambled to save as many sites as possible before they disappeared. A large part of what they were able to rescue has now been deposited, together with objects from the old Chongqing Museum, in this massive new museum. Opened in 2005 and stretching one whole side of a pedestrian plaza, this nondescript concrete-and-glass refuge displays at any one time around 17,000 objects over four floors. Despite getting carried away with one too many lengthy galleries hosting interactive dioramas and floor-to-ceiling photographic panoramas of the Three Gorges (which consists of the Qutang, Wuxia and Xiling Gorges along the 200 km stretch of the Yangtze), the museum displays many exceptional items and offers a good overview of the area's rich ancient civilization and equally important plant and animal life.

The first galleries are reconstructions of historic scenes – coolies pulling boats along rugged shorelines and models of boat-shaped coffins used in Ba kingdom burials. Also displayed are a selection of mounted specimens

Top of a bronze *chunyu* or bell with suspension hook in the shape of a tiger

from the hundreds of known species of fish and animals living in the Three Gorges, from golden eagles, porcupines and mountain goats to the now extinct White Fin Dolphin and currently protected White Sturgeon. Further on is a cursory mention of the towns lost and people displaced when the dam was built.

The third floor galleries display the treasure trove of Palaeolithic finds from the Three Gorges area. Among the most spectacular are those from the Longgupo Site in Wushan, which have caused China's history to be rewritten. These are fossilized remains of a primitive human species dating to about two million years BC. Pictures and replicas of some of the more than 230 finds include a lower jawbone fragment and stone tools. Excavations of caves such as Xinglongdong Cave in Fengjie County produced a human tooth, mammalian fossils, stone artefacts and an ivory Stegodon tusk engraved with abstract patterns – the earliest known engravings by humans. This site dates to 120,000–150,000 years ago. Fengdu is home to the important Palaeolithic sites of Jingshuiwan, Yandunbao and Ranjialukou in nearby Gaojia, the most spectacular of which

Museum façade

is Jinshuiwan, dating from the middle phase of the Palaeolithic (around 100,000 years ago) where stone tools including cores, flakes and scrapers were found as well as animal fossils. This is the earliest and only site in the Three Gorges area where tools have been found.

Most famous of the Neolithic sites, also in Wushan County, is that of the people who lived along the middle reaches of the Yangtze River; the Daxi (5000–3000 BC) and the Qujialing (4000–3000 BC) Cultures. Numerous excavations of the Daxi graves have revealed an abundance of artefacts from pottery, stone and bone to jade and also fish bones. Photographs of these excavations are on display along with examples of their pottery identifiable by their reddish brown colour over-painted with geometric patterns including a pot belly shaped-stove. The Daxi appear not only to have been fishing and hunting, but archaeological evidence points to farming too.

This floor also showcases spectacular objects from the Ba Culture dating from the Shang, Spring and Autumn and Warring States periods (Zhou dynasty) displayed by theme. These include a large bronze bell, or *chunyu*, with a suspension loop in the form of a tiger, its long, curled tail extended and mouth open. This curious creature might have been a symbol of the ancient Ba people. (The decoration also includes small designs and graphics which might have been the Ba's set of characters.) Here too is a bronze *zhong*, or hand

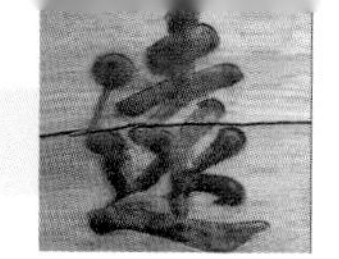

bell, also used for signalling; wonderful bronze dagger axes known as *ge*, some triangular in shape, others decorated with a deer motif or cloud designs; and spearheads with silver inlays and animal-mask designs. Notice the excellent craftsmanship of the weapons. Another superb bronze item relating to war is the rare undecorated conical bronze helmet. Many of these were unearthed at Xiaotianxi Village in Fuling, built on a mound near the Wujiang River. Numerous tombs of what are believed by some to be former Ba kings who stayed on the land after the Ba kingdom was conquered by the Qin state, have been excavated since its discovery in 1972 and likely to date from the middle and late Warring States period. Other highlights include the very large Shang dynasty *zun* with its flaring undecorated mouth and sheep sitting on its shoulder, decorated with a single-horned dragon. Found at Dachang in Wushan, this is one of the oldest vessels discovered in the area. One of the small tombs at Xiaotianxi yielded yet another prized item, a bird-shaped *zun* with duck's feet and decorated with feather designs, some of which still exhibit their original turquoise inlays.

A large display of small round-bottomed pots discovered by the hundreds at the Zhongba Site near the Yangtze are displayed hanging on poles. Although this is not how they were found, this might have been how they were used, for this site, with a sequence from the late Neolithic to the Shang, was also once home to the Ba and a source of salt water. Could these pots have held brine and been left in the sun to harvest salt? Note also the long boat-shaped coffins (here 4.7 m, but they were often longer) hollowed out from single logs where the Bronze Age Ba and Shu buried their dead, along with artefacts placed at both head and feet. Unique to eastern Sichuan, this type of burial had never been found elsewhere in China and survived a bit longer in Ba than in Shu.

The fourth floor galleries host a great display of Han dynasty pottery, and although there is little English signage, the objects speak for themselves, among them wonderful figurines dancing, playing a zither and drumming, all placed in the tombs of their patrons to entertain them in the afterlife. Cases display fearsome grave guardians, a bird-shaped pedestal, a pottery horse with inscriptions down its back leg and bricks with impressions illustrating the region's industries.

The final floor features a selection of works donated by Li Chuli, a native of Jiangjin in Chongqing (Li and his wife donated 600 items to the museum). Notable among them are paintings by renowned artists of the Ming and Qing periods. The porcelain galleries exhibit pieces in exceptionally well-lit cases and with English signage. Featured are ceramics from local kilns, including those from the Qiong or Qionglai site, identifiable by their opaque green glazes, and the Longquan Kiln, reknowned for its celadon jars and vases. There is also a gallery devoted to the history of Chongqing during the War against Japan.

Keen to show as many artefacts as possible, the museum rotates the main exhibition spaces every four years and has plans to display work by contemporary local artists. There are audio and tour guides available in English, as well as an IMAX 3D cinema showing the Three Gorges prior to dam construction.

A bronze sword with animal mask designs, Ba-Shu State

A bronze spear incised with abstract designs

Bird-shaped *zun* with duck's feet, Warring Sates period

162 Hall of Inscribed Boards in the Huguang Guildhall Complex

湖广会馆 匾额博物馆 *Huguang huiguan bian'e bowuguan*

1 Bajiaoyuan, Changbin Road, Yuzhong, Chongqing

重庆市渝中区长滨路芭蕉园1号

Tel: (023) 6392 9011
Open: 9.00–18.00; last entry 17.00
www.cqhuguang.com
Audio guides in English and Chinese for all parts of the complex, although they are not highly recommended

The end of the Ming dynasty and beginning of the Qing saw Manchu troops enter Sichuan and raze the area to the ground. To repopulate the province, the new rulers ordered millions of residents from Guangdong, Guangxi, Jiangxi, Hunan and Hubei to relocate. These immigrants needed a place to meet, conduct business and be entertained. What is known today as the Huguang Guildhall is in fact a series of halls built by merchants from the various provinces with these purposes in mind. Taking pride of place is the main hall with its various rooms, platforms and courtyard. The beams, window frames and door surrounds are decorated with vividly carved animals, plants and people. There is also a temple where people would pray for good fortune.

This complex is home to a museum documenting the migration, as well as an outstanding museum of traditional carved and decorated boards (right wing of the main hall). Suspended above the lintels of halls, pavilions or gardens, they were fashioned from wood of various kinds and carved with two, three or four characters. Some are signed and dated. Simple looking at first glance, they were in fact the product of skilled artisans. Often one person would do the carving of the characters and another would apply the gold leaf. The calligraphy was considered the 'soul' of the board, and their making a prestigious career for an artisan. The actual sayings were considered an art in themselves and reflected the writing ability of their authors.

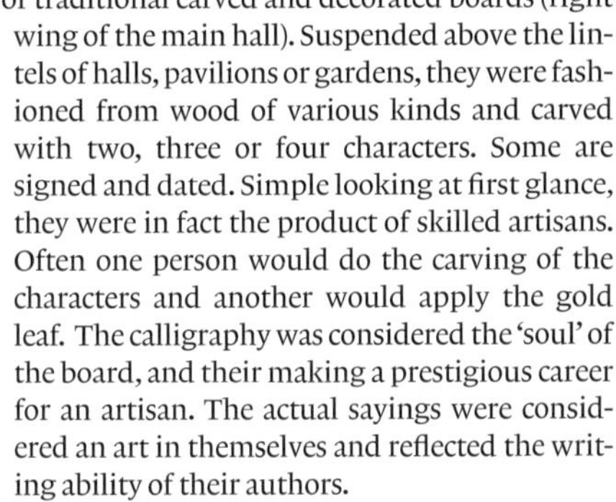

This collection was amassed by the father and son team, Liu Shaolin and Liu Guangrui, both well-known local doctors of traditional Chinese medicine. Obsessed with saving these boards from being used as firewood, they set about collecting them from all over Sichuan. Currently there are over 300 examples from the Ming and Qing dynasties, as well as later examples from the Republic of China; however, the collection is still growing. Displayed are around seventy examples covering five types, from those praising excellence and encouraging business and study, to messages of congratulation on birthdays and those used to identify buildings or residences. To eulogize someone's success or character, it might say 'being honest in performing official duties'

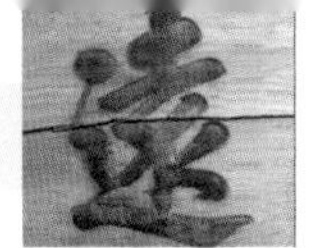

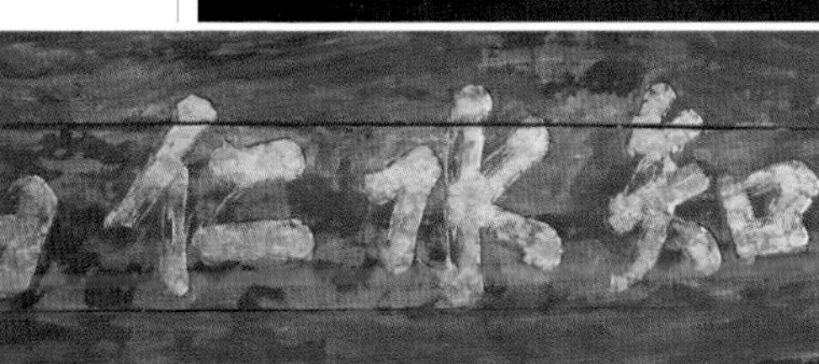

Details of wooden signs displayed in the Guildhall

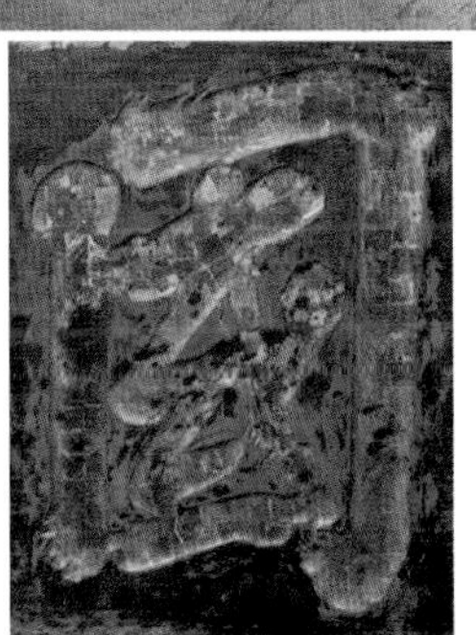

and could be presented by a person at a lower level to someone more senior. These were often hung inside the central living space to flaunt the person's status. Those crafted as a present to a newly opened shop were very carefully created as they became the public 'face' of a business. The owners are currently constructing a new museum near the Stilwell Museum, in order to show more of their collection. The new museum will open imminently at Liziba Ercun (李子坝二村). Signage is in English and Chinese.

163 **Museum of Chinese Medicine**

中国民间医药博物馆 *Zhongguo minjian yiyao bowuguan*

101 Pipa Mountain Main Street, Yuzhong, Chongqing

Tel: (023) 6352 8755

Open: 9.00–17.00

重庆市渝中区枇杷山正街101号

At first glance this slightly dusty Aladdin's cave of medical paraphernalia might not look very inviting, but if you enjoy less sanitized displays and have an interest in seeing a traditional Chinese medical practice, this is the place for you. Following family tradition, Mr Liu trained as a doctor and, like his father, is hooked on collecting. Together they are responsible for another museum in the city, the Hall of Inscribed Boards in the Huguang Guildhall Complex and, what's more, are avidly amassing objects and books relating to Sichuan Opera. To keep their collecting passions alive and their various museums, they produce a range of natural herb-based cosmetics which they export abroad.

The first of the three floors is used as a reception and treatment room; however, the public is allowed to walk around and learn more by reading information panels in English and Chinese. On the pharmacy counter is a

Basket used for drying herbs with information stating which months of the year are best for drying particular herbs

Acupuncture chart referring to painless Chinese acupuncture

dragon-shaped implement used to cut herbs, as well as hand-grinders of all shapes and sizes. Behind on shelves are rows of glass containers spilling over with herbal remedies.

The museum proper begins on the second floor. The collection of more than 20,000 ancient texts recording medical treatments dating back to the Song dynasty has pride of place. Among them is a copy of the classic divination manual *Book of Changes*, the premise of which is the balance of opposites and harmony, the basic principles of good health according to Chinese medicine. Displayed in a seemingly random manner on the third floor are incense burners, old medicine cabinets beautifully crafted with small drawers and compartments, and implements for collecting and processing herbs, including a large partitioned circular basket painted with Chinese characters informing its user at what time of the year particular herbs are best harvested.

164 Residence and Headquarters of General Joseph Warren Stilwell

史迪威博物馆 *Shidiwei bowuguan*

63 Jialing New Road, Liziba, Yuzhong, Chongqing
重庆市渝中区嘉陵新路63号

Tel: (023) 6387 2794 / 6360 9515; call ahead for group visits
Open: 9.00–17.00

Walking through the entrance gates of this beautiful hillside site, you are immediately struck by the expansive view of the River Yangtze and, as far as the eye can see, the dense skyline of modern skyscrapers which blanket the city. But then your gaze is swiftly drawn to the larger-than-life-size bronze bust of General Joseph Stilwell (1883–1946) and the 1930s modernist house nearby. This was Stilwell's official residence and office when he was commander of the US forces in the China–Burma–India Theatre and, by permission of Chiang Kai-shek, the Chinese 5th and 6th Armies operating in Burma during the War

against Japan (1942–44). Having been used by the Kuomintang government to house their VIPs, it became Stilwell's official residence in 1942, when he agreed to go to China at the request of the American President Franklin Roosevelt.

Stilwell's knowledge of the Chinese language (he could write in Chinese with a brush), which he had learned on visits in the 1920s, prepared him well for his new assignments. He also understood the complexities of Chinese politics, and the strengths and weaknesses of the Chinese soldiers. Despite these attributes, however, he was also known to be short-tempered, earning his nick-name, 'Vinegar Joe', for his often caustic remarks. Arriving in India in 1942, Stilwell was placed in charge of the American forces in China, Burma and India and was then sent to Burma, where the Japanese had already captured Rangoon. Stilwell and his troops tried to defend Burma but were badly defeated and had to retreat more than 225 km by foot to India. By now the Japanese had also blocked the overland supply route through Burma, leaving the precarious air route over the Himalayas and the Hengduan Mountains to Kunming in Yunnan Province the only way for supplies to reach China. Stilwell set out to establish an alternative route and was put in charge of the Ledo Road (later renamed the Stilwell Road in his honour) which extended from northeast India across Burma to southwest Yunnan. Just over two years later, and after thousands of Americans and locals had lost their lives, the road extending from Assam to Kunming – a total of 1,736 km in length – permitted the first convoy of 113 vehicles to bring much-needed supplies into China. Towards the end of 1944 Stilwell was recalled by Roosevelt, having fallen out with both the British leaders in India and Chiang Kai-shek as well. He had one more wartime post, as commander in Okinawa in 1945. He died a year later of stomach cancer having earned a whole host of military decorations.

General Joseph Stilwell and Admiral Louis Mountbatten in Burma 1943

The ground floor of the house is arranged as it was when Stilwell lived there. Visitors can make their way round the various rooms, ranging from the Military Meeting Room – bedecked with a large table and chairs, and decorated with pictures of the general meeting various dignitaries – to his rather spartan office, with just his desk, a typewriter and a couple of chairs. Only a few very brief signs give you any hints as to what you are looking at, although you can easily determine the function of each of the six rooms by their furnishings.

Downstairs are several halls and rooms covered wall-to-wall with photographs and information panels describing the key moments in Stilwell's tenure in China, including pictures he took on his visits in the 1920s. Other images show him with Chiang Kai-shek, whom he distrusted; one shows him standing among a group of high-ranking Party leaders; many show him inspecting personnel, including meeting with the 14th Air Force led by the American veteran Claire Chennault. Although Chennault and Stilwell had a well-known prickly relationship due to their tactical differences (Stilwell called Chennault a 'jackass'), Chennault became a legend in China. As an adviser to Chiang Kai-shek he set up a training school for Chinese pilots in 1937. In 1941 he convinced retired American pilots to volunteer to airlift supplies into the country via the

Bust of General Stilwell at the museum

Yunnan–Burma Highway over the Himalayas, known as the 500-mile 'Hump' route (because the mountain pass looked like a camel's hump) and fight the Japanese. Their success, despite the odds, made them heroes and earned them the Chinese name 'Flying Tigers'. Some of the most spirited images on display are those of the 'Flying Tiger' pilots standing in front of their P-40 fighter aircraft painted with their highly recognizable shark-face emblems.

Although the bulk of the visitors to this museum are currently American veterans of World War II who call this their 'second hometown', anyone with an interest in the events that shaped modern history should plan to see this site and others in Chongqing related to the war. There are bilingual labels and information panels.

WWII Sites in Chongqing

Besides General Stilwell's house, Chongqing – formerly known as Chungking – is home to numerous museums, parks and residences of famous people relating to its role as the capital of Chiang Kai-shek's Nationalist government. Some are better known, like the Museum of the Provisional Government of the Republic of Korea, while others are rarely mentioned or off the beaten track. A selection includes:

Eling Park: (峨岭公园; *Eling gongyuan*) 176 Zheng Street, Eling, Yuzhong District, with fabulous views of the city, built in 1909. Originally the home of Lee, a wealthy businessman, during the war Chiang Kai-shek and his wife lived here.

Gele Mountain Revolutionary War Sites: hilly area with several sites relating to the war between the Kuomintang and the Communist Party, including Red Cliff Martyrs Memorial Museum (红岩魂陈列馆; *Hongyanhun chenlieguan*); Chiang Kai-shek's Hideout (蒋家院子; *Jiangjiayuanzi*); and Songlin Execution Grounds (松林坡; *Songlin po*).

SACO (Sino-American Co-operation Organization) Prisons (also known as KMT Prisons): located at the base of the Gele Mountain includes two prisons (白公馆; *Baigongguan*, and 渣滓洞; Zhazidong). SACO was operated by the US and Chiang Kai-shek from 1943 to 1946 for the training of intelligence agents. When the Americans withdrew it was used by the Nationalists as a political prison. Photographs of Americans training Chinese officers and highly emotive images of those later murdered by the Kuomintang are on display along with instruments of torture used on the Communist prisoners. The cells are now memorials to the victims who were held here and then massacred by the Kuomintang after the Communist victory in the 1940s. Some distance away is an exhibition hall often referred to as the US Chiang Kai-shek Criminal Acts Exhibition Hall.

Red Crag Memorial Museum, also known as the Hongyan Revolutionary Memorial Museum (红岩革命纪念馆; *Hongyan geming jinianguan*), Hongyan (Red Crag) Village (No. 52 Yuzhong): site of the former headquarters of the Southern Bureau of the Central Committee of the Communist Party and the office of the Eight Route Army. Besides this newer red-brick building there is also the Zhou Residence (周公馆), or *Zhougongguan*, the Mansion of the Zhou, at No. 50 Zengjiayan Street located at Zhongshan Xilu. This is where Zhou Enlai lived and worked as the representative of the Communist Party. It also was the Party's main centre. Two hundred

metres from this site at 64 Zhongshansi Road is the Gui Garden (桂园; *Guiyuan*), which was the residence of the Kuomintang member Zhang Zhizhong. Zhang moved out in 1945 and allowed Mao Zedong to live here when he came to negotiate with the Kuomintang. The hall on the ground floor is where Mao and Zhou Enlai negotiated and finally signed an agreement with the Kuomintang. Signage is in Chinese only.

Nanshan Park (南山公园; *Nanshan gongyuan*): large mountainous area on the southern bank of the Changjiang (Yangtze) River where, during the War against Japan, important Kuomintang officials and foreign envoys built their villas. The house of Chiang Kai-shek can be seen here.

Soong Ching Ling's Residence (宋庆龄故居; *Song Qingling guju*): near the Hilton Hotel in the centre of Chongqing, her residence during World War II and a good example of the pre-liberation colonial architecture that can be seen in and around the city.

Liberation Monument (解放碑; *Jiefangbei*): at the heart of the Jiefangbei shopping square, erected to celebrate the end of China's war with Japan and formerly known as the 'Monument of Victory in the War of Resistance'.

There is also an air-raid shelter in the centre of Chongqing, which is now a memorial to the victims following a bombing by Japanese planes.

165 Site Museum of the Provisional Government of the Republic of Korea

大韩民国临时政府旧址陈列馆 *Dahan minguo linshizhengfujiuzhi chenlieguan*

Near Jiefang Bei shopping centre, Chongqing
38 Lianhuachi, Qixinggang, Yuzhong District, Chongqing
重庆市渝中区七星岗莲花池38号

Tel: (023) 6382 0752
Open: 9.00–17.00 except Mon
Shop sells Chinese and Korean books

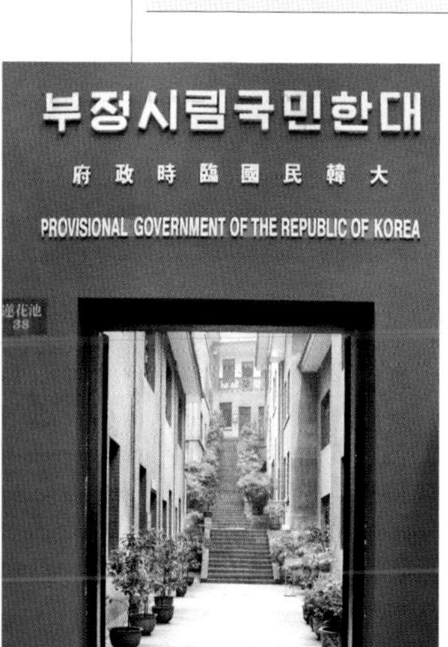

Despite its location in the middle of bustling Chongqing, this tranquil site was home to historical events which resonate powerfully for Koreans. From 1939 until 1945, this was the headquarters of the Korean Provisional Government (KPG), which had been relocated from its original command centre in the French Concession of Shanghai and then from other cities as Japanese forces advanced into China. Despite the endless bombing and destruction of Chongqing by the Japanese during this period, they held out until 1945 when the Japanese surrendered.

The KPG had been established in 1919 with the help of the Chinese. Its main aim was to strive for the liberation of Korea from Japanese occupation, which lasted from 1910 until 1945. The incident that caused the exodus of the KPG from Shanghai occurred in 1932, when a bomb thrown

The central figure is Kim Gu (金九), President of the Provisional Government of Korea taken at the government headquarters

during a Japanese ceremony killed senior officials and wounded the Japanese commander-in-chief in China, General Shirakawa (who was aboard the *USS Missouri* when the Japanese signed the surrender). The hunt for Koreans by the Japanese drove them eastwards; eventually they positioned themselves in Chongqing in 1939, which had also become China's wartime and concomitant capital when the Kuomintang capital, Nanjing, was captured by the Japanese in 1937.

This delightful complex, originally owned by a wealthy Chinese entrepreneur, was rented by the Chinese government for the Koreans. It has been refurbished to a high standard and in 1995 opened as a museum. Using excellent copies of historic photographs, film footage of harrowing events, and numerous reproductions of historic documents and furniture, the museum does an excellent job of conveying the history of this period. Even if you are unable to read Korean or Chinese (there's no English signage), much can be gleaned from looking at the images and documents in the two well-laid-out exhibition halls and by wandering through the complex of rooms which reconstruct various offices and private rooms.

KPG buildings in Hangzhou and Shanghai have also been refurbished and opened as museums, and the Hangzhou residence of Kim Gu (Kim Koo) has also opened as a memorial to the Premier of the KPG.

166 Sanxingdui Museum

三星堆博物馆 *Sanxingdui bowuguan*

Near Guanghan (about 30 km northeast of Chengdu)

邻近广汉，距离成都约30公里

Tel: (0838) 5510 399
Open: 8.30–17.30
www.sxd.cn/page/default.asp

Sanxingdui is one of the great museum destinations in China, rivalling the Terracotta Warriors in Xi'an. If you find yourself in Sichuan, do not pass up the opportunity to see the museum.

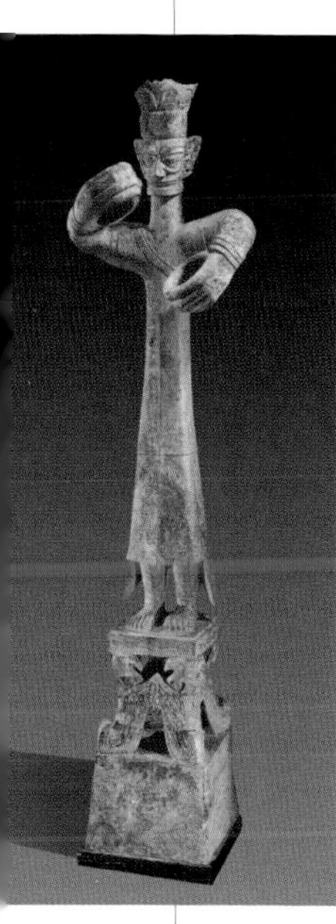

Shu Culture bronze 2.6-m high – regarded as the masterpiece from the excavation

The Shu Culture (Shu is the ancient name for the area now known as Sichuan – a large, fertile region surrounded by mountains and known as the Red Basin) was wrapped in mystery until the discovery of this site. Although the archaeological evidence shows that it existed from the Late Neolithic (equivalent to the Longshan Culture in the northern plains) through to the Eastern Zhou, very little mention is made of it in the historical record before the Spring and Autumn period, and to date no written records exist. In fact, no system of writing has been found, with the exception of seven glyphs.

The first breakthrough came in 1929 when a Sichuan farmer digging on his land found a pit containing several hundred jade and stone artefacts. Subsequent archaeological investigations uncovered more objects and structures. Then in 1986 two Shang dynasty sacrificial pits were found. Pit I contained bronzes, jade, gold, elephant tusks, and burnt bones and associated objects, some of which are spectacular, such as a life-size bronze human head, a gold mask and a dragon-shaped bronze column. Breaking and burning were common practices for sacrificial offerings at the time.

Pit II, some metres away, contained objects even more dazzling. They too had been burnt and broken before burial, but no bones were found here. The objects were neatly organized: on the top, sixty-seven elephant tusks, then bronzes, gold, jade ware, turquoise ornaments, stone implements and seashells. Some of the finds are of the sort common in Xia and Shang burials, but others are exquisite and unique artefacts such as a 2.6-m-high bronze statue of a human, a divine tree made of bronze nearly 4 m high, a 1.9-m-wide bronze mask with bulging eyes, and a bronze human head with a gilded mask. The purpose of these pits is debated – it is thought there is a hundred-year difference in their ages. Whether they are themselves a tomb, subordinate to a tomb or a storehouse is not clear.

The site of Sanxingdui covers an area of approximately 12 sq km. Only the museum is open to the public. The archaeological evidence reveals an ambitious scale of city planning including traces of a wall, roads, a palace site, residences, workshops and sacrificial sites.

Close-up of bronze above in a pose that suggests he is exercising magic at a mystic ceremony (note the mystic band on his shoulder decorated with rectangular motifs)

Many of the objects are of spectacular workmanship and unsurpassed beauty. The bronze figures differ in visage, dress, hairstyle and stance, and seem to portray different classes of society. Most have large almond-shaped eyes. The eye motif, prevalent in Shu Culture, seems to have had some association with supernatural power, perhaps due to the eye's connection with the image of the sun and to light. Another theory involves an early chronicle of the Shu kingdom which states that the Shu people's ancestral deity and earliest king, Cancong, had 'protruding eyes'. Bronze eyes or rhomboid objects (which look like beautiful pieces of contemporary sculpture) were also discovered, further indicating some concept of ocular divinity.

Bronze animal masks and animals, vessels, decorations and spears also abound.

Small ritual items made of pounded gold foil

were also found at the site. The craftsmanship is sophisticated and technically advanced. The gold wares were exclusively for ritual purposes; no gold for personal adornment has been discovered.

The 'divine tree' found in Pit II is the largest ancient bronze artefact ever found in China. The elaborate decoration includes a pedestal, and coming off the main trunk are branches bearing fruit with crested birds perched on the ends. Scholars do not agree on the purpose of this object, but it does have many references to cosmology, a common feature of ancient religions. The excavations have uncovered about a thousand jade and stone artefacts, again made to an exquisite standard. They include shapes such as the *zhang*, *bi*, *yuan*, *cong* and *ge*. Many ritual tools and weapons were found, giving credence to the theory that the Shu kingdom had a large and active ritual system. Interestingly, no actual weapons were found here, nor is there any other evidence of conflict, unlike for other Shang groups. Finally, a great deal of earthenware was excavated here, some types of which are rare at other sites: small, flat-based, high-stemmed bowls and ladles with bird-headed handles.

Ritual masks found at the site with large almond-shaped eyes

Also on exhibit are jade jewellery, seashells – probably offerings – elephant tusks and tiger teeth.

167

China Lantern Museum

中国彩灯博物馆 *Zhongguo caideng bowuguan*

6 Gongyuan Road, Zigong
自贡市公园路6号

Tel: (0813) 2305 061 / 2304 003
Open: 9.00–17.30
www.lantern-museum.com
Guides are available but must be arranged in advanced

Set in Lantern Park in the centre of Zigong, this low-lying concrete museum punctuated with large windows in the shape of a classic Chinese lantern sits handsomely facing a man-made lake surrounded by parkland. It is the perfect setting for the annual Zigong Lantern Festival (February to early March) as well as the Zigong International Dinosaur Lantern Show (one month between January and March), which attract thousands of visitors. Not only do the park and museum light up with glistening coloured lanterns in all shapes and sizes, but the whole town becomes a riot of colour and light.

Zigong is hailed as the 'Capital of Lanterns' and over the past several decades has taken what was once a folk-craft industry built around small groups of artisans and made it into a major industry. Today there are more than ninety lantern-making companies in the city, which have revitalized the local economy and put Zigong on the cultural map. Such is the success of Zigong's festivals that groups of local lantern-makers now stage similar events in cities around China and abroad. The craft has gone from the simple bamboo and coloured-paper lanterns first fashioned in the Han dynasty to complicated three-dimensional lanterns, often larger than life, representing well-known characters from cartoons or legends fitted with electronic chips to control moving parts.

Over five floors and eight exhibition halls, displays of historic and modern examples supported by interactive screens tell the origin of lanterns, the history of their construction from the Warring States period to the present day, explain modern methods of fashioning lanterns, describe the various festivals in Zigong and elsewhere, and show the best examples created for the annual festivals. These masterpieces are ingenious creations, from the dragon-and-phoenix lantern made by stringing together thousands of china plates to the flying-dragon realized from numerous silk cocoons. Displays of lanterns from other provinces, countries and across time surprise by their diversity. Finer lanterns were fashioned with frames of carved wood covered in silk and glass, others from slices of sheep horn moulded and shaped, or painted with flowers or birds and dangling with tassels. There are lanterns that float on water (popular in Guizhou and Yunnan), ice lanterns from Harbin, and those festooned with braided beads from Wanzhou. There is even a workshop where you can try your hand at fabricating you own lantern from a myriad of materials!

The Zigong Lantern Festival lights up the night sky

Lantern Festivals

Lanterns in Chinese culture are usually connected with two main festivals. The first is the Lantern Festival held on the fifteenth day of the first month of the Chinese lunar calendar and marks not only the end of the fifteen-day celebration of Chinese New Year but also the first full moon in the lunar New Year. The origins of this festival are many but were always marked by displays of lanterns in limitless shapes and sizes from gates, overhangs and even trees. Celebrations extend to composing poetry, parading lanterns around town and eating *tangyuan*. These balls of sticky rice with various fillings symbolize important family values such as unity. The second celebration, the Mid-Autumn Festival, highlights the fullest moon of the year and takes place on the fifteenth day of the eighth month in the lunar calendar. This marks the end of the harvest and, like harvest festivals elsewhere, is celebrated with food offerings, the eating of special foods – such as moon cakes or round cakes made with various fillings either sweet or salty, and the staging of lantern shows.

168 **Zigong Dinosaur Museum**

自贡恐龙博物馆 *Zigong konglong bowuguan*

238 Dashanpu, Da'an, Zigong
四川省自贡市大山铺238号

Tel: (0813) 580 1235 / 2095 / 1234
Open: 8.30–17.30; last entry 17.00
www.zdm.cn
Café / shop selling books, salt, and all things related to dinosaurs
Kids

The dinosaur-shaped visitor's centre

Mid Jurassic *Yandusaurus hongheensis*

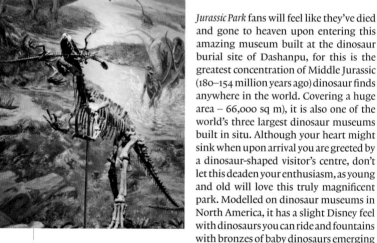

Jurassic Park fans will feel like they've died and gone to heaven upon entering this amazing museum built at the dinosaur burial site of Dashanpu, for this is the greatest concentration of Middle Jurassic (180–154 million years ago) dinosaur finds anywhere in the world. Covering a huge area – 66,000 sq m), it is also one of the world's three largest dinosaur museums built in situ. Although your heart might sink when upon arrival you are greeted by a dinosaur-shaped visitor's centre, don't let this deaden your enthusiasm, as young and old will love this truly magnificent park. Modelled on dinosaur museums in North America, it has a slight Disney feel with dinosaurs you can ride and fountains with bronzes of baby dinosaurs emerging from eggs. These delights aside, it has been designed to the highest level with first-rate information panels and labels throughout. Leave at least two hours to view it properly, as there is a fair bit of walking between the exhibition halls and the open pits where you can see excavations in progress.

When the dinosaurs roamed the area around Zigong, it was even more lush and fertile than it is today, resulting in river, lake and floodplain deposits over four strata, or layers – the most perfect environment for dinosaurs, bony fish and marine reptiles imaginable. This explains the mother load of finds that have been excavated here since the first hint of a 'dinosaur graveyard' was discovered by China's greatest dinosaur hunter, Dong Zhiming, in the 1970s.

After fighting off an oil-and-gas company that was already bulldozing the site, Dong rallied officials and got permission to excavate. When the museum complex opened in 1987, a selection of the 40 tons of fossils and tens of thousands of bones was put on display or placed in store for palaeontologists from abroad and China's universities to examine.

After picking up a map of the park in the visitor's centre and a walking stick, umbrella or pushchair, make your way outside and walk behind the building to the right towards the main exhibition building. Along the way you will pass a large, raised circular grassy area containing large-scale dinosaur models. Further on there is a living garden planted with Mesozoic trees, ferns, gingkoes and cypresses, very like the flora that would have existed at the time in the lush forests. Ahead is a rather massive, sandstone-coloured building – the heart of the museum-park complex – containing two floors of displays and an exposed section of the original excavated site.

Upon entering, your eyes will be drawn to the breathtaking display of eighteen dinosaur skeletons in the Dinosaur World exhibition space. It is, however, worth taking a moment to first study the nearby world-distribution map of dinosaur bones covering the Triassic, Jurassic and Cretaceous periods and having a look at the images of the skeletons being excavated. There are too many highlights to list, but do be sure to see an extremely well-preserved specimen of the herbivore *Huayangosaurus* (160 million years old), one of the most primitive of the stegosauruses. Around 4.5 m in length, it had two sets of huge bony plates running the length of its spine with spikes at the end of its tail, most likely for protection. Look also at the *Yangchuanosaurus*, a carnivorous monster from the Upper Jurassic period extending 10 m and to date the largest and best-preserved meat-eater found in Asia.

Best not to linger too long in the main hall, as there's lot more to see. Around the corner in the central hall you can look down onto ten dinosaur skeletons piled upon one another, perhaps caught in the swirl of the waters during a flood. Stop here too if you'd like to envision yourself thirty million years ago in the darkest depths of the Jurassic period – for you can step inside a simulated composition and have yourself filmed and take home a DVD to show your friends. Waiting on the other side of this central area is the 2,800-sq-m dinosaur graveyard exposing more than a hundred individual bones and fossils such as turtles. You are able to walk not only around the entire preserved site but also down into it via stairs and a viewing platform.

Huayangosaurus taibaii

The second floor contains the gallery devoted to the Mesozoic (250–65 million years ago) fauna and flora – this was the true 'Age of the Dinosaurs'. Displayed here are specimens of crocodiles, fishes, early birds, mammals, and flora of all types which existed alongside the dinosaurs over the Triassic, Jurassic and Cretaceous periods. Particularly spectacular are the well-preserved fossils of turtles from Liaoxi (west of Liaoning Province), as well as the aquatic reptile *Hyphalosaurus lingyuanensis*, with paddle-like limbs and a long serpentine neck, and the fish-shaped reptile with four fin-shaped limbs known as an ichthyosaur.

The Treasure Hall in the next gallery is a must, for here are some of the prizes of the museum rightly displayed on red velvet in specially lit glass cases. Sadly not all of these are original as security demands that the real ones are kept in store. The beauties include the best-preserved fossil of *Agilisaurus louderbacki* (named after the American geologist Dr Louderback, who first recognized dinosaur fossils from Sichuan Province in 1915), the small dinosaur which looks like a lizard lying curled up. It was found 90 per cent complete and adds tremendously to our evolutionary knowledge of this genus. The skull of the *Shunosaurus,* the best-preserved specimen known is sensational, as almost 100 per cent of it was found, and in the next case is a fossil of its club-shaped tail, the first discovery of this type anywhere. The skin impression of the *Mamenchisaurus youngi* covered in polygonal scales was the first example of such a find from a sauropod in China.

Finally, outside and a bit of a walk from the main museum is a slice of earth exposing the Xiashaximiao formation of the Middle Jurassic, which covers a wide area of the Sichuan Basin. Composed of several large sedimentary rhythms, it contains the most diverse dinosaur fauna before the Late Jurassic and is best known for its sauropods, including the one here in view, the *Omisauraus*, the long-necked herbivore that stretched to over 20 m in length.

169

Zigong Salt History Museum

自贡市盐业历史博物馆 *Zigongshi yanye lishi bowuguan*

107 Jiefang Road, Ziliujing District, Zigong

自贡市自流井区解放路107号

Tel: (0813) 220 4385
Open: 8.30–17.30 except New Year's Eve
www.saltmuseum.cn
English-speaking guide available without booking

Not only was Zigong one of the Sichuan Basin's centres for inland salt production, but it is credited with an array of spectacular technological breakthroughs which have had lasting impact world-wide. The most impressive has to be the invention of deep drilling in the mid eleventh century AD, listed by the famous historian of technology Joseph Needham in his summary of twenty of China's most important inventions to have entered Europe. Later, this technique would be instrumental in the advance of drilling technology for the oil and gas industries. If that were not enough, the area around Zigong saw the drilling of the first-ever wells to a depth of more than 1,000 m (in the early nineteenth century), and goes down in history as using coal and natural gas as fuel for salt production for the first time.

The museum is in the eighteenth-century Guildhall of the Shanxi Merchants

Salt has been one of the most traded commodities, whether for food preservation or as a condiment, at least since Neolithic times. As in many parts of the world, archaeological evidence points to salt being produced in Zigong by the evaporation of briny water in wide-mouthed shallow wells, or by using pottery vessels and boiling away the water content. Here in the Sichuan Basin, around 2,250 years ago, the first salt well was recorded in China, exploiting the thick, black salt-brine layers formed hundreds of metres below the surface during the Jurassic and Cretaceous periods.

Over time, drilling technology developed, and so did salt production. During the Tang dynasty a well reached a depth of

A 1950s photo captures the wooden derricks which once stood in the Zigong Saltern

A 1982 photo of Derrick workers repairing a 'Heaven Cart', which could reach more than 100 m in height

250 m, but it was not until the invention of a new cable-drilling method between 1041 and 1048 that production took off. This, coupled with the discovery of natural gas in the Zigong area in the early seventeenth century and, later, new gas-production techniques, moved production on to a different level, producing sufficient heat for more than 700 salt pans. By the middle of the nineteenth century, the industry was employing tens of thousands, dozens of wooden derricks (tall wooden structures made of hundreds of fir trees bundled together) could be seen across the landscape, and the River Fuxi was crowded with salt boats exporting some 150,000 tons of edible salt. Zigong City became the salt-production capital of southwestern China, its name the combination of two famous salt-production areas, Ziliujing and Gongjing.

This fascinating history of salt-well production and its cultural, economic and environmental impact is told in chronological order over two floors in the completely original Shanxi Guildhall, built from 1736 to 1752 by the rich Shanxi merchants who were active in the salt industry in the Ziliujing area. Displayed are cases filled with scores of tools for opening the well-heads and drilling the wells. Numerous models allow visitors to work a lever or press a button and watch how various tools removed mud and stones from the bore-hole, or corrected deviations to ensure the well-bore was vertical. Others show how dozens of tools perfected for fishing out objects which fell into the bore-holes were used. Fallen chisels would be retrieved using the 'king of fishing tools', the Fixture. Its bamboo shell would be manoeuvred until the chisel shaft slid into the narrow section of the shell.

Tools used to repair and drill wells

Illustrations from *The Annals of Salt Law of Sichuan Province* show the elaborate but advanced method of cable drilling, which with the help of gravity drove an iron chisel at the bottom of the hole, thus deepening the well and cutting the time needed to drill one down from ten to between three and five years. Others demonstrate how wooden columns were made and mud was lifted from the wells as they were dug. Equally informative are the historic images showing the forest of wooden derricks or tall wooden structures used for drilling and brine-lifting, which, in the 1950s covered the Zigong saltern, nineteen of which can still be seen today dotting the landscape. The collection extends to salt-industry contracts, marketing accounts and records of well-digging. Huang Jian, associate professor and curator of the museum, has made the history of salt production in this region his life's work and is worth speaking to if you have a translator. The Shenghai Well, the first to exceed 1,000 m in depth, can be visited in the nearby Da'an District of Zigong.

170 Gulangyu Guanfu Classic Art Museum

鼓浪屿 观复古典艺术博物馆 *Gulangyu guanfu gudian yishu bowuguan*

Shuzhuang Huayuan, 7 Gangzai Hou Road, Siming District, Gulangyu, Xiamen, Fujian

福建省厦门市鼓浪屿思明区港仔后路7号 菽庄花园

Tel: (0592) 2570 858
Open: 8.00–17.30
www.guanfumuseum.org.cn
English audio guide / multimedia information screens

The Guanfu Classic Art Museum, located just inside the entrance to the Shuguang Garden, is a small private museum, with some interesting pieces of mainly Ming and Qing furniture and porcelain.

The museum, established by Ma Weidu, a well-known collector of antiques, opens with a collection of beautiful chairs from the Ming and Qing dynasties. There are horseshoe-shaped chairs with rounded backs, rectangular chairs with the longevity motif, arm chairs with a curved top rail and a foot base, the official's hat armchair with an angular scroll, a folding horseshoe-backed chair with a dragon and cloud motif, and a large elaborate canopy bed with a swastika motif. There is also a small table with horsehoof feet, humpback stretchers and interlocking rings. Of special interest is a set of furniture from the Liao dynasty (916–1125) that includes a Luohan couch bed and lantern hook chairs.

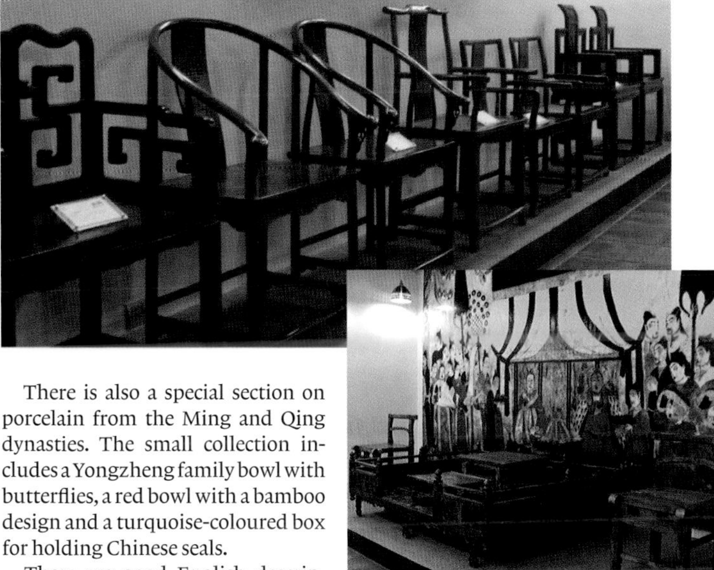

Ming and Qing dynasty chairs

Rare Liao dynasty couch bed and lantern hook chairs

There is also a special section on porcelain from the Ming and Qing dynasties. The small collection includes a Yongzheng family bowl with butterflies, a red bowl with a bamboo design and a turquoise-coloured box for holding Chinese seals.

There are good English descriptions for each of the items.

171 **Gulangyu Piano Museum**

厦门鼓浪屿钢琴博物馆 *Xiamen gulangyu gangqin bowuguan*

No. 45 Huangyan Road, Shuzhuang Garden, Gulangyu, Xiamen, Fujian

福建省厦门市鼓浪屿 晃岩路45号 菽庄花园

Tel: (0592) 2570 331

Open: 8.15–19.45

Gift shop down from the museum sells music boxes made in the shapes of pianos and other musical instruments

The Xiamen Gulangyu Piano Museum, located on sleepy Gulangyu off the coast of Xiamen, is situated on a hill with beautiful views of the sea below. The existence of the museum here on Gulangyu, and the fact that the island has a century-old love affair with music and the piano (there are said to be more than 600 privately owned pianos on Gulangyu), have won the islet the nickname Piano Island.

The museum, located in two separate houses on the hilltop, was established in 2000 by Hu Youyi, a native of the island who studied music at the Royal Academy of Brussels and later migrated to Australia. The original building was constructed in 1913 and modelled after Youyi's father's villa in Taipei, Taiwan.

The collection includes some one hundred pianos of all shapes and sizes made by famous piano makers from Europe, Australia and the USA; some are more than a century old and there are a few beautiful reproductions. The oldest piano in the collection is a Clementi square piano from London that dates

Gulangyu Island has both a piano and an organ museum

back to 1801. Other interesting pieces include a French street musician's barrel piano, a grand piano with ivory keys made in England, a piano that was treasured by US President, Abraham Lincoln, an 1824 Broadwood & Sons piano from London that is said to be the tallest upright piano in existence, and a number of old Steinway models. There is also a collection of miniature and custom-made pianos. The automatic 1928 Haines, which imitates the styles of famous pianists, can be heard each day at 16.00.

Music lovers who enjoy the piano museum should also visit the Gulangyu Organ Museum, located in a once stately mansion that has fallen into disrepair. Also founded by Hu Youyi, the museum has a dusty collection of antique organs, but unfortunately sparse explanations in either Chinese or English. The collection includes a Norman & Beard organ that was made in 1909, two years after the building it now sits in. The pipe organ was originally housed in Cradley Heath Methodist Church in the UK. The museum is located at 43 Gu Xin Lu (鼓新路43号) and is open from 9.30 to 16.30.

172

Xiamen Culture and Arts Centre

厦门文化艺术中心 *Xiamen wenhua yishu zhongxin*

95 Tiyu Road, Xiamen, Fujian
福建省厦门市 体育路95号 厦门科技馆

Tel: (0592) 514 7666 / 8555
Open: 9.00–17.00 except Mon
www.xmstm.com.cn (Chinese only)

This impressive, sprawling complex made of painted white metal and glass opened in 2007 and comprises three museums: The Xiamen Science and

Stone sculpture in the History Museum

Optical illusion in the Science Museum (see over)

The physics of water (see over)

Technology Museum, The Xiamen History Museum and the Xiamen Art Museum.

The Xiamen Science and Technology Museum is interesting because of the many interactive exhibits (around 80 per cent are interactive) that allow children (and their parents) to get a hands-on feel for science. The displays have limited but useful English explanations. Exhibits focus on moving robots, two of which engage in jousting with Chinese swords. An exhibit on universal gravitation allows visitors to manipulate a large metal top that seemingly slides on its own to a higher position.

The second floor has an exhibition on insects, with models of various bugs that are bigger than humans so children can get a close look. The insects also emit their unique sounds. In the 'Water Works Park' visitors can get a first-hand look at how water pressure works and an indoor playground area on the same floor has a wooden jungle gym. The 4D Theater shows science films that appear to leap right out of the screen, with screenings several times a day (10.00, 11.00, 15.00 and 16.00; additional showings at noon and 2pm during holidays). When you exit the museum on the first floor, remember to take a look at the giant water clock.

The Xiamen History Museum examines the history of Xiamen, from the Stone Age to its place as a modern seaport. Unfortunately, there are few descriptions in English. The outside of the modern-looking museum is nicely prefaced by antique stone gates and stone statues of officials, guardians and animals, in many cases their facial features erased by time.

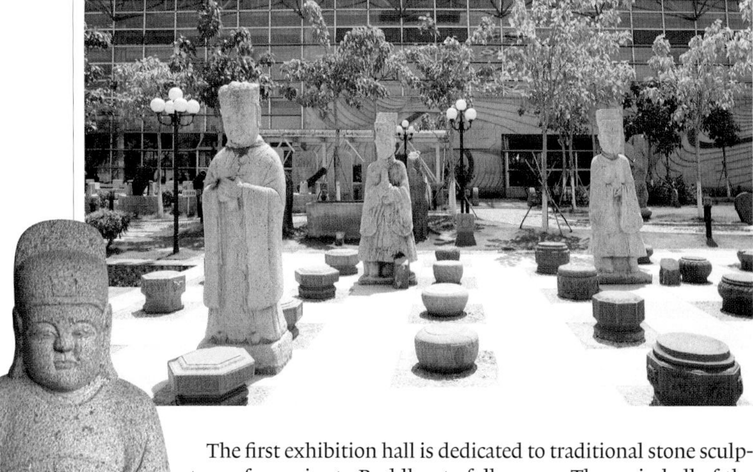

The first exhibition hall is dedicated to traditional stone sculptures, from pigs to Buddhas to folk scenes. The main hall of the museum opens with bronze statues of famous former residents, the most notable of whom is Koxinga (or Zheng Chenggong) the half-Chinese, half-Japanese pirate who sailed his fleet of tens of thousands of ships from this area to wrestle control of Taiwan from the Dutch during the Qing dynasty. Also on display are ancient clay figurines, pottery pieces, an old-fashioned 'fire truck' and a walkway made to look like an old-fashioned cobblestone street, lined with various traditional shops: tea, wicker, ghost money (paper money burned as an offering to the dead and used in the afterlife) and a blacksmith. The museum also looks

at the local resistances in operation against the Japanese during World War II and the civil war between the Communists and the Nationalists.

The adjoining Xiamen Art Museum is a large space featuring travelling exhibitions and the work of local artists.

173

Xiamen Overseas Chinese Museum

厦门华侨博物院 *Xiamen huaqiao bowuguan*

493 Siming South Road, Xiamen, Fujian
福建省厦门市思明南路493号

Tel: (0592) 208 4028
Open: 9.30–16.00
www.huagqiaobowuyuan.org.cn

The Overseas Chinese Museum tells the story of the native sons of Fujian who left here in search of their fortune a century or longer ago. The museum was built with funding from Chen Jiageng, an overseas Chinese philanthropist, and it opened in 1959. The museum is organized into three sections: one explores the Chinese overseas, the second displays Chen Jiageng's private collection and the third is the Natural Science Museum.

Chinese emigrants panning for gold abroad

At the heart of this museum is the Hall of Overseas Chinese, which tells the story of Chinese emigrants through photographs, art and bronze reproductions demonstrating how life was lived by the early waves of Chinese people who travelled abroad. In the main hall there are several wooden boats, models of the types that took the Chinese to Southeast Asia and other neighbouring parts of the world. There is a mock of a ship's hold, with life-like models of people sitting on the floor of the boat, complemented by paintings on the wall. Other models include a Chinese school, a tailor's shop and a printer's, as well as a gold miner and a rickshaw puller. On the second floor there are scenes of

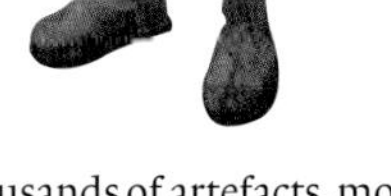

Diorama showing Chinese sorting type at a publisher overseas

the Chinese people who helped to build the US railroad, and of rubber harvesting from rubber trees in Malaysia.

The Hall of Relics, on the third floor, displays thousands of artefacts, most of which were collected by Mr Chen, including pottery, bronze ware, sculpture and art. The Natural Science Museum, on the second floor, has displays of rare animals, plants, aquatic life and the skeleton of a large whale.

174

Opium War Museum

鸦片战争博物馆 *Yapian zhanzheng bowuguan*

88 Jiefang Road, Humen Town, Dongguan, Guangdong

Tel: (0769) 5512 065
Open: 7.00–17.00

广东省东莞市虎门镇解放路88号

Lin Zexu was an imperial commissioner in the Qing court. In 1838, he was sent to Guangdong to deal with the illegal importation of opium from India into China by the British. Not only was opium addiction sapping the energy of the population, it was also undermining the economy, as silver was sucked out to pay for the growing trade. He ultimately rid Guangzhou of over one million kilos of opium, which he had burnt in pits in Humen. Lin is well known for writing a letter to Queen Victoria in which he asks her to stop the trade in opium on moral grounds. He is now regarded as the quintessential 'patriotic' official. In fact, his destruction of the opium actually drove the price of it up,

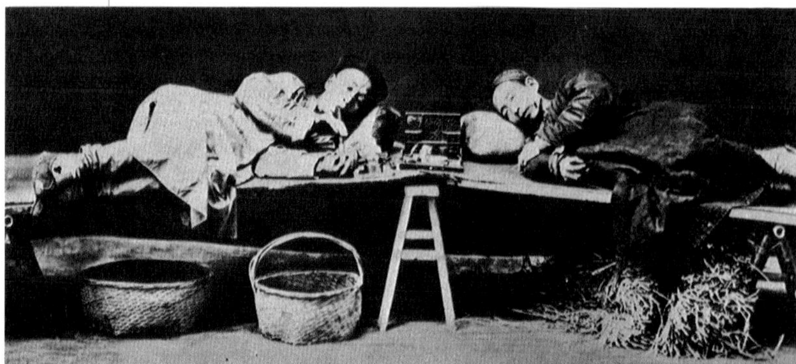

Addiction to opium was rampant in nineteenth-century China

thus benefiting the British. It also provided the excuse to the British for starting the First Opium War.

On display are cannons, cannonballs and other weapons of the Chinese, British and Americans. These are complemented by documents, photos and illustrations. Some displays are interactive but in Chinese only.

Besides the museum building, it is possible to visit the pits in which Lin burnt the opium and several old batteries along the coastline constructed during the Opium Wars.

Junks in battle during the First Opium War

175

Guangdong Museum of Art

广东美术馆 *Guangdong meishuguan*

38 Yanyu Road, Ersha Island, Guangzhou, Guangdong

广东省广州市二沙岛烟雨路38号

Tel: (020) 8735 1361
Open: 9.00–17.00
www.gdmoa.org
English audio guide / multimedia information screens

This painting pays tribute to the armed forces during the Sichuan earthquake (top right)

This contemporary art museum, located on Ersha Island in the centre of the Pearl River, has twelve exhibition halls featuring both permanent and temporary exhibitions, and an outdoor sculpture garden. Each year, the museum hosts a large exhibition of its permanent collection of sculpture, painting and ceramics, which includes contemporary artistic works of the coastal areas of China and Guangdong Province, as well as work by overseas Chinese artists. The museum also hosts exhibitions of artwork from various countries around the world.

176

Guangdong Provincial Museum

广东省博物馆 *Guangdongsheng bowuguan*

215 Wenming Road, Guangzhou, Guangdong

广东省广州市文明路215号

Tel: (020) 8382 8776

Open: 9.00–17.00

English audio guide / multimedia information screens

The Guangdong Provincial Museum is a comprehensive museum that includes exhibition halls, the site of the Kuomintang's First National Congress and the Lu Xun Memorial Hall (located in the Bell Tower), dedicated to the memory of one of China's most famous modern writers.

The highlight of the museum is its wonderful collection of Chaozhou wood carvings and furniture, Chaozhou being one of the oldest and most famous schools of woodcarving in China. The elaborately carved gold window lattice and panels depicting ancient Chinese tales are especially fine.

There are also displays on Guangdong history, ceramics, calligraphy, paintings and handicrafts. The ceramics collection includes pieces from many famous ancient kilns, and the calligraphy exhibition contains sutras written in the Sui and Tang dynasties, and pieces created by some of China's most famous calligraphers. On the second floor is a section dedicated to the history of Guangzhou city, from prehistoric to modern times, including ancient bronzes and clay figurines. Especially interesting is a Han dynasty clay reproduction of a banquet scene.

Qing dynasty gilt wood carving

Detail of Qing carved wood

The Lu Xun Memorial Hall presents the life of Lu Xun (1881–1936), China's most influential modern writer. The complex also houses the hall where the First Kuomintang, or Nationalist, Congress took place, as well as meetings between the Kuomintang and the Communist Party.

There is also a Nature Hall that has simple examples of the natural ecological environment of Guangdong.

Descriptions are all in Chinese.

A new museum building is under construction and will be completed in the summer of 2009 (see Stop Press). It will be located at Zhujiang New Town and will feature Guangdong history, folk arts, natural science and more.

177

Guangzhou City Museum

广州博物馆 *Guangzhou bowuguan*

Zhenhai Tower, inside Yuexiu Park, 988 Jiefang North Road, Guangzhou, Guangdong

广东省广州市解放北路988号 越秀公园内镇海楼

Tel: (020) 8355 0627
Open: 9.00–17.30
English audio guide / multimedia information screens

Western Han clay figures

The Guangzhou Museum is located in the historic Zhenhai Tower (or Tower Controlling the Sea), which sits on the last remaining part of the old city wall. The tower was first built here on a hill in Yuexiu Park in 1380 by Zhu Liangzu, a general of the Ming dynasty, and was rebuilt a total of five times after that.

The museum focuses on the history of the Guangzhou area, with 1,000 exhibits covering 2,000 years of history spread out over its five floors. On the first floor there is simply a large map of the city and an old anchor dating back to the Ming dynasty. The second floor displays items from the Han dynasty, including two statues of Persian men – ancient visitors to the region. The third and fourth floors focus on the city's role as a trading

centre in the nineteenth century and the Western influence on Guangzhou. The fifth floor has a gift shop and a balcony with excellent views of the city.

Just outside the museum is a collection of steles, several old canons from the Opium War and a large wooden tomb.

There are no descriptions in English.

178

Guangzhou Museum of Art

广州艺术博物院 *Guangzhou yishu bowuyuan*

13 Luhu Road, Guangzhou, Guangdong
广东省广州市麓湖路13号

Tel: (020) 8365 9202
Open: 9.00–17.00
www.gzam.com.cn
English audio guide / multimedia information screens

Clockwise from top right:

Print by Lai Shaoqi

Watercolour by Liao Bingxiong

Painting by Liao Bingxiong

The Guangzhou Museum of Art is one of the biggest and best art museums in southern China, known for its diverse range of ancient and contemporary pieces created by artists from the region. The collection includes paintings, calligraphy, woodblock prints, watercolours, gouache, powder paintings, cartoons, sculpture, *thangkas*, Tibetan religious tapestry and ceramics.

Both permanent and special exhibitions are housed over the three floors of this sprawling museum. Particularly good is a special collection of Liao Bingxiong's political cartoons and drawings of people, such as opera performers. The Zhao Tailai Collection Hall features a varied, private antique collection, including an ivory fan with an embroidered peacock from the Qing dynasty, a pearly sphere vase from France, Tibetan religious items, bamboo and ivory carvings, jade and bronzes. Wonderful pieces of sculpture are scattered throughout the museum. You will need at least half a day to view all that's on display here.

179

The Museum of the Mausoleum of the Nanyue King of the Western Han Dynasty

西汉南越王博物馆 *Xihan nanyuewang bowuguan*

867 Jiefang North Road, Guangzhou, Guangdong

广东省广州市解放北路867号

Tel: (020) 3618 2865
Open: 9.00–17.30
www.gznywmuseum.com
English audio guide / multimedia information screens

This museum is located in a modern building situated against Xianggang Hill, which was the original site of the tomb of the second Nanyue King (the Nanyue kingdom was established in 203 BC). Enter the museum building and proceed to the third floor, where you exit outside to the site of the tomb, which has seven underground chambers guarded by heavy stone slab doors. The tomb, which was discovered by accident in 1983, had fortunately never been plundered and so was intact when opened, making it one of the largest and best protected tombs of its kind found in southern China. In the middle of the burial room once stood the inner and outer coffins, which have disintegrated. The vestiges of the king's corpse remained when found, the body dressed in a jade shroud made of 2,291 pieces of jade sewn with silk thread. At the time of the death of the king, it was believed that jade could prevent the body from decaying. At the time of excavation, the body had disintegrated and the jade pieces of the shroud lay scattered around the burial chamber. It took archaeologists three years to restore the shroud. The king's body had ten iron swords at his waist, and his head rested on a pearl-embroidered pillow.

Jade ornament with dragon and phoenix pattern found on the King's right eye

The collection contains over 10,000 relics, including the gold seal of Emperor Wen, one of the earliest imperial seals ever discovered. The seal, which has a dragon-shaped handle, is evidence that the inhabitant of the tomb is the second Nanyue King, Zhao Mo. Fifteen sacrificial victims were also found buried in the tomb with the late Emperor. In the Western Chamber seven more sacrificial victims were found buried without coffins; these included cooks and servants. Four concubines were buried in the Eastern Chamber. Each of them was buried with a seal identifying who they were. In the Rear Storeroom, 155 large cooking vessels were found, along with food for the deceased royal family, including remains of fruit, fish-bones, rice, birds, domestic animals and shells. Seals found here bear the inscription 'Officer Tai', who was the director in charge of the kitchen. It's believed that Officer Tai, one of the sacrificial victims found in the Western Chamber, placed these items here before the burial.

After visiting the tomb, proceed to the exhibition halls where many of the excavated items are on display. In the first exhibition room is a reproduction of the jade shroud that covered the body of the king, as well as his dragon seal and many other pieces of jade unearthed from the tomb.

The museum also houses a collection of over 400 ceramic pillows, 200 of which were donated by Mr and Mrs Yueng Wing Tak, prominent Hong Kong collectors. The pillows date from the Tang dynasty to modern times, but the

majority are from the Song and Jin dynasties. As they were produced by different provincial kilns at different times, their shapes and motifs reflect the designs that were favoured when they were made.

180

Cultural Revolution Museum

文革博物馆 *Wenge bowuguan*

Tashan Scenic Zone, Lianshang Town, Chenghai District, Shantou, Guangdong

广东省汕头市澄海区莲上镇塔山风景区

Tel: (0754) 8510 0434 (Administrative Office of the Scenic Zone)
Open: 9.00–17.30

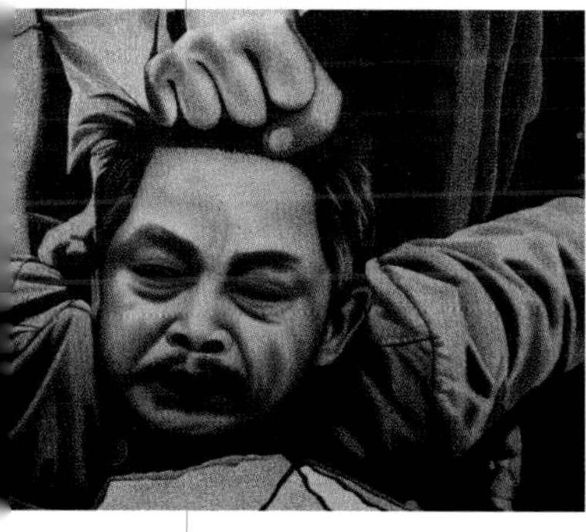

A struggle session etched into stone with the victim in the 'airplane position'

It has been more than thirty years since the end of the Cultural Revolution, yet the subject remains highly sensitive in this country. This bloody, violent and cruel period of modern history is not a subject the government wishes anyone to revisit in depth, as it not only defiles the legacy of Mao Zedong but also undermines the credibility of the Communist Party. That is why the continued existence of this museum, opened in 2005, is so amazing and so curious.

This private museum was created by the ex-mayor of Shantou, Peng Qi'an, who was reportedly 'struggled against' 300 times and even put on a Red Guard death-list, which was later revoked. The park in which the museum is located was the scene of pitched battles between warring factions of the Red Guards, and many people died and were buried in the hills and along the trails of the Tashan Forest. The point of the memorial is expressed in the words of Guangdong Provincial Party Secretary and liberal reformer, Ren Zongyi: 'Take history as a mirror and never again allow the tragedy of the Cultural Revolution to repeat itself.'

Set within the forest, the museum is a circular pagoda-style building. Inside, 623 dark-grey granite slabs are etched with scenes of the Cultural Revolution, which come from a book published in Hong Kong called *Cultural Revolution Museum*. These chilling and graphic scenes recording the barbarous acts of the Red Guards, as well as the humiliation and even suicides of their victims, leave little to the imagination. Also surprisingly explicit are the depictions of Mao himself, at first shown as a strong and virile man swimming the Yangtze and finally as a fat and exhausted shadow of himself, slumped in an armchair.

Beyond the pagoda the memorial park continues, displaying plaques, sculptures and other exhibits within the grounds.

Some say the museum has been allowed to remain open due to its location far from the corridors of central power. Still, the government does not allow the museum to publicize itself and therefore it is not well known within the country. Those who visit cannot fail to be moved.

181

Guangdong Marine Silk Road Museum

广东海上丝绸之路博物馆 *Guangdong haishang sichouzhilu bowuguan*

Shiliyintan, Hailing Island, Yangjiang, Guangdong
广东省阳江市海陵岛十里银滩

Open: Scheduled for early 2009
Kids

It was not until treasure hunters started finding Chinese merchant shipwreck in the South China Sea full to the gunnels with cargos of eighteenth-centur porcelain that archaeologists realized China had set up marine trading route 200 years before those of the Spanish, Portuguese and British. Wrecks like th Tang dynasty *Batu Hitam* provided evidence that over 1,200 years ago the Chi nese began trading by sea as an alternative to the famous overland Silk Roac The Marine Silk Road took porcelain, tea and silk from the southern ports i Guangdong and Fujian for export to countries in the Middle East, India an Europe.

This enormous, purpose-built museum on the beach on Hailing Island ad jacent to Yangjiang city will tell the story of China's success and the wealth i accumulated while trading with the world via its marine routes in the Tan and Song dynasties. The building overlooks the ancient waterways that wer once the start of the Marine Silk Road and some of the busiest sea lanes in an cient times. Consisting of five interlinking ellipse-shaped halls, the structur bears a resemblance to a seagull in flight.

The museum's star attraction will undoubtedly be the Nanhai No. 1 (Sout China Sea No. 1) shipwreck, which will be displayed in 'Crystal Palace', th largest of the halls. Dating from the early Southern Song dynasty, it was foun lying upright in silt off the coast of Guangdong. Its fine state of preserva tion, complete with a stunning cargo of mostly export porcelain produced a China's southern kilns, gold and silver containers and jewellery, urged archae ologists to consider raising it as a whole so it could be excavated in controlle conditions. After years of planning, a huge steel cage was engineered to rais the wreck and its tens of thousands of artefacts to the surface. It is in a holdin tank prior to being transferred to the museum's giant sealed salt-water aqua ium, where it will be stored underwater in conditions that mimic those wher it lay on the seabed. Visitors will then be able to watch underwater archaeolo gists measure, draw and photograph the vessel before it is excavated.

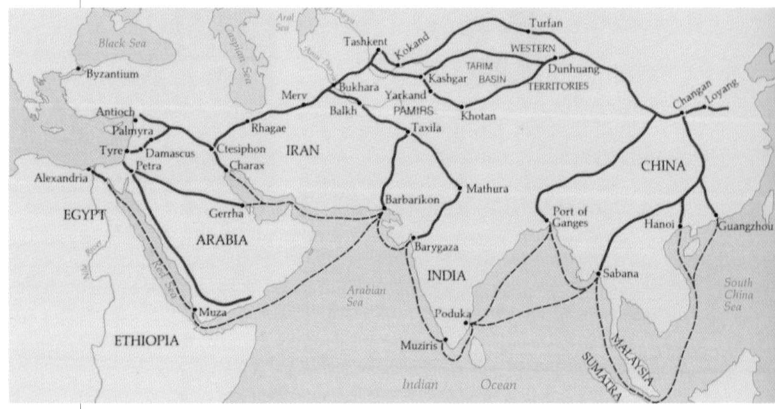

East–West trade routes by land and sea, known as the Silk Roads

182

Hunan Provincial Museum

湖南省博物馆 *Hunansheng bowuguan*

No. 50 Dongfeng Road, Changsha, Hunan

湖南省长沙市东风路50号

Tel: (0731) 4514 630
Open: 8.30–17.30, last entry 16.30, 10 Oct–31 Mar; 8.00–18.00, last entry 17.00, 1 Apr–9 Oct
English audio guide / English-speaking guide can be arranged by calling one day in advance
Book / gift shops

T-shaped painting on silk banner carried in funeral procession, from Tomb No. I Mawangdui

The well-preserved female corpse of Lady Xin from Han Tomb No. 1, found buried with close to 2,000 funerary objects including well-preserved lacquer and slips of bamboo listing all the goods placed in the tomb

Painted figurines from Tomb No. I Mawangdui (see over)

The Hunan Provincial Museum first opened in Changsha, the capital of Hunan Province, in 1956. The discovery and excavation of the Mawangdui Han Tombs (the tomb of Marquise Dai's family in the Western Han dynasty) in 1972–74 was of major significance for the Provincial Museum, adding to its collection thousands of precious relics and the well-preserved corpse of a female member of the Dai family. In order to display the enlarged and valuable collection properly, a new exhibition hall was opened in 1973. Then, around 2000, a state-of-the-art exhibition centre was added, with excellent displays and brief descriptions in English.

The Exhibition of the Mawangdui Han Tombs, including more than 3,000 cultural relics taken from three tombs, is the major attraction here, representing, as it does, one of the most significant archaeological discoveries in twentieth-century China. The most important piece is the well-preserved corpse of a female member of the family of Marquise Dai. Around 2,000 years old, it rests in a glass coffin and can be viewed from overhead. The cultural relics include three beautiful gauze gowns that the museum describes as 'thin as a cicada's wing', and a selection of silk robes. There are also wonderful wooden figurines of singers, dancers and musicians, some colourfully painted or wearing silk clothing. In addition, there is well-preserved lacquer ware, silk embroidery, socks and shoes, as well as paintings on silk and brightly painted inner coffins.

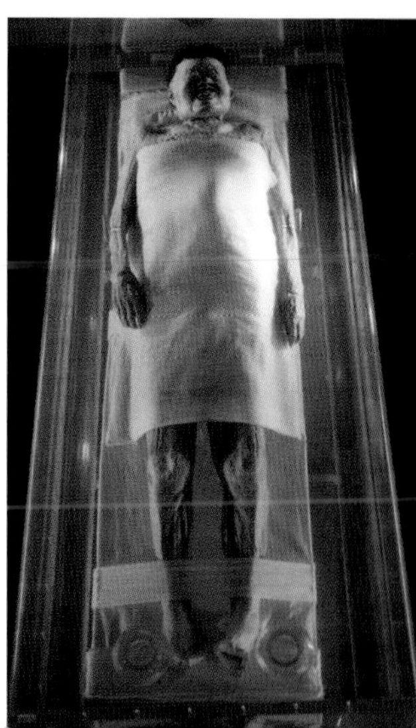

The Exhibition of Shang and Zhou Bronzes includes the earliest bronzes found in Hunan, some dating back around 3,500

years. The Exhibition of Ceramics from Famous Kilns in Hunan has on display shards excavated at Yuchanyan, in Dao County, which are among the earliest ever found in China. There are also separate exhibitions of calligraphy and paintings from the Ming and Qing dynasties. The second floor holds the Exhibition of Ten New Major Archaeological Discoveries in Hunan as well as space for temporary exhibitions.

The Mawangdui Han Tombs, located east of Changsha, are open to the public. Only the objects excavated from the site are exhibited here at the Provincial Museum.

183 Mao Zedong's Former Residence

毛泽东故居 *Mao Zedong guju*

Shangwuchang, Tudichong, Shaoshan, Hunan

湖南省韶山市韶山乡土地冲上屋场

Tel: (0732) 565 1288
Open: 9.00–17.00, closed on Mon
Gift shop at museum / English and Japanese guides available at house / refreshments

Trays dating to the Cultural Revolution celebrate Mao's birthplace at Shaoshan

Shaoshan, located in the countryside approximately 100 km southwest of Changsha, was the birthplace of Mao Zedong and, while it may no longer be the pilgrimage site that it once was, it continues to attract a few million visitors per year. The 'Great Helmsman' was born here on 26 December 1893 to a relatively wealthy peasant family. The thirteen-room farmhouse is spacious and sparsely furnished with purportedly original furniture, and there are a few photographs of Mao as a young man, as well as his parents and his brother. Here, there is not the sense of voyeurism that permeates Xikou, Chiang Kai-shek's hometown, but rather a thoughtful solemnity, as if we might somehow wrap our minds – Chinese and Western alike – around the contradictory elements of Mao's legacy. It is clear that Mao did not like return-

ing to his home, only visiting a handful of times during the decades after his rise to power, yet his political understandings and core beliefs were indelibly shaped by this humble rustic setting.

Next door to the house is the primary school that Mao attended. Further down the road is Comrade Mao's Memorial Hall, which was empty on the day of the author's visit. Despite the photographs, examples of his calligraphy and some books he read, the exhibits do not really illuminate this man who was to dominate Chinese politics for so many decades. Passing by Mao's shaving kit, bathrobe and slippers, and an enormous pair of swimming trunks, one cannot help but be struck by the contrast between these ordinary items and the god-like marble statue posed in front of a rainbow-coloured China in the grand foyer.

184

Jingdezhen Ceramic History Museum

景德镇陶瓷历史博览区 *Jingdezhen taoci wenhua bolanqu*

Panlonggang, Fengshushan, Xishi District, Jingdezhen, Jiangxi

江西省景德镇市 西市区枫树山蟠龙岗

Tel: (0798) 852 1594 / 3541
Open: 8.00–17.00
Kids

Jingdezhen Kiln

Potter at work on site

This 'living history' museum is actually a park in the Panlong Mountains, on the outskirts of Jingdezhen. The highlight here is the opportunity to see potters produce ceramic ware from start to finish, using traditional techniques and materials.

The three main types of kilns are on site – bun, gourd and dragon – as well as the Jingdezhen Kiln, which combines the best attributes of them all. This huge kiln is about 20 m in length and visitors can step inside (it's not firing!) to see how the ceramics are fired.

There are several well-preserved buildings in traditional Ming and Qing styles, displaying ceramics and other objects. There are also gardens to enjoy, a teahouse, gift shops and a post office from which to ship your porcelain.

Traditional techniques are demonstrated

Detail from Qing dynasty ceramic plaque illustrating ceramic production

185 Jingdezhen Chinese Porcelain Museum

景德镇中国陶瓷博物馆 *Jingdezhen zhongguo taoci bowuguan*

21 Lianshe North Road, Jingdezhen, Jiangxi

江西省景德镇市 莲社北路21号

Tel: (0798) 822 9784
Open: 8.00–17.00
Shop selling reproduction Jingdezhen wares and books on all aspects of ceramics

The Jingdezhen Chinese Porcelain Museum first opened in 1954. There are about 19,000 objects in its inventory and, of these, about 2,000 have come from the collection of the Palace Museum in Beijing. As Jingdezhen was the centre of imperial porcelain production during the Song dynasty, most of the objects produced here were sent out of the city. Therefore, the finest examples of Jingdezhen porcelain cannot be seen in the place of its manufacture.

The oldest pieces from the collection are displayed on the ground floor and date from the first century BC. A Song dynasty bisque porcelain jar with a square lid is an important piece as it is unglazed, which is unusual for this period. In the same room is a Yuan dynasty blue and white jar decorated in a flower and plant pattern – the earliest example of cobalt blue with pale celadon in the museum. Most experts agree that blue and white ware, although

most prevalent in the Ming, originated in the Yuan dynasty, with the cobalt mainly imported from Persia.

There is a Ming dynasty blue and white lidded pot from the Wangli Reign (1573–1620) decorated with a five-clawed dragon and phoenix pattern (a five-clawed dragon denotes imperial use). Also on display is a jar decorated with beautiful girls from the Chongzhen Reign (1628–44). Chongzhen was the last Ming Emperor and during this period of the collapse of the dynasty, potters were turning to popular production as they no longer had the patronage of the court.

Upstairs, Qing dynasty ware is exhibited. The number of pieces on view is not very large but examples from most reigns are represented. Be sure to see the extraordinary Lang Kiln red ware, or ox blood, vase. This glaze, first made in the Kangxi Reign, is very unstable and tends to roll and gather at the foot

Detail from Qing dynasty plaque of snow scene

of the pot. Therefore these vessels usually have a lip at the bottom to catch the glaze. They also often have tiny little spots where gaps are left in the glaze.

There is a charming blue and white plate showing a scene from the romantic play, *Xi Xiang Ji*. The image depicts a girl and her nurse craning their necks to hear the music her lover is playing on the opposite side of the wall.

During the Qianlong period (1736–95) in Jingdezhen, wares from many different areas were copied, such as Jun ware and Ru ware. Examples of these pots are also on display.

Finally, Republican period and post-1949 period pottery is also represented at the museum. At the end of the Opium Wars many painters came to Jingdezhen and painting became a major feature of ceramic production – a tradition that continues today.

At the time of writing, a new museum was soon to open which will include the work of contemporary Jingdezhen potters. Twenty-six nationally recognized 'masters' live and work in Jingdezhen, and their work will be included.

Qing plate with scene showing the girl and nurse listening to music played by lover on opposite side of wall from the romantic play *Xi Xiang Ji*

186

Jingdezhen Folk Kiln Museum (Hutian Kiln Site)

景德镇民窑博物馆 *Jingdezhen minyao bowuguan*

No. 18, Hangkong Avenue, Jingdezhen, Jiangxi

江西省景德镇市航空大道18号

Tel: (0798) 8481 071
Open: 8.30–17.00

The Hutian Kiln produced pottery here for over 700 years, from 907 to 1644. It was not an imperial kiln but it did produce porcelain for the court, most notably the thin-walled *qingbai* wares of the Northern Song.

The site includes a small museum with a few objects and limited English signage. The collection includes some very early celadon pieces from the Five Dynasties period, and Northern Song wares such as bowls, pillows, cups and jars. Note the especially elegant and simple pale celadon carved and impressed *qingbai* glazed ewer. There is also a lovely *qingbai* Guanyin fragment in the position known as 'Royal Ease', often seen during the Song dynasty. Yuan dynasty porcelain and examples of Ming dynasty blue and white porcelain are also on display.

The kiln excavations are on view and the excavated levels are marked as Song, Yuan and Ming.

Jingdezhen Porcelain

The environmental conditions in the area surrounding Jingdezhen make it ideal for the development of its ceramic culture which has been synonymous with high-quality porcelain production and innovation for over 1,000 years.

The region is rich in porcelain stone and kaolin clay – the two ingredients essential to create the delicate and translucent final product. The surrounding mountains and forests provide plentiful wood to feed the kilns. In earlier times, the Changjiang River and its tributaries allowed for convenient transportation of both raw materials and finished products. Before the Song dynasty, the town was known as Changnan (south of the Chang), referring to its position on the river. Some believe that the English word 'china' is, in fact, a garbled pronunciation of Changnan.

During the Jingde Reign of the Song dynasty, the name of the town was changed to Jingdezhen and from this time through the Yuan, Ming and Qing dynasties, Jingdezhen became the centre of imperial porcelain production. During the Yuan, the famous 'blue and white' porcelain appeared, using cobalt sourced from western Asia as trade increased with Mongol rule.

As orders for imperial porcelain increased, production was expanded beyond the official imperial kilns and outsourced to family workshops and kilns in the area. A governmental agency – the Porcelain Office – was set up to ensure quality control at kilns. The porcelain business became global: by the seventeenth century, more than 10,000 craftsmen were working in Jingdezhen, creating elaborate porcelains

using sophisticated techniques and exporting them beyond the domestic market to Southeast Asia, Europe and the New World. A highly efficient system of mass production was developed, in which each step of the process was handled by a separate individual. It has been reported that as many as seventy people could be involved in the creation of a single item.

Today, the art and craft of porcelain production still oozes from the pores of the city. 'Biscuit carriers' haul unfinished wares in carts or on pallets to kilns or decoration houses. Porcelain shops line the road and stacks of colourfully glazed pots in every conceivable shape fill the street markets. Trucks and scooters are piled high with pots wrapped traditionally in rice straw packing. Even the lampposts are porcelain. Wander through the narrow hilly streets and you will find small family workshops, some many generations old, still creating porcelain ware according to traditions begun centuries ago.

Porcelain stone is ground into fine powder in the traditional method using water-powered 'trip stampers', followed by washing, precipitating and drawing off the clay to make bricks called *dunzi* (this and next page)

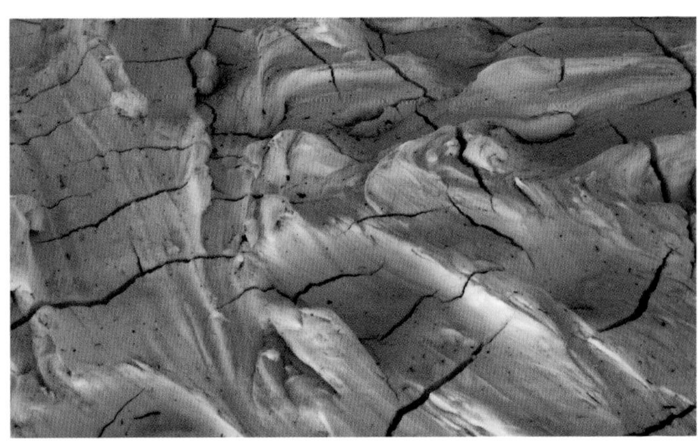

187 Jingdezhen Imperial Porcelain Museum

景德镇官窑博物馆 *Jingdezhen guanyao bowuguan*

Longzhuge, Jingdezhen, Jiangxi
江西省景德镇市龙珠阁

Tel: (0798) 822 9784
Open: 8.00–17.00

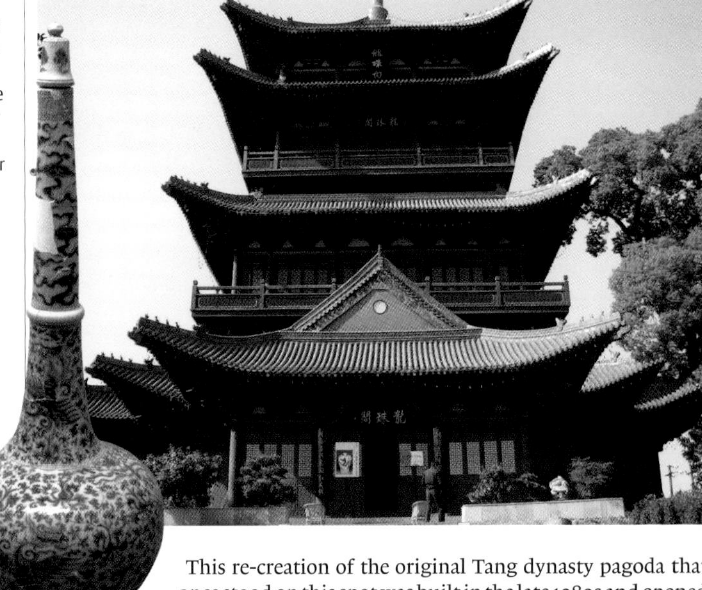

Crane-neck bottle from Chenghua Reign made as a gift for the Korean ambassador

This re-creation of the original Tang dynasty pagoda that once stood on this spot was built in the late 1980s and opened in 1990. At the time of the author's visit a new building was under construction next door promising a more state-of-the-art approach to conservation and display.

The objects in the museum date primarily from the Ming dynasty and were all excavated in the centre of Jingdezhen. These ceramics, usually found smashed and buried, were rejects due to misfiring or poor colour, failed experiments or over-supply. In large part, the pottery excavated in Jingdezhen had been thrown out (had the objects been perfect, they would have been shipped out for imperial use). Some of the shards carry reign seals and, interestingly, some of these depict a previous reign, i.e. they are fake old.

Yongle period tripod vessel for imperial ritual use

The collection holds shards and conserved objects from many periods. There is a blue and white ritual *jue* and dish decorated with dragons and clouds from the Yongle period, which is of special interest because in earlier times, bronze was generally used for ritual vessels, but at this time ceramics begin to be used for imperial rituals.

The crane-neck bottle from the Chenghua Reign (1447–87) is also of note. Made for the Korean ambassador as a gift, the vessel was created in a traditional Korean shape as a gesture.

The top floor holds objects that have recently been excavated, including many examples of red glazes. Some of these shards are from rejected vessels intended for ritual use in the Temple of Heaven in Beijing.

188

Lushan Conference Site

庐山会议旧址 *Lushanhuiyi jiuzhi*

504 Hexi Road, Lushan, Jiujiang, Jiangxi
江西省九江市庐山河西路504号

Open: 8.15–15.15
www.china-lushan.com/

Beginning in 1957, the Great Leap Forward was promoted by Mao Zedong to accelerate China's development as a leading industrial nation and to cement the Communist revolution through collectivization and the establishment of People's Communes. This utopian dream turned into a nightmare as the central leadership grew increasingly out of touch with reality. By 1958, Mao revised his earlier estimate for China to overtake Britain in steel production from fifteen years, insisting that it should be done in one. Peasants were mobilized to smelt iron and steel, building backyard furnaces and neglecting crops in the fields, and within a few short months, widespread food shortages were already in evidence. Party officials were afraid to report the truth, however, for fear of being labelled a rightist and 'spraying cold water on the enthusiasm of the masses'.

The Lushan Conference took place from 2 July to 16 August and consisted of an enlarged meeting of the Central Committee Political Bureau. At first, the main topic of discussion was how to correct leftist errors in the Great Leap Forward. However, Peng Dehuai, vice-premier and Minister of National Defence, handed Mao a letter criticizing aspects of the Great Leap, such as 'the wind

Lushan

Lushan, a beautiful mountainous area in northern Jiangxi Province, has a long and illustrious history. It was an educational and religious centre of ancient China and is home to the country's oldest institute of higher learning. The Bailudong (White Deer Academy) was founded in 940 and is one of China's four most prestigious academies. During the Southern Song, a neo-Confucianist educator at White Deer, Zhu Xi, proposed educational guidelines which went on to form the basis for teaching in ancient China. These included the philosophy that one should never impose upon others what one dislikes oneself; that we are the only ones to be blamed for our mistakes; and that one should raise questions and let those who know teach.

Lushan is also known as a centre for a number of ancient religions. Hui Yuan (334–416), a monk during the Eastern Jin, established Donglin Temple, initiating the Pure-Land Sect (sometimes known as the White Lotus Sect) of Buddhism, which had a profound influence on the development of Buddhism in Japan. During the Southern dynasties (fifth century), Lu Xiujing founded the Nantianshi Sect of Taoism. During the Ming and Qing, Islam and Christianity found their way here, and by the early part of the twentieth century, churches and mosques were added to the many temples dotting the hillsides.

Over the centuries, numerous eminent writers and scholars have been attracted to Lushan's natural beauty and intellectual atmosphere, from poets of the Tang and Song, such as Li Bai (701–762), Bai Juyi (772–846) and Su Shi (1037–1101), to modern authors such as Guo Moruo. After 1885, Lushan became a popular resort for foreign nationals seeking respite from steamy south China summers, and by the early twentieth century there were over 1,000 villas here. From the 1930s, Lushan served as a 'Camp David' for China's political elite, with both Chiang Kai-shek and Mao Zedong maintaining villas, and the Communist Party's Central Committee meeting here.

of boastfulness' that overestimated the agricultural production, the wasteful steel campaign, the lack of truth as basis for policy-making and the dangers of political belief clouding the 'scientific rule of economy'. Mao saw this letter as

an attack on his leadership, and Peng Dehuai, along with others who shared his views, were criticized, demoted and imprisoned. This was the beginning of a rift in the communist leadership that culminated in the Cultural Revolution. Scholars have estimated that somewhere between 16.5 million and 40 million people died before the experiment came to an end in 1961, making the Great Leap famine the largest in world history. By 1961, Mao was forced to admit that the Great Leap Forward had been a failure.

The exhibits are primarily labelled in Chinese, but they have been recently updated and include interactive screens and a large number of photographs. Perhaps the most interesting aspect of the museum is the film theatre on the first floor, which continuously runs documentaries and footage of the meetings held in Lushan. One can only imagine what it feels like to have lived through the excesses of political zealotry and yet to simultaneously believe that Chairman Mao was a great leader, knowing that this was the moment when it went so horribly wrong. On the second floor, the conference room has been preserved as it looked in 1959, with name cards and teacups.

189

Lushan Museum

庐山博物馆 *Lushan bowugan*

1 Lulin Road, Lushan, Jiujiang, Jiangxi
江西省九江市庐山庐林路1号

Tel: (0792) 828 2341 / 1331
Open: 8.30–17.00
www.china-lushan.com/
Gift shop

The museum is Mao Zedong's former residence here and his living quarters are preserved. There is a small collection of antiquities, numerous examples of Mao's calligraphy and a long photo gallery illustrating diplomatic and political events. Mao's living quarters include a plastic shrouded bedroom and a very large Western-style bathroom, but there is nothing more personal than the pictures of Mao shaking hands with various world leaders. There is also a small exhibit detailing features of the geological park.

Other villas scattered around the village include Villa 359, where Zhu De stayed during meetings of the Central Committee of the Communist Party of China, and Villa 286, where Deng Xiaoping and Dong Biwu stayed. Gen. Marshall stayed in Villa 442 a number of times, as did Zhou Enlai and Deng Yinchao during Party meetings.

Mao's bedroom wrapped in plastic

190

Lushan Old Villas (including Pearl S Buck's Villa)

庐山别墅群 *Lushan bieshuqun*

Mt Lushan, Jiujiang, Jiangxi
江西省九江市庐山区

Open: 8.00–17.00
www.china-lushan.com/

The church built by Edward Selby Little

This is a complex of six villas built on the slopes of Lushan. Besides the childhood home of Pearl S Buck (called 'Meilu'), one can also visit the Villa of the Missionary, the Memorial Hall of Edward Selby Little, the Cathedral, the Villa of Open-Air Bar, and the Villa of Kuomintang Officer. The community was the brainchild of Edward Selby Little, a British missionary who was able to obtain a lease for the resort concession in 1885. He named the area 'Kuling', which sounds similar to the actual Chinese name of Guling, and at the same time is a reference to its cool mountain air. The rustic and unassuming houses are all built in a Western style. The six villas are open to the public and contain period furnishings, wax figures and scenes of the daily life of the inhabitants.

The exhibits in the Memorial Hall of Edward Selby Little detail his biography, the purchase of the land and the development of Kuling. Little is depicted in various scenes negotiating and overseeing construction.

Pearl S Buck's home, built in 1897, contains exhibits related to her life and work, telling the story of her life as a child and her development as a writer.

Despite the kitsch elements, this is an altogether charming jaunt through local history and a glimpse into the world of a nineteenth-century missionary.

191

Meilu Villa (Chiang Kai-shek's and Madam Chiang's Villa)

美庐别墅 *Meilu bieshu*

180 Hedong Road, Lushan, Jiujiang, Jiangxi
江西省九江市庐山河东路180号

Tel: (0792) 828 2315
Open: 8.00–17.30
Gift shop / restaurant with advance reservation only
www.china-lushan.com/

This mountain getaway, built in 1903 and set within the woods of Lushan, was one of the homes of Soong Mei Ling and her husband, Chiang Kai-shek, and became their official summer residence in 1934. Due to the subsequent Japanese invasion, they did not return until the summer of 1946, when they inscribed the name of the house 'Meilu' on a stone at the entrance. When the Communists came to power, Mao Zedong used the house, and many important party members visited. Some felt the inscription should

Chiang Kai-shek and Soong Mei Ling on their wedding day

Meilu Villa

be erased, but Mao was not offended and insisted that it remain.

The spacious and originally well-appointed interiors are in need of painting, but they still convey the air of a gracious estate intended for the top echelons of Chinese society. There is a small exhibition of photos and other personal memorabilia, including books by Strindberg and Dorothy L Sayers, and paintings by Soong Mei Ling. On the rooftop balcony you can have your picture taken in KMT uniform or in a traditional *qipao*.

192

Bada Shanren Memorial Hall

八大山人纪念馆 *Bada shanren jinianguan*

259 Qingyunpu Road, Nanchang, Jiangxi
江西省南昌市青云谱路 *259*号

Tel: (0791) 527 3565
Open: 8.30–17.00
Gift shop

The museum is located in the Qingyun Pu Pavilion, a tranquil 2,500-year-old Taoist temple that was the artist's home and studio in his later years. Legend has it that Qiao, son of King Ling of the Eastern Zhou dynasty (700–221 BC), came here seeking immortality. Bada Shanren (1626–1705), as he is usually referred to, was a descendant of the imperial Zhu family of the Ming dynasty and an influential Chinese painter and poet of the early Qing. His distinctive calligraphic style was influential both in China and Japan, and his early extant work is in the National Palace Museum in Taipei. In addition to the calligraphy and paintings by Bada Shanren and Niu Shihui, there are works by later famous artists inspired by Bada Shanren's style of freehand brushwork, including Qi Baishi and Wu Changshuo.

Painting by Bada Shanren, also known as Zhu Da, ink and colour on paper

193 Nanchang Bayi (August 1st) Uprising Museum

南昌八一起义纪念馆 *Nanchang bayi qiyi jinianguan*

380 Zhongshan Road, Nanchang, Jiangxi

江西省南昌市中山路380号

Tel: (0791) 661 3323

Open: 8.00–18.00 summer; 17.00 winter

English audio guide

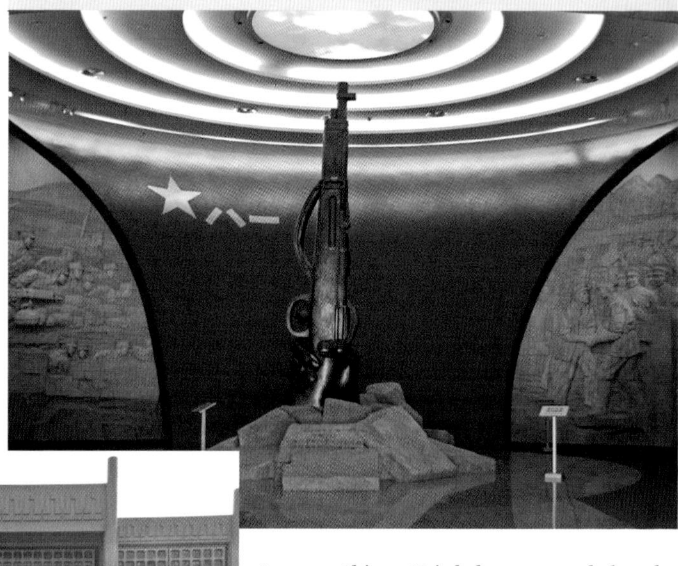

In 1927, Chiang Kai-shek announced that the Communists were the enemies of the Nationalists and should be denied any say in the political future of China. This prompted the Bayi, or August 1st Uprising, during which the Communists captured and briefly held Nanchang. Despite the failure of the CCP to hold Nanchang, it was a pivotal historical development marking the beginning of hostilities between the Communists and the Kuomintang (KMT), and the growing ideological conviction among the Communists that they should focus on a peasant revolution rather than the Soviet model of a revolution of the workers.

Previously, the museum was housed in what had been the Communist headquarters during the Uprising, but a new museum was built next door in June 2007 and the old headquarters are undergoing renovation. The English audio, which provides interesting background details, including revolutionary songs, is recommended, as there is only limited English signage.

The exhibits detail events surrounding the Bayi Uprising and subsequent historical events, up to the founding of the People's Republic of China in 1949, using a variety of state-of-the-art techniques. As with the Huaihai Memorial Museum in Xuzhou, the People's Liberation Army is attempting to retell, and, in subtle ways, rebalance views of recent history. The standard story on

the hostilities between the Communists and the KMT and the development of a split within the Party is presented, but the role of Mao Zedong in the 1930s has been adjusted to more realistic proportions, with the roles of other figures such as Zhu De and Zhou Enlai made more of, presenting a more nuanced view than has been previously available.

194

Jiangxi Provincial Museum

江西省博物馆 *Jiangxisheng bowuguan*

2 Xinzhou Road, Nanchang, Jiangxi
江西省南昌市新洲路2号

Tel: (0791) 659 5424
Open: 9.00–16.15
www.jxmuseum.cn
Kids

This museum is housed in a new building opened in 1999, located on a sand bar between the Gan and Fu Rivers. It is divided into three parts: historic, revolutionary and natural history. At the time of writing, the buildings were looking a little tired and poorly maintained but the value of the collection makes the museum well worth seeing.

The Provincial Revolutionary Museum has exhibits on the history of the Communist Party and local revolutionary events. These are in Chinese only. The Natural History hall contains an assortment of Paleozoic fossils, dinosaur skeletons – notably a 2.2-m-high ichthyosaurus – a minerals display, marine animals, insects and information about local topography. And there is an ethnographic exhibition concentrating on the Hakka minority, a prevalent peoples in southern Jiangxi.

The museum has a fine collection of Jiangxi ceramics exhibited in a timeline from the Neolithic to the late Qing, including examples from the Tang dynasty Hongzhou Kiln and of course, Ming and Qing examples from Jingdezhen, Jiangxi's premier porcelain centre.

Bronze mask from Dayangzhou

Bronze tiger with resting bird from Dayangzhou

The most compelling reason to visit this museum, however, is to see the artefacts found at Dayangzhou, south of Nanchang. In September 1989, farmers found some bronze objects while digging on a construction site, which led to the excavation of a large royal burial chamber containing approximately 1,300 magnificently crafted bronzes, jades and ceramics dating from the period between *c.* 1200 BC and 1046 BC.

During the Shang dynasty, with its capitals at Zhengzhou and then Anyang on the Yellow River, Bronze Age civilization in China was at its height. It was previously believed that during this period the southern Yangtze River Valley was underdeveloped and uncivilized compared to the great capitals to the north, but discoveries at Sanxingdui, Jinsha and Dayangzhou have belied this assumption and proven that Bronze Age civilization in China was much more complex than was previously thought, and that other highly developed centres did indeed co-exist with the Shang kingdoms.

The marvellous and intricately patterned bronzes from Dayangzhou include sacrificial vessels, weapons, tools, cooking vessels and bells. Unique to this area, the tiger motif can be seen on many of the bronze and jade objects. Flat-legged vessels common here are rare at other Chinese sites. Don't miss the bronze, two-tailed tiger with a bird calmly resting on his back or the bronze double-faced mask with bulging eyes, reminiscent of those found at Sanxingdui.

Ceramics and jade artefacts from the site are also on display.

One can also visit the site of Dayangzhou and the Dayangzhou Bronze Museum: Chengjia village, Dayangzhou town, Xin'gan county, Jiangxi Province, along the No. 105 National Expressway.

All the objects on display here, however, are reproductions; the originals are housed at the Jiangxi Provincial Museum.

195 Kunming City Museum

昆明市博物館 *Kunmingshi bowuguan*

71 Tuodong Road, Kunming, Yunnan

云南省昆明市拓东路71号

Tel: (0871) 3153 256

Open: 10.00–17.00 except Mon

A large and somewhat idiosyncratic 'folk collection / shop' displays the usual jade, porcelain and furniture (only some of which is for sale – ask the assistant) / Green tea is free to visitors

Sutra stone from the Dali kingdom

An attractive model of old Kunming greets you in the entrance hall of this museum, allowing for an interesting comparison between the modern metropolis of today and the walled Ming city as depicted in the model. To the left is a dimly lit hall dedicated to the ancient bronze and ironware of the Dian kingdom; many pieces are in fact reconstructions of the best pieces housed in the Yunnan Provincial Museum, but there are some beautiful daggers, swords, bronze bulls' heads and gold ornaments.

On the first floor is an exhibition room devoted to dinosaurs discovered in Yunnan – five skeletons line up for inspection, four of which are replicas (with the real bones under glass around the room's periphery) but the fifth, *Dilophosaurus*, is constructed from real bones. Sadly, there is not much written in English but this is not the case in the auditorium on the ground floor to the right of the entrance, where an impressive 6.6 m octagonal Sutra Stone Pillar stands alone, dating back to the kingdom of Dali (937–1253) and covered with Buddhist images and rare scriptures, as well as a good caption in English.

196 Yunnan Nationalities Museum

云南民族博物馆 *Yunnan minzu bowuguan*

Dianchi National Tourist and Holiday Zone, Haigeng, Kunming, Yunnan

云南省昆明市滇池国家旅游度假区

Tel: (0871) 4311 216
Open: 9.00–16.30 except Mon
www.ynnmuseum.com
Bookshop / coffee shop in inner quadrangle

Tibetan scriptures for redeeming lost souls

Opened in 2004 near the northern shore of Dianchi Lake, this expansive museum is set around a green quadrangle and comprises seven exhibition halls that together house over 10,000 exhibits detailing the history and everyday life of Yunnan's twenty-two ethnic nationalities. Room 1 focuses on clothing and textiles, and is filled with a plethora of fantastically coloured traditional dress, weaving machines and examples of dyeing, appliqué and cross-stitching techniques. Other rooms exhibit musical instruments, minerals and precious stones, folk masks and ancient documents – twenty-three written languages exist in this province alone and the Tibetan scrolls and Naxi Dongba pictograph scripts are excellent. There are halls illustrating the diverse architecture and differing lifestyles of the various ethnic groups according to geographical location, from tropical hunting and fishing to mountain terrace agriculture.

Throughout the museum, large pictures on the walls behind the objects illustrate the objects being used in real-life situations, revealing a genuine connection between the exhibits and the modern world. Well worth at least half a day's exploration.

Tibetan mask

197

Yunnan Provincial Museum

云南省博物馆 *Yunnansheng bowuguan*

118 Wuyi Road, Kunming, Yunnan

云南省昆明市五一路118号

Tel: (0871) 3645 655
Open 9.00–17.00
www.ynbwg.cn

Song dynasty gold Acarya statue from the Dali kingdom

Situated in central Kunming and newly renovated, the excellent Yunnan Provincial Museum focuses on the mysterious Bronze Age kingdom of Dian and the later Nanzhao kingdom (649–1253) centred around Erhai Lake and Dali, which flourished during the Tang and Song dynasties. The white-walled, brightly lit first floor 'Yunnan Bronze Civilization' gallery is packed full of interesting artefacts dating from the eighth century BC through to the end of the Han dynasty in the third century AD. Prize exhibits include huge bronze drums, cowrie shell containers with intricate lids and superb bronze and gold work illustrating how technologically advanced the Dian were.

On the second floor, the 'Regimes Illuminating Buddha's Light' gallery is moodily lit, with religious statues, scripts and pottery ranging from the seventh-century heyday of the Buddhist Nanzhao kingdom through to the Ming and Qing periods. Also on the second floor is a room titled simply 'Treasures', and it lives up to its name, being full of exquisite decorative and religious pieces made from all manner of materials, from gold and silver to ivory, bamboo, rhino horn, amber and sandalwood.

The Dian Kingdom

The Dian reigned in southwest China (current day Yunnan) for around 500 years from the Warring States period to the Western Han, before being absorbed by the Eastern Han. It was not until excavations began in the 1950s of Dian burial sites located on and around Lake Dian (near Kunming) that more was discovered about this mystical kingdom, as they had no written language and only a few historical records referred to them. The most opulent and famous site is the cemetery of Shizhaishan where the Dian buried their kings and elite members of their kingdom. Among the forty-eight burials unearthed was one containing a rich range of offerings placed around the coffin, including beads, gold, bronze mirrors and weapons, as well as a gold seal bearing an inscription which reads 'The seal of the King of Dian'. Spectacular bronzes, which the Dian are renowned for, were also found in this grave and many of the others. They included drums and drum-shaped bronze vessels containing cowries (possibly to indicate status rather than for use as currency), their tops decorated with detailed scenes of miniature figures of humans and animals hunting, conducting sacrifices or at war. Bronze models of houses provide a unique opportunity to learn about the domestic life and architecture of the Dian, while other bronze objects such as plaques and weapons engraved with motifs confirm they primarily hunted, but were also agriculturally quite advanced. The bronze tableaux and engravings provide further visual clues to the Dian people's absorption of surrounding cultural influences from Central and Southeast Asia, south China and beyond.

Bronze cowrie container with handles in the form of tigers and lid adorned with buffalo

198

Lijiang Municipal Museum

丽江市博物院 *Lijiangshi bowuguan*

North entrance of Black Dragon Pool Park, Heilongtan, Lijiang, Yunnan
云南省丽江市黑龙潭 黑龙潭公园北端入口

Tel: (0888) 5180 270
Open: 8.30–17.30
www.lijiangmuseum.com
English-speaking guides are free of charge
Book / gift shop serves free Pu'er tea to visitors

Originally called the Museum of Naxi Dongba Culture, in 2006 a new building was inaugurated at the same picturesque site, sporting a different name but still dedicated to the celebration of the unique Naxi Culture and, in particular, the Dongba religion that was brought to the world's attention by Joseph Rock in the early twentieth century.

The rectangular museum constitutes four halls set around an inner courtyard: the 'First Exhibition Hall' contains a huge 3D map of the mountainous region surrounding Lijiang, as well as detailed notice boards (in good English), photographs and bronze and clothing items that reveal the early history of the region dating from the Warring States period. The 'Life Rite Exhibition Hall' explains the importance of the shaman-like *Dongba*, or 'educated one', in Naxi Culture, and the divination techniques and religious instruments he uses.

The 'Dongba Manuscripts Exhibition Hall' and the 'Dongba Art Exhibition Hall' are filled with superb examples of how tree-bark paper is made, interesting comparisons between Babylonian and Egyptian pictographic alphabets and the Dongba system (the sole remaining pictographic writing system still in use today), and wood, paper and cloth panels and books (up to 1,500 years old) illustrating this rich and fascinating culture. Not to be missed.

Dongba painted wooden stakes used at sacred ritual sites

Joseph Rock

Joseph Rock (1884–1962) was a botanist, adventurer, ethnographer, photographer, cartographer, linguist and journalist – in short a renaissance man. Born in Vienna in 1884, he emigrated to the USA at age 21. While working in Hawaii as a botanist, he was sent to China by the US State Department to collect seeds used in the treatment of leprosy. This led to a lifetime dedicated to travel and discovery in Asia. Through his life, he collected and studied flora and fauna for various American universities and institutions, including the Museum of Comparative Zoology and the Arnold Arboretum of Harvard University and the Smithsonian. Besides his work in the field of biology and zoology, *National Geographic Magazine* regularly published reports and photos of his extensive travels through southwest China and Tibet. He died in Hawaii in 1962.

Rock's ethnographic studies and photographs of the various minority groups in Tibet, Yunnan, Gansu and Sichuan, as well as in Vietnam and Cambodia, remain an invaluable resource to this day. Perhaps his greatest legacy, however, is his collection and translations of thousands of volumes of Naxi literature and religious texts, as well as his Naxi dictionary published posthumously.

Naxi *Dongba* pictographic script is the only living pictographic script in the world

The Naxi language is a subset of the Tibeto–Burman language family and was spoken predominantly in Yunnan, especially in Lijiang, but also by Naxi in parts of Sichuan and Tibet. Today, only a small number of people can understand it. The Naxi Dongba script ('Dongba' refers to the religion, priests and written language of the Naxi), mostly comprising pictograms, was used by Dongba priests in religious ceremonies and rituals.

Just outside of Lijiang, on the slopes of the gorgeous Jade Dragon Snow Mountain, is Yuhu village, where you can visit Rock's house. There is also a small museum containing photographs and some of his belongings.

199

Dunhuang Museum

敦煌博物馆 *Dunhuang bowuguan*

Yangguan Dong Road, Dunhuang, Gansu
甘肃省敦煌市阳关东路

Tel: (0937) 8822 981
Open: 8.00–18.00

A sole, Han dynasty, left; and a pair of woven hemp socks, Western Han dynasty, right

This important collection has been housed in a rather cramped, unsuitable building in the city centre, and, although the displays have been improved in recent years, it was still felt necessary to commission a new museum. It is, however, not known where the museum will be built or when it is scheduled to open.

The collection encompasses the history of the city and county of Dunhuang and also the extraordinary wealth of objects found at the sites and excavations in the area.

The wealth of the local culture is illustrated in a display of local history spanning the Neolithic period to the nineteenth century; a miscellany including ceramics, old Chinese scrolls, coins, tools, tiles, bricks, bronzes, fabrics, jades and precious stones.

Of greater artistic and literary importance are some fine examples of classic Chinese and, in particular, Tibetan Buddhist manuscripts from the Library Cave (Cave 17) at Mogao, as well as hemp scrolls and other written and printed rarities.

There is a comprehensive and absorbing selection of locally excavated burial artefacts, including stone tablets, pagodas and pottery, and tomb guardians from the Han through to the Tang dynasties. Of particular interest are the decorative construction materials – lotus bricks and rare *qilin* bricks bearing a mythical deer-like animal sculpted in high relief.

The collection includes objects used for trade along the Silk Road, including fabrics, silks, Han bamboo strip documents, metal tools and weapons. There is also a reconstruction of the early Great Wall of the Han dynasty, together with objects and relics from its garrisons. Now in ruins, the wall once extended west even of Dunhuang to Yumenguan (the Jade Pass).

The cliffs on the west bank of the Daquan River into which are carved hundreds of caves

200 **Mogao Grottoes**

莫高窟 *Mogaoku*

25 km from Dunhuang centre by bus or minibus, Gansu

距离敦煌市中心25公里

Open: 8.00–17.00
www.friendsofdunhuang.org/ &
http://idp.bl.uk/
English audio guide and written guide
Gift shop / book shop / restaurant / snack bar

The Dunhuang Caves consist of various Buddhist cave sites within the ancient county boundaries of the oasis trading city of Dunhuang, at the extreme western end of the Silk Road in China. Of these, the cave temples of Mogao, a World Heritage Site, provide one of the great experiences of China – indeed, one of the wonders of the world. The site itself, on the fringes of the Gobi Desert, is one of great beauty and resonance. The flat, reddish desert, pulsating with heat in summer, snow clad in winter, gives way suddenly to a wide valley carved out by the Daquan River.

On the west bank are cliffs varying in height from 15 to 30 metres. Into these, in four uneven layers, are carved a multitude of caves, of which 735 are extant, which contain no less than 45,000 sq m of wall paintings, more than 2,000 painted sculptures and some 50,000 manuscripts, works on silk and paper, and other precious artefacts.

Dunhuang is at the western end of modern Gansu Province – the western border of Chinese civilization. Beyond lay the barbarian world; and beyond that, the great civilizations of the Indian subcontinent to the southwest and the civilizations of western Asia and Europe in the distant west.

Dunhuang was not just a frontier town. It was a vital stage on the Silk Route – the great trading highway, arduous, perilous and time-consuming, but full of the promise of profit – that linked Rome, in the west, to Xi'an and Luoyang, the great capital cities of China, in the east.

Mogao was a meeting point for Indian Buddhist art and culture with

Cave 130, large Buddha statue

Chinese civilization. The caves, founded by Buddhist monks in the fourth century, were inhabited as an isolated monastery for over 1,000 years. The murals with which they are decorated include some of the finest examples of Buddhist art in China, reflecting the changing style of Chinese art for more than a millennium, and ultimately, with a further move eastwards, providing the founding impetus for Japanese Zen Buddhism and for the creation of Japanese Buddhist art.

Five other major religions or systems are represented in the art of Mogao: Confucianism and Daoism from Central China, and Manichaeism, Zoroastrianism and Nestorian Christianity from Persia and Central Asia.

Dunhuang was the place where the economy, culture, technology and social life of China met and mixed with that of Eurasia. This meeting had a dramatic effect on the appearance and development of Chinese Buddhist art.

The first cave was dug in 366 by a monk called Yuezun from central China who had a vision of multiple golden Buddhas appearing in a cloud of golden light above the Sanwei Mountains. Shortly thereafter, a monk named Faliang joined him there from the east.

Mogao cave art flourished for more than 1,000 years, reaching its apogee during the early Tang period (618–755).

The essentials of Buddhist iconography had developed in India and Gandhara and changed little at Mogao, but the style and method of representation altered dramatically to create a uniquely Chinese version of Buddhist art.

The Mogao cliffs were composed of a friable conglomerate which defied carving – hence the decorative use of wall painting and clay painted statues as opposed to the earlier stone carved caves in India such as at Ajanta, or in Central China at Datong (the Yungang Caves of the fifth century).

The exteriors originally had wooden framed façades to simulate conventional buildings (although constant erosion has left only five caves with their external eaves intact). Inside, the decoration simulates a regular Chinese architectural structure with beams and rafters. There are five different types of cave, with uses ranging from group meditation, to cells for individual monks, to the great Buddha caves with massive figures, some over 35 m in height.

Apart from the giant Buddhas, which have stone cores, most of the statues

have wooden skeletons, padded with reeds and covered with a mixture of clay and straw, which was then painted. Originally, the standing figures were broad-shouldered and Indian in style; over time they became more Chinese in appearance, with leaner, more square faces and flatter bodies. Under the Sui and Tang they come in groups of seven or nine. The mourners have exquisitely expressive features which contrast with the tranquil naturalness of Buddha's features as he enters *nirvana*.

The wall paintings were an integral – indeed the dominant – factor in the design. The cave walls were prepared with layers of mixed straw and clay which was then plastered. A great variety of both mineral and organic pigments were used to cover the whole area inside the cave. The total effect is truly extraordinary.

The paintings have seven different types of subject matter:

1. Paintings of Buddhas and other sacred figures such as boddhisatvas, disciples, *yaksas* (spirits) and *apsaras* (flying dancers and musicians who act as celestial servants to the gods).
2. Narrative paintings such as the *Jataka* stories of the life and acts of Buddha.
3. Paintings of gods and spirits, both Indian and traditional Chinese.
4. Sutra stories – the Buddhist scriptures visualized. At Mogao, these are transformed into large, complete series of narrative painting, illustrated here with a uniquely Chinese mastery of narrative and complex subject matter.
5. The story of Buddhism's journey east: the stories and myths of Buddhism's arrival in China, its power and efficacy, and the monks such as Xuanzang (602–664), who travelled to India in search of enlightenment and scripture.
6. Donor paintings: the portraits of the lay donors – both local and national – of Han, Tibetan, Tangut, Uighur and Mongol peoples, giving a fascinating record of the dress and appearance of men of power over a 1,000-year period.
7. Illusionistic architectural and decorative features of an extraordinary richness of detail and overall effect.

Cave 57, central double niche in main chamber

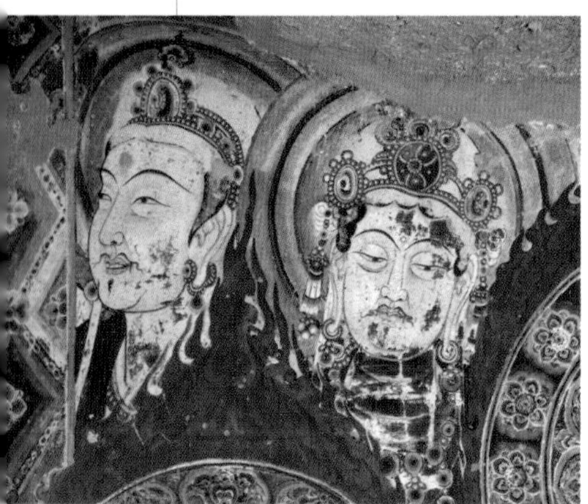

Mogao Cave 217, Early Tang (618–704)

Mogao has a major problem of conservation. Many of the paintings have over the years oxidized and become discoloured. Their preservation, and that of their ground, is a constant battle. Earthquakes and sand have taken a further toll. Wind erosion has weakened the ceilings of the caves and water has seeped down through cracks in the cliff, dissolving salts within the rocks near the wall paintings and causing further damage.

Furthermore, mass tourism would, if uncontrolled, cause the temperature, relative humidity and the carbon dioxide density within the caves to rise dramatically, further endangering the already seriously weakened wall paintings.

Mogao Cave 320, ceiling with multiple Buddha design

As a result, only twenty caves are open to the public, of which only ten can be visited, with a guide, at any given time. There is no choice offered as to which ones can be visited, although for a small additional fee a few more than ten caves can be seen.

The visitor should not be put off by this. Simply to visit some of these caves as part of a small group with an excellently informed guide in this remote site is experience enough.

In addition, there are eight reproduction caves, each beautifully executed and representing a significant period of art at Dunhuang, arranged by the Dunhuang Research Centre – together with an exhibition of objects from the caves. Both are highly recommended. Visit the museum that houses these after your tour of the actual caves.

The tour will definitely include a visit to Cave 17 – the Library Cave – the second reason for Mogao's international fame and importance.

In 1900, a small side cave was discovered off the corridor of Cave 16 during renovation work. It contained tens of thousands of ancient manuscripts, printed documents and paintings. The British and French explorers, Sir Aurel

Stein and Paul Pelliot, with the help of a resident Daoist monk, Wang Yuanlu, acquired large numbers, mainly in Chinese and Tibetan, which were dispatched to the British Library and the French Bibliothèque nationale in 1907 and 1908.

The cave must have been either a Buddhist library, or at least a source of ex-library copies from a local monastery.

Amongst its other treasures it contained the earliest complete printed book in the world, a copy of the *Diamond Sutra*, which was commissioned by a man called Wang Jie in memory of his parents in May 868.

Outside, there is a permanent exhibition on the manuscripts related to the Library Cave.

There are a number of other cave sites in the Dunhuang region, although Mogao is justifiably the most famous and the most worthy of a visit. Of these, the visitor may want to take in the Yulin Caves (75 km west of Guazhou), with a site on the Yulin River almost as striking as Mogao itself; it is deeper and somewhat narrower. Yulin has forty-two extant caves, ranging from the seventh to the fourteenth century, containing 4,200 sq m of wall painting and 259 sculptures.

The true afficionado can also take in the Western Thousand Buddha Caves (33 km southwest of Dunhuang) and the Five Temple Site (40 km south of Mogao in present day Subei Mongolian Autonomous County).

201

Jiayuguan Great Wall Museum

嘉峪关长城博物馆 *Jiayuguan changcheng bowuguan*

Southwest side of Xinhua Nan Road 新华南路, Jiayuguan, Gansu (bus from city centre / get off at 'Xinhua Nan Road' or 'Xinhua Shangchang' 新华南路西南方

Open: 8.30–12.30 & 14.30–18.30 summer & autumn;
12.00 & 18.00 winter & spring
www.friendsofgreatwall.org/english/
Bookshop / gift shop

Jiayuguan Fortress

The middle gate tower, the Rouyuan Tower (see over)

Jiayuguan was the Ming fort at the western end of the Hexi corridor in Gansu Province. With its 17-m towers with upturned eaves, it is one of the iconic images of Chinese history, situated at the western end of the Great Wall, the ultimate western frontier established in the Ming dynasty (1367–1644). Earlier, during the heyday of Dunhuang, the frontier extended westwards of that city to the Jade Gate Pass (Yumenguan).

Intermittently for 2,000 years, with a policy that operates once again in the twenty-first century, this frontier 'where Spring winds never blow' was repopulated by Han Chinese farmers relocated from central China, and defended by Han Chinese soldiers who lamented their lot of near exile and constant danger – their experience recorded in some of the most moving of Chinese poetry.

The Ming fort at Jiayuguan has been heavily restored but it is still a potent symbol of the extremity of Chinese power, lying in an open valley with the snow-covered Qilian Shan mountains to the north and the black Mazong (horse's mane) mountains to the south.

The new Jiayuguan Great Wall Museum has a series of fascinating reconstructions of military life on the Great Wall, its defences, and the tools and artefacts that were used by its garrisons.

Jiayuguan is not worth a special visit, but for the traveller by road coming westwards up the Hexi Corridor from Lanzhou to Dunhuang, it provides a breathtaking piece of historical evidence.

202

Gansu Provincial Museum

甘肃省博物馆 *Gansusheng bowuguan*

3 West Xijin Road, Lanzhou, Gansu
甘肃省兰州市西津西路3号

Tel: (931) 2335 151 / 2346 306
Open: 9.00–17.00 except Mon
English- and Japanese-speaking guides are available
Shop / bookshop / coffee bar

Built in 1956, this massive, dour, Russian-style building covers 18,000 sq m (almost four acres) of downtown Lanzhou. Until recently, the galleries had been decrepit and dusty but the interior was redesigned and the museum re-opened in 2006. It houses a very important collection, reflecting both the historical and cultural importance of Gansu Province.

Gansu is old China's most northwestern province, a narrow strip of land that follows the course of the Yellow River from its emergence from the mountains eastwards for more than 800 miles along the Silk Road, taking in the Hexi Corridor – the 'throat of China'. It has proved a fertile source of prehistoric excavations, both of fossils and of very early cultural artefacts, in particular pottery. In historic times, Gansu came to prominence

Scroll painting of 'Special Envoys', by Xiao Yi showing foreign envoys sent to China during the Liang period of the Southern dynasties

under the Han dynasty (206 BC – AD 220), with the growth of the importance of the Silk Road, and the Great Wall was extended westward through the province to Yumenguan (the Jade Gate Pass). Its importance declined during the Ming (1368–1644), in part due to the neglect of the Silk Road, but it became a separate province in 1666 under the Qing (1644–1911), with Lanzhou as its capital. In the 1920s and 1930s, Lanzhou was a centre of Russian influence and was very badly bombed by the Japanese during the war.

The museum directly reflects the cultural history of the province and the collection is divided into three main areas: the fossils of prehistoric animals; the ancient painted pottery of Gansu; and the culture and treasures of the Silk Road. All the objects have clear English signage.

The impressive fossil gallery houses some huge dinosaur skeletons along with what is reputed to be the largest complete fossilized skeleton in the world, of a mammoth (*Stegodon hunghoensis*), found in 1973.

Historically, the most important part of the collection is that of the primitive agricultural stone tools and early red-grey vessels from the Dadiwan site, which are 6,000–12,000 years old; and the Neolithic painted pottery, which is the chief local treasure of Gansu. The black and red painted pottery, some of it considerably sophisticated, includes magnificent examples from all the local cultures from 7000 to 476 BC – Yangshao, Majiayao, Miaodigou, Qija, Banshan, Siwa and Xindian.

The museum's displays including the skeleton of a mammoth found in Gansu province

The exhibition of the Silk Road treasures has its highlights in the Han dynasty. Of historical interest are more than 20,000 wooden tablets inscribed in ink recording the region's history, the fortunes of the garrisons, and events that took place along the Silk Road.

Bronze Flying Horse from Wuwei, Eastern Han dynasty

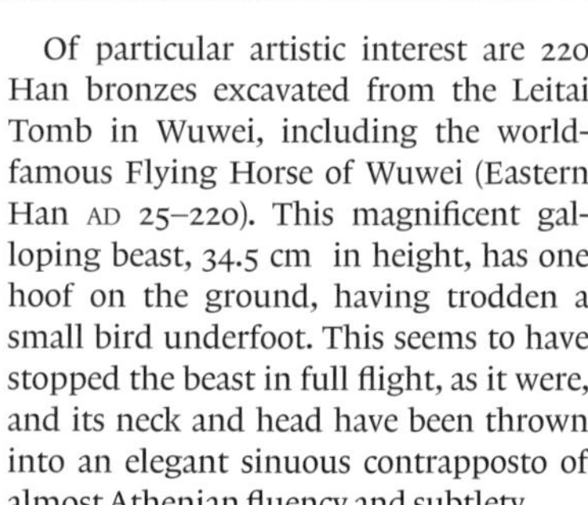

Bronze guard of honour

Of particular artistic interest are 220 Han bronzes excavated from the Leitai Tomb in Wuwei, including the world-famous Flying Horse of Wuwei (Eastern Han AD 25–220). This magnificent galloping beast, 34.5 cm in height, has one hoof on the ground, having trodden a small bird underfoot. This seems to have stopped the beast in full flight, as it were, and its neck and head have been thrown into an elegant sinuous contrapposto of almost Athenian fluency and subtlety.

There are many other national treasures, including many from the Mongol Yuan dynasty (1279–1368), the Mongols having conquered Gansu in 1235.

203 Baoji Bronze Museum

宝鸡青铜器博物馆 *Baoji qingtongqi bowuguan*

West side of Gongyuan West Road, Baoji, Shaanxi

宝鸡市公园南路西侧

Tel: (0917) 281 6289
Open: 9.00–17.00
www.bronze.org.cn (Chinese only)

The small city of Baoji sits on the western edge of the Guanzhong Plain, which was the birthplace of the Zhou and Qin dynasties. Chinese archaeologists have excavated a large quantity of bronze ware of the Western Zhou dynasty in this

One of the numerous bronzes on display from the Western Zhou dynasty

area, and many of these pieces are on display in the little-known museum. The first floor houses the museum's collection of bronze ware; on the second floor, there is an exhibition on ancient Chinese calligraphy and on the use of knotting for record keeping in the selling and buying of land. The museum is just 40 minutes' southwest of the Famen Temple, and can be combined with a visit to the temple.

204

Famen Temple Museum

法门寺博物馆 *Famensi bowuguan*

Famen Town, Chengbei, 10 km north of Fufeng County, Shaanxi

陕西省扶风县北10公里法门镇 法门寺

Tel: (0912) 5254 002 / 154
Open: 9.00–17.00
www.famensi.cn (Chinese only)

Gilded silver Buddha

The Famen Temple, some 118 km (73 miles) west of Xi'an, dates back to the Eastern Han dynasty, between AD 147 and 189. However, the structure has undergone many renovations over succeeding dynasties. The temple houses one of Sakyamuni Buddha's finger bones, said to have been distributed by the Indian King Asoka (d. AD 232). During the Tang dynasty, the temple's pagoda was rebuilt and relics were tucked away in a crypt underneath it. In 1609, during the Ming dynasty, a 45-m octagonal brick pagoda was built above the crypt.

On 24 August 1981, the Ming dynasty pagoda partially collapsed, leaving exactly half the structure standing and the other half a pile of rubble. By 1987, the damaged pagoda had been completely cleared away, leaving the stairway to the underground vault exposed. Four finger-bone relics of

To the left of the Famen Temple Pagoda is the Famen Temple Museum opened in 1988

Sakyamuni Buddha were discovered: one was found in the front chamber, in a reliquary known as 'the Asoka Pagoda'; one was discovered in a marble bier in the middle chamber; the back chamber held another in an eight-fold casket; and the last one was found in a secret shrine underneath the back chamber, in a five-fold casket. As only one of the bones is a genuine *sarira*, the other three are known as 'shadow bones'. They are meant to protect the genuine one in case of persecution of Buddhism. Visitors enter the renovated crypt via stairs leading inside and downwards.

The unearthed treasures are held in the museum, just next door to the temple. The museum is made up of three structures built in the architectural style of the Tang dynasty. The objects are nicely displayed and there are good explanations in Chinese and English.

A succession of emperors either visited the Famen Temple themselves or arranged for the famous finger-bone relic to be taken to Chang'an so they could view it. The temple underground vault included many artefacts for daily use offered by the royal families, such as tableware, tea items, censers, clothes, coins and jewellery.

The exhibition hall to the right of the Treasure Hall exhibits an excellent collection of Tang gold and silverware, demonstrating the advanced metalworking techniques and skills of the craftsmen of that period. Some one hundred of the gold and silver vessels, mainly imperial wares made in the royal workshop, were offered by Emperor Yizong (r. 859–873) and his son Emperor Xizong (r. 873–888). Examples include a gilded silver bowl with an overlapping lotus petal design; the four gilded silver ewers (ritual vessels for the consecration of the image of Buddha; an exquisite gilded silver basket decorated with geese in flight; eight small gilded silver plates with a peony design. In addition to the wares from the imperial workshops, there are also objects of tribute from southern China, and a special section dedicated to teaware. These include a silver tea mortar decorated with a gold-gilt design of wild geese and a silver tea strainer with a design of an immortal on a flying crane, both dated 869.

Other rare objects include the *mise* or 'secret colour' celadon ceramics and more than 700 pieces of silk, including brocade, satin, embroidery, thin silk, gauze and many other types. Many of the textiles were donated by the imperi-

The Wufu stone casket decorated with pearls and gold fitting, the last casket of the eight-fold casket, Tang dynasty

Tea basket woven with gold and silver wires, Tang dynasty

al family or the aristocracy. Other textiles had been used to wrap objects. Some were imperially consecrated by Empress Wu Zetian (684–705). The best piece may be the miniature garment embroidered in gold-wrapped thread (even finer than strands of hair) and lined in red silk.

205

Fuping Pottery Art Village

富平陶艺村 *Fuping taoyicun*

1 Qiaoshan Road, Fuping, Shaanxi

陕西省富平乔山路1号

Tel: (0913) 822 8161

Call ahead for a reservation

Some of the galleries are designed after traditional kilns

Ceramic sculpture by a visiting Mexican artist

There has been an explosion of creativity in all mediums of Chinese contemporary art but the ceramic arts have been slower to move away from traditional forms and design. This complex of museums, called the Fule International Ceramics Arts Museums (FLICAM), was created in 2004 to encourage the development of Chinese ceramics as a vital art form and to expose Chinese potters and the public to trends and influences from abroad.

The art village, 70 km northeast of Xi'an, consists of seven museums, all imaginatively designed, some inspired by the forms of traditional Chinese kilns. The exhibition spaces, arranged by country, show the works of potters from France, Australia, Scandinavia, New Zealand and Canada. Another gallery includes the works of potters from a selection of other countries, including Mexico and China. More galleries covering African, Asian and other European countries were in the process of being set up during the author's visit.

All the pottery exhibited is created in Fuping – the artists come here to work.

Sculpture by American potter, Rimas Visgirda

Besides being a showcase for the pottery, the complex supports an artist-in-residence programme, as well as providing pottery studios for visiting artists.

The museum was initiated by the commercial tile factory located in the grounds which continues to support the art galleries and studios of the village.

206 Hanyangling Museum

汉阳陵博物馆 *Hanyangling bowuguan*

East side of the Xianyang International Airport Road, Xi'an, Shaanxi

西安咸阳国际机场专线公路东段

Tel: (029) 8603 1470
Open: 8.30–17.30

A walking pottery figure originally clothed, height: 55 cm

Yangling is the tomb of Liu Qi, the fourth Han Emperor Jingdi, who reigned from 157 to 141 BC. The tomb was discovered by accident in 1990, by workers building a road to the new airport. On the south side of the road is the Yangling Museum, which opened in September 1999 and is home to thousands of pottery figurines and animals. The Emperor's tomb mound sits on the north side of the road, opposite the museum. Archaeologists have focused on excavating pits in the nearby surrounding area and, as with the mausoleum of Qin Shihuangdi, they have left the Emperor's tomb untouched for the time being while they wait for more advanced scientific methods of excavation to become available.

The mausoleum's south gate ruins were excavated from 1997 to 1998. Since 2001, the remains of the gate have been housed inside a large structure that resembles the original Han dynasty building. The rammed earth, pieces of tile and the post-holes of the original gate can be seen inside the structure, along with illustrations of gates throughout Chinese history. The Yangling South Gate is the first gate to be found; it is the most complete, and offers important information on traditional Chinese architecture. A pottery weiqi chessboard, which was found in the area around the south gate, and is the oldest of its kind, is exhibited in the main museum.

One of the highlights at Yangling are the pottery figures from the excavated tombs. A glass walkway has been built at the foot of the eighteen furrows, giving visitors a bird's eye view of the pits. Their number of figurines is impressive, with some 50,000 scattered around the site. When excavation work began on twenty-four pits containing the Emperor's army, which were to the south of the road, thousands of pottery warriors were discovered. Their bodies are approximately one-third life size, without arms and naked. Their arms and hands were made of wood, with moveable joints, but these, together with the leather armour and silk clothing they once wore, have long since decayed. There are, however, traces of red silk remaining on some of the figurines. There are patches of bright vermillion around the heads of some, with traces of woven silk fabric – apparently the remains of a kind of headband worn during this period. Some eunuch figures have also been found, providing the earliest known example of the existence of eunuchs in China.

All the figures were painted and many still retain at least their original basic ochre colouring, representing the

Ruins of the South Gate of the Emperor's tomb

skin. Features such as hair, eyebrows, moustaches and pupils were painted in black. Archaeologists have concluded that the nude figures, which were originally clothed, were intended as burial objects for the royal family alone, as they were found in pits accompanying the Emperor's tomb. It is thought that the practice of enrobing burial figures in textiles, which is characteristic in the Chu tombs, illustrates the influence of that culture, whereas the figures with sculpted clothes are similar to the figures in Qin Shihuangdi's tomb.

The figures include soldiers, archers on horseback, servants, musicians and dancers. Some servant figurines have been unearthed in almost perfect condition, wearing moulded clothes with white painted robes and yellow belts. In some pits, the figures lay stacked on one another. In Pit No. 17 and No. 14, only the heads stick out of the earth, the bodies still buried from the neck down.

Pottery figurines unearthed in burial pit No. 17 in the southern area of the Mausoleum

The excavated domesticated animals include horses, cows, pigs (some of which appear to be pregnant), sheep, goats, dogs and chickens. The horses have a slot along the back of their necks where a mane was once fixed, and a hole for a tail, but these have decayed, perhaps because they were originally made from real horse's hair. It appears that each pit represents a division or department of the Emperor's palace. In fact, some of the pits have revealed rooms complete with servants and everyday utensils. The inclusion of domestic animals is of particular interest to archaeologists as this is the first time such a quantity and variety has been discovered. Following the unification and standardization of the Qin dynasty, the Chinese under the Han Emperors experienced a relatively stable and prosperous period, in which the development of agriculture progressed rapidly.

At the end of your tour of the underground exhibit, visit the small theatre where a 20-minute 3D video is shown on the history of the tomb.

With its convenient location beside the airport road, Yangling is a convenient stop for tourists flying into or out of Xi'an.

207

Museum of the Terracotta Warriors and Horses of Emperor Qin Shihuangdi

秦始皇兵马俑博物馆 *Qinshihuang bingmayong bowuguan*

Lintong County, 30 km east of Xi'an, Shaanxi

西安市临潼区，距西安以东30公里

Tel: (029) 839 4462 / 2542
Open: 7.30–18.30
www.bmy.com.cn/index.htm

Warriors in the eighth and ninth columns of Pit No. 1; notice they are not wearing helmets which accords with historical records which state that the Qin army fought without helmets

In 1974, some farmers were digging a well at Lintong, 35 km east of Xi'an, when they stumbled upon one of the greatest archaeological discoveries of history: the buried army of Qin Shihuangdi.

The larger-than-life-size terracotta figures were found in a vault 5 m (16 ft) below the surface, 1.5 km (less than a mile) east of the Emperor's tomb itself. The positions of the three pits discovered correspond to the prescribed military formation of a battle-ready army during the Warring States period and Qin dynasty times. The museum opened in 1979, and the area was declared a UNESCO World Heritage Site in 1987.

The terracotta soldiers are remarkably realistic pieces of sculpture. Each soldier's face has individual features, prompting speculation that they were based on living models. They have square faces with broad foreheads and large, thick-lipped mouths; they wear neat moustaches, and a number have beards; some of them have their hair in a topknot. The figures stand between 1.72 and 2 m (nearly 5 ft 8 in. and 6 ft 7 in.) tall.

There is a 360-degree cinema behind Pit No. 1 showing dramatizations of scenes from Qin Shihuangdi's conquering of the six independent states, the construction of his mausoleum, the making of the terracotta figures and their eventual destruction by soldiers of the rebel general Xiang Yu. It is useful to see this film before visiting the museum, as it provides a background to what is on display.

Pit No. 1 is the first of the three pits to be discovered and forms the main exhibition hall. Extensive excavation in the eastern half of the pit uncovered 1,087 warriors, thirty-two horses and the traces of eight chariots. The display consists of infantry and charioteers arranged in battle formation. So far, over 1,000 soldiers have been restored to standing position on the original brick floor, in columns four abreast. At the head, facing east, is the vanguard, consisting of three rows of seventy archers each. They are followed by thirty-eight columns of more heavily armoured infantry interspersed with some forty war chariots, of which only the pottery horses remain. The south and north flanks are defended by a single column of spearmen facing outwards, some in armour and holding weapons, while more warriors on the west flank form the rearguard. In the centre of the formation, the warriors are lined up in nine columns, and among them are interspersed impressions of eight wooden chariots, now decayed. Each chariot is drawn by four horses and would have borne a driver and two warriors.

The entrance to the vault is through the west door, and from there one heads north. At the foot of a staircase, the spot is marked where the original discovery was made back in the drought-stricken spring of 1974. Proceeding down the northern flank of the vault you cross the excavations on an elevated walkway which affords views of both the wholly excavated area looking west and the partially excavated area to the eastern end of the vault. The grooves

across the tops of the walls separating the corridors are the marks left by the decayed wooden beams.

At the unexcavated western end of the pit stand many half-reconstructed soldiers. As each piece is unearthed, it is coded, marking where it was found and to which statue it might belong. Archaeologists have estimated that, if completely excavated, the pit would yield more than 6,000 warriors, 160 horses and forty chariots.

Pit No. 2 is 20 m (65 ft) south of Pit No. 1. This L-shaped pit was discovered in 1976 after extensive test drilling, although the official excavation did not begin until March 1994. Pit No. 2 houses around 900 soldiers, including kneeling and standing archers, infantrymen and charioteers, together with some 350 chariot horses, 116 cavalry horses and the remains of eighty-nine wooden chariots.

The pit, which is only partially excavated, is contained in a modern building that allows visitors to walk around it and observe the ongoing excavations. The collection of figures here includes a higher number with vestiges of their original colouring. This pit has eleven sloping entrances, down which the terracotta warriors are believed to have been carried. Trial digging at several places unearthed seventy archers, some kneeling, others standing. Some fifty-two horses were also discovered. On the north side of the building, examples of some of the warriors unearthed in this pit are on display in glass cases. A stairway leads to a second-floor exhibition hall where more exhibits are on display, including some of the more than 30,000 pieces of Qin weaponry discovered in the three pits.

Archaeologists say the military formation of Pit No. 2 is far more complex than that in Pit No. 1. The larger quantity of archers, chariots and cavalry suggests that in the battles of the day those troops in Pit No. 2 would have been engaged in launching offensives and breaking up the enemy ranks. Once the enemy troops were on the run the cavalry would have given chase.

Pit No. 3 is the smallest of the three, strategically the most important since the command of the entire terracotta army was based here. Excavation of this battle headquarters has revealed the traces of a chariot, four horses and sixty-eight warriors. The four horses pulling the chariot and the four warriors behind it are in good condition, but many of the pit's other figures are headless or smashed completely. Numerous bronze weapons, and fragments of deer horn and animal bone have also been found. Animal sacrifice was probably part of the rites performed by commanders of a real army, who would have prayed to the gods for victory before a battle.

Pit No. 3 is housed within a modern building. Terracotta warriors, mainly headless, and the four draught horses of a chariot, stand upon a Qin brick floor. Within the pit, rammed earth walls form chambers housing small detachments. Timber once completed this subterranean vault structure, but these collapsed and damaged the warriors beneath.

A kneeling archer excavated from Pit No. 2

Every figure is different. Their facial features and clothing reveal differences in age, function and rank; however, collectively, the figures do exhibit some general racial characteristics: they have squar-

ish faces, wide foreheads, thick lips, moustaches and beards.

The figures are all fairly tall, with generals and commanders being the tallest and most portly. Apart from their larger size, generals can be clearly identified by their double-tailed headgear, longer tunics falling to below the knee, and minimal fish-scale-pattern armour on their midriff, which hangs in an inverted V-shape a little below the waist. On the chest and neck they have bow-like decorations, while their feet are shod in boots with upturned toes. The sleeves of the generals' tunics are usually long enough to partly cover the hands, since generals directed their troops and rarely engaged in direct combat themselves.

Officers have simpler headgear and usually wear a little more armour, sometimes on the shoulders, but not on the chest. Boots are flat-toed and box-shaped. Sleeves leave the hands clear and free, for the officer both directs his troops and may need to lead them by example into combat.

Cavalrymen are seen dismounted in front of their terracotta horses. They can be recognized by their sleeveless jackets of armour, which appear thick and are composed of quite large, squarish plates that seem to be riveted together. Headgear is extremely simple and close fitting, and is secured with a chin strap to prevent it blowing off while riding. Shoes are the lightest and smallest of all the figures.

Detail of the battle chariot, known as the *liche*, showing the remarkable craftsmanship required in its creation

Archers usually wear simple battle robes with no armour, and their arms are in the process of drawing back their bows. Kneeling archers are more plentiful. They are crouched down on one knee in readiness for combat and wear quite heavy armour. Viewed from the rear, their boots can be seen to have a distinct tread.

The infantry wear either battle robes or bulkier armour. Their hair is usually tied into topknots and their hands are poised to carry spears. The charioteers are in more active poses, with both arms stretched out slightly so as to hold the reins to drive their vehicles.

Two magnificent bronze chariots are housed in a relatively new exhibition hall, which stands to the right as you first enter the museum complex. In December 1980, two chariots, each with two-spoked wheels and drawn by four horses, were unearthed – totally smashed, apart from the solid bronze steeds and charioteers. These chariots were about half the size of the actual chariots used by Emperor Qin Shihuangdi on his inspection tours of the empire. They were certainly crafted specifically for Qin Shihuangdi's afterlife.

Bronze chariot, half life size designed to carry the spirit of Qin Shihuangdi in the afterlife

One was made of bronze, gold and silver components (about 3,462 separate metallic parts in all). The second chariot, the *gaoche*, which was found in front of the other, may have been a vanguard vehicle. It is also called a *liche* (a battle chariot), and like the second, is drawn by four horses. The chariot carries a pair of bronze shields, a crossbow and arrow, and a box containing sixty-six bronze arrowheads.

Both chariots highlight the excellent metallurgical and metal-shaping technology of the Qin period, as well as its high artistic standards. Most chariot fittings are of solid bronze, while the harness and reins are inlaid with gold and silver. A tassel hangs down from each horse's neck. The chariot drivers and horses are also of solid bronze, and yet appear very life-like.

208

Shaanxi History Museum

陕西历史博物馆 *Shaanxi lishi bowuguan*

91 Xiaozai East Road, Xi'an, Shaanxi
陕西省西安市小寨东路91号

Tel: (029) 8521 9422
Open: 9.00–17.30, 15 Nov–15 Mar; 8.30–18.00, 16 Mar–14 Nov
www.sxhm.com
Free pamphlet / wheelchairs available
English guide book

The creation of the Shaanxi History Museum, the final wish of Premier Zhou Enlai, began in 1983 and was opened to the public in 1991. It was the first major state museum built with modern facilities in China, designed in a mixture of traditional Tang and modern building styles. It is a massive structure with 8,000 sq m of exhibition space. Its remit is the explanation of the history and culture of Shaanxi Province, and the repository for its art.

A close-up of the rider holding a banner, one of some fifty horsemen depicted in the mural

Polo Players (detail), from the Tang wall paintings decorating Prince Zhang Huai's tomb

Shaanxi, and its capital city Xi'an (originally Chang'an), was the heartland of ancient Chinese civilization. Details of its 150,000-year past continue to emerge from province-wide excavations in the loess – the dry sandy soil which has nearly perfectly preserved its past. Situated to the north and west, Xi'an had been the capital of the province, intermittently, since the time of the ancient Zhou. Thirteen dynasties had made their capitals here, as did the Qin Emperor, Qin Shihuangdi, who brought the period of the Warring States to a close by suppressing and unifying the other six states into a centralized China for the first time. It was outside Xi'an that he built his tomb with the famous Terracotta Warrior Army.

Xi'an reached the height of its wealth and power in the Tang dynasty, when it was laid out on a grid pattern, still extant today, with rectangular blocks of streets spreading out on the compass points from the Bell Tower at its centre. It was surrounded by walls, which were completed by the Ming and which still stand today. Situated at the eastern end of the Silk Road, which brought it great wealth, Xi'an alternated as the capital with Luoyang to the east for generations.

The permanent collection sets out to explain the rich legacy of Shaanxi's history and is divided historically into seven sections: prehistory, Zhou, Qin, Han, Wei–Jin, the Northern and Southern dynasties, and the Sui–Tang and Song–Yuan–Ming–Qing, giving a panoramic picture of Shaanxi's past, from the earliest times to the mid nineteenth century. The display of objects is enlivened by models of archaeological sites, explanatory drawings and photographs. Here, one can put into context painted Neolithic ceramics, bronzes that show the rise of the Zhou, the weapons, horses and soldiers of the Qin, the daily life of the Han dynasty seen from the minute detail of its funerary objects, and the gold and silverware and *sancai* ceramics of the Tang.

It is no surprise therefore that over 370,000 relics have been unearthed in this province, including bronzes, pottery, stoneware, oracle bones, Han and Tang figurines, jade, copper, mirrors and brick tiles. There are pottery figurines from the Han and the Tang, as well as some of the finest gold and silverware, and a spectacular series of murals, from the Tang.

The collection contains 762 pieces of first class, 2,242 pieces of second class and 4,205 pieces of third class. The earliest exhibit is the prehistoric Lantian Apeman of 1,000,000 years ago; the latest relate to the Opium War of 1840.

The exhibition area of the museum is divided into three halls. The permanent collection is on display in the central Main Exhibition Hall, arranged

The Hunt (detail), murals painted on the passage wall of Prince Zhang Huai's tomb

historically and emphasizing some of the great achievements of art in Shaanxi, including the capital city Chang'an, the gold and silverware of the Tang dynasty, as well as its pottery figures, and the pottery figures and porcelain of the Song, Yuan and Ming dynasties. Throughout, the important role of the Shaanxi province in the development of Chinese history is traced.

One of the glories of the Shaanxi History Museum is a spectacular collection of Tang tomb frescoes, for which, at the time of writing, a new purpose-built exhibition hall is under construction. The murals come from more then twenty Tang tombs and cover more than 1000 sq m, delineating in vivid and elegant detail the court life, military, sports and pastimes of China's wealthiest dynasty. There are also pictures of foreigners who have arrived on the Silk Road. The tomb frescoes have been brilliantly preserved, having been peeled off the walls of the tombs to a depth of 5–10 mm, mounted on new backing and now conserved with the most advanced museum technology here – controlled temperature and humidity, and non-ultraviolet lighting system. The Tang murals alone are worth a visit to this museum.

Two other pieces are particularly treasured: one is a Tang dynasty animal-headed agate cup designed in the shape of a horn, with an antelope head and gold fittings. The other is the ingenious Dao Liu Hu pot; designed in one piece without any moveable lid, there is only one hole at the bottom of the pot through which it is filled, but which retains the contents when placed upright.

209

Xi'an Banpo Museum

半坡博物馆 *Xi'an Banpo bowuguan*

155 Banpo Road, Dongjiao, Xi'an, Shaanxi

西安市东郊半坡路155号

Tel: (029) 8351 2807 / 8353 2482
Open: 8.00–17.00 Mon–Fri; 7.30–17.00 Sat, Sun & holidays
www.bpmuseum.com/

Most of the pots that excavators could restore from the site came from graves where breakage was less

Banpo is one of the earliest and finest Chinese archaeological site museums. The site itself is vast, with an excavated area of 50,000 sq m over various levels. The layout and topography is extremely interesting and there is so much to see, creating a vivid picture of the life of the original Neolithic inhabitants.

Banpo people lived 6,000 years ago, the biggest group yet known of the Yellow River Neolithic peoples. They were not only fishermen and hunters, but also early farmers. Some idea of their culture had been known about for some time, notably during the War of Liberation when Marshal Chenyi had excavated some artefacts as his troops were digging trenches in the area, but the existence of Banpo as the major identifiable culture of the Yellow River Neolithic world was established only by the excavation of this site, which began in 1953.

Opened to the public in 1958, the site is elegantly covered in a steel and glass structure with walls in pale stucco reflecting the colour of the soil beneath. It was restored and re-opened in 2006. The grey-brown loess from which these remnants of Neolithic life emerge gives off a dusty impression of immense age, and, as always in Shaanxi Province, creates a sense of the layer upon layer of ancient civilizations lying underneath our own.

The visitor can choose whether to begin with the site itself at the end of the main courtyard facing the entrance, or to start with the two galleries of important excavated artefacts that are on the left of the main courtyard. There is much to be said for getting a feel for the site first. In any event, the two displays – the site and the artefacts – must be linked in the mind for the visitor to get the maximum from the experience.

The site is surrounded by a huge trench, which covers an area of some 30,000 sq m containing residential areas within. These residential areas are clearly separated from others used for worship, pottery-making and burial. There are remains of more than forty houses, 200 cellars and storage pits, 200 adult tombs, some children's burial urns, two ditches, two pens, one worship site and six pottery kilns.

The remains of the houses are semi-subterranean, some square, some circular; their outlines are clearly delineated by post-holes. Given the date and their physical nature, they give a fascinating insight into the evolutionary moment that mankind moved from cave dwellings into housing. In particular, it is easy to imagine the reality of the circular houses, which were supported by six beams, with sloping sides and a flat roof.

Neolithic Kiln

The square houses, with twelve posts arranged in three straight lines, are quite evidently the ancestors of the basic Chinese house and hall structure, which became the standard from the beginning of Chinese history to the twentieth century.

The storage pits were of many shapes and sizes and were scattered amongst the houses – some in the shape of a bag with a small mouth and big belly. Their inner walls were either plastered or burnt to help preserve their contents.

The kilns were either horizontal or vertical, mostly small, with space for not more than ten objects each. The most impressive remains of a kiln are housed separately in a building behind the main site.

There are two semi-circular pens near the ditches, which could have been fortifications or alternatively cattle pens. The function of the small ditch is unclear but the big ditch, sliced massively and deeply through the compacted soil, was clearly used for defence.

The graves were neatly dug, mostly individual but a few for group burial. Bodies were laid in deep soil facing west. Children were buried in small urns or jars.

There is also a standing stone pillar, 65 cm in height, which stands like a mystic sentinel with an apparently ovoid cross-section, and polished with striations on its surface. Its function is unknown.

The Exhibition Galleries

More than 30,000 objects have been excavated on site; the finest, or most representative of these are displayed in two exhibition halls on the left-hand side of the main entrance. The first hall has objects such as stone tools, fishing implements, jade, and pottery rings. The second hall is dedicated to the very high quality red and black Neolithic pottery found at Banpo.

Almost without exception, the originality of the design and execution of these objects transcends their humble utilitarian function. Like the semi-subterranean houses of the site, they have a quality which exemplifies the emerging skill of 'man the designer'.

Amongst the artefacts illustrating the daily life of Banpo people are bone needles, bone shuttles and earthen spinning wheels, cooking ware, food vessels and pottery stoves for cooking, and fishhooks and other tools for fishing. There are also decorative pottery rings of elaborate design, and stone beads.

It is the pottery that is of the highest quality. Outstanding examples include a pottery basin painted with a human face and fish, showing a human face with a triangular headdress, with semi-abstract fish on each side of the mouth. The subject matter and the style of its execution is the source of intense speculation amongst archaeologists, both for the strength and originality of its imagery and also because of the light it shed on the possible role of the fish in the shamanistic religion of Banpo Culture.

Banpo pottery usually consists of black painted decoration – mostly of human heads, fishes and birds – on a reddish ground. The style is geometric. Also not to be missed are some quite extraordinarily realistic pottery sculptured human heads, and human and animal figures.

210

Xi'an Beilin Museum

西安碑林博物馆 *Xi'an beilin bowuguan*

15 Sanxue Road, Xi'an, Shaanxi

西安市内三学街15号

Tel: (029) 8721 0764 / 8526 5711
Open: 8.00–17.00
English audio guide
Small book and gift shop

Aerial view of the museum complex

The Forest of Steles Museum, known in Chinese as the Beilin Museum, is one of the key depositories of Chinese culture – its core being an indispensable collection of classic texts and of masterpieces of calligraphy engraved on stones – or stele. It offers a graphic insight into the role of calligraphy – the most prominent art in Chinese culture.

Opened in 1952, in the former Temple of Confucius, it is located beside the southern section of the city wall. Its collection of more than 1,000 inscribed stones started in 1090, when a large collection of steles carved in AD 837 – of the oldest existing texts of the Confucian classics – was moved to the back of the temple for safekeeping.

The art of inscribing on stone began in China at least as early as the fourth century BC.

From the Han dynasty onwards, flat stones were cut with either text or pictures for commemorative purposes, and to make it possible to reproduce them on paper by taking rubbings.

The museum's collection is divided into four basic categories: literature and philosophy, historical records, calligraphy and pictorial stones. Especially interesting are the pictorial stones in Room 4, almost all dating back to the Ming (1368–1644) or Qing (1644–1911).

In Room 1 there is a set of 114 stones engraved in AD 837, which are known as the Kaicheng Classics. These include the Book of Changes, the Book of History, the Book of Songs and the Analects of Confucius. An impressive 650,252 characters are inscribed on the front and back of just one stele.

Tang stone tomb sculpture of a rhinoceros, from the Xianling mausoleum of Li Yuan, Emperor Gaozu, Sanyuan county

Room 2 holds a valuable Nestorian stele, carved in 781. The stele bears the history of the Nestorian Christian community in Chang'an, beginning with its founding by a Syrian missionary in the seventh

The fifth exhibition room displaying stone stele

century. Notice the small cross inscribed at the top, and the Arabic script at the bottom. There are also examples of calligraphy by many of the Tang dynasty's leading calligraphers. The stele have served as models for students practising calligraphy.

Room 3 houses an important calligraphy collection. A stone carved by Shi Mengying in 999, during the Northern Song dynasty, bears characters in the ancient seal script, with the corresponding character in the later normal script inscribed immediately below each ancient character.

Room 4 displays examples of poetry from the Song to the Qing dynasties, in the original handwriting of the authors.

Tang dynasty tablet of Daode Temple, calligrapher Dao Fan

In Room 5 are stele of the Song, Yuan, Ming and Qing dynasties, primarily dealing with temple renovation and individual merit.

Most of the inscriptions in Room 6 are poetry, written by the literati of the Yuan, Ming and Qing periods.

Room 7 exhibits inscriptions by emperors, famous ministers and calligraphers throughout Chinese history.

The Stone Sculpture Gallery, just beside the museum, was built in 1963 and renovated in 1999. It houses some seventy excellent sculptures and relief carvings, the most famous among them being the six bas-reliefs from Zhao Ling, the Mausoleum of Emperor Tang Taizong.

A number of large animals that once lined the approaches to imperial tombs of the Han and Tang are also on display, including lions, a tiger, a rhinoceros and an ostrich.

The exhibition also contains several Buddhist statues, including a very beautiful torso of a bodhisattva, showing the strong Indian influence typical of the Tang dynasty, and an Avalokitesvara on an elaborate lotus throne from the same period. Outside the sculpture gallery stands a collection of dozens of stone hitching posts, used during the Ming and Qing dynasties for tethering horses. The tops are decorated with carved animals and people.

211 Xi'an Museum

西安博物馆 *Xi'an bowuguan*

72 Youyi West Road, Xi'an, Shaanxi
西安市友谊西路72号

Tel: (029) 6890 1980
Open: 9.00–18.00

Gilt bronze figure of Buddha Dao Fan

The very impressive new Xi'an Museum opened in 2007 in the park surrounding the Small Goose Pagoda. In the large lobby there is a marble map on the floor showing the layout of the city in different historical periods. Overhead, the ceiling is covered with a stylized lily.

The basement is a good place to begin a tour of the museum, presenting an excellent introduction to the history of the Xi'an city wall at different periods in Chinese history. Here, there are several wooden models of the ancient city. The first illustrates the walled city as it looked in the Han dynasty. The wall is not square, as it had to follow the contours of the Wei River. The Tang dynasty wall was quite large. The wonderful 1:1500 scale model shows a pagoda standing in each district of Chang'an, as Xi'an was then known. There were five gates in the wall and only the Emperor could enter through the south gate. Daming Palace, the home of the imperial court, can be seen in a separate enclosure to the northeast. Markets are visible outside the east and west gates of the wall. A third wooden model shows the city wall in the Ming and Qing periods, which represents the present-day shape of the wall.

The basement also has a section on ancient bronze ware from the Zhou to the Tang dynasties, including an elaborate bronze mirror. The collection includes a statue of a Qin charioteer, chariot parts, and tools, including axes, chisels and knives.

Of particular interest is a Hu pot in the shape of a silk worm, which was buried in the ground as a listening device to alert the military that the enemy was approaching. The museum also has what may be the world's first ever air conditioner – a metal box that contained pieces of ice.

An exhibition of pottery shows statues of the typically chubby women that were so admired in the Tang dynasty. The women wear long skirts and their shoes, which peak out from beneath their skirts, are curved. The elaborate hairstyles are particularly interesting. There are also tri-coloured galloping horses from the Tang dynasty. A number of foreigners can also be seen. One notable tri-colour features a foreign boy wearing a gown with a rounded collar while sitting on a horse. A model of a Ming dynasty funeral procession has seventy-seven figures, including one empty horse representing the deceased. Another Tang dynasty tri-colour shows a girl sleeping on the back of a camel. There is a coffin carved with intricate flowers and dragons and a coffin with a door.

The first floor has a wonderful collection of Buddhist statues. There is one

Tang tri-coloured glazed pottery figure of galloping horse and rider, excavated in the outskirts of Xi'an

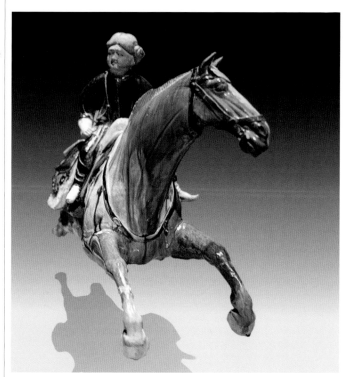

stone statue from the Northern Wei dynasty and a beautiful statue of Guanyin, the Goddess of Mercy, from the Tang dynasty, which is gilded and painted, still showing traces of gold. The iron Buddha on display here is said to be the only one made of iron in China.

The second floor is devoted to Chinese calligraphy scrolls, including works by the legendary Zhang Daqian, as well as one Yuan dynasty scroll. There is also a collection of jade ware, including jade pigs from the Han dynasty, and all sorts of seals made from a wide variety of materials. Some of the characters on the seals are quite difficult to read, and so only recognizable to experts.

There are brief English descriptions with most exhibits.

There is also a 3D theatre here that shows a film introducing the history of the Small Goose Pagoda, a short walk from the museum in the park.

A fierce tomb guardian figure

Xi'an Film Studio

In the mid 1980s, some young graduates of the Beijing Film Academy, China's premier film school, began to look for an alternative to the stultifying atmosphere in the Chinese capital. These members of China's Fifth Generation of filmmakers, post-Cultural Revolution graduates of the film school, wanted more space to practise their craft. They soon found what they were looking for at the Xi'an Film Studio, which offered a creative environment to produce films based on art rather than politics. The studio soon became the spiritual home of these young directors.

In 1985, Wu Tianming, the director of the studio, invited the cinematographer, Zhang Yimou, to work on *Old Well*. The Xi'an native agreed to take on the project but asked Wu to support him in his own directorial debut. After completing *Old Well*, Zhang launched his own career as a director with *Red Sorghum*, a moving film shot in the Shandong countryside, which uses minimal dialogue, rich cinematography and evocative music to tell the story of a young woman who rises to the task of running her husband's winery after he passes away. The film won Zhang the Berlin Gold Bear and an Oscar nomination.

Mama, directed by Zhang Yuan and distributed by the Xi'an Film Studio, marked a break from traditional cinema in China. The first film independent of government assistance since the Communists came to power in 1949, *Mama* examined the lack of government assistance for families with mentally handicapped children. The film uses a combination of real documentary interviews filmed in colour, with fiction filmed in black and white.

Zhang Yimou is the Xi'an Film Studio's most famous son. After *Red Sorghum*, he directed *Judou*, *Raise the Red Lantern* and *The Story of Qiu Ju* (winner of the Golden Lion Award at the Venice Film Festival in 1992). He then won a second Golden Lion Award at the 1999 Venice Film Festival with *Not One Less*. Part of the charm of this moving film, based on a true story about a thirteen-year-old primary school teacher, lies in the performances of its cast of non-professional children, whose interactions with people on the streets were captured by hidden cameras. In 2002, Zhang returned to Xi'an to film *I Love You*, a realistic look at a young couple's disintegrating marriage. Zhang's *Hero* (2003) and *House of Flying Daggers* (2004) were panned by local audiences unhappy with the story lines. However, the two films received international acclaim for their beautiful cinematography. *House of Flying Daggers* was nominated for an Oscar (neither film was produced at the Xi'an Film Studio). Zhang Yimou directed the spectacular opening ceremony of the 2008 Beijing Olympics.

The controversial *Warriors of Heaven and Earth*, directed by He Ping, which was co-produced by Xi'an Film Studio and Columbia Pictures Film Production Asia, was nominated for an Academy Award in 2004. The lush action film is the story of battle and comradeship between two heroic figures that takes place in the harsh Gobi Desert.

Tuya's Marriage, directed by Wang Quanan, won the Golden Bear award at the 2007 Berlin International Film Festival, and the Special Jury Prize at the 2007 Chicago International Film Festival. The film is the story of Tuya, a hardworking and beautiful shepherdess who is forced to look for a new spouse to take care of her family after she and her husband are injured.

212 Hotan Museum

和田博物館 *Hetian bowuguan*

342 Beijing West Road, Hetian, Xinjiang
新疆省和田市北京西路342号

Tel: (0903) 251 9286
Open: 9.30–13.00 & 16.00–20.00 summer; 10.30–13.30 & 15.30–19.00 winter
www.htww.gov.cn

Turkish forms and Muslim influences in Xinjiang art

The Southern Silk Road town of Hotan (Hetian) in the Uighur heartland has been renowned for its jade and silk products for more than 2,000 years. It is also home to the compact but rewarding Hotan Museum, comprising a ground-floor hall that highlights the development of human civilization along the southern edges of the Taklamakan Desert, and a first-floor display of all things related to Uighur Culture.

Downstairs, fossilized sea shells, Stone Age tools and Bronze Age pottery make way for Han period bracelets and carved pillars from the ancient ruins of Niya; wooden bowls, spoons and brocades showing intricate animal motifs and Chinese characters from the Sampul cemetery (created by the Udun people); and bone, jade, wood and clay artefacts from the ancient Silk Road cities of Karadong, Yotkan, Mazar Tagh and Rawak. Of special note are two Five Dynasties period (907–960) mummies from the Imam Musa Kazim cemetery and a fantastic ship-like wooden coffin still graced with colourful paintings of birds, dragons, snakes and tigers.

The upstairs Uighur gallery (photography permitted) has an excellent selection of carpets and jade carvings, as well as rows of *doppis* (Uighur caps), robes, a silk loom and examples of household goods and utensils, all of which help to create a picture of everyday life on the edge of the great Taklamakan Desert.

213

Turpan Prefecture Museum

吐魯番地區博物館 *Tulufan diqu bowuguan*

224 Gaochang Road, Turpan, Xinjiang (5-minute walk north of the main Public Square)

吐鲁番市高昌路224号

Open: 9.30–19.00
www.turfanological.com

Turpan (Tulufan) is a popular Xinjiang tourist destination, but with so many nearby attractions its museum gets less traffic than it deserves (unfortunately, English is used only for exhibit headings and not for detailed explanations). Of the two halls on the ground floor, on the left is the Dinosaur Fossil Hall, containing a number of huge skeletons, the main one comprising actual bones discovered by railroad workers in 1993 of a 24-million-year-old creature named *Paraceratherium tienshanensis*. A first-floor open gallery around this shows the evolution of life and change in geography of the Turpan Basin, from lush swampy jungle 20 million years ago to dry desert today.

Also on the ground floor is the Culture and History Hall, with exhibits from archaeological digs at the major local sites of Jiaohe, Astana, Karakhoja and

Gaochang period embroidered boot

Mummy from Astana cemetery displayed as he was found, with knees drawn up and clothing still clearly visible (see over)

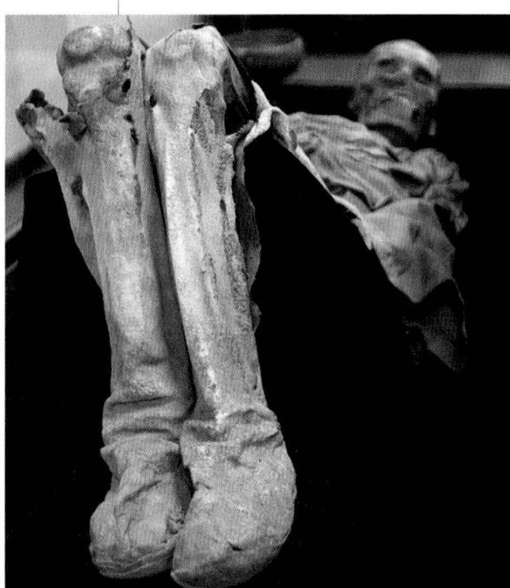

Silk fragment from the Gaochang Uighur period

Gaochang. Upstairs is a room called The Ancient Corpses of Turpan, which were discovered only in the last few decades. There are twelve mummies in total (including two infants); a couple discovered in Astana cemetery in 1972 had documents buried with them showing dates (AD 502–640) and their family name – they are very well preserved, with the man's thin moustache still clearly visible. A nice touch is replicas of the couple in lavish Tang clothing standing next to the bodies, illustrating how they looked in life. Photography is allowed throughout the museum.

214

Xinjiang Uighur Autonomous Region Museum

新疆自治区博物馆 *Xinjiang xìzhìqu bowuguan*

581 Xibei Road, Urumqi, Xinjiang
新疆维吾尔自治区乌鲁木齐市西北路581号

Tel: (0991) 453 6436
Open: 10.30–18.00, last ticket sold at 17.00

More than 2,000 years ago, as China began to develop into an empire of global significance under the Qin and Han dynasties, the empty land beyond its western borders was known simply as 'the Western Regions', a vast forbidding wilderness of mountain and desert, populated by 'savages' and all manner of demons. Today, the bulk of this region falls within the borders of the Xinjiang Uighur Autonomous Region.

The famous – and hugely important – Silk Road trade routes traversed Xinjiang's territory, skirting the infamous Taklamakan Desert and crossing high mountain passes on to farther lands. Along the way, caravans passed through

oasis city-states that grew rich from the two-way traffic of merchant goods. These kingdoms also benefited from the ideas, technologies and religious beliefs that flowed between the major civilizations of East and West.

Over the centuries, the importance of the Silk Road waxed and waned, with the Xinjiang region's Buddhist kingdoms influencing Tang dynasty China (AD 618–907) heavily in religion, art and music, then playing host to the Mongol hordes of Genghis Khan, the conquering armies of Islam, and ultimately the military might of the Qing dynasty. But it wasn't until the late nineteenth and early twentieth centuries that foreign explorers began to unearth the immense cultural, historical and archaeological wealth that put Xinjiang at the forefront of Chinese anthropological exploration.

The best place to get a detailed overview of this fascinating legacy of many millennia of human civilization is in Urumqi at the Xinjiang Uighur Autonomous Region Museum. The museum's large new complex took five years to build, and was finished and opened in 2005. Its central domed entrance hall contains a 3D relief map of Xinjiang that immediately gives an insight into the importance of the region's topography in determining where and how humans could live and prosper.

The two-storey building is split neatly into four sections: on the ground floor, the subjects are the Silk Road and ethnic minorities, while upstairs a large room is devoted to Xinjiang's famous mummies and another contains memorabilia of the Chinese liberation of Xinjiang. It's best to visit the displays in chronological order, so first turn right and enter the 'Silk Road' down a tunnel-like corridor, walking on a Perspex layer over a sandy 'desert' floor.

This section actually covers a much greater time frame than its name implies – the first exhibit is an 8,000-year-old skull from Artux City, followed by pottery, wool and felt hats, and a dyed corduroy-style trouser leg from 1000 BC. A host of Bronze Age implements, colourful clothing and weapons are all in amazingly good condition and show excellent craftsmanship, but it is when you move on to the collection of items from the Western Han through to Tang dynasties that the incredible wealth of ancient artefacts becomes apparent. The dry desert conditions helped to preserve an amazing array of items that detail life in the oasis kingdoms, from silk brocades and copper seals to wooden tablets and official paper records; from Buddhist mural paintings to cakes and twisted dough sticks.

There are superb examples of Yuan dynasty horse halters, coins, gold figures and porcelain from the Middle kingdom, as well as rare Buddhist scriptures written in early Uighur Mongolian characters. The final section of the 'Silk Road' display shows Qing dynasty items such as jade and silver carvings, stone stelae and beautiful multicoloured silks from Hotan on the Southern Silk Road.

As comprehensive and compelling as the 'Silk Road' display is, above it on the first floor of the museum lies Xinjiang's highlight exhibit and its signature displays. A sign at the entrance to the temperature-regulated room says: 'Passed Away but Amaze the World Immortally [sic]'. This is your introduction to the famous Xinjiang mummies, and the first glass case contains the prize exhibit, the 'Loulan Beauty from Tiebanhe Riverside'. Excavated from Tieban River, north of Lop Nor, in 1980, with skin smooth and blackened by dessication, the corpse is a forty-five-year-old woman of Europoid origin, with red hair, a thin aquiline nose, and covered with a red-brown, rough wool blanket. Dated to 1800 BC, her features are delicate, her lips drawn back in a tiny, enigmatic smile, while fur-topped, leather-soled shoes cover her feet, and a feather, comb and woven basket are arranged around her exactly as they were when she was found.

Other mummies include a child, a boy of four to five years, swaddled in a wool blanket fastened with sixteen wooden pins; a long-haired adult female from 1800 BC discovered in the desert at the Xiaohe Graveyard and wearing a pointed felt hat with a weasel skin trim; and the dessicated corpse of one Zhang Xiong (583–633), whose feet retain incredible detail in the skin and toenails. Some of the mummies were excavated from the Astana tombs, Tang Chinese governors or military staff buried with bows and arrows alongside them, while a beautifully caparisoned male and female Europoid couple were exhumed from Qiemo in southern Xinjiang, buried alongside each other and dating to 800 BC.

After this emotive insight into Xinjiang's past, the 'Liberation' room on the same floor catapults you into the modern era. Unfortunately, where all the museum's other sections are clearly and informatively explained in English, this room has no English signage. So the military artefacts and memorabilia, including photographs and contract documents between the factions who fought for control of Xinjiang in the twentieth century, lose their potency.

Downstairs, however, the final section entitled 'Display of Xinjiang Nationality Custom', is well worth exploring in full, as it explores each of Xinjiang's twelve ethnic groups. You enter into a replica of a Uighur courtyard

Ethnic Minorities in China

The population of China is not a single homogeneous culture but is made up of many separate ethnic groups. The official count is fifty-six, the largest group of which is the dominant Han, making up about 92 per cent of the population. Many of these groups, such as the Tibetans, Uighurs and Miao fiercely guard their identity and may not even think of themselves as Chinese. This is obviously a highly political and sometimes incendiary topic.

A number of these groups, such as the Tibetans and the Uighurs, have their own territories, called Autonomous Regions, but in fact these regions are closely controlled by the central government.

The figure of fifty-six minority groups is a disputed number as there are countless subdivisions between some of these groups who would not necessarily want to count themselves amongst the larger culture. Examples of such 'undistinguished groups', as they are known, would be the Musuo within the Miao or Oirat within the Mongols.

Some of these minorities have their own language (not a Chinese dialect). In addition, there are twenty-one unique systems of writing amongst China's ethnic minorities. Additionally, each group has its distinctive customs in terms of dress, religion, social mores, cuisine etc., giving them a strong sense of individual cultural identity.

and house, with a wonderful display of Uighur musical instruments and then pass through rooms highlighting each nationality's unique dress and customs, from Kazakh yurts to dummies of Mongolian wrestlers, Kyrgyz livestock and Xibe archers, and from Russian iron-and-brass beds to Daur hanging cradles.

A modern, well-planned museum, this is an essential stop on any Xinjiang tour, preferably visited before you move on to the region's main historical sites. The insight you gain here will augment your subsequent experiences.

215 Xinjiang Ili Kazakh Autonomous Prefecture Museum

新疆伊犁哈萨克自治区博物馆 *Xinjiang Ili Hasake zìzhiqu bowuguan*

122 Feijichang Road (Airport Road), Yining, Ili Kazakh Autonomous Prefecture, Xinjiang

新疆伊宁市飞机场路122号

Open: 9.40–13.30 & 16.30–20.00 summer;10.00–12.00 & 15.30–17.30 winter

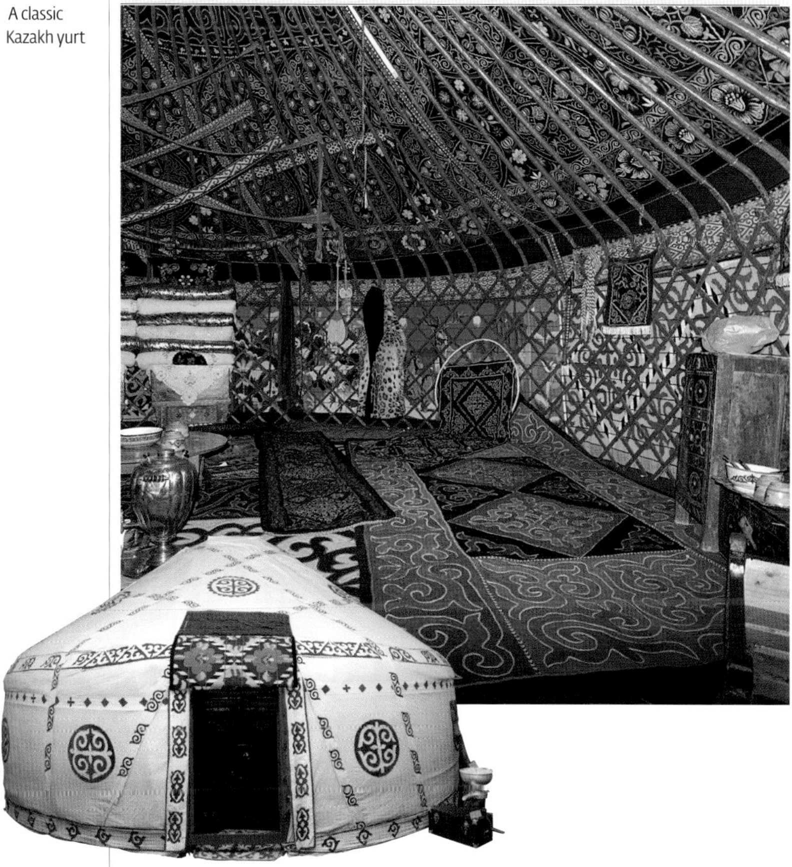

A classic Kazakh yurt

A street musician in Xinjiang and a case of traditional instruments at the museum

A small but bright gem in a remote corner of China, this museum focuses on the history and culture of the Ili Kazakh Autonomous Prefecture, which includes all of northwest Xinjiang, from the fertile Ili Valley within the northern Tien Shan mountains to the Junggar Basin and Altai range in the far north. Of the three galleries, the first covers the prehistory period, displaying mammoth teeth from the Pleistocene era of a million years ago, petroglyphs from 8000 BC and early Bronze Age axes, sickles, arrowheads etc. The second details the rise of the great nomadic steppe cultures, showing skeletons, weapons, utensils and beautifully wrought gold work (look out for the superb fifth-century gold mask unearthed at the Boma Tomb in the Ili Valley), as well as a row of Altai anthropomorphic stone statues. The third gallery, the 'Gallery of Nations and Folkways', displays mannequins clothed in the various traditional dress of the thirteen indigenous ethnic groups (including the Han) of the region, with a centrepiece of a glorious Kazakh yurt surrounded by animal furs, horse harnesses, houseware and handicrafts. Photography is permitted only in the third gallery. A small but immensely interesting museum that is a must-see destination if you're in Yining.

216

Potala Palace

布达拉宫 *Budala Gong*

No. 1 Gongqianxiang, Beijing Zhong Road, Lhasa, Tibet

拉萨北京中路宫前巷1号

Tel: (0891) 682 2896 / 683 0427
Open: 8.00–17.30 (opening times are due to change); tickets are limited, best to buy a day ahead in peak season
Tibetan and Mandarin guides are available
Gift shop

The thirteen-storey palace soars 117 m from the top of Marpo Ri, the 'Red Hill', and was the chief residence of the Dalai Lama until the 14th Dalai Lama fled to India in 1959

The palace's sloping stone walls are 3 m thick and 5 m thick at the base

With the increase in tourism, both Chinese and international, and the opening of the railway from Beijing, the number of visitors to the palace has increased to such levels that the number of visitors has had to be rationed daily to about 2,000. Booking in advance is therefore recommended. Passport is required. Duration of visit is limited. Individuals have two hours and groups one hour. All bags (including cosmetics) must be checked. Remember that this is not just a museum but also a place of worship for many Tibetan pilgrims. Be respectful and honour their privacy.

The original palace that stood on this site was built by the seventh-century King, Songsten Gampo (r. AD 627–49), who also built the two holiest temples in Tibet – the Jokhang and Ramoche. A new palace was built in the same location 1,000 years later by the illustrious 5th Dalai Lama, Ngawang Losang Gyatso (1617–1682). Work began on the construction of the Potrang Karpo, or White Palace, in 1645. It was completed three years later, and in 1649 the 5th Dalai Lama moved from the Gelupa Order, Drepung Monastery, to his new residence. The building was then further enlarged with the construction of the Potrang Marpo, or Red Palace. The White Palace was used for secular purposes, both residential and bureaucratic, as it served as the seat of Tibetan government, while the Red Palace was used for

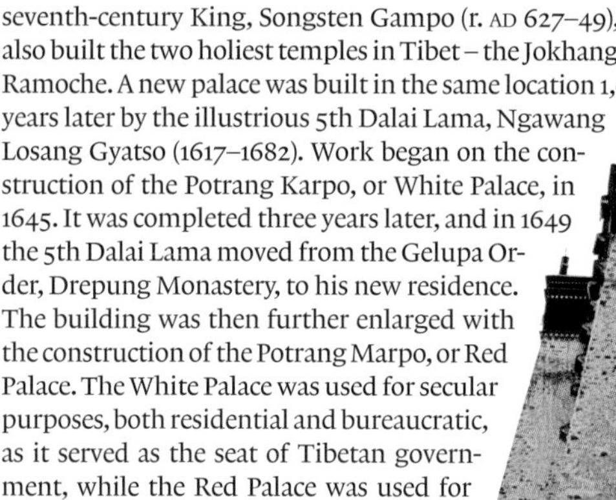

religious affairs. It contains chapels, schools, libraries and even the tombs of several Dalai Lamas.

The 5th Dalai Lama was a charismatic and scholarly leader who united Tibet under the Gelug – or Yellow-Hat Sect – of Buddhism, made Lhasa the capital and was responsible for combining the secular and religious leadership roles of the Dalai Lama, which is maintained to this day. In an effort to avoid conflict or chaos, his death in 1682 was concealed for twelve years until the Red Palace was completed in 1694.

Since its construction, the Potala has been the home of all the Dalai Lamas, although since the building of the Norbulingka summer palace in the late eighteenth century, it has served solely as a winter residence. The 13th Dalai Lama undertook some renovation work in the early twentieth century, demolishing sections of the White Palace to expand some chapels and in 1959, the Potala sustained some damage during the Tibetan Revolt. Unlike most of the other holy sites in Tibet, the Potala was spared during the Cultural Revolution, reportedly at the insistence of Zhou Enlai, who is said to have deployed his own troops to protect it. The palace is now a UNESCO World Heritage Site.

A visit to the Potala is overwhelming. The colourful palace is brimming with murals, paintings, pillars, statues, furniture, rugs, jewellery and more. The air is rich with the smell of yak butter which burns in the hundreds of lamps set before holy statues bedecked with the ubiquitous white ceremonial scarves; at their bases, cases stuffed with cash offered in the hopes of wishes being granted. The halls are crowded with an incongruous mix of Western and Chinese tourists and incessantly chanting Tibetan pilgrims, many of whom have travelled in arduous conditions to pray here. You will not see all 1,000 rooms in a visit of two hours – best to simply soak in the extraordinary atmosphere. For the voyeur, look at the private rooms of past Dalai Lamas, including that of the present 14th Dalai Lama as it was when he fled to India in 1959. And from the roof there is a magnificent view of Lhasa below.

The main attractions on the third floor are the Chapel of Maitreya, the Tomb of the 13th Dalai Lama, the Chapel of Three-Dimensional Mandalas, the Chapel of Victory over the World and the Chapel of Immortal Happiness.

The highlight on the second floor is the small, seventh-century chapel of Arya Lokeshvara – Potala's most sacred image. The chapel is one of the palace's oldest surviving rooms.

Tibetan monks live in the White Palace within the Potala Palace

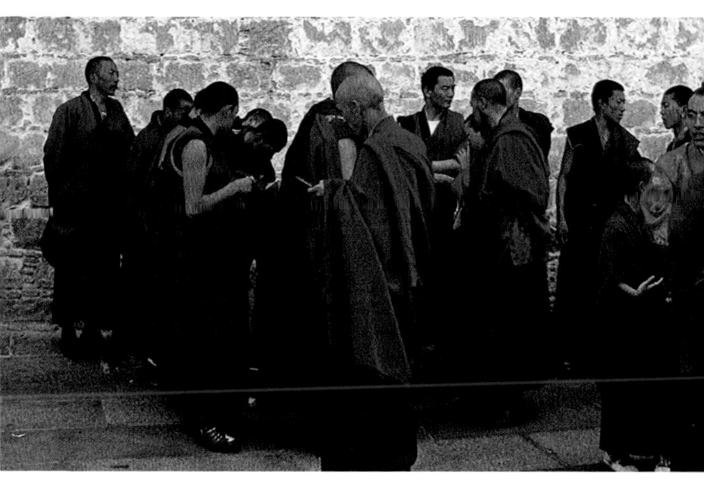

A monk sits in front of the windows in the Red Palace reading scripture and prayers

Ghee lamps burn continuously in front of the palace's many shrines

217

Tibet Museum

西藏博物馆 *Xizang bowuguan*

19 Luobukalin Road, Lhasa, Tibet
拉萨市罗布卡林路19号

Tel: (0891) 681 2211/ 683 9222
Open: 9.00–17.00 except Mon
www.tibet.cn
English audio guide

Tibetan drama costume

This museum building, in style a combination of Tibetan and Chinese, was designed by a Han Chinese architect from Sichuan Province and was opened in October 1999 with great fanfare. As the sign says at the entrance, the museum was 'built under the kind care of the Central Committee of the Communist Party of China'. The history of the Sino-Tibetan relationship, and reminders of China's righteous hegemony, is the message running throughout the museum's choices of exhibits as well as its signage. Notwithstanding the tremendously unsubtle political subtext, many of the objects here are of great interest. The Prehistoric Gallery exhibits material from the Paleolithic, Neolithic and Bronze Age, with the highlight being the Neolithic pottery excavated in the 1970s from the Eastern Tibetan site of Karo.

The Tibetan History and Culture Gallery has many highlights, among them the Golden Vase. There are two copies of this, one originally in the Jokhang Temple and one in the Lama Temple (Yonghe Gong) in Beijing. It was a gift from the Qianlong Emperor, and from it was drawn the lots determining the appointment of the Dalai Lama's reincarnation. This vase was also used in 1995 to determine the government-sanctioned selection of the 11th Panchen Lama.

Weapons from the Western Tibetan kingdom of Guge, which flourished from the ninth to the seventeenth centuries are exhibited. This kingdom was a centre of foreign trade and strong supporter of Buddhism, and was influential in the spread of Buddhism throughout Tibet.

Rare pattra sutras – Buddhist scriptures written in Sanskrit on the leaves of the Indian palmyra palm – are also on display. Very few still survive. There is a birch bark Tang dynasty sutra which is labelled as the 'testament of Songtsen Gampo' who was the seventh-century King and founder of the Tibetan empire.

The museum also holds a gold seal given to the 5th Dalai Lama, Ngawang Lozang Gyatso (1617–1682) in 1653 by the Shunzhi Emperor when he went to Beijing. He is one of the greatest and most revered of the Dalai Lamas and was responsible for unifying Tibet and combining the spiritual role of the position with political leadership. Among the accomplishments of this intellectual leader was declaring Lhasa the capital and being responsible for the rebuilding of the Potala Palace. Construction began in 1645 and wasn't completed until 1694. His death, which came before completion of the project, was kept secret for twelve years in order to prevent unrest. More recent history is also represented, such as the 'Agreement for the Peaceful Liberation of Tibet', signed in May 1951.

Gilt Buddha in the Sino-Tibetan style

Bronze Buddha from Western Tibet

Buddhist metal sculptures, musical instruments, astrological and cosmological paintings, mandalas and examples of Tibetan calligraphy are exhibited. One of the finest pieces in the museum is the Tsurphu Scroll, which was discovered in 1949 by the British scholar, Hugh Richardson, in the Tsurphu Monastery, west of Lhasa. This Ming dynasty silk-backed scroll is 15.2 m (50 ft) long and 76 cm (2.5 ft) high, with inscriptions in Chinese, Tibetan, Mongolian, Uighur and Arabic. The inscriptions alternate with elegantly painted panels depicting the miracles performed by the 5th Karmapa Dezhin Shekpa during his visit to the Yongle Emperor in Nanjing in 1407.

Painted, as well as *kesi* embroidered *thangkas* from as early as the thirteenth century are exhibited, some of which are very fine.

In the Folk Custom gallery, ethnographic handicrafts, jewellery, textiles and jade are represented. There is a reproduction of a typical Tibetan house, as well as a yak skin boat. On the third floor is a special display of imperial porcelain from the Ming and Qing periods, many of which were given as gifts to Tibet's nobles.

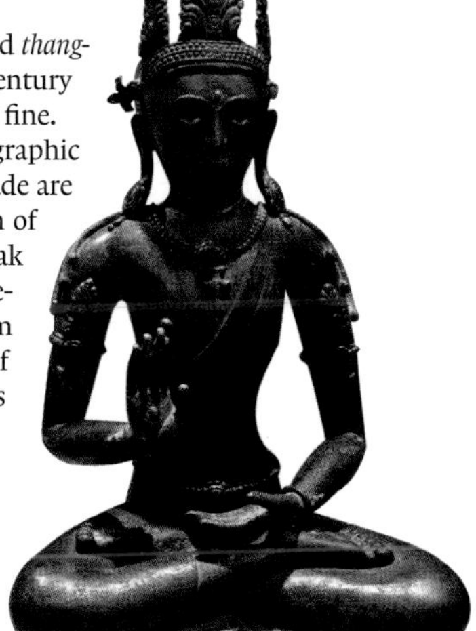

218

National Palace Museum

国立故宫博物院 *Guoli gugong bowugua*

221 Zhishan Road, Sec. 2, Shilin District, Taipei
台北市士林区至善路二段221号

Tel: (+886) 2 2881 2021
Open: 9.00–17.00, late opening Sat until 20.30
www.npm.gov.tw/en/home.htm
Restaurants / cafés / book & gift shop
English guide books / audio guide

This museum houses some of the greatest examples of Chinese art from almost all periods; yet its very existence has also resulted in something of a political football match being played out between Beijing and Taipei for the last half century. It contains many of the greatest treasures from the old imperial collection in Beijing. Even more than the imperial treasures that ended up in the Nanjing Museum after the end of the Civil War, these in Taipei represent *hua-xia*, a term that means 'China' both in a political sense and also in the broadest cultural sense – the representatives of Chinese art and culture from the Shang and the Zhou dynasties to the downfall of the Qing in 1911.

The National Palace Museum was founded in the Forbidden City in 1926 after the expulsion of the last Emperor, Puyi. When Beijing was threatened during the War against Japan, the Nationalist government of Chiang Kai-shek took with it as much as possible of the collection, first to Nanjing, then to Chongqing, then back to Nanjing. The possession of the collection was considered almost as a seal of power proclaiming the authenticity of the Nationalist government. In 1948, when the Civil War was drawing to a close and it was clear to Chiang Kai-shek that he would lose Nanjing, he ordered as much as possible of the cream of the collection to be shipped to the island of Taiwan, where he was preparing to remove his government. This included some sixty boxes of paintings and objects that had been exhibited at the Royal Academy in London in 1935–36 – a collection which had given to many in the West their first glimpse of the nature, quality and range of Chinese art. Between 1948 and 1949, no less than 3,248 crates were shipped to Taiwan, where on arrival they were stored in caves in the Taichung area of the island.

Chun ware dish with rich purple glaze boldy applied to opalescent blue glaze ground, Song to Yuan dynasties

The building of the current museum was completed in 1965, and is situated in the northwest area of Taipei City, facing Shuangxi Park, in a luxuriously wooded and hilly area. The design of the building was based loosely on the Palace Museum in Beijing, with green tiles, yellow walls and white staircases. Today, it houses a collection of some 650,000 items, of which 240,000 came from the imperial collection in Beijing. The museum has been constantly expanded and improved, with the final restoration completed in 2006. Important pieces are shown for three months at a time over a ten-year cycle, to ensure that all the greatest of the treasures are seen by the public at least once in a decade.

The permanent collection is on show in the main four-storey exhibition hall (there is a high-quality restaurant on the fourth floor). There is another

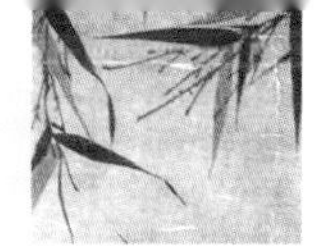

building for temporary exhibitions, and a library which is open to the public. The grounds contain three separate Chinese gardens and a memorial hall to the modern master from Sichuan, Zhang Daqian, built on the site of his former residence (booking is required for the memorial hall; it is closed Sundays and national holidays).

The main entrance to the museum is on the first floor, where the visitor is greeted by a bronze bust of Sun Yat-sen, the founder of the Republic in 1911. It is a replica of the bust at his tomb in Nanjing. Here, there is also a selection of some of the finest pieces of calligraphy and paintings in the collection, including the two most famous long scrolls in the history of Chinese art.

The national treasures in the collection include the Mao Gong *ding*, a Western Zhou bronze excavated in Shaanxi province in 1850. It is 53.8 cm in height, and while the interior and exterior decoration is relatively plain, on the inside is an inscription of 491 characters (the longest inscription known on any ancient bronze), making it a priceless record of ancient Chinese language and history, as well as a magnificent object in itself. The collection also contains a further 2,382 ancient bronzes.

Other galleries contain jades, calligraphy from the Jin and Tang dynasties onwards, paintings starting from the Tang and Song dynasties, ceramics from the Song and Yuan dynasties onwards, bamboo items, objects from the

Wen Tong (1018–1079), hanging scroll, Bamboo, *c.* 1070

Fan Kuan (d. after 1023), hanging scroll, *Travellers amid Streams and Mountains* (see over, left)

Anonymous, eleventh-century hanging scroll, Portrait of the Emperor Renzong, great-grandson of Emperor Taizu (r. 960–76), founder of the Song dynasty (see over, right)

Emperor Huizong (1082–1135; r. 1101–25) Hand scroll; Two Poems (detail of one poem) (see over, bottom)

scholar's table, rare books and lacquer ware.

The outstanding national treasures include paintings and calligraphy by the master calligrapher Wang Xizhi (303–381); Fan Kuan (*c.* 950–1027, Song dynasty painter); Guo Xi (1023 to *c.* 1085, Song dynasty painter); Li Gonglin (1049–1106, Song dynasty painter); Qiu Ying (*c.* 1509–1551, Ming dynasty painter); and Wang Hui (1632–1717, early Qing dynasty painter).

Among the scholar's objects is the inkstone of Su Dongpu (1037–1101), one of the most famous of the Song dynasty literati and a great calligrapher; and the inkstone of Zhao Mengfu (1254–1322), a famous Yuan dynasty calligrapher.

There is a magnificent collection of Northern Song imperial ceramics, and also representative collections of objects from all later dynasties. Among the most popular and well-known objects is the Qing dynasty imperial Jade Cabbage; 19-cm high and made of jadeite it is carved with exquisite virtuosity to show the green and white colours of a fresh cabbage, and two grasshoppers.

The Picture Gallery

Images of China and selected artefacts from museums and collections throughout China

Tang dynasty *sancai* glaze tomb guardian. Arthur M Sackler Museum of Art and Archaeology at Beijing University (no. 2)

Left:
Wanshou Temple. Beijing Art Museum, (no. 6)

Opposite:
Tang dynasty tomb figurine. Arthur M Sackler Museum of Art and Archaeology, (no.2)

Above:
Votive offerings at the Wanshou Temple. Beijing Art Museum, (no. 6)

60066

Left:
This An-2 (Antonov) is shown with the markings of the Chinese People's Liberation Army. China Aviation Museum (no. 15)

Bottom left:
The An-2 was a Russian-designed multi-purpose biplane which first flew in 1951. It played a variety of roles from carrying passengers to crop spraying and came either with wheels, skis or, as in this case, floats. It was built in China under license. China Aviation Museum (no. 15)

Detail from a Liao dynasty stone *sarira* casket. Capital Museum (no. 14)

Below:
Remains of sacrificed horses – buried alive – with chariots. Linzi Museum of Chinese Ancient Chariots (no. 68)

Right:
Detail from Tang dynasty head of Bodisattva. Poly Museum (no. 40)

Bottom right:
Three Shadows Photography Art Centre, Beijing. Dashanzi and Caochangdi (no. 25)

Left:
Bodisattva in Contemplation, Northern Qi Dynasty. Poly Art Museum (no. 40)

Above:
Class Zhu De locomotive. China Railway Museum (no. 20)

Photographic Credits

The authors wish to thank all contributors for their kind permission to reproduce the images which appear in this book. Every effort has been made to credit and trace the copyright holders of all images and we apologize in advance for any unintentional omissions. The publishers will be happy to amend any errors or omissions in subsequent editions of this publication.

Except for those noted below all photographs are by © Miriam Clifford. All rights reserved. © Cathy Giangrande **14, 15, 18, 19, 33.** © Fuxing Photo **36 top.** © Paul Mooney **26, 27 top, 52, 72, 100 top, 107, 174, 175, 179, 193, 216 bottom, 217, 225, 276–79, 281–83, 287 bottom.** © Antony White **37 bottom right, 50 top, 155, 201, 313, 314 top, 328 bottom to 330.** © Elissa Jaffe Cohen **85, 86, 101, 213, 232 bottom, 291 top left, 296–98, 300.** © Edward Denison **104, 148–49 top, 186, 188 bottom, 189.** © Gary L Todd **122.** © Gemma Thorpe **140 top.** © Guoyang **140 bottom.** © Preston Scott Cohen **146 bottom, 147.** © Pat Wang **149 bottom, 150 bottom.** © Gavin A Fernandes **150 top.** © Deke Erh **20, 168–69.** © Peter Ellegard **197.** © Wang Lu **233.** © Christian Richters **235.** © Clifford Coonan **285.** © Richard Beck **299 top right.** © Jeremy Tredinnick **302–07, 336–41, 342 right, 343.** © Kaizheng Yuan **344–47.**

Courtesy of the following individuals, museums, architectural firms, businesses, libraries and institutions: SOAS (School of Oriental and African Studies) Library, University of London **32 top, 44–45, 51, 73 top, 82 top, 83, 92 bottom, 96, 99, 100 bottom, 141, 164 bottom, 166, 170, 173, 190, 195, 196, 210 centre, 232 top, 234, 237–39, 280, 286, 299 bottom.** Shangai Postal Museum **42–43, 183.** Fahai Temple **55, 56 top.** LEHK (London Editions (HK) Ltd) **57–64.** Guanfu Classic Art Museum **69, 70, 274–75.** Mei Lanfang Memorial Museum **74.** Museum of Ethnic Costume **79.** Guy and Myriam Ullens Foundation **93 bottom, 94.** Tianjin Museum **103 bottom left & right.** Hebei Provincial Museum **109.** Yinxu Museum **110 top.** Luoyang Ancient Tombs Museum **116.** Luoyang Museum **119–21.** Qi State History Museum **129.** Shandong Provincial Museum **130–32.** Qingzhou Municipal Museum **136–37.** Shanxi Museum **143–46.** September 18 History Museum **156 top.** Shenyang Palace Museum **156 bottom, 157 top.** Jewish Refugee Museum / Ohel Moishe Synagogue **162.** Shanghai Auto Museum **167 right.** From an exhibition in Mianzhu, Sichuan **172.** Lu Xun Memorial Museum and Final Residence **176.** Shanghai Museum **176 bottom to 178.** *Le 70 anniversaire du Musée Heude, 1868–1938*, Shanghai, Musée Heude, 1939 **182.** Dr Alfreda Murck **185.** Changfengtang Museum **194, 195.** Nanjing Museum **198–99.** Nantong Textile Museum **207.** Suzhou Museum **208–09.** Xuzhou Cultural Site of the Han Dynasty **214.** Xuzhou Museum **215, 216 top.** Ningbo Museum of Art **231.** Sutherland Hussey **243.** Jinsha Archaeological Site Museum **246–47.** Sichuan Provincial Museum **252.** Chongqing Three Gorges Museum **257–59.** Residence and Headquarters of General Joseph Warren Stilwell **263.** Site Museum of the Provisional Government of the Republic of Korea **266.** Sanxingdui Museum **267–68.** China Lantern Museum **269.** Zigong Salt History Museum **273.** Museum of the Mausoleum of the Nanyue King of the Western Han Dynasty **284.** Hunan Provincial Museum **287 top, 288 top.** Jiangxi Provincial Museum **301.** Mogao Grottoes **309–12, 360.** Gansu Provincial Museum **314 bottom to 316.** Baoji Bronze Museum **317 top.** Famen Temple Museum **317 centre & bottom, 318.** Hanyangling Museum **320–21.** Museum of the Terracotta Warriors and Horses of Emperor Qin Shihuangdi **323–25.** Shaanxi History Museum **326–28.** Xi'an Beilin Museum **331–32.** Xi'an Museum **333–34.** National Palace Museum **348–50.** Three Shadows Photography Art Centre **356 bottom right.**

Cave 57. Mogao Grottoes (no. 200)

Temirtau
Qaraghandy
Kazakhstan
Irtys
Ob
Malyj Jenisej
Lake Balkhash
Ertix
Bishkek
Ili
Yining
Shihezi
Urumqi
Kyrgyzstan
Naryn
Aksu
Korla
Hami
Tarim
Kashi
Kongi
Yarkant
Golmud
Indus
Moron Us
Tongtian
China
Sengge
Sutlej
Gar
Za
Zi
Yangtze
Salween Nu
Chandigarh
Dehra Dun
Meerut
New Delhi
Karnali
Shahjahanpur
Agra
Bhind
Lucknow
Faizabad
Kanpur
Gorakhpur
Yamuna
Jaunpur
Allahabad
Mau
Varanasi
Patna
Ganges
Murwara
Ranchi
Korba
Gondia
Raurkela
India
Brahmaputra
Lhasa
Brahmaputra
Kathmandu
Nepal
Muzaffarpur
Bhutan
Thimphu
Dibrugarh
Purnia
Guwahati
Brahmaputra
Ingraj Bazar
Balurghat
Shillong
Rajshahi
Sirajganj
Sylhet
Bangladesh
Dhaka
Durgapur
Agartala
Imphal
Haora
Narayanganj
Kolkata
(Calcutta)
Khulna
Chittagong
Chindwin
Nmai
Mekong
Ayeyarwady
Burma
Sagaing
Mandalay
Pakokku
Myingyan
Meiktila
Cuttack
Puri
Bhubaneshwar
Brahmapur
Sittwe
Minbu
Salween
Bay of Bengal
Pye
Sandoway
Henzada
Chiang Mai

Komsomol'sk-n
Lake Baikal
Vitim
Chita
Ulan-Ude
Ingoda
Silka
Argun
Amur
Blagoveshchensk
Jagdaqi
Khabar
Selenga
Manzhouli
Hailar
Yakeshi
Onon
Bei'an
Yichun
Hegang
Zalantun
Nen
Shuar
Ulan Bator
Qiqihar
Suihua
Daqing
Anda
Jixi
Harbin
Ulan Hot
Mudanj
Fuyu
olia
Changchun
Jilin
Gongzhuling
Dunhua
Tongliao
Yanji
Xiliao
Xar Moron
Kaiyuan
Siping
Hunjiang
Shenyang
Fushun
Chifeng
Kanggye
Anshan
Luan
Jinzhou
Benxi
North Korea
Hamhung
Chengde
Sinuiju
Jinxi
Hungnam
Zhangjiakou
Wonsan
Xuanhua
Qinhuangdao
Pyongyang
Baotou
Huang Yellow
Beijing
Tangshan
Jinzhou
Dalian
Sariwon
Seoul
Wuhai
Baoding
Tianjin
Inch'on
Suwon
Shizuishan
Yinchuan
Shijiazhuang
Yantai
Taejon
Taiyuan
Wuding
Binzhou
Linyi
Xishe
Xingtai
Zhangdian
Chonju
South Korea
Jinan
Yellow Sea
Tianshuibu
Handan
Tai'an
Laiwu
Qingdao
Mokp'o
Lanzhou
Xiping
Qufu
Huang Yellow
Xinpu
Cheju
Zhengzhou
Xuzhou
Zaozhuang
Jeju-Do
Tongchuan
Luoyang
Yancheng
Wei
Xianyang
Suzhou
Xi'an
Luohe
Guozhen
Huai
Fuyang
Yangzhou
Hanzhong
Han
Zhumadian
Nanjing
Shanghai
Ankang
Xinyang
Suzhou
Hefei
Huzhou
Xiangfan
Jiaxing
Yichang
Yangtze
Wuhan
Hangzhou
Shaoxing
Suining
Shashi
East China S
Huangshi
Quzhou
Jiaojiang
Jingdezhen
Chongqing
Changde
Xuri
Yiyang
Nanchang
Luzhou
Wenzhou
Xiangtan
Yichun
Xiamen
Zunyi
Lengshuijiang
Pingxiang
Bijie
Shaoyang
Nanping
Yong'an
Fuzhou
Kaili
Hengyang
Taipei
Chi-lung
Guiyang
Chenzhou
Ganzhou
Panxian
Guilin
Wuling
Xunwu
Xiamen
T'ai-chung
Taiwan
Yuanlin
Sakishima Shoto
Chia-i
T'ai-nan
Linzhou
Wuzhou
T'ai-tung
Nanning
Guangzhou
Shenzhen
Kao-hsiung
Yulin
Zhuhai
Hong Kong
Maoming
Hanoi
Hong Gai
Zhanjiang
Hai Phong
Nam Dinh
Haikou
Thanh Hoa
Laoag
Hainan
Vinh
South China Sea
Philippine
Luzon

Glossary

bi	disc with a hole in the centre – often made of jade or stone
bianzhong	musical instrument – a set of chime bells hung on a wooden frame
bixie	'averter of evil' winged mythological animal with two horns – often a tomb guardian
blanc de chine	white porcelain made in Dehua, Fujian Province and exported widely
celadon	a European term referring to a green glaze and ware, sometimes crackled that became very popular as an export – green is most prevalent, but it also appears as yellow, grey, blue and white
cloisonné	decoration made using copper or bronze wire on a metal base and filled in with molten coloured enamel
cong	tall tube-shaped inner vessel with square outer walls, symbol of heaven and earth
ding	round or square ritual vessel or kettle – often three-legged, but also four-legged
dou	food container on a stem, usually bowl-shaped with bowl-shaped lid
doucai	designs on porcelain which are first painted in underglaze blue, glazed and then fired at a high temperature, with outlines then filled in with red, green, yellow and aubergine overglaze enamels and fired again at a lower temperature
famille jaune	predominance of yellow in decoration
famille rose	predominance of pink enamel in decoration
famille verte	predominance of green in decoration
fangding	is a square, four-legged *ding* vessel
fenghuang	Chinese mythological bird often translated as 'phoenix' although it is not the same as the Western version
fengshui	geomantic science of matching spaces to forces of nature
ge	a weapon originally stone and later bronze blade attached to the top of a long staff
gu	wine container with tall, thin stem which flares into cup
guang	wine vessel – shape similar to a modern gravy boat
Guanyin	bodhisattva of compassion or goddess of mercy, one of the attendants of Amitabha Buddha – originally the male Indian god *Avalokitesvara*
gui	food container with handles; seen in a variety of shapes
he	box
hu	jar or pot
jia	wine vessel on legs for storing or warming wine
jian	double-edged sword
jin-silk	complex warp faced polychrome woven silks

jue	libation vessel
kaolin	a fine white clay, essential ingredient to create porcelain
kesi	highly prized and intricately styled woven silk
lei	tall wine jar with narrow neck – usually four-sided or round
leiwen	spiral pattern seen on bronze objects
li	round-bellied tripod vessel, more delicate than a *ding* in design
luohan (arhat)	disciple of Buddha
meiping	gracefully proportioned narrow-necked vase on a flat base designed to hold one flowering branch
nao	bell with curved lip
qi	battle axe
qilin	mythical creature with hooves and horns – a good omen
qingbai glaze	porcelain glaze that is a pale and delicate bluish-green colour
qipao	long, tight-fitting woman's garment often with high side slits, based on traditional Manchu dress – the modern version became very popular in 1930s Shanghai
Sakyamuni	'Sage of the Sakyas' – one of the names for Gautama Buddha, the historical figure
samite	heavy silk fabric often interwoven with gold or silver threads
sancai glaze	'tri-colour' glaze – although in fact not limited to three colours – particularly used in Tang dynasty
sarira	Buddhist relic
si	Buddhist temple – e.g. Famen Si and Fahai Si
stela (e) also stele (s)	large upright inscribed stone or slab
sutra	the holy scriptures and teachings of the Buddha
taotie	animal-like mask
yan	steamer – both utilitarian and ritual
you	wine container
yu	bowl-shaped food container with handles
yue	broad axe – often ritual
zhi	wine vessel or cup
zun	urn which can be in the shape of an animal

Chronology

Neolithic period	c. 12000–2000 BC
Yangshao Culture	c. 5000–3000 BC
Hongshan Culture	c. 4500–2900 BC
Dawenkou Culture	c. 4300–2500 BC
Liangzhu Culture	c. 3300–2200 BC
Majiayao Culture	c. 3100–2700 BC
Shandong Longshan Culture	c. 2500–2000 BC
Central Plain Longshan Culture	c. 2500–1900 BC
Qijia Culture	c. 2400–1900 BC
Xia dynasty	c. 2070–1600 BC
Erlitou Culture	c. 1800–1600 BC
Ba	c. 2000–220 BC
Bronze Age	21st to 5th centuries BC
Shang dynasty	c. 1600–1046 BC
Zhou dynasty	c. 1046–221 BC
Western Zhou	c. 1046–771 BC
Eastern Zhou	770–221 BC
Spring and Autumn period	770–476 BC
Warring States period	475–221 BC
Qin dynasty	221–207 BC
Han dynasty	206 BC – AD 220
Western Han	206 BC – AD 8
Xin or Interregnum of Wang Mang	AD 9–23
Eastern Han	AD 25–220
Three Kingdoms period	AD 220–265
Western Jin	AD 265–316
Eastern Jin	AD 317–420
Southern and Northern dynasties	AD 420–589
Southern dynasties	
Song	AD 420–479
Qi	AD 479–502
Liang	AD 502–557
Chen	AD 557–589
Northern dynasties	
Northern Wei	AD 386–534
Eastern Wei	AD 534–549
Western Wei	AD 535–557
Northern Qi	AD 550–577
Northern Zhou	AD 557–581

Sui dynasty	AD 581–618
Tang dynasty	AD 618–907
Five Dynasties and Ten Kingdoms	AD 907–960
Liao dynasty	AD 916–1125
Song dynasty	AD 960–1279
Northern Song	AD 960–1127
Southern Song	AD 1127–1279
Western Xia dynasty	AD 1038–1227
Jin dynasty	AD 1115–1234
Yuan dynasty	AD 1206–1368
Ming dynasty	AD 1368–1644
Qing dynasty	AD 1644–1911
Republic of China	1912–
People's Republic of China (PRC)	1949–

Cultural, Heritage and Tourism Websites and Blogs

These are sites we have used and can recommend; however, new sites are springing up daily!

General Cultural

www.chinaculture.org
Culture and history of China

http://whc.unesco.org
UNESCO's official site

http://china.icom.museum
International Council of Museums

http://icom.museum/disaster_relief
ICOM Disaster Relief for Museums

www.cnta.org.cn
The China National Tourism Administration

http://etcweb.princeton.edu/asianart/china.jsp
Princeton University Art Museum

www.artsmia.org/art-of-asia/introduction/
Minneapolis Institute of Arts site

www.britishmuseum.org/explore/online_tours
British Museum tours relating to Chinese art

www.orientations.com
Leading magazine on Asian art

www.chinaheritagenewsletter.org
Research School of Pacific and Asian Studies, The Australian National University

http://chineseculture.about.com
Chinese cultural, history and more

www.aasianst.org
Association for Asian Studies

www.tibetan-museum-society.org
Tibet

www.asiahouse.org/net/
Asia House, London

www.asiasociety.org
Asia Society, New York

News

http://cnreviews.com
Blog about Chinese travel, technology and art

http://time-blog.com/china_blog/
Time China Blog

http://english.peopledaily.com.cn
Daily news from China's leading English language newspaper

www.xinhuanet.com/English
Chinese and international news

www.gbcc.org.uk/
Great Britain China Society

Regions and Cities

http://english.bjww.gov.cn/
Beijing Administration of Cultural Heritage

www.beijingpage.com
Beijing listings

http://en.beijingology.com
A site on everything related to Beijing

www.cityweekend.com.cn/beijing
Feeds to information on Beijing

www.chengdu.gov.cn/echangdu
Chengdu

www.expo2010china.com
Official site for the 2010 World Expo in Shanghai

www.shanghai.gov.cn
Shanghai

www.yunnantourism.net
Yunnan Province

Specific Topics – including Contemporary Art

www.chineseclayart.com
All about Chinese ceramic arts

http://bbs.keyhole.com/ubb/showflat.php?Cat=0&Number=1201174
Google Earth Community Collection of Chinese Navy Ships

www.railwaysofchina.com
All about railways in China

www.cbs.columbia.edu/weblog/
Center for Buddhist Studies Weblog, Columbia University

www.thebuddhistsociety.org/
Buddhist Society

www.bl.uk/onlinegallery/features/silkroad/main.html
British Library, Silk Road

http://artradarasia.wordpress.com/
Free site on the contemporary art scene across Asia

www.artrealization.com
Contemporary galleries and museums in China

www.yishujournal.com
Quarterly journal on contemporary Chinese art

www.artzinechina.com
Chinese contemporary art portal

www.aaa.org.hk
Contemporary Asian art portal

http://review.redboxstudio.cn
Bilingual information on Chinese contemporary art

www.shanghai-jews.com/index.htm
History of Jews in Shanghai

Suggested Reading

Bagley, Robert (ed.), *Ancient Sichuan, Treasures from a Lost Civilization*, Seattle Art Museum in association with Princeton University Press, 2001

Barnes, Gina L, *China, Korea and Japan: The Rise of Civilization in East Asia*, Thames and Hudson, 1993

Cahill, James, *Chinese Painting*, Skira/Rizzoli, 1985

Capon, Joanna, *Guide to Museums in China*, Orientations Magazine Ltd, 2002

Chang, Iris, *The Rape of Nanking: The Forgotten Holocaust of World War II*, Basic Books, 1997

Chang, Kwang-chih, *The Archaeology of Ancient China*, 4th edn, Yale University Press, 1986

Clunas, Craig, *Art In China*, Oxford University Press, 1997

Denison, Edward and Ren, Guang Yu, *Building Shanghai: the Story of China's Gateway*, Wiley-Academy, 2006

Denison, Edward and Ren, Guang Yu, *Modernism in China*, John Wiley & Sons, Ltd, 2008

Dunlop, Fuchsia, *Shark's Fin & Sichuan Pepper*, Ebury Press, 2008

Ebrey, Patricia Buckley, *The Cambridge Illustrated History of China*, Cambridge University Press, 2002

Garret, Valery M, *Chinese Clothing: An Illustrated Guide*, Oxford University Press (USA), 1994

Gernet, Jacques, *A History of Chinese Civilization*, Cambridge University Press, 1989

Haw, Stephen G, *China: A Traveller's History*, 5th edn, Interlink Publishing Group, 2008

Hibbard, Peter, *The Bund: Shanghai*, Odyssey Books & Guides, 2007

Hung, Wu (ed.), *Chinese Art at the Crossroads: Between Past and Future, Between East and West*, New Art Media, 2001

Jinshi, Fan, *The Caves of Dunhuang*, Scala Publishers Ltd, 2009

Keay, John, *China: A History*, Harper Press, 2008

Mallory JP and Mair, Victor, *The Tarim Mummies: Ancient China and the Mystery of the Earliest Peoples from the West*, Thames and Hudson, 2000

Ming, Bai, *The Traditional Crafts of Porcelain Making in Jingdezhen*, Jiangxi Fine Arts Publishing House, 2002

Mooney, Paul et al, *Xi'an, Shaanxi and the Terracotta Army*, Odyssey Books & Guides, 2005

Murck, Alfreda, *Poetry and Painting in Song China: The Subtle Art of Dissent*, Harvard University Press, 2000

Musée d'Art Contemporain de Lyon, *The Monk and the Demon: Contemporary Chinese Art*, 5 Continents Editions, 2004

Ng, Henry et al, *Juanqinzhai in the Qianlong Garden, The Forbidden City*, Scala Publishers Ltd, 2008

Nuridsany, Michel, *China Art Now*, Flammarion, 2004

Puyi, Aisen Gioro, *From Emperor to Citizen: The Autobiography of Aisen Gioro Puyi*, Foreign Languages Press, 2002

Rawson, Jessica, *Mysteries of Ancient China*, British Museum Press, 1996

Ronan, Colin A, *The Shorter Science and Civilisation in China: An Abridgement of Joseph Needham's Original Text*, Cambridge University Press, 1981

Rui, Huang (Editor-in-Chief), *Beijing 798, Reflections on Art, Architecture and Society in China*, Timezone 8 Ltd and Thinking Hands, 2004

Smith, Karen, *Nine Lives: The Birth of the Avant-Garde in New China*, Timezone 8, 2008
Snow, Edgar, *Red Star over China*, Random House, 1938
Spence, Jonathan D, *The Search for Modern China*, Hutchinson, 1990
Sullivan, Michael, *The Arts of China*, 4th edn, University of California Press, 1999
Tadgell, Christopher, *The East: Buddhists, Hindus & the Sons of Heaven – Architecture in Context II*, Routledge, 2007
Thorp, Robert L, *Visiting China's Past: A Guide to Sites and Resources*, Floating Word Editions, Inc., 2006
Thorp, Robert L and Vinograd, Richard Ellis, *Chinese Art and Culture*, Harry N Abrams, Inc., 2001
Thubron, Colin, *Behind the Wall: Journey Through China*, William Heinemann Ltd, 1987
Thubron, Colin, *Shadow of the Silk Road*, Chatto & Windus, 2006
Tuchman, Barbara W, *Sand against the Wind: Stilwell and the American Experience in China, 1911–1945*, Macmillan, 1971
Watt, James CY (ed.), *China: Dawn of a Golden Age, 200–750* AD, Metropolitan Museum of Art, 2004
White, Antony, *The Forbidden City*, Scala Publishers Ltd, 2002
Whitfield, Susan, *The Silk Road: Trade, Travel, War and Faith*, British Library, 2004
Winchester, Simon, *The Man who Loved China: The Fantastic Story of the Eccentric Scientist Who Unlocked the Mysteries of the Middle Kingdom*, Harper Collins, 2008
Wood, Frances, *A Companion to China*, Weidenfeld and Nicolson, 1988
Zhensheng, Li, *Red-Colour News Soldier: A Chinese Photographer's Odyssey through the Cultural Revolution*, Phaidon Press, 2003

Stop Press: Museums Opening Shortly

These museums are due to open shortly, or have been announced officially and will open in the next couple of years. The most up-to-date information is given; however, changes occur rapidly, so it is recommended that you check the web, ask the local tourist office, or the director or senior curator in the nearby provincial or city museum.

Section 1

Beijing

Contemporary Museum and Sculpture Park: Opening: Not announced. It will be located in the Beigao District, between the contemporary art area 798 and the airport. Guan Yi, one of China's top collectors of contemporary art, plans to showcase a large portion of his holdings of over 800 works. Aiming to be environmentally friendly, the complex will use solar power among other green technologies.

The National Art Museum of China: Opening: 2011/12. A new museum building to house the museum's growing collection of contemporary and international art. It will be built next to the Bird's Nest Olympic Stadium.

Moon River Museum of Contemporary Art (MR MoCA): Opened as this publication went to press in the autumn of 2008. Address: No. 1, Moon River Hebin Road, Tongzhou District. Part of a large, luxury lifestyle group and run privately, it is located in one of the city's designated cultural zones. It displays regional and international art including pan-Asian art, as well as hosting fashion and design shows. Education and research also feature, all under the guiding eye of Victoria Lu, former director of MoCA Shanghai.

Qingdao

Olympic Sailing Museum: Opening: 2009. Qingdao International Yacht Club, Fushan Bay Area, Qingdao, Shandong Tel: (532) 8309 2020. As one of China's premier port cities it's not surprising that Qingdao was chosen by the Beijing Olympic Committee to host the 2008 sailing competitions. The former Beihai Shipyard was transformed into a world-class centre for the Olympic and future sailing regattas. Post-Olympic redundant buildings have been assigned new uses. The Athletes' Centre will become a museum on the history of Olympic sailing.

Section 2

Liaoning Province

Yizhou Fossil and Geology Park: Opening: Imminently. He Jia Xin Village, Tou Tai Town, Yi County (416) 278 1383 (www.liaoningdinosaurpark.com/museum.htm). Built of environmentally friendly materials, painted with non-toxic paints and lit with energy from a windmill, this museum with an educational bent will focus on what the province is best known for – unique dinosaur finds – which have offered strong evidence of an evolutionary link between dinosaurs and birds. The museum will also feature a large tank in which endangered species that lived at the time of the dinosaurs will be reared.

Section 3

Shanghai

China Maritime Museum: Opening: July 2009. Nanhui District (www.mmc.gov.cn). This is China's first national maritime museum. It will showcase China's maritime history, industry and contributions to the world of maritime science. A public appeal has brought in numerous donations and the museum is relying on additional donations in the coming years to assemble their collection. It will also contain a hall dedicated to astronomy and a movie theatre.

Jackie Chan Film Art Museum: Opening: October 2009. Changfen Ecology Commercial District, Putuo District. Work began in 2008 on this museum, which will be housed in a renovated factory building. It will track the career path of martial art's actor-cum-charity-supporter, Jackie Chan, using awards, costumes and props from his movies, as well as images and additional memorabilia.

Metro Museum: Opening: 2010. To be located near the Wuzhong Road Station of the Metro Line 10, currently under construction. Through documents, images and artefacts it will tell the history of the city's Metro and its construction, and will include a section for simulating disaster situations and emergency drills for earthquakes and the like.

Yuan Dynasty River Control Site Museum: Opening: 2010. Zhidanyuan residential quarter. Over the last six years, archaeologists have been excavating this site, which dates to the Yuan and includes the remains of river control systems. The main section consists of a large stone gate and pillars close to the old course of the Wusong River, also called the Suzhou River. It was a major waterway to the East China Sea and past records point to the importance of this water control facility. The site museum will be bow-shaped – a reference to the bows and arrows used by the ruling Mongols in the Yuan dynasty.

Zendai Museum of Modern Art: Opening: 2010. It will be part of the new Zendai Himalayas Centre designed by the Japanese architect Arata Isozaki in the Pudong New Area, near the current museum with the same name. Both are the brainchild of the businessman and philanthropist, Dai Zhikang; however, this next-generation museum will be the focal point of an arts and cultural centre, which will include a hotel, artists' studios, performance hall and shops. The old museum will remain and become an art archive.

Nanjing

Nanjing Museum of Art and Architecture: Opened as this publication went to press in the autumn of 2008. Located in Pearl Spring near Nanjing, New York-based Steven Holl Architects have used spatial ploys and suspended rectangular spaces to create a museum complex with its visual axis focused on the city centre beyond. Besides the 3000 sq m exhibition space there is a tea house and curator's residence.

Section 4
Sichuan Province
Art Museum of Yue Minjun: Opening: Early 2009. However, the devastating quake has meant the other seven museums earmarked for the same site and dedicated to contemporary artists including – Zhou Chunya, He Duoling, Wang Guangyi, Fang Lijun, Zhang Peili, Wu Shanzhuan and Zhang Xiaogang – have been delayed. Eventually, they will be built on an 18-acre site, near Qingcheng Mountains adjacent to the Shimeng River, near Sichuan. This first one, designed by the Beijing-based Studio Pei-Zhu (designers of the Digital Building for the 2008 Olympics), will display works by Yue Minjun, known for his large, repetitive smiling figures. Its futuristic design – an organic-shaped sphere clad in polished zinc – is, according to the architects, designed to blend into its natural surroundings. The local government of Dujiangyan is behind the development, which was conceived by Lu Peng, an art professor at the China Central Academy of Fine Art.

Section 5
Fujian Province
Xiamen City Museum: Opening: Not announced. Located on a man-made island in the centre of Xiamen, this space-age looking museum, designed by the Chinese architectural firm, MAD Ltd, will consist of five platforms on stalks. At ground level there will be public spaces and the stalks will transport visitors to the platforms on top, which will house the museum's exhibition areas and restaurants. Finally, the roof will be accessible as a space from which to admire the surrounding landscape and will also hold the solar panels.

Guangdong Province
New Guangdong Provincial Museum: Opening: June 2009. The New City Centre Plaza of Culture and Art, southern waterfront of Zhujiang New City, Guangzhou. This huge 'treasure box' designed by Hong Kong's Rocco Yim is slated to open as part of a large arts and culture complex, including China's third largest opera house designed by the British architect, Zaha Hadid. Designed in the shape of a modern red lacquered box, it will house tens of thousands of 'precious' objects ranging from modern folk art and paintings to ancient pottery, bronzes and jades, as well as fossils and natural history displays. It will replace the current Guangdong Provincial Museum (see no. 176).

Dafen Art Museum: Opening: Building completed, but at time of publication had not yet opened. Located in the centre of Shenzhen. Created by Urbanus Architecture and Design for the municipal government, it is what they call a mixed-use arts centre designed with each of the three floors serving a specific function, including a floor for local artists who specialize in quality copies of paintings to display their wares. Dafen is best known for its vast production of thousands of low-end fakes scooped up by decorators from across the globe.

Shenzhen Museum of Contemporary Art and Planning Exhibition: Opening: Not yet announced. The design competition was won by Coop Himmelb(l)au Design as part of the city's new centre dubbed the 'Futian Cultural Centre'.

Hunan Province

Nushu Language Museum: Opening: Imminently. Located in Jiangyong County. Made possible by a grant from the US Ford Foundation, this museum aims to conserve this rare language of the Yao minority from extinction. Spoken and written only by women, Nushu was discovered by linguists in the 1980s, but will soon die out, as Nushu speakers are passing away. Through displays of manuscripts, recordings of songs and spoken words, as well as other artefacts, a permanent record of the language will be saved for posterity.

Yunnan Province

Ancient Dian Kingdom Cultural Park: Opening: Announced in 2008 by the Jiangchuan Bureau of Commerce. To be built in Yuxi, Jiangchuan County. Building on the historical importance of the ancient Dian kingdom, not only as a key component of Chinese bronze culture, but also connecting other cultures both in this province and those in Southeast Asia and Japan, the city has sought funding for the construction of this park, which will display scenes of the daily lives of the Dian, a bronze workshop, and link it to the Dian tomb site in Lijiashan Mountain to form a core of tourist sites all relating to this ancient kingdom.

Inner Mongolia Autonomous Region

Ordos

Ordos Museum: Opening: 2009. This is the second museum to be built as part of a master plan, known as the *Ordos 100* urban planning project (http://movingcities.org/embedded/ordos100/phase1/), where one hundred international architects have been invited to build a villa as part of a new city centre development away from the current city. Ordos is an empty desert town rich in natural resources, but short on good architecture and culture. Along with the villas will be this museum designed by the Chinese architectural firm, MAD, created at the centre of this new city. Irregular in shape and clad in reflective metal it will contain exhibition halls and a public space. It joins the Ordos Art Museum, designed by DnA Beijing and opened in 2007, which showcases contemporary Chinese and Western artists.

Watch this space for podcast tours of the sites listed in this book, art tours and more.

Acknowledgements

During the lengthy and demanding process of compiling this book, we collected along our journey a host of individuals to whom we owe a great deal of gratitude. Firstly, our sponsor, Gazeley – in particular Pat McGillycuddy, Chief Executive – who believed in this project enough to finance it from its earliest days; a very big thank you! And his team, including Jack Yang, Managing Director Gazeley China; Magalie Milo, Global Marketing Manager; and Yolanda Yang, Marketing/Business Development (China). Outstanding support in so many ways came from Dr Paul Clifford, whose knowledge of China which he generously shared from start to finish was invaluable and much appreciated. MC and CG are profoundly grateful to Wang Yi, our Project Assistant in China. His tireless and efficient help and guidance on museum matters, as well as his marvellous skill as an interpreter and facilitator on our travels is incalculable. So, too, was Ching-Yi Huang, our dependable assistant in London who spent endless hours researching and translating, helping us most brilliantly – thank you both. Special thanks goes to Paul Mooney (thank you too, Elaine!), an associate writer and researcher in China who, at the drop of the hat, travelled far and wide to reach museums we might otherwise have left out and did so with a professionalism now rarely encountered: quel homme! Others who assisted with writing, photography and research include Edward Denison, Jeremy Tredinnick and Elissa Jaffe-Cohen; thank you for your willingness and spirit of adventure. Space does not allow us to personally thank the numerous museum directors and owners, curators, assistants and archaeologists who generously gave us their time to guide us through their collections, granted oral interviews, plied us with useful catalogues and DVDs and countless times many kindly invited us to share a meal; to all of them we offer a heart-felt collective thanks. Architectural firms and photographers kindly supplied us with images of artists' renderings of new museums, or out-of-the way ones without which this book would have been less visually pleasing. Our design wonder, Misha Anikst, and his team worked incessantly to produce with panache the volume you now hold in your hand, thank you. Sandra Pisano deserves thanks for her editing skills and patience, as does Julie Pickard, our copy editor. Magnus Bartlett and his team at Odyssey Books & Guides were enormously supportive from the beginning, thank you. An endless stream of colleagues and friends helped us with their skills, encouragement, friendship and contacts; to them we offer our deepest appreciation. They include Nancy Abella, Clifford Coonan, Cindy Cui, Chengxi Dong, Deke Erh, Ulrika Fornaeus, Amy Gendler, Rupert Grey, Fan Jianchuan, Wang Jie, Roger Keverne, Tang Liang, Francine and Robert Martin, Enrico Perlo, Jiang Ping (Charissa), Zhang He Ping, Guang Yu Ren, Yueying Shan, Dr Wang Tao, Didi Kirsten Tatlow, Julie and Megan Upton Wang, Pat Wang, Ma Weidu, Suzhen Xie, Kaizheng Yuan and Dr Xiaodong Zhu of the State Administration of Cultural Heritage. MC would personally like to thank Dr Alfreda Murck for her encouragement and confidence from the very beginning of this project and sage advice throughout. To her family – Paul, Jasper, Hugo and Zoë who have been so supportive and patient throughout this very long process – she sends her love and thanks. CG would like to thank her friends and colleagues both past and present at the World Monuments Fund. Boundless support and encouragement was lovingly provided by her husband, Paul Hodgkinson: it would not have been possible without him. And her sons, Chris and Alex, will be happy to know they no longer have to tolerate burnt hamburgers!

Index to Art Spaces, Museums and Sites